MARITIME SAFETY, SECURITY AND PIRACY

Related Titles

From The Grammenos Library

Commodity Trade and Finance
By Michael N. Tamvakis
(2007)

Future Challenges in the Port and Shipping Sector
By Hilde Meersman, Eddy Van de Voorde and Thierry Vanelslander
(2009)

From the Lloyd's Practical Shipping Guides

The Handbook of Maritime Economics and Business
By Professor Costas Th. Grammenos
(2002)

ISM Code: A Guide to the Legal and Insurance Implications, 2nd edition
By Dr Philip Anderson
(2005)

Risk Management in Port Operations, Logistics and Supply Chain Security
By Khalid Bichou, Mike G.H. Bell and Andrew Evans
(2007)

From the Essential Maritime and Transport Law Series

War, Terror and Carriage by Sea
By Keith Michel
(2004)

MARITIME SAFETY, SECURITY AND PIRACY

BY

WAYNE K. TALLEY, Ph.D.

informa

LONDON
2008

Informa Law
Mortimer House
37–41 Mortimer Street
London W1T 3JH
law.enquiries@informa.com

an Informa business

First published 2008

British Library Cataloguing in Publication Data
A catalogue record for this book
is available from the
British Library

ISBN 978–1–84311–767–4

Text set in 10/12pt Plantin
by Interactive Sciences Ltd, Gloucester
Printed in Great Britain by
MPG, Bodmin, Cornwall

Printed on paper from sustainable sources

To my children and their spouses,

Wynn Talley Perkins, Ian Mark Perkins,
Joseph Cordle Talley, Tanya Wooten Talley,
Jason Wayne Talley and Megan Rounds Talley

CONTENTS

CHAPTER 4   US SHIP ACCIDENT RESEARCH
Di Jin, Hauke Kite-Powell and Wayne K. Talley

CHAPTER 5   SECURITY OF SHIPS AND SHIPPING
            OPERATIONS
Khalid Bichou

CHAPTER 9   PORT STATE CONTROL INSPECTION AND
VESSEL DETENTION
Pierre Cariou, Maximo Q. Mejia Jr. and Francois-Charles Wolff

CHAPTER 10   PORT SHIP ACCIDENTS AND RISKS
Tsz Leung Yip

CHAPTER 11   PORT SECURITY: A RISK BASED PERSPECTIVE
Mary R. Brooks and Ronald Pelot

CHAPTER 12   US PORT SECURITY
C. Ariel Pinto, Ghaith Rabadi and Wayne K. Talley

LIST OF CONTRIBUTORS

Khalid Bichou	Imperial College London, UK
Mary R. Brooks	Dalhousie University, Halifax, Canada
Pierre Cariou	World Maritime University, Malmo, Sweden
Eric Custar	Old Dominion University, Norfolk, Virginia, USA
Devinder Grewal	Canberra Institute of Technology, Canberra, Australia
Girish C. Gujar	Erasmus University Rotterdam, Rotterdam, The Netherlands
Di Jin	Woods Hole Oceanographic Institution, Woods Hole, Massachusetts, USA
Hauke Kite-Powell	Woods Hole Oceanographic Institution, Woods Hole, Massachusetts, USA
Maximo Q. Mejia Jr.	Lund University, Lund, Sweden
Koi Yu Adolf Ng	The Hong Kong Polytechnic University, Hong Kong
Athanasios A. Pallis	University of the Aegean, Greece
Ronald Pelot	Dalhousie University, Halifax, Canada
C. Ariel Pinto	Old Dominion University, Norfolk, Virginia, USA
Ghaith Rabadi	Old Dominion University, Norfolk, Virginia, USA
Ethan M. Rule	United States Navy, Norfolk, Virginia USA
Sara E. Russell	Old Dominion University, Norfolk, Virginia, USA
Wayne K. Talley	Old Dominion University, Norfolk, Virginia, USA
George K. Vaggelas	University of the Aegean, Greece

Jin Wang — Liverpool John Moores University, Liverpool, UK

Francois-Charles Wolff — University of Nantes, Nantes, France

Zaili Yang — Liverpool John Moores University, Liverpool, UK

Tsz Leung Yip — The Hong Kong Polytechnic University, Hong Kong

LIST OF FIGURES

LIST OF TABLES

CHAPTER 1

INTRODUCTION

Wayne K. Talley

Maritime Safety, Security and Piracy is a peer-reviewed book that examines the maritime topics of safety, security and piracy. Maritime safety accidents are unintentional, while maritime security and piracy incidents are intentional. Maritime security and piracy incidents differ in that the focus of the former is damage to property and/or injury to individuals for political reasons while that of the latter is theft. Maritime safety accidents, security incidents and piracy incidents, however, may have the same outcomes—injuries and property damage. The book is divided into two parts. Part I discusses maritime safety, security and piracy from the standpoint of ships and Part II discusses maritime safety, security and theft from the standpoint of ports. The book is written so that it may be read and be of value to both practitioners and academicians.

Chapter 2 provides an overview of international ship safety regulations. The International Maritime Organization (IMO) was established in 1948 to provide international standards of maritime safety, efficiency of navigation and prevention and control of marine pollution from ships. The IMO is not a policing body. Rather, implementations of IMO conventions remain within the province of IMO member sovereign states (or countries). Member states agree to register ships (i.e., to flag them) in order to monitor and control safety aspects of ships. The most important IMO safety convention is the Safety of Life at Sea (SOLAS) convention, which specifies minimum safety standards for ship construction, equipment and operation. Compliance of standards is the responsibility of the flag states (i.e., flag state control). Since states have not always honoured the terms and conditions of IMO conventions, member states are allowed to inspect foreign ships that visit their ports if there is concern that the ships are unsafe (i.e., port state control).

State ship registries may be closed or open. State closed registries are those that stipulate that vessels flying the flag of the state must be owned by residents of the state. State open registries allow the registration and the flying of the state flag (upon payment of a fee) on vessels for which the owners are not residents of the state. The advantages of registering a ship in a state with an open register (i.e., flagging out) include flexibility in investment decisions, the ability to use less costly crews and lower tax and legal environments. Classification societies inspect vessels to ensure that they are seaworthy, meet flag state requirements and conform to international safety standards.

1

Chapter 3 describes the Formal Safety Assessment (FSA) framework that was adopted by the IMO to improve shipping safety. Specifically, the FSA has been used by the IMO to review and evaluate safety and environmental protection regulations. The review and evaluative process for a given regulation consists of five steps: hazard identification (step 1), risk assessment (step 2), risk control options (step 3), cost benefit assessment (step 4) and decision-making recommendations (step 5).

In the FSA of ships, a hazard (or accident) is a physical situation with the potential for human injury, property damage, and damage to the environment. Once various types of hazards (or accidents) are identified (e.g., collision, explosion, flooding and grounding), the risk of accidents occurring is assessed. This risk is with respect to various ship functions—e.g., entering port, berthing, un-berthing, leaving a port, and loading and unloading. From the information in step 2, risk control options are identified for preventing and mitigating possible negative effects of ship accidents (i.e., step 3). In step 4, cost-benefit assessments of risk control measures are undertaken, i.e., the benefits and costs in reducing ship accident risks for each risk control option are identified and compared. The most attractive risk control option is that option for which its benefits are greater than the financial cost to be incurred (in its adoption) than any other measure. In step 5, the information from the previous steps are used to select the best (based upon stated criteria) risk control option.

Chapter 4 provides a review of the US ship accident research literature. Investigations into the severity of ship accidents often hypothesise that the injury or damage severity of a ship accident is a function of the type of ship accident (collision), ship characteristics (ship size), ship operation phase (underway), weather condition (high winds), type of waterway (river), type of ship propulsion (diesel), type of ship hull construction (steel) and cause of ship accident (human cause). With respect to accident injury severity, the literature's empirical results suggest that: (1) fatal injuries for cargo ships are higher for older ships and for fire accidents; and (2) fatal injuries for passenger ships are higher when precipitation and poor visibility exist at the time of the ship accident.

With respect to the vessel damage severity of ship accidents, the literature's empirical results suggest that commercial cargo ship accidents incur the largest vessel damage costs from fire/explosion accidents. Containerships tend to incur more vessel damage cost per vessel gross ton for ship accidents than tankers; tankers incur more vessel damage cost per vessel gross ton than bulk ships. Oil spillage in a tanker accident is greater when the tanker is adrift and when the accident occurs on a coastal waterway, but less for larger and for US flag tankers. For tank barge accidents, oil spillage is greater for collision and material/equipment failure accidents. The probability of a vessel fishing accident is higher for higher wind speeds, higher the closer to shore than offshore, and lower in spring and autumn.

Chapter 5 explores security risk in shipping. This risk can be reduced by additional documentation and screening of sea cargo. A drawback to warning thresholds and security event-reporting is that they may have errors. If thresholds are set too high, significant risk events may not be reported. In complying with shipping security initiatives, shipping companies incur *ex ante* costs related to the investment in security equipment and recruiting and training security personnel. Also, shipping companies incur *ex post* costs when involved in compliance assessments.

Adherence to security regulations may negatively affect the operations of shipping companies and shippers. For example, the 24-hour rule may result in shipping companies declining late cargo bookings. Also, shippers may have to adjust their production and inventory management practices accordingly. Alternatively, shipping companies and shippers may benefit from security regulations in terms of reduced insurance costs and risk exposure.

Piracy in shipping is presented in Chapter 6. Piracy is an act of boarding or an attempt to board a ship with the intent to commit theft. Unlike ship accidents that are unintentional, piracy incidents are intentional. Piracy may involve petty thieves who look for easy ship targets, taking money and other valuables from the ship's safe or an organised-crime syndicate that seeks to take possession of ships and hold the crew hostage for ransom. Regions of the world that are most likely to attract piracy ship attacks have a high volume of ship traffic (e.g., the Malacca Straits and the South China Sea), are sheltered from high seas, low-economic regions and are regions in political turmoil (e.g., Somalia). In 2006, the South China Sea had the highest number of reported and attempted piracy attacks (66), followed by 53 attacks for the Indian Ocean.

Security against piracy attacks includes patrols and the use of security equipment. US and foreign military ships, for example, often escort commercial ships through the Straits of Bab el Mandeb, Gibraltar, Hormuz and Malacca. Security equipment includes ship alarms that notify the ship's crew of an approaching piracy attack and sonic equipment that blasts ear-splitting noise in the direction of the attackers. An analysis of the number of monthly reported and attempted piracy attacks worldwide from April 2000 to August 2007 indicates a declining trend over this period. The highest number of attacks occurs in the month of May.

Chapter 7 analyses worldwide piracy attacks for the period 1996–2005, taken from the piracy database of the International Maritime Bureau (IMB). The attacks are only those that are reported (actual or attempted) to the IMB. However, it is widely acknowledged that there is under-reporting of these attacks due to the complex reporting procedures imposed on ship captains, concerns about commercial reputations, and time delays to ships from lengthy investigations. In 1996–2005, 0.74% of the world's commercial shipping fleet was subjected to actual or attempted piracy attacks. Bulk vessels were subject to the greatest number of attacks, followed by general cargo vessels, containerships and tankers. As a percentage of a vessel's total fleet, containerships had the greatest number of attacks or 1.6% of the containership fleet. Most reported attacks are in Asia.

A Probit estimation of the determinants of the probability of a vessel being subjected to a piracy attack was obtained utilizing data on the world's commercial shipping fleet for 1996–2005. These data consist of vessels that were and were not subjected to piracy attacks. The empirical results suggest that containerships are more likely to be subjected to piracy attacks than other types of vessels. Further, vessels flying the Malaysian, Singaporean and Indian flags are more likely to be attacked by pirates than those flying flags of other registries.

The safety of port workers is explored in Chapter 8. Prior to World War II, port workers worked in physically demanding conditions that routinely subjected them to accidents and personal injuries. In loading/unloading ships carrying bulk cargoes (such as cement, talcum powder and cocoa), port workers often inhaled dust. With the advent of international ocean container transportation in 1966, ports became more capital intensive in the handling of general cargo. The jobs of port workers became less physically demanding and safer. Also, the safety efforts of unions, port authorities and governments have resulted in significant improvements in the safety of port workers. In the US, the Department of Labor instituted the Occupational Health and Safety Act (OHSA) in 1970, creating national workplace safety standards for US workers in all industries.

A number of innovations have contributed to the improvement in port worker safety. For example, Automated Guided Vehicles (AGVs) have reduced the risk of accidents to port workers. AGVs are controlled by centralised-located automatic control systems, enabled by a Global Positioning System, for transporting containers within a container terminal. Automatic mooring systems also reduce the safety risk of port workers in mooring vessels. These systems eliminate the need for vessel line handlers, thereby reducing the likelihood of port quayside accidents.

Chapter 9 discusses port state control and analyses a database of port-control vessel detentions. The ineffective enforcement of international safety rules for ships by some countries was addressed with the establishment of port state control (PSC) systems. In 1982, 12 European countries signed the Paris PSC Memorandum of Understanding that arranged for the safety inspection of ships of all flags (including each other's) visiting their ports, and to insist, by detention if necessary, on deficiencies being rectified. The effectiveness of most PSC MoUs (Memoranda of Understanding on Port State Control) relates to the ability of PSC systems to target vessels in port that might be detained, i.e., vessels for which inspections would lead to deficiencies being identified that are hazardous to safety, health and the environment.

Data from 26,515 PSC vessel inspections within the Indian MoU region for the period 2002–2006 were used to investigate determinants of whether a vessel is detained following a PSC inspection. In 2002 the number of vessels detained following an inspection was 5.6%, reaching a maximum of 9.1% in 2003; the average percentage was 7.7% for all years. The empirical results from the Probit estimation suggest that the likelihood of a vessel being detained following a PSC inspection increases: (1) with the age of the vessel; (2) if inspected in India versus Australia, Iran and South Africa; (3) if the vessel flies the Panama flag; and (4) if the vessel is a chemical tanker. The detention is less likely if the vessel is classified by the Nippon Kaiji Kyokai classification society.

Port ship accidents and their risks are discussed in Chapter 10. Most databases of ship accidents are recorded by nation for which the nation's port accidents represent less than one-half of the nation's total ship accidents. However, there is often no distinction between port and non-port accidents in these databases, thereby preventing an analysis of the nation's port accidents. Japan is an exception where approximately 30% of the nation's ship accidents occur in port. The risk of ship accidents in port may be reduced by controlling ship speed, providing ship routing and traffic separation, reallocating anchorage and other water sites, utilizing vessel traffic service systems and providing navigational aids.

In the Port of Hong Kong, 68% of the recorded ship accidents in 2001–2005 were collision/contact ship accidents, followed by 8%, 7% and 7% for grounding/stranding, foundering/sinking and fire/explosion ship accidents, respectively. In comparison, 29% of the recorded ship accidents in Taiwanese ports in 1992–2003 were machinery failure ship accidents, followed by 23%, 9%, 7% and 7% for collision/contact, fire/explosion, grounding/stranding and heavy weather damage, respectively. Human error is the primary contributing factor for traffic-related port ship accidents, followed by the density of port traffic. In the Port of Hong Kong, the types of ship accidents that result in the highest numbers of fatalities are collision, foundering and capsizing accidents; for ship collision accidents, the non-fatality injury rate is 0.16 and the fatality injury rate is 0.02.

Chapter 11 provides an overview of risk concepts and approaches to port security. Port security risk differs from typical risk management problems in that: (1) there is deliberate intent to cause harm; (2) threats are unpredictable; and (3) terrorists may circumvent new security measures. Port security strategies have focused on external activities, e.g., identification of threats and system vulnerability. Less emphasis has been placed on the end of the process, i.e., dealing with a security incident once it occurs.

Port security is a component of international supply chain security. The US sees security threats coming from foreign sources, whereas the EU sees the threat coming from intra-European trade. Therefore, the EU has included cabotage trades in its port security programme. Information-sharing by supply chain partners for prevention of security incidents has its own risks. The sharing of too much information increases the risk of terrorists obtaining this information, whereas the sharing of too little information increases the risk of a security incident. A port security performance evaluation system may address, for example, whether a disaster recovery plan exists, whether certain types of security training sessions are held and the number of false positives and false negatives for scanned containers.

US port security is explored in Chapter 12. Since 11 September 2001, the US has established numerous programmes to prevent and detect port security threats. In 2001 the US Congress created the Transportation Security Administration (TSA) to ensure the security of US passenger and freight transportation. The 2002 Maritime Transportation Security Act (MTSA) is designed to prevent security incidents in the maritime supply chain by focusing on the higher security-risk sectors of the maritime industry. There are three major US maritime cargo security initiatives—two voluntary security programmes, the Container Security Initiative (CSI) and the Customs-Trade Partnership Against Terrorism (C-TPAT), and the 24-Hour Advance Manifest Rule (24-hour rule). The voluntary security programs are designed to provide origin-to-final destination visibility and control over containerised freight movements. The purpose of the 2006 SAFE Port Act is to strengthen port security by enacting technology initiatives and better data-collection programs.

US port security is financed in part by Department of Homeland Security grants that are allocated to ports based upon port security risk assessments. A port security incident cycle has four stages: (1) prevention of the incident; (2) detection of a possible incident; (3) response to the occurrence of an incident; and (4) recovery from an incident. If port security has a negative impact on a port's throughput, throughput will be highest when no security activities are conducted and lowest when security is extremely tight, i.e., higher the security level, less the throughput. Alternatively, the existence of a securitised port might be a competitive advantage for the port and thus attract more cargo than its competitors.

In Chapter 13 EU port and shipping security are discussed. Regulations for securing EU ports include Regulation 725/2004 (in force since 2004) that requires enforcement of the IMO ISPS Code. Specifically, the Regulation requires that ports have security plans, identify and monitor restricted areas, and prevent dangerous materials from being taken onto ships or into port facilities. The Regulation also covers ship voyages within the EU and their ports. Directive 65/2005 (in force since June 2007) secures aspects of the port not covered by Regulation 725/2004, e.g., requiring a security plan that contains actions and necessary procedures to be undertaken in the event of a security incident. If a port is subject to Regulation 725/2004, it is also subject to Directive 65/2005.

The EU maritime security programme was initially designed after the US maritime security programme, e.g., both endorsed the ISPS Code. Recently, however, the EU and the US security programmes have taken different paths. The US has passed additional regulations to enhance maritime transportation and supply chain security, e.g., the 2006 SAFE Port Act and its TWIC (Transport Worker Identification Credential) programme. EU maritime stakeholders, however, have criticised the SAFE Port Act for requiring foreign ports to install scanning equipment for scanning US-bound containers. The EU notes that the problem with 100% scanning of US-bound containers is that this ruling is not a risk-based approach to port security.

Port security in Asia is explored in Chapter 14. The focus of Asia's port security programme is slightly different from that of the US and the EU. Specifically, the focus of US and EU port security has been to fight terrorism, unlike that in Asia. That is to say, terrorism is perceived as a problem for the US and the West, but not a problem for Asia. Asian governments also regard port security as a problem to be solved rather than an added-value opportunity for shippers. A number of countries and regions in Asia, especially developing countries and regions, have found it difficult to comply with ISPS Code requirements due to the lack of information-sharing, regional co-operation and technical knowledge, and the low priority of port security as a political issue.

Since no significant maritime-related terrorist attacks have occurred in Asia and the political implications of such attacks are largely hypothetical, the emergency levels for introducing port security in Asia are low. This view is supported by the fact that port security managers often occupy junior positions. At the Port of Hong Kong, for example, none of the security managers at the Port's marine terminals have reached the senior grade level; also, their responsibilities are often execution as opposed to decision making. In Hong Kong, port terminal operators are expected to cover all of the financial costs in the execution of their port facility security assessments and the preparation of port facility security plans and their actions. The intent of the Hong Kong government is neither to subsidise nor provide loans to any port security projects (unlike the situation in the US).

Chapter 15 examines landside cargo theft, i.e., cargo that has been stolen at some point either between its origin and stowage on a vessel at a port or between its discharge from a vessel at a port and its ultimate destination. Cargo thieves typically seek low-volume and high-valued cargoes, e.g., hi-tech equipment, consumer electronics, alcohol and cigarettes, and pharmaceutical goods, that have a ready black market distribution network and are not easily identifiable as stolen. The three components of a cargo theft market are the customer of stolen goods, the criminal who steals the goods and the fence, a distributor of stolen goods. Cargo thieves employ a number of strategies, e.g., document fraud or the creation of a false document to increase the opportunity to steal cargo.

The way in which international maritime containers are transported and processed provides cargo thieves with opportunities to steal their cargoes. To reduce the risk of cargo theft, insurers may recommend that shippers make the contents of containers as anonymous as possible, frequently change coding schemes and avoid routine shipping schedules. Shippers may demand that carriers: (1) provide direct routeing of their cargo from origin to destination; (2) eliminate as many stops and transhipment points as possible; (3) provide real-time tracking capabilities; and (4) use tamper-evident seals on containers. It was not until 2007 that the US implemented legislation that established uniformity in reporting cargo crimes.

PART I

SHIPS

CHAPTER 2

INTERNATIONAL SHIP SAFETY REGULATIONS

Devinder Grewal

1. INTRODUCTION

Treaties between shipping states have a long history, as have attempts to regulate for safety at sea. However, efforts to establish uniform sea safety regulations only occurred piecemeal until the establishment of the United Nations in 1945. With the impetus provided by this international organisation of co-operative, or at least generally civil, states, the IMO was created in 1948 in order to set the highest practicable "standards of maritime safety, efficiency of navigation and prevention and control of marine pollution from ships" (IMO, online). In this role, the IMO develops the instruments by which activity on the seas can be monitored and regulated. The IMO conventions provide a body of international regulations that guide member states in terms of their use of the sea, and the safety of ships and the seafarers who sail them. The IMO, however, is not a policing body and the implementation of any IMO conventions relating to safety at sea remains the province of sovereign states worldwide. Thus, while member states agreed to register ships (flag them) as a mechanism for monitoring and controlling ships' activities in terms of safe conduct, it is the responsibility of the state with which the vessel is registered to set the acceptable standard of safety onboard ships sailing under that flag. However, while the IMO conventions are very sound in what they demand from flag states, the states have not always sufficiently exercised their responsibility for honouring the terms and conditions of IMO conventions. Nor have the terms of the UN's Convention on the Law of the Sea always been enacted into state legislation, in spite of its importance in maintaining good order and safety on the high seas. Flag state control (FSC) of ships and shipping, therefore, has been augmented by port state control (PSC) in order to spread the responsibility for safety at sea more widely.[1]

This chapter will review some of the IMO conventions designed to ensure a high level of safety at sea, and consider the success, or otherwise, of the FSC

---

1. I am indebted to my friend and colleague, Dr Detlef Nielsen, for reading a draft of this chapter and providing useful comments for improvement. I retain full responsibility for any inaccuracies that may still remain.

or PSC regimes as enforcers of IMO policy in an effort to determine if the reality at sea matches the ideal.

2. SAFETY CONVENTIONS OF THE IMO

Nation states have signed a variety of IMO conventions since 1948 with the understanding that each sovereign state will go on to shape national regulation to achieve the desired outcomes of the conventions. A brief outline of each of the salient safety conventions is given below:

1. The most important of the safety conventions produced by the IMO is the SOLAS convention. The technical provisions of SOLAS specify minimum standards that must apply to the construction, equipment and operations of ships, as well as the defining of certificates that a ship must carry to prove that this has been done. Responsibility for ensuring compliance with these requirements is given to flag states that will register the ships, thus defining flag state control.

   Control provisions within SOLAS allow countries to inspect foreign ships when they visit their ports if there are grounds to believe that a ship does comply with the requirements of the convention. This is port state control. A detailed description of the SOLAS Convention can be found on the IMO website (www.imo.org).

2. Following the sinking of *Herald of Free Enterprise*, the IMO adopted Guidelines on Management for the Safe Operation of Ships and for Pollution Prevention in 1989. The purpose was to ensure safety, prevent injury or loss of life, and avoid damage to the environment or property. After a period of refinement in the use of the guidelines, they were adopted as the International Management Code for the Safe Operation of Ships and for Pollution Prevention (the ISM Code) in 1993 and became mandatory in 1998. The ISM Code forms Chapter IX of the SOLAS Convention.

3. The International Convention on Standards of Training, Certification and Watch-keeping for Seafarers (STCW) (1978) establishes basic requirements in these areas on an international level. Before this convention came into being, each country had its own standards, leading to wide disparity in seafarers' capabilities and practice. Adopted in 1978, this convention came into force in 1984.

4. The Convention on the International Regulations for Preventing Collisions at Sea (COLREG) was adopted in 1972 and came into force in 1977.

5. The International Convention on Loadlines (Loadlines Convention) defines minimum freeboards and watertight integrity and survivability of ships.

6. The International Convention for the Prevention of Pollution from Ships (1973), modified by the Protocol of 1978 (MARPOL 73/78), covers

pollution by oil, chemicals, harmful substances and garbage. The Protocol of 1978, which included measures of tanker design (hence the connection with ship safety), was adopted into the convention following a spate of tanker accidents. The convention came into force in 1983.

7. The Convention for the Suppression of Unlawful Acts against the Safety of Maritime Navigation (SUA) was developed to ensure that appropriate action is taken against persons committing unlawful acts against ships. These include the seizure of ships by force; acts of violence against persons on board ships; and the placing of devices on board a ship which are likely to destroy or damage it.

8. Other safety-related conventions of the IMO include the International Convention on Maritime Search and Rescue (SAR), International Convention on the Maritime Satellite Organisation (INMARSAT), and the International Convention for Safe Containers (CSC).

With no policing powers, the IMO can only urge the implementation of these conventions and rely on the efficacy of flag and port state control.

3. THE FLAG STATE AND ITS RESPONSIBILITIES

Today, more than 90% of international trade is carried on ships. In some cases, such as that of Australia, this figure is close to 99% (BITRE, 2007). Today, there are nearly 50,000 ships trading internationally, registered in nearly every country in the world (ICS, 2007), manned by around a million seafarers. Article 91 of the Law of the Sea Convention (LOSC) provides that a sovereign state must fix conditions under which ships can register and fly its flag and carry documentary proof of such registration; and states exercise their right to own and register ships that engage in various functions, including, *inter alia*, international trade, passenger transport, marine activities and exploitation of marine resources. Ships, therefore, fly the state's flag on their masts to indicate the country of registry, making the country of registry the "flag state".

In addition, customary law that has governed shipping for many centuries has provided that a state can register the ships of any ship owner willing to pay a fee, granting their ships the nationality of the registering state, regardless of the nationality of the ship owner. In effect, a flag state might exercise jurisdiction over a very multicultural fleet belonging to many non-citizens since, as early as the 14th century, customary law provided the basis for flag state jurisdiction, with associated responsibilities, such as ensuring ship safety.

3.1 Development of ships' registries and "flagging"

Shipping is the first truly global industry which has served the function of commerce and travel from the time humans started to trade. Laws relating to safety and the resolution of disputes date back to very early times. No known written records exist of the earliest, e.g., Rhodian, rules but reference to them is found in various later laws, such as the Roman and Byzantine (Ashburner, 1909). It is known that special tribunals existed in the Mediterranean Sea ports to hear cases of disputing seafarers. The general average, still in practice today, comes from Rhodian law. These were adopted into the York/Antwerp Rules in 1890 by the International Law Association (www.comitemaritime. org/histo/his.html).

Contemporary maritime law is rooted in English law based on laws introduced to England by Eleanor of Aquitaine, who had earlier established them on the island of Oleron, circa 1266, as the Rolls of Oleron, which make very interesting reading for students of maritime law (www.admiraltylawguide .com/documents/oleron.htm).

The history of ship registration can also be traced to England. King Edward I, in 1302, imposed a tax on wine imports into the country. Wine was carried in *tuns*, a legal measure of not less than 252 gallons. Piracy and war dictated that ships sail in convoy between Europe and England and a tax was levied on the "tunnage" carried to pay for the cost of protection. During the reign of Henry V (1387–1422), tonnage measurement requiring ships carrying coal from Newcastle was enacted in 1421 (Campbell, 1980). This required ships employed in this trade to be measured and marked. This practice has remained and evolved to all ships being measured internally and given a "tonnage" based on 100 cubic feet to each ton. From this are derived gross and net tons, measurements that are used to calculate dues charged to ships.

Flag state protection and control of trade can also be identified in English practices of this period. In 1381, legislation was enacted to reserve English cargo for the nation's own ships. However, the insufficient number of ships to serve national trade ensured that this legislation was not enacted. As English colonial power and trade grew, the number of ships increased and the law was brought into force, foreign ships being forbidden from entering the trade between the colonies and the home country. In 1660, the Navigation Act was enacted and this document provided a template for ship registration, at least to the countries that came under English influence.

As English colonial power and shipping grew over the next two hundred years, further Acts of Parliament were passed to protect trade, administration, national interest and national shipping. These Acts brought about requirements that are taken to be the norm today, including the provision of a unique number, to be permanently marked on the main beam of the ship for purposes of identification in the case of a shipwreck, the display and location of the ship's name and port of registry, recording of change of ownership after the first registry, location of build, and the name of the Master. The ship carried the documents but a record was also maintained in the state's administrative department ashore. This department was formally established in 1850 through the enactment of the Mercantile Marine Act.

The following years saw rapid development in various sectors. In 1854, consolidation of the Merchant Shipping Act saw the ability to register ships that were not only trading to the home country, recognising that ships may trade worldwide among the colonies and with other countries without ever coming to England. This Act, in 1872, also defined the measurement of tonnage and its use in charging port and light dues. Permanent marking of ships' identity marks (name, port of registry and official number) became a prerequisite in 1873. The Plimsoll mark, with its accompanying requirement to mark permanently the loadline on the side of every ship, became a requirement in 1875, resulting in the preservation of countless lives of seafarers who until then had been regularly lost with overloaded ships.

The various changes to the Merchant Shipping Act were consolidated and included in the Imperial Merchant Shipping Act of 1894, which reflected Britain's administrative aspirations to rule the colonies, requiring that all ships owned in the colonies be registered as British ships. In 1988, the Merchant Shipping Act removed this requirement, recognising the changed situation of the colonies now being, by and large, independent countries, and restricting its authority to the UK.

3.2 Closed and open registers

Technically, ship registry, as it has evolved from early English and European developments, can take place in any shipping nation, regardless of the origin and ownership of the vessel. However, some nations stipulate that their flags may only fly on vessels belonging to owners who are resident in the country. These are closed flags or registers. Open flags or open registers belong to nations that will allow the registration of ships, upon payment of a fee, by owners who do not live in or have any great business dealings with that country. Between these two extremes can be found second registers or international ship registers.

The term "national flag" is broadly taken to mean closed flag, that is, a closed register. Such a flag is understood to provide a tradition of administrative control that has matured and achieved a state of effectiveness in implementing its regulations on the ships under its responsibility. The key benefit of a national register is the ability of the country to implement its laws on the ships as well as on the managers who operate them. The purpose of closed flags is to maintain social, commercial and environmental national interest as well as international treaty obligations. The ability of the state to implement its laws effectively, many of which will be reflective of IMO conventions, is the key to successfully achieving the outcomes desired.

However, before registering with a national flag, a ship owner weighs up the costs and benefits of being there, like any other business owner. Essentially, this decision follows the principles of the economic theory of the firm—a strategic decision to maximise profits. When deciding to go with a national flag, the ship owner knows that his factors of production—the number of crew, their costs and quality, and the stores, supplies and fuel—are controlled to some extent. The other areas of business operations where some control may exist include degree of government control, role of unions, level of profit retainable and attitude of financial institutions (Bergantino and Marlow, 1996).

In most traditional maritime countries, of both the old and the new world, staying with the national flag, unless supported by considerable subsidies, has usually been less attractive to ship owners than registering under a convenient foreign flag offered by a country that will allow considerable freedom of activity, turning a differentially blind eye to the niceties of IMO conventions on ship safety and safe passage.

3.3 Open registers and flags of convenience: "flagging out"

Registering in a state with an open register can be extremely advantageous, depending on the nature of the state, its attitudes towards IMO conventions and regulations, and its taxation and legal practices. For the ship owner, "flagging out", that is moving to an open register, allows flexibility in investment decisions, selection of the best crew to suit their needs (whether cost, output, or a mix of both), and the ability to choose the desired returns in terms of legal and tax regimes and national support.

Internationally, ship owners have used the ability to flag out over many centuries. Colonial powers imposed restrictions on trade with their colonies that reserved cargo for their own ships. In the 16th century, Spain, for example, had similar restrictions to the UK—only Spanish ships would trade with the West Indies. To get into this lucrative trade, British ship owners often flagged their ships under the Spanish flag. Not only is flagging out used to obtain entry into a restricted market, it is most often used to escape what ship owners consider onerous regulation or taxation. Evidence of this is found in British fishing vessels registered under the French flag to escape British regulations (Llacer, 2003).

Open registers are, therefore, useful to ship owners in a variety of commercial ways. Unfortunately, however, some open registers have become infamous for failing to put into effect any of the regulations proposed by the IMO to ensure safety at sea. These registers, which exist largely to avoid any regulatory regime, are often referred to as "flags of convenience" (FOCs); and since the cost of compliance with existing regulations is quite high, ship owners are generally happy to flag out their ships with a FOC as a means of escaping "onerous regulation". The most frequently heard criticism of FOCs, in fact, is that they do not implement international conventions and that the conditions and safety of the mariners on board are compromised. Moreover, it is argued that the increasing pollution of oceans and beaches is the result of poorly maintained and operated vessels flagged by FOCs.

Flagging out under a FOC, then, generally leaves the responsibility for the implementation of international regulations with the ship operator, since neither the flag state nor the owner will take responsibility. This abrogation of duty means, therefore, that some ships, indeed entire shipping fleets, may be operated to abysmal standards by shady operators able to act outside the spirit of international law. It is worth noting, however, that some ships flying the flag of an open registry operate to the highest standards of the industry and in compliance with IMO conventions and state regulations.

According to the UNCTAD Review of Maritime Transport (2007), 66.35% of the global deadweight tonnage is registered under foreign flags. Among them, Panama and Liberia, the largest open registers, have 32.4% of the fleet. Open registries in countries like Liberia and Panama provide a large amount of income for their nations. This income, coupled with the fact that the role of surveying ships to ensure compliance with national and international regulations can be devolved to classification societies, is becoming more and more attractive to many governments and authorities. This is resulting in competition to attract ships to open registers, including some in landlocked countries.

There is some truth in the argument that FOCs exist because national policymakers were out of touch with the reality of the needs of the very competitive shipping market. Many governments have, in fact, set up "off shore registries" themselves, aware of the impact of international law on ship operators. These are half-way houses between open registries and national flag regimes. The idea is to provide the attractions of open registries while retaining shipping under the national flag. In some cases, national social security arrangements apply to such registries. The success of these registers has not been as great as that of open registers, however, although they remain attractive for generating economic benefits at a micro level.

Keeping all the pros and cons of registering ships under FOCs in mind, and realising that ship operators are not convinced by the campaigns launched by ITF and some governments against these flags, national authorities are coming round to reconsidering their policy towards shipping. Taking a pragmatic view, this review is overdue.

3.4 Classification societies and their use by flag states

The history of Lloyd's Register (LR) (www.lr.org) makes informative reading. This provides the background to the development of Lloyd's Register and the evolution of rules for the registry of ships. The first register of ships was published by Lloyd's in 1764. Other ship registers followed. Bureau Veritas (BV) came into existence in 1828, American Bureau of Shipping (ABS) in 1862 and Det Norske Veritas (DNV) in 1864. The founders of these classification societies were marine insurers, who set them up as non-profit organisations whose purpose was to provide assurance about the hull and construction of ships so that insurance cover could be issued to the ship owner. This meant that the clients of classification societies were underwriters, not shipowners.

However, in 1834, Lloyd's Register started a trend to charge shipowners for surveys.

After World War II, as many countries became independent and registered ships under their flag without the infrastructure to administer this responsibility, classification societies became the natural recipients of delegation to act on behalf of governments.

Classification societies provide the service that most flag states whose ships trade internationally are not able to deliver—regular audits and inspections of their ships, in various contexts, as needed by the ship or the flag state. Since classification societies usually have surveyors based in most ports, and possess the necessary expertise, they are able to provide this service, under a contract, to a regulatory agency of any government.

In 1969, the International Association of Classification Societies (IACS) (www.iacs.org.uk) was formed by the key societies to provide some discrimination against the proliferation of new societies of indifferent quality and ability. IACS members classify around 95% of international shipping tonnage, and, through their position as a non-governmental organisation (NGO) at the IMO, exercise considerable influence in the development of instruments produced by the IMO.

Variation in the output of classification societies, including the ease with which ship owners ejected from one society are allowed to join another, has led to sharp criticism from marine insurers, who finally insure risk. This, in turn, has led to the creation of inspections carried out by P&I clubs into areas like hatch covers, cargo holds, and safety equipment, not covered by classification societies.

Large numbers of accidents on board oil tankers in the 1970s and early 1980s led to a questioning of the work of classification societies. This led to the oil majors developing their own vetting system of ships.

Classification societies, owing to the nature of their work, possess immense knowledge and the ability to deliver almost any survey-related service. They are, for example, involved in developing ship design, ensuring the ships are constructed to the design through regular and timely surveys, classification surveys leading to the registration of ships following the guidelines of flag states (often these guidelines are recommended by classification societies), periodic statutory surveys to remain "in class", surveys on behalf of governments if the ship changes flag during the course of its life, and surveys following any major repairs (Abe, 2000). Following accidents, classification societies may be involved in investigations for their own intelligence-gathering to learn lessons or on behalf of insurance companies. In short, there is not much among the needs of flag states in the realm of hull, machinery and safety that classification societies cannot provide. Over recent years, there have been developments in their participation in human factors research, again to use their expertise to advise both flag state regimes and ship owners about this crucial element in the operations of ships and their safety.

While the stated role of classification societies remains to enhance safety of life and property at sea through high standards in design, construction and maintenance of ships, it is clear that they are becoming a one-stop shop to flag states in the regulatory function, making it easy for any state to set up registry and delegate the responsibility for implementing relevant national regulation to classification societies. On the other hand, they are also an instrument in the hands of ship owners in the design, construction and operations of ships. It is apparent that they have a very powerful, if somewhat schizophrenic, role in the operation of ships. Goss's (1993) comments on classification societies are worthy of note (" . . . they have excluded all consumers, all seafarers and practically all governments or other public sector bodies"). The International Ship Management Code (ISM) and the International Ship and Port Facility Security Code (ISPS) have both resulted in classification societies taking on a more regulatory delegation in their functions than ever before, creating more "evidence" of conflict of interest in the eyes of the wider industry regarding the role that classification societies are now expected to play in the effective outcomes of safety and compliance with IMO instruments.

Essentially, classification societies are commercial undertakings that are operating in a competitive market. Like other commercial businesses, they are subject to the same pressures and norms. BV, for instance, is a listed company on the Paris stock exchange. In 2006, it made a hostile takeover bid for GL, which was rejected by GL stakeholders (Marine Log, 2006).

Going back to the fundamental issue of flag state responsibility in ship safety and marine pollution, a sub-committee on Flag State Implementation (FSI) was set up in 1992 by the Maritime Safety Committee (MSC 61) and the Marine Environment Protection Committee (MEPC 33). The aim of the FSI was to consider effective implementation of IMO instruments, flag state, port state and coastal state measures and the difficulties experienced by some countries, analysis of casualty statistics and the convergence with the Law of the Sea Convention. In 1993, the FSI developed draft guidelines for, *inter alia*, minimum standards for organisations acting on behalf of governments, i.e., classification societies (IMO Res A 739 (18)), specifications on the survey and certification functions of recognised organisations (IMO Res A 789 (19)), model agreement for the authorisation of recognised organisations (www.imo.org).

In 1997, FSI introduced possible criteria for, *inter alia*, assessing flag state performance and producing a list of countries that were not meeting the minimum standards. The following year saw the circulation of a self-assessment form for member states. The use of this form would allow member states to identify capability gaps and seek assistance from the IMO. No clear outcomes have been achieved so far on this issue since the IMO does not publish the results and few member governments have volunteered any information. In 2003, a Voluntary IMO Member State Audit Scheme (VIMSAS) was introduced by the FSI. However, this scheme was soon in need of expansion in response to the 2004 implementation of the ISPS Code and other requirements of safety. Voluntary audits commenced during the closing months of 2006 but the number of volunteering countries remains very small. Most countries continue to depend on classification societies for delivering their international treaty responsibilities.

A new initiative in the cause of ship safety is the draft new code casualty investigation, and amendments to SOLAS to make it mandatory, that were approved by FSI in June 2007. The code will recommend investigation, by the flag state, into marine casualties that involve death, total loss of ship or severe damage to the environment (International Group of P&I Clubs, 2008).

3.5 Ultimate responsibility for safety at sea

Shipping nations are well aware of the negative effects of shipowners flagging out with FOCs. They understand that the governance of safety exists at two levels—the international conventions of the IMO to which countries become signatories, and the national law that is developed to allow the implementation of these conventions in the jurisdiction of a country. While the processes of developing a convention at the IMO and the shaping of national regulation to implement the requirements of the convention are well developed, albeit vast in the task of engaging sovereign countries to agree on the outcomes, less clear is the effectiveness of the implementing of national regulations. While flag states clearly have sovereign rights, they also have responsibilities under international treaty obligations.

Thus, while the delegation of surveys to classification societies remains the right of the state, the responsibility to monitor the working of the delegate remains clearly with flag states. The Round Table of International Shipping associations—BIMCO, INTERCARGO, International Chamber of Shipping/International Shipping Federation and INTERTANKO—have jointly published Shipping Industry Guidelines for Flag State Performance (ICS-ISF 2007), that are updated regularly. The purpose is:

- To encourage ship owners and operators to examine whether a flag state has sufficient substance before using it.
- To encourage ship owners and operators to put pressure on their flag administrations to effect any improvements that might be necessary, especially in relation to safety of life at sea, the protection of the marine environment and the provision of decent working and living conditions for seafarers (p. 5, Shipping Industry Guidelines for Flag State Performance).

Data for measurement of flag state performance are obtained from various sources, including port state records, use of classification societies by various flag states, fleet profile, mandatory reporting mechanisms of the IMO and attendance at IMO meetings.

The ratification of IMO and ILO conventions does not guarantee effective control of ships or commitment to safety and efficient performance. However, ratification does put some responsibility on the states to perform as required by the convention. This initially led to some states not ratifying some conventions, which meant that their ships did not have to conform to the requirements contained in them. This advantage was soon lost as the "no-more-favourable treatment" doctrine in port states evolved, under which ships registered in a state not party to a convention were not to be treated differently than those ships which were registered in a state which was party to the convention (Nielsen, 2004).

4. PORT STATE CONTROL

Port state control (PSC) is a response to flag states not being able or being unwilling to exercise effectively their responsibility in implementing international conventions on ships flying their flags. As attention has focused on the wider cost of accidents, welfare and safety of the crew, and protection of the natural environment from the risks generated by the operations of ships, and recognising that flag states have not always been effective in carrying out their responsibilities, a regime of PSC has come into being. The Law of the Sea Convention gives port states the right to exercise some level of control on visiting ships. The IMO resolution A. 787 (19) Procedures for Port State Control (1995), as amended by Resolution A. 882 (21), provides the necessary operational framework under which ship inspections can be carried out of foreign ships in host countries. This makes PSC an important and effective link in the regulatory oversight and control of ships trading in all parts of the world. It would be very costly, if not impossible, for flag states to implement their rules through the inspection and detention in foreign ports of ships registered under their flags.

Various memoranda of agreement cover nearly all the sectors of the world where trading ships operate. The first of these was signed in 1982 in Paris (referred to as the Paris MoU), by 14 EU member states. Over the next two decades, eight other MoUs have come into effect in different parts of the world. The US takes on this task unilaterally.

As MoUs mature and states gain and share experience, the implementation has become better and more targeted. The IMO provides technical assistance in capability development through workshops for managers of regional MoUs and harmonisation efforts of PSC activities across various parts of the world.

Broadly, the process of inspection includes an initial check of the statutory documents and certificates of the ship. This is followed by a broad impression of maintenance. If this is of a reasonable standard, the inspector usually focuses on any earlier reported deficiencies to confirm that they have been addressed. If the impression is that the standards of maintenance are not reasonable, then a more detailed inspection may be carried out to uncover deficiencies or defects. If any are detected, the ship may be detained until they are remedied. If a ship is detained, this fact must be reported to the flag state and the relevant classification society. On average, detention rates in the main MoU sectors (Paris and Tokyo) are just below 5%. Shipowners do have the ability to protest detention of their ship(s) through review panels which have been set up for this purpose.

It must be remembered that PSC is a second line of control over ships—the first line is flag state control. Serious defects in ships and their operations are expected to be picked up during statutory surveys and periodic checks by the flag state, with port states being the follow-up to ensure that ships are operated in a safe and defect-free state as they go about their business.

The total percentage of bulk carriers that were inspected of ships visiting Australian ports was 58.05%. Of these, 69.57% were detained[2] [bulk shipping is the major shipping activity, over 60% of all ship calls, in Australia by volume of cargo]. Australia has 37.7% of world market share of iron ore exports and 9.5% of grain exports (UNCTAD, 2007). Given this large share of the dry bulk market, and recognising that bulk carriers have high risks of catastrophic failure and foundering, with heavy loss of human life, Australia has established a PSC regime that pays particular attention to this kind of ship through the Australian Maritime Safety Authority (AMSA).

In Tokyo MoU countries, from 2000 to 2007, the average inspection rate of bulk carriers was 26.73% and the detention rate was 16.79%. In Paris MoU countries, from 2000–2007, the average inspection rate of bulk carriers was 16.18% and detention rate was 15.11%. In these two regions, detention rate of bulk carriers tends to be 9.95% and 1.06% lower than their inspection rate. However, Australia shows an opposite trend, as its average detention rate is 4.32% higher than its average inspection rate, according to Tokyo MoU (2008) records in 2000–2007, and is 3.13% higher according to AMSA Port State Control (PSC) annual reports 1998–2006.

These results show that either these targeted bulk carriers trading to Australia have detainable qualities, or the Australian PSC inspectors have set higher standards for bulk carriers than other PSC regimes in the region (see Table 2.1). In response to the increased shipping activity since 2004, the market for shipping has been very tight, leading to a postponing of scrapping by many shipowners. AMSA has intensified its risk profiling of bulk carriers during these years to ensure that unsafe ships do not find their way to Australian ports. According to the data retrieved from Tokyo MoU and Paris MoU websites on PSC inspection, the detention rates of bulk carriers to total inspection of all ships was 0.97% from 2000 to 2007 and 0.84% from 2004 to 2007. The detention rate of deficient bulk carriers to total numbers of bulk carriers inspected was 3.61% between 2000 and 2007 in Tokyo MoU and 5.18% between 2004 and 2007 in Paris MoU. In Australia, the detention rate

2. I am indebted to my friend and colleague, Prof Solomon Chen, currently at the Australian Maritime College, for sharing with me a snapshot of his current research into PSC inspection activity in Australia, in particular relation to bulk carrier detentions.

of bulk carriers to total numbers of bulk carriers inspected was 4.59% (2000–2007, Tokyo MoU Data) and 5.65% (1998–2006, AMSA Data).

Table 2.1 Inspection and detention rate

	Tokyo MoU – Bulk	*Tokyo MoU – Total*	*Paris MoU – Bulk*	*Paris MoU – Total*	*Australia – Bulk*	*Australia – Total*	*Australia – Bulk (AMSA)*	*Australia – Total (AMSA)*
1998	n.a.	n.a.	n.a.	n.a.	n.a.	n.a.	7.62%	4.28%
1999	n.a.	n.a.	n.a.	n.a.	n.a.	n.a.	5.41%	3.09%
2000	3.80%	1.17%	n.a.	n.a.	3.62%	2.12%	4.64%	2.73%
2001	2.96%	0.86%	n.a.	n.a.	3.17%	1.89%	3.93%	2.37%
2002	3.77%	1.05%	n.a.	n.a.	4.98%	2.91%	6.08%	3.62%
2003	4.15%	1.11%	n.a.	n.a.	5.74%	3.13%	6.99%	3.96%
2004	3.75%	0.98%	5.55%	0.93%	4.36%	2.55%	5.02%	3.03%
2005	3.48%	0.88%	4.25%	0.70%	5.23%	2.97%	5.78%	3.39%
2006	3.61%	0.88%	5.06%	0.82%	4.79%	2.71%	5.37%	3.12%
2007	3.37%	0.79%	5.85%	0.89%	4.79%	2.70%	n.a.	n.a.
2008	5.09%	1.19%	5.13%	0.72%	8.08%	4.29%	n.a.	n.a.
Average	3.61%	0.97%	5.18%	0.84%	4.59%	2.62%	5.65%	3.29%

Compiled from: AMSA PSC annual reports, Paris MoU annual reports and Tokyo MoU annual reports.

According to data retrieved from the online LR ClassDirect LIVE database (2008) from 1 January 2001 to 28 February 2008, a total of 2,399 ships, classed with Lloyd's Register, were detained by PSC inspectors worldwide. The top six countries where detentions took place were: Italy (223), Australia (206), USA (177), Spain (152), China (109) and Netherlands (108). These six countries accounted for 40.64% of total detentions. The main six detained ship types were: general cargo (926), bulk carrier (715), oil tanker (231), container ship (136), refrigerated cargo ship (95), and Ro-Ro cargo ship (58). These six ship types accounted for 90.08% of total detentions. Among these, the 715 detained bulk carriers shared 29.8% of 2,399 detentions (Table 2.2).

Table 2.2 Port state control detentions and Australia's share

	Total	*2001*	*2002*	*2003*	*2004*	*2005*	*2006*	*2007*	*2008*
Total ships detained	2,399	382	325	363	373	303	302	310	41
BULK CARRIER	715	119	87	103	119	84	94	96	13
	29.80%	31.15%	26.77%	28.37%	31.90%	27.72%	31.13%	30.97%	31.71%
AUSTRALIA	206	26	35	46	37	20	18	20	4
	8.59%	6.81%	10.77%	12.67%	9.92%	6.60%	5.96%	6.45%	9.76%
Total deficiencies	30,594	4,795	4,031	4,804	4,242	4,116	3,736	4,297	573

Derived from: LR ClassDirect LIVE database.

Among these, bulk carriers shared 35.32% of deficiencies, at a total of 20,072 items. The main six groups of deficiency were: fire safety measures, life-saving appliances, safety in general, load lines, propulsion and auxiliary machinery, and safety of navigation.

AMSA uses a ship risk profiling system that defines the risk of non-compliance that a ship holds, based on its age, type and inspection history including any deficiencies or detentions. This Ship Inspection Decision Support System (SIDSS) provides PSC inspection resources to be focused where they are most needed. Currently, AMSA targets 80% of high risk ships and 60–80% of medium to high risk ships. Through the risk-based targeting approach, limited inspection resources can be effectively allocated to higher risk vessels. Table 2.3 shows the target groups and the inspection rates achieved.

Table 2.3 Risk groups and inspection rate

	Target	Average	2001	2002	2003	2004	2005	2006
High risk ships	80	94.67	95	95	96	96	94	92
Medium to high risk	60	81.83	81	86	70	86	82	86
Low to medium risk	40	66.17	68	74	40	73	71	71
Low risk	25	53.33	63	63	27	60	56	51
Overall target	50	73.83	77	80	58	79	75	74

Source: AMSA Annual Reports, 2001–2002 (12), 2002–2003 (13), 2003–2004 (14), 2004–2005 (15), 2005–2006 (16), 2006–2007 (17).

5. TRENDS IN APPLICATION OF REGULATION

Historically, accidents that have shocked the maritime world and the world ashore have led to conventions. The large numbers of collisions in the 18th and nineteenth centuries led to the development of regulations to prevent that happening. Samuel Plimsoll's efforts to address the loss of lives from dangerously overloaded ships resulted in the load line regulation being introduced in 1876 for the UK flag ships, with criminal sanctions available to be imposed against the guilty party. The sinking of *Titanic* resulted in the SOLAS Convention and the capsizing of *Herald of Free Enterprise* led to the ISM Code, linking responsibility between ship and shore management.

Herald of Free Enterprise was perhaps the first attempt to link management to accidents. It led to the creation of new statutory offences (s. 30, MSA 1988) under which an owner, demised charterer, or Master may be criminally liable for a dangerously unsafe ship and liable to a maximum of two years' imprisonment or unlimited fine. This applies to British ships worldwide and foreign ships in British waters with the aim of making everyone connected with ship management, not only the Master and crew, subject to prosecution, including having criminal sanctions brought against them. Corporate manslaughter came to being recognised, but no successful prosecutions happened in this case because *mens rea* could be attributable to individuals, not corporations. Another important outcome from this accident was the establishment of the Marine Accident Investigation Branch (MAIB) to learn from accidents. An important aspect of the work of the MAIB was that any investigations carried out by it would be used to learn from accidents and not made available to the Maritime and Coastguard Agency (MCA) for use in prosecution. This allowed the MAIB to collect information that was given without fear and in the ambience of a community of practice in which learning from mistakes will happen.

A unique feature of maritime law is the ability of a ship owner to limit his liability to the value of a ship after a major accident. This is based on the theory that once a ship owner has properly equipped and crewed his ship, he should not be liable for something that happens when the ship is out of his direct control. Using this feature, many unsafe ships are able to weave their way through the flag state and port state controls, perhaps supported by officials who are not honestly and effectively carrying out their responsibilities, pass classification society surveys and oil company vetting regimes. In response to accidents happening or impacting on their shores, various countries have moved from global response to safety and protection of life and property, through IMO instruments, to individual nations (or groups like the EU) adopting unilateral positions that are severe and punitive towards ships and seafarers. Sometimes they have been in response to accidents but, in other cases, also in anticipation of them. The precedence was, perhaps, set by the US through the Oil Pollution Act. In Europe, following the sinkings of *Herald of Free Enterprise* and *Marchioness* (which sank in 1989 after collision with the dredger *Bowbelle* on the Thames), the (British) Law Commission proposed the creation of a new offence—that of corporate killing where death can be caused by management failure. Criminalisation, in effect, has now progressed further than culpable negligence in operations!

This trend is more developed in the US than most other parts of the world, where it is evidenced in relation to pollution. Criminal liability there can arise from violation of state and federal environmental statutes. Issues that can lead to criminal liability include false record-keeping (for ships, log books not being accurate), making false statements, particularly in relation to oily water discharge monitoring equipment, hiding of such operations that can lead to obstruction of justice, and conspiracy charges. If discovered, shipowners, Masters and chief engineers can be convicted of criminal behaviour, even in the absence of any proof of pollution having taken place (for example on high seas) or in US territorial waters.

The US Coast Guard (USCG) uses sophisticated computer programs to compare the ships' bilge sounding logs with oil record book entries with the expected waste oil production of the ship, tank capacities and incinerator use to determine if the entries are "correct". While it may be pointed out that the US government has no jurisdiction over unauthorised discharges by foreign flag ships in international waters in violation of MARPOL, the practice is that the USCG and the Department of Justice (DoJ) are extremely zealous in their investigation and prosecution of owners for any suspected pollution, using document subpoena, crew interview, grand jury subpoena/appearance, vessel searches, seizure of documents or equipment, and detention of the crew as material witnesses (Legal Information Institute (LII), 2008). The investigations can be extremely intimidating for the ship's crew who are aggressively investigated and prosecuted for spoiled record book entries, obstruction of justice and witness tampering. Sometimes the mistake is made of trying to conceal innocent or minor regulatory breaches, inadvertently giving rise to more serious charges involving obstruction of justice.

The legislation most frequently used by the USCG and Justice Department is the False Statement Act 18 USC 1001 (LII, 2008), conspiracy to defraud the United States 18 USC 371, witness tampering and obstruction of justice 18 USC 1505 and 1512, and destruction of evidence 18 USC 1519 (US DoJ, 2008). The US Act to Prevent Pollution from Ships 1901 (APPS—US version of MARPOL) applies to acts committed within US jurisdictional waters (12 miles) and provides that US authorities may refer the matter to the flag state or deal with it themselves. Maximum fines allowed are "USD 500,000 per charge or twice the gain obtained (or twice the loss caused) by the offender, whichever is the greater". This enables authorities to offer very substantial rewards to whistleblowers, forming a very real temptation to crew members. Some large fines have resulted because of this legislation, e.g., Evergreen was fined $25m in April 2005 for illegal discharges from seven ships and concealment by the keeping of false logbooks. At the same time, many seafarers have been detained and penalised on grounds that were not established as clear.

Similar developments have taken place in Canada, albeit with respect to the protection of the environment and the enactment of Bill C-15 (May 2005) to amend the Migratory Birds Convention Act, 1994 (Government of Canada, 2004). This amendment allows that a discharge (including accidental) can be a criminal offence and criminal charges can be brought not only against the person who commits the discharge but also against the "master, chief engineer, owner and operator of a ship—and, if the owner or operator is a corporation, against any director and officer of the corporation who is in a position to direct or influence its policies or activities relating to prohibited conduct and who fails to take all reasonable care to ensure that the vessel and all persons on board the vessel do not cause the discharge". The amendment also allows for increased penalties, including an unprecedented system of minimum fines.

In the EU, Directive 2005/35/EC of 7 September 2005 is currently (March 2008) being amended "to ensure that penalties are 'adequate in severity to discourage' potential polluters, as provided for in Article 4(4) of MARPOL, the deterrent effect of the system of penalties must be reinforced, sending a strong signal, with a much greater dissuasive effect, to potential offenders. Furthermore, criminal investigation and prosecution and judicial co-operation between member states can be essential and more powerful than administrative action" (p. 3, amending Directive 2005/35/EC on Ship-source Pollution and on the Introduction of Penalties for Infringements (CEU 2008)).

The approach, as in other cases mentioned earlier, is to have a "dissuasive" effect on marine pollution through severe legislation. "Member States are required to lay down that any ship-source discharge of polluting substances, as defined in Article 2 of Directive 2005/35/EC, into any of the areas referred to in Article 3(1) of Directive 2005/35/EC, if committed with intent, recklessly or with serious negligence, is to be considered a criminal offence" (p 6). Under the Directive, sanctions can be applied not only to the ship owner or the Master of the ship, but also to the owner of the cargo, the classification society or any other person involved. Port authorities—but not salvors—are specifically excluded from the application of this directive.

Such unilateral positions, taken by countries or groups like the EU, stand separate from, and not always in conformance with, the outcomes sought by the IMO. For instance, MARPOL does not provide for any criminal sanctions for accidental discharges and expressly excludes discharges for safety reasons.

This development of stringent requirements is part of a new trend of regulation by coastal states who want to protect their environment from unsafe shipping, particularly in the aftermath of spectacular accidents, such as *Erika* and *Prestige*. France, Spain and Portugal have excluded single hull tankers carrying fuel oil from operating within their exclusive economic zone. UNCLOS provides that a coastal state may impose more stringent requirements and standards to ships flying its flag. However, the coastal state is not entitled to apply such additional standards to the ships of other states even when those foreign ships are operating within its territorial sea.

Japan, on the other hand, has had a requirement since March 2005 that all ships of over 100 GRT coming to Japanese ports must have insurance cover from one of the approved/designated insurers. This insurance cover addresses the additional problem of shipwrecks that may be abandoned by the owners and need to be removed by the Japanese authorities.

It is necessary to consider the effects of this trend on shipping operations and ship safety. Most companies have appointed a director responsible for safety and the enforcement of company policy, particularly as a result of the ISM Code. The weight of the responsibility that goes with this role is now making it unattractive for senior executives to be the "front man" for the company. The consequences of these trends to criminalise maritime endeavours are strongly negative, driving expertise away from the industry. On ships, chief officers prefer not to move up to the role of Master because of the personal risk of prosecution and direct scrutiny from regulators ashore. The skilled seafarer shortage is likely to be worsened with these new national regulations as those with the skills and aptitude will continue to exit the industry. The wider impact is that the world is likely to become segregated into areas where the regulation is onerous and "dissuasive" to participants while the rest of the world will work on a different level. Shipowners or their representatives will be reluctant to attend any scenes of casualties for fear of personal risk, and comment will increasingly only be made on advice of lawyers.

Outside the shipping industry itself, but closely working with it, are salvors who will be deterred in participating in any activity that may release pollution into the sea and may not attend accidents or wrecks quickly and fearlessly. Overall, the effect will be to reduce the ability to learn from accidents and incidents and so multilaterally improve personal, environmental and ship safety—key goals of the IMO. Until the ability of unsafe ships to operate is removed through effective implementation of regulations, these incentives to develop new harsher laws will merely add to the burden of regulation, not make shipping safer.

6. CONCLUSION

The implementation of IMO conventions through flag state control is clearly not happening to the desired level. The critical weakness in the system is that the IMO itself has no powers to impose its conventions. This is left to member states, making enforcement of legislation non-uniform across the world. The requirement that ships be surveyed before registration and periodically after-wards has not been shown to be effective by itself. At the same time, ship owners have seen benefits in flagging out, moving their commercial assets to where they have most operational freedom in their business. This has resulted in ships not always being operated at the internationally accepted level of social and environmental safety. Owing to the very wide and costly admin-istrative task of surveying ships as they trade around the world, flag states have delegated their responsibilities to classification societies, who not only have a wide presence through their offices in many countries, but also the expertise to do the work. However, this delegation is not always followed up by checks from the flag state to confirm that the delegation is accurately conducted.

This situation has led to an obvious concern from port and coastal states who want to protect their coastlines and their people from the risk of unsafe ships operating near their coasts. These states have set up their own protection regimes.

The port state control regime is seen to be an effective second line of defence against unsafe ships and the various PSC MoUs around the world work effectively under IMO guidelines in sharing information and targeting unsafe ships.

While ships are given the right of innocent passage under LOSC, coastal states also have the right to protect their waters from pollution and other unwelcome effects of shipping traffic. This has been taken quite seriously by some states, who have developed severe and "dissuasive" legislation to criminally prosecute ships, their Masters and responsible operators. These unilateral measures, contrary to the multilateral approach taken by the IMO to address unsafe shipping, merely drive unsafe shipping to other parts of the world, not help to get rid of it.

In conclusion, the existing regulatory framework is adequate in that the LOSC clearly requires flag states to exercise their responsibilities. This is a multilateral approach which can achieve much more than any set of unilateral measures by any group of countries can. The IMO is not able to exercise any influence over flag states (other than a name and shame through white, grey and black lists in the future). While this may give some information about how various flags perform in their responsibilities, it still does not stop ship owners from registering their ships where they like. The tightening of PSC regimes around the world will address the ability of unsafe ships to trade. Classification societies remain a powerful player in this game, playing on both sides—those of the flag state and of the ship owner.

CHAPTER 3

SHIP FORMAL SAFETY ASSESSMENT

Zaili Yang and Jin Wang

1. INTRODUCTION

The business of shipping is governed by a multitude of statutory regulations that support ship safety at both national and international levels. The safety-related rules have predominately been prescriptive, quite often derived as a reaction to a major incident at sea in order to prevent similar accidents from occurring again (Rosqvist and Tuominen, 2004). For example, the capsize of *Herald of Free Enterprise* in 1987 greatly affected the rule-developing activities of the IMO (Cowley, 1995; Sekimizu, 1997). The accident certainly raised serious questions on operation requirements and the role of management, and stimulated discussions in those areas at the IMO. This eventually resulted in the adoption of the International Safety Management (ISM) Code. The *Exxon Valdez* accident in 1989 seriously damaged the environment by a large scale oil spill. It facilitated the implementation of the international convention on Oil Pollution Preparedness, Response and Co-operation (OPRC) in 1990. Double hull or mid-deck structural requirements for new and existing oil tankers were subsequently applied (Sekimizu, 1997). The *Scandinavian Star* disaster in 1990 resulted in the loss of 158 lives. Furthermore, the catastrophic disaster of *Estonia*, which capsized in the Baltic Sea in September 1994, caused around 900 people to lose their lives (Wang, 2001 and 2002). The accidents highlighted the role of human error in marine casualties, and, as a result, the new Standards for Training, Certificates and Watchkeeping (STCW) for seafarers were subsequently introduced (Wang, 2006).

The above-mentioned accidents have shocked the public and attracted great attention to ship safety. This facilitates and stimulates the move from a largely prescriptive and reactive safety scheme to a risk-based proactive regime in the marine industry. The adoption of the safety case approach in the UK offshore industry also motivated marine safety analysts to look at the possibility of employing a similar "goal-setting" regime (Wang, 2001). The responsibility for safety is being placed on those in the industry to set out and justify their basis for managing the risks. Such a change should create new perspectives on risk-based decision making. It is believed that marine safety may be significantly improved by introducing a formal "goal-setting" safety assessment approach so that the challenge of new technologies and their application to ship design and operation may be dealt with properly (Wang, 2001).

In 1992, Lord Carver's report on the investigation of the capsize of *Herald of Free Enterprise* raised the issue of a more scientific approach to the ship safety subject and recommended that emphasis should be given to a perform-ance-based regulatory approach (House of Lords, 1992). The UK Maritime & Coastguard Agency (UK MCA, previously known as Marine Safety Agency) quickly responded and in 1993 proposed to the IMO that formal safety assessment (FSA) should be applied to ships to ensure a strategic oversight of safety and pollution prevention. The UK MCA also proposed that the IMO should explore the concept of FSA and introduce it in relation to ship design and operation. The IMO reacted favourably to the UK's FSA submis-sion. Since then, substantial work including the demonstration of FSA's practicability by trial applications has been done. Eventually, guidelines for FSA in the IMO rule-making process were approved by the IMO in 2002. However, new research is still required to appropriately address the potential problems related to the supporting techniques used in FSA and to facilitate its applications to ship design and operation.

2. A BRIEF REVIEW OF SOME NOTEWORTHY MARINE ACCIDENTS

2.1 The capsize of Herald of Free Enterprise

On 6 March 1987, four minutes after leaving the Harbour of Zeebrugge *Herald of Free Enterprise* capsized. As a result, at least 150 passengers and 38 crew members lost their lives (UK DpT, 1987). The capsizing of *Herald of Free Enterprise* was caused by a combination of adverse factors. Those which have been identified were the trim by the bow, the bow door being left open, the speed of the vessel just before capsizing and the location of the ship's centre of gravity. Their combined effect was to cause a quantity of water to enter G-deck and loss of the vessel's stability (Wang, 2002; Wang and Trbojevic, 2007). The findings of the inquiry clearly demonstrated the contributions of human actions and decisions to the accident. These ranged from weakness in the management of safety to human errors, caused by various factors includ-ing a heavy workload. The basic Ro-Ro ferry design was questioned, in particular the single compartment standard for G-deck. There were no water-tight bulkheads at all on this deck to prevent the free surface effect along the full length of the vessel.

The public inquiry into the accident of *Herald of Free Enterprise* led by Lord Carver was a stepping-stone in ship safety. It has resulted in changes of marine safety-related regulations, demonstrated by the adoption of the enhanced damage stability and watertight closure provisions in SOLAS '90, the intro-duction of the ISM Code for the Safe Operations and for Pollution Preven-tion, and the development of the FSA framework in the shipping industry (Wang, 2002; Wang and Trbojevic, 2007).

2.2 The Estonia accident

The passenger ferry *Estonia* departed from Tallinn, the capital of Estonia, on 27 September 1994 at 19.15 hours for a voyage to Stockholm, Sweden. She carried 989 people, 803 of whom were passengers. She sank in the northern Baltic Sea in the early hours of 28 September 1994. Only 137 passengers survived. According to the Accident Commission, the cause of the accident was that the design and manufacture of the bow visor locks were wrongly conducted, resulting in the locks being too weak. During bad weather conditions the locks were broken and the visor fell off and pulled open the inner bow ramp (Wang, 2006). Water flooded the main Ro-Ro deck and the vessel lost stability and sank. *Estonia*, at her last voyage, was not seaworthy and she did not fulfil the SOLAS requirements. The crew also made mistakes, which partially contributed to the loss of so many lives (Wang, 2002; Wang and Trbojevic, 2007).

The *Estonia* tragedy also resulted in a surge of research into the phenomenon of Ro-Ro damage survivability and was instrumental in the adoption of the North European regional damage stability standard in SOLAS'95 and the Stockholm Agreement. These standards require the upgrading of virtually every passenger Ro-Ro ship operating in Northern Europe (English Channel, North Sea, Irish Sea, and Baltic Sea) (Wang, 2006).

2.3 The Prestige accident

Prestige, a 26-year-old Bahamian-registered and American Bureau of Shipping (ABS)-classed single hull tanker, carrying 77,000 tonnes of heavy oil, departed its loading port of Riga, Latvia, on 5 November 2002. On 13 November, *Prestige* developed a substantial starboard list when she was underway in heavy seas and high winds in the region of Cape Finisterre, between 25 to 30 nautical miles off the coast of Galicia in the north-west of Spain (ABS, 2002). A large crack was found in the starboard side of the hull and with the loss of her main propulsion due to list she began to drift. The ship was towed out to sea into heavy weather away from the Spanish coast. The condition, however, deteriorated onboard. Consequently, *Prestige* structure gave way and collapsed, subsequently the vessel broke into two and sank about 133 nautical miles off the coast of Spain on 19 November 2002 (Wang, 2006).

The *Prestige* tanker accident seriously polluted the Spanish coast by oil spills. It has shocked the public and focused attention on tanker safety. Under new rules adopted by the EU, single hull tankers carrying heavy oil have already been banned from EU ports. The ban brings the EU in line with the US, which restricted single-hull tankers carrying heavy oil from its waters three years after the 1989 *Exxon Valdez* disaster. The EU's ban came a year after the *Prestige* tanker accident (Wang, 2002 and 2006; Wang and Trbojevic, 2007).

3. CURRENT STATUS OF FORMAL SAFETY ASSESSMENT OF SHIPS

As serious public concern is raised on the safety of ships all over the world, the IMO has continuously dealt with safety problems in the context of operations, management, surveying, ship registration and the role of administration (Wang, 2006). Improving safety at sea has been highly emphasised. The international safety-related marine regulations are guided by lessons learned from serious marine accidents.

Following the tragedy of *Herald of Free Enterprise*, an FSA framework was proposed to the IMO in order to ensure a strategic oversight of safety and pollution prevention. The FSA framework that has been proposed by the UK MCA consists of the following five steps (MCA, 1993): (1) identification of hazards; (2) assessment of risks associated with those hazards; (3) ways of managing the risks estimated; (4) cost-benefit analysis of the risk control options (RCOs); and (5) decisions on which options to select.

The above framework was initially studied at the IMO Maritime Safety Committee (MSC) meeting number 62 in May 1993. At the 65th meeting of the MSC in May 1995, strong support was received from the member countries, and a decision was taken to make the FSA a high-priority item on the MSC's agenda. Accordingly, the UK decided to embark on a major series of research projects to further develop an appropriate framework and to conduct a trial application on the selected subject of high-speed passenger catamaran ferries. The framework produced was delivered to MSC number 66 in May 1996, with the trial application programmed for delivery to MSC number 68 in May 1997. An international FSA working group was formulated at MSC number 66 and MSC number 67 where draft international guidelines were generated. The IMO eventually approved the application of the FSA for supporting the rule-making process in 2002 (Wang, 2006).

It has been noted that there is the potential or possibility of using the FSA in a wider context in ship design and operation. The application of the framework in ship design and operation may offer great potential incentives and may lead to benefits (MCA, 1993; Wang, 2001), including: (1) improved performance of the current fleet and then be able to measure the performance change so ensuring that new ships are of good design; (2) ensure that experience from the operational field is used in the current fleet, and that any lessons learnt are incorporated into new ships; and (3) provide a mechanism for predicting and controlling the most likely scenarios that could result in incidents.

The possible benefits indicated have already been realised by many shipping companies. For example, P&O Cruises Ltd in the UK has reviewed the implementation of risk assurance methods as a strategic project and proposed short-term/medium-term and long-term objectives (Vie and Stemp, 1997; Wang, 2001). Its short-term/medium-term objectives are to provide a reference point for all future risk assurance work; to develop a structure chart that completely describes vessel operation; to complete a meaningful hazard identification as the foundation of the data set; to enable identification of realistic options for vessel improvement; to be a justified record of modifications adopted or rejected; and to be capable of incorporating and recording field experience to ensure that the knowledge is not lost. Its long-term objectives are to provide a mechanism for understanding the effect of modifications on total vessel performance; to be capable of future development; to provide a basis for total valuation of identified improvements using cost-benefit analysis; to generate a meaningful risk profile for vessel operation; and to provide a monitor for evaluation of modification effectiveness. The philosophy of FSA may well be fitted into the above objectives (Wang, 2001; Wang and Trbojevic, 2007).

Ship safety is also significantly driven by classification. Current classification society rules have evolved over many years and have been mainly developed on an empirical basis (Card et al., 2004). The basis of the rules is not always transparent to the users. There have been many calls from the marine industry for classification societies to adopt an approach that would lead to the development of rules that are more easily understood and based on clearly identifiable scientific principles (Card et al., 2004). Recently, there have been positive developments on this aspect led by some leading classification societies such as the ABS, DNV and Lloyd's Register (LR). For example, to meet the expectations of the marine industry and to make use of the best standards practice, ABS, DNV and LR have jointly developed a new set of classification rules for oil tankers that would provide, through transparency, a better understanding of the design principles underpinning the rules (Wang, 2006).

Although showing much attractiveness, FSA as a newly developed systemic maritime safety assessment methodology still arguably has some space for improvement on its applications. Areas where improvement can be achieved include risk criterion acceptance, cost-benefit analysis, uncertainty and expert judgement, life-saving equipment, human reliability and information availability, etc. (Wang, 2006) while much research has been seen to address such areas. In recent years, many test cases of FSA have been conducted to improve and enhance the application of ship safety. Those include (Wang, 2006) a trial study on high-speed craft (IMO, 1997a); a trial study on bulk carrier (IMO, 1998a, 2002a and 2002b); a trial study on passenger Ro-Ro vessels with dangerous goods (IMO, 1998b); its application to fishing vessels (Loughran et al., 2003; Pillay, 2001); its application to offshore support vessels (Sii, 2001); its application to cruise ships (Lois et al., 2004; Lois, 2004); its application to ports (Trbojevic, 2002); its application to containerships (Wang and Foinikis, 2001); and its application to liner shipping (Yang et al., 2005b).

It should be pointed out that the above only constitutes an incomplete list of investigations selected. Researchers worldwide have investigated safety assessment and its applications to maritime systems such as ballast tanks, helicopter landing areas, oil tankers, floating, processing, storage and off-loading vessels, etc. There are many advanced risk modelling and decision-making techniques developed/being developed, that may be applied to facilitate maritime risk-based design and operation (Wang, 2006).

4. FORMAL SAFETY ASSESSMENT

FSA is a new approach to marine safety which involves using the techniques of risk and cost-benefit assessment to assist in the process of decision making. It should be noted that there is a significant difference between a safety case approach and FSA. The safety case approach is applied to a particular ship, whereas FSA is designed to be applied to safety issues common to a ship type (such as high-speed passenger vessel) or to a particular hazard (such as fire), often for rule-making purposes.

The philosophies of FSA and the safety case approach are essentially the same. Many ship owners have begun to develop their ship safety cases. The major difference between such ship specific and generic applications of the approach is that whilst features specific to a particular ship cannot be taken into account in a generic application, the commonalities and common factors which influence risk and its reduction can be identified and reflected in the generic approach for all ships of that type (Sekimizu, 1997). This should result in a more rational and transparent regulatory regime. Use of FSA by an individual owner for an individual ship on the one hand and by a regulator for deriving the appropriate regulatory requirements on the other hand, are entirely consistent (Wang, 2006).

It has been noted that many leading classification societies are moving towards a risk-based regime. It is believed that the framework of FSA can facilitate such a move. This may be due mainly to the fact that FSA involves much more scientific aspects than previous conventions. According to the benefits identified by UK MCA (MCA, 1993), adopting FSA as a regulatory tool will effectively address all aspects of safety in an integrated way, present a pro-active approach, enabling hazards that have not yet given rise to accidents to be properly considered and provide a rational basis for addressing new risks posed by ever-changing marine technology.

Guidelines for FSA in the IMO rule-making process approved by the IMO in 2002 incorporate all the key elements of the FSA framework proposed by the UK MCA including the five steps introduced in section 3. Figure 3.1 can be used to describe a flowchart of the FSA methodology. Within the methodology, Step 5 can interact with each of the other steps in arriving at decision-making recommendations (Loughran et al., 2003). The FSA process, therefore, can be flexibly carried out to deal with safety analysis and management of various generic ships without the strict requirement of the presentation of a full five-step framework.

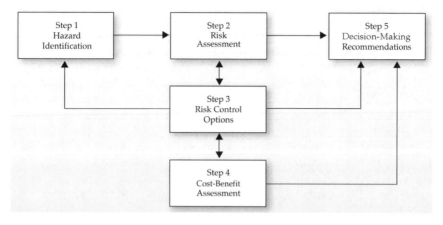

Figure 3.1 Flowchart of the FSA process (IMO, 1997b)

4.1 Identification of hazards

The first step to achieve effective risk assessment and management is to identify and generate a selected list of hazards specific to the problem under review. In FSA of ships, a hazard is defined as "a physical situation with potential for human injury, damage to property, damage to the environment or some combination" (MCA, 1993). Hazard identification is concerned with using the "brainstorming" technique involving trained and experienced personnel to determine the hazards. In FSA of ships, an accident is defined as "a status of the vessel, at the stage where it becomes a reportable incident which has the potential to progress to loss of life, major environmental damage and/ or loss of the vessel" (MCA, 1993). The accident categories include contact or collision, explosion, external hazards, fire, flooding, grounding or stranding, hazardous substance-related failure, loss of hull integrity, machinery failure and loading and unloading-related failure (Wang, 2001).

Human error issues should be systematically dealt with in the FSA framework. Various scientific safety assessment approaches such as Preliminary Hazard Analysis (PHA), Failure Mode, Effects and Criticality Analysis (FMECA), and Hazard and Operability (HAZOP) study, can be applied in this step (Wang, 2001). Once the hazards are identified with respect to each of the above accident categories, significant risks can be chosen using screening techniques. One way of classifying risks is to use the "Risk Matrix" approach (Wang et al., 1999), in which the frequency and consequence ranking values of the risks can be estimated and combined to produce risk ranking numbers on the basis of a mixture of empirical data and expert judgement. As a primary estimation method, the "Risk Matrix" can provide safety engineers with an effective reference to exclude the trivial risks from further investigation. An example of the "Risk Matrix" table and its explanatory notes can be seen in Table 3.1.

Table 3.1 An example of risk matrix table

Frequency / Severity	Extr. remote (F1)	Remote (F2)	Occas. (F3)	Likely (F4)	Reasonably probable (F5)	Freq. (F6)	Extr. freq. (F7)
Negligible (S1)	1	2	3	4	5	6	7
Marginal (S2)	2	3	4	5	6	7	8
Critical (S3)	3	4	5	6	7	8	9
Catastrophic (S4)	4	5	6	7	8	9	10

Negligible risks (1–3); ALARP risks (4–7) (As Low As Reasonably Practicable); Intolerable risks (8–10).

4.2 Assessment of risks

This step aims at estimating risks and factors influencing the level of safety. The assessment of risks involves studying how hazardous events or states develop and interact to cause an accident. Shipping consists of a sequence of distinct phases between which the status of ship functions changes. The major phases include design, construction and commissioning, entering port, berthing, unberthing and leaving port, loading and unloading, dry-docking and decommissioning and disposal.

A ship consists of a set of systems such as machinery, control system, electrical system, communication system, navigation system, piping and pumping system and pressure plant. A serious failure of a system may cause disastrous consequences. Risk estimation may be carried out with respect to each phase of shipping and each such system. The occurrence likelihood of each failure event and its possible consequences can be assessed using various safety assessment techniques (MCA, 1993). For example, an influence diagram, which is a combination of fault tree analysis and event tree analysis, may be used to deal with the escalation of an accident and mitigation aspects such as the evacuation of people, and containment of oil pollutants. Generic data or expert judgements may be used in this step.

4.3 Risk control options

This step aims at proposing effective and practical risk control options (RCOs). High risk areas can be identified from the information produced in Step 2 and then the identification of risk control measures (RCMs) can be initiated. In general, RCMs have a range of attributes including: (1) those relating to the fundamental type of risk reduction (i.e., preventative or mitigating); (2) those relating to the type of action required and therefore to the costs of the action (i.e., engineering or procedural); and (3) those relating to the confidence that can be placed in the measure (i.e., active or passive, single or redundant) (Wang et al., 1999).

RCMs can reduce frequencies of failures and/or mitigate their possible effects and consequences. Structural review techniques may be used to identify all possible RCMs for decision making. For example, a casual chain-based RCMs analysis technique has been developed and well used in practice (PVA, 1997). The identified RCMs can be chosen and categorised to form appropriate RCOs according to the requirement of specific safety strategies in different applications.

4.4 Cost-benefit assessment

Selected RCMs must also be cost-effective (attractive) so that the benefits gained will be greater than the financial loss incurred as a result of the adoption (IMO, 1997b; UK MCA, 1993; Kuo, 1998; Wang, et al., 1999). Therefore, this step aims at identifying benefits from reduced risks and costs associated with the implementation of each RCO for comparisons. To conduct cost-benefit assessment, it is required to set a base case that can be used as a reference for comparisons. A base case is the baseline for analysis reflecting the existing situation and what actually happens rather than what is supposed to happen. A base case reflects the existing level of risk associated with the shipping activity before the implementation of RCOs. The costs and benefits associated with each option can be estimated. The evaluation of costs and benefits may be conducted using various methods and techniques. It should be carried out initially for the overall situation and then for those interested entities associated with the problem.

4.5 Decision-making

This step aims at making decisions and giving recommendations for safety improvement taking into consideration the findings obtained. The information generated in the previous steps can be used to assist in the choice of cost-effective and equitable changes and to select the best RCO.

5. FORMAL SAFETY ASSESSMENT OF A GENERIC FISHING VESSEL

The generic fishing vessel is a hypothetical vessel of any size and method of fishing. It is an appraisal of the functions of operation that is necessary for any fishing vessel. Fishing being a combined production and transport operation is cyclic with the following distinct phases (Loughran et al., 2003): design, construction and commissioning, entering port, berthing, unberthing and leaving port, fish loading and unloading, passage, dry dock and maintenance period and decommissioning and scrapping.

Figure 3.2 shows the considerations when defining a generic fishing vessel based on the following estimations for safety analysis purposes: vessel life expectancy: 25 years, operational days per year: 250, operational hours per day: 13 and major maintenance per year: 1.

A generic fishing vessel may also be considered as being a combination of hard and soft systems such as communication, control, electrical, human, lifting, machinery, management, navigation, piping and pumping and safety.

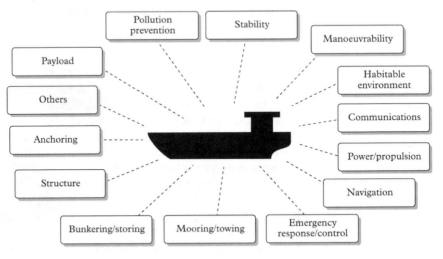

Figure 3.2 Generic fishing vessel (Loughran et al., 2003)

In many cases of fishing vessel accidents, information is incomplete or totally lacking. This makes it difficult to analyse the events that lead to accidents. Accurate historical and current data on vessels, fishermen, professional experience, hours and nature of exposure and safety performance of personnel and equipment are fundamental to assessing safety problems, monitoring results of safety programmes and measuring the effectiveness of safety improvement strategies. Very few data are regularly collected or published on these parameters. The limited data make it difficult to quantify safety problems, determine casual relations and assess safety improvement strategies. However, the data available indicate that significant safety problems exist and that human error, vessels and equipment inadequacies and environmental conditions all contribute to them (Loughran et al., 2003).

From the literature survey, it was found that safety assessment of fishing vessels had been limited to stability considerations and very little work had been carried out on the operational and equipment safety assessment. A full FSA application to a fishing vessel is yet to be carried out. In this chapter, considering the current situation of fishing vessel safety, the FSA methodology proposed by the MCA cannot be directly applied to a generic fishing vessel. It may be more appropriate to concentrate on the first two steps in the FSA framework. As a result, a formal safety analysis for a generic fishing vessel is proposed (Loughran et al., 2003). The proposed formal safety analysis based on the FSA principle considers the characteristics of fishing vessels to identify high risk areas which need design and/or operational attention. The formal safety analysis for fishing vessels can be developed into five steps for ease of understanding as follows: (1) hazard identification (HAZID); (2) risk quantification; (3) risk ranking; (4) recommendations; and (5) decision making.

A test case study on a generic fishing vessel as defined earlier is used to demonstrate its application. The first step is to identify relevant hazards. This consists of determining which hazards affect the fishing vessel's activities under consideration using a "brainstorming" technique involving trained and experienced personnel. In the hazard identification phase, the combined experience and insight of engineers is required to systematically identify all potential failure events at each required level with a view to assessing their influences on system safety and performance.

Information produced from the hazard identification phase will be processed to estimate risk. In the risk quantification phase, the likelihood and possible consequences of each system failure event will be estimated either on a qualitative basis or a quantitative basis (if the events are readily quantified). The level of potential consequences of a system failure event may be quantified in economic terms with regard to loss of lives/property and the degradation of the environment caused by the occurrence of the system failure event. The results produced from the risk quantification phase may be used through the risk ranking phase to assist designers and operators in developing maintenance and operation policies. Risk ranking can be undertaken on a qualitative basis if only qualitative safety information is available.

Accident categories considered in this analysis include capsizing and listing, collisions and contacts, fires and explosions, heavy weather damage, foundering and flooding, loss of hull integrity, machinery damage, missing vessels, stranding and grounding and others.

Having identified the accident categories, the causes are then grouped into the following risk exposure groups in Table 3.2.

Table 3.2 Risk exposure groups in terms of causes of accident categories

1. Human errors	
Human performance	– Abandonment
	– Anchoring
	– Communication
	– Competency
	– Fishing
	– Mooring
	– Navigation
Commercial pressures	– Company or firm procedures
	– Finance
	– Manning
Management systems	– Loading fish
	– Onboard management
	– Shore side systems
2. Hardware failures	
	– Bunkering and storage
	– Control
	– Diagnostic system
	– Electrical
	– Emission control
	– Habitable environment
	– Maintenance systems
	– Material of construction
	– Piping and plumbing
	– Propulsion
	– Refrigeration
	– Safety
	– Steering
	– Structure
3. External events	
Environment	– Climatic variations
	– Pollution prevention
Payload	– Berthing
	– Crane/lifting mechanisms
	– Fish handling and storage

In order to sort the large amount of information collected at the HAZID meeting, a set of accident sub-categories is established in Table 3.3.

Table 3.3 Accident sub-categories

1. Collision and contact accident sub-category	
	– Abnormal operation
	– Anchored
	– Arrival manoeuvring close to the berth
	– Berthed
	– Departing and manoeuvring close to the berth
	– Dry-docked
	– Entering harbour
	– Loading and unloading in port
	– Loading fish at sea
	– Maintenance
	– Manoeuvring in harbour and close to harbour
	– Passage in open sea
	– Shutdown
	– Starting up
2. Fire accident sub-category	
	– Accommodation
	– Engine room
	– Fish room space
	– Galley
	– Wheelhouse
3. Loss of hull integrity accident sub-category	
	– Appendages
	– Bulkheads
	– Framing
	– Hull plating
	– Opening or failure of doors
	– Opening or failure of scuttles
	– Penetrations
	– Seals
	– Welds and joints
	– Others

The risk matrix approach is used in the hazard screening process. For each appropriate combination, an assessment is made of the frequency (F) of the accident, and the severity (S) of the consequences in terms of human injuries/deaths, property damage/loss and the degradation of the environment (Loughran et al., 2003; Pillay, 2001). The corresponding risk ranking number (RRN) is then selected from the risk matrix table. This method allows for expert judgements where detailed data is unavailable. Table 3.1 (in section 4.1) shows the risk matrix table that gives in a tabular format, a risk level related to the frequency and severity of an accident. RRN ranges from 1 (least frequent and least severe consequence) to 10 (most frequent and most severe consequence).

Table 3.4 gives the interpretation of the frequencies F1 to F7. Using the risk matrix approach, for each accident category a ranked risk table is produced, listing all accident sub-categories against each generic location. An example of this is seen in Table 3.5. The number in the brackets is the corresponding RRN obtained from Table 3.1. Upon completing the risk table, the next task is to determine the "Equivalent Total" for each accident category.

Table 3.4 Key to risk matrix table

Likely to happen on a vessel once	General Interpretation	Generic fishing vessel Interpretation
F1 10,000–100,000 years	Extremely remote to extremely improbable	Likely to happen every 20 yrs in the industry
F2 1,000–10,000 years	Remote to extremely remote	Likely to happen every 2 yrs in the industry
F3 100–1,000 years	Occasional	Likely to happen 5 times per yr in the industry
F4 10–100 years	Likely	Likely up to 3 times per vessel life
F5 1–10 years	Reasonably probable	Likely up to 30 times per vessel life
F6 Yearly	Frequent	Likely annually per vessel
F7 Monthly	Extremely frequent	Likely monthly per vessel

Table 3.5 Example of a risk table

Accident sub-category	Generic location				
	Berth	Harbour	Coastal	At sea	Dry dock
Engine room	F5 S1 (5)	F5 S2 (6)	F5 S3 (7)	....	....
Bridge	F1 S2 (2)	F1 S3 (3)	....	....	....
Cargo hold	....	....	....	....	....

The purpose for calculating the "Equivalent Total" is to provide a means of integrating the risks evaluated for each hazard of the accident sub-category. It will also provide a means of estimating each accident category to determine and justify the allocation of resources—to eliminate or reduce the risk.

Table 3.6 represents an example for a fire accident category. The data have been drawn from the MAIB (Marine Accident Investigation Branch) reports. Tables 3.1 and 3.4 are used to assign the values of S and F (Loughran et al., 2003). A RRN is assigned for each accident sub-category at different generic locations. Table 3.6 can be generated for each accident category by analysing the incident/accident data in terms of its occurrence likelihood and severity of possible consequences.

Table 3.6 Fire risk ranking

Accident sub-category	Generic location				
	Berthing/ unberthing	Manoeuvring (harbour)	At sea (coastal)	At sea (open sea)	Dry dock maintenance
Fish room space	F4 S1 (4)	F4 S2 (5)	F4 S3 (6)	F4 S3 (6)	F4 S1 (4)
Galley	F4 S1 (4)	F4 S2 (5)	F4 S3 (6)	F4 S4 (7)	F4 S1 (4)
Crew accomm.	F4 S2 (5)	F4 S2 (5)	F4 S3 (6)	F4 S3 (6)	F4 S1 (4)
Bridge	F3 S1 (3)	F3 S1 (3)	F3 S1 (3)	F3 S1 (3)	F3 S1 (3)
Engine room	F5 S1 (5)	F5 S2 (6)	F5 S3 (7)	F5 S3 (7)	F5 S2 (6)

Table 3.7 shows the number of times each RRN appears within an accident category (only those with RRN values larger than 3 are considered). For example, RRN 4 appears five times (as highlighted in Table 3.6). As the RRN for each accident sub-category is considered for different generic locations, an "Equivalent Total" is calculated to give the accident category an index which will be used later to compare against other accident categories.

Table 3.7 Number of occurrences of fire risk ranking scores

RRN	No. of occurrences for accident category, fire
4	5
5	5
6	7
7	3

The calculation makes use of the fact that both the frequency and severity bands of the risk matrix are approximately logarithmic (e.g. a risk level of 6 is treated as 10^6) (IMO, 1997b). Using 7 as a base then the following can be obtained from Table 3.7:

$$\text{"Equivalent Total"} = 7 + \text{Log} \ (3.000 + 0.700 + 0.050 + 0.005) = \\ 7 + \text{Log} \ (3.755) = 7.57 \tag{1}$$

Alternatively using the risk ranking score of 4 as the base, then:

$$\text{"Equivalent Total"} = 4 + \text{Log} \ (3000 + 700 + 40 + 5) = \\ 4 + \text{Log} \ (3755) = 7.57 \tag{2}$$

It can be noted that the risk ranking score does not change with the base chosen. Similarly, for each of other accident categories an "Equivalent Total" can be calculated and the value obtained will give a direct indication of the areas needing attention. The higher the value of the "Equivalent Total", the higher the associated risk with reference to that category.

For particular risk factors, there is a range of RCOs. It is most cost-effective to reduce risk factors at the early design stages. Additional costs are incurred in redesigning or modifying plant or processes once they are being used.

At this stage, practical RCOs are recommended while considering the effectiveness of each option. An RCO could be in the form of a preventive measure—where the RCO reduces the probability of occurrence of an undesirable event, and/or a mitigating measure—where the RCO reduces the severity of its possible consequences. Other factors that need to be considered are the cost of the RCO and the stakeholders who will be affected by its implementations.

Stakeholders can be defined to be any entity (e.g., person, organisation, company, nation state or grouping of these), who is directly affected by accidents or by the cost effectiveness of the industry. For any particular stakeholder, its stake in a generic vessel can be a definite committed monetary value such as an investment or payment. Stakeholders can be voluntary, involuntary or a mixture of both. In the decision-making process, the stakeholders may be affected directly, indirectly or by representative groupings. The stakeholders are identified for a generic fishing vessel as classification society, coastal state, crew, designer/constructor, emergency services, flag state, insurance companies, other vessels, owner, port authority, port state and suppliers.

The best RCO for the estimated risks of the generic vessel can be identified by determining the cost and benefit of each RCO with respect to the stakeholders mentioned above.

Each RCO needs to be evaluated in accordance with the costs for its implementation and maintenance through the vessel's lifetime, as well as the benefits received for the same period. This evaluation is required to be carried out at two levels, primarily for the overall situation and then for each of the parties concerned and/or affected (stakeholders) with respect to the problem under review (IMO, 1997b; MSC, 1998a and 1998b; Wang, 2001). The cost and benefit for each RCO have to be calculated in terms of its Net Present Value (NPV). NPV can be numerically represented as:

$$NPV = \sum_{t=1}^{n} [(B_t - C_t)(1 + r)^{-t}] \tag{3}$$

where: t = time horizon for the assesment, starting in year 1.

B_t = the sum of benefits in year t.

C_t = the sum of costs in year t.

r = the discount rate.

n = the number of years in the vessel's lifetime.

A positive NPV suggests that the implementation of the RCO would be financially beneficial (cost-effective). All the RCOs can be ranked in terms of their NPVs and the most appropriate RCO with the largest value can then be chosen.

It is then required to determine the possible RCOs for the generic vessel considered. As data for quantifying each RCO are difficult to obtain, hypothetical RCOs are considered for the demonstration of this method. The cost and benefit columns in Table 3.8 represent the cumulative values for all the stakeholders involved in the study. The views presented by each stakeholder may considerably affect the outcome of the NPV. Considering the four RCOs given, and the associated cost and benefit, an NPV for each RCO can be obtained.

Table 3.8 RCOs determined for generic vessel

Risk Control Options	Cost (each year)	Benefit (each year)
RCO 1	£50,000	£25,000
RCO 2	£10,000	£25,000
RCO 3	£10,000	£15,000
RCO 4	£30,000	£40,000

Assuming that the time horizon for the safety assessment is for 25 years at a discount rate of 3%, and using equation (1), the NPV calculation for each RCO is given as follows:

$$NPV_1 = \sum_{t=1}^{25} [(25,000 - 50,000)(1 + 0.03)^{-t}] = -435,329 \tag{4}$$

$$NPV_2 = \sum_{t=1}^{25} [(25,000 - 10,000)(1 + 0.03)^{-t}] = 261,198 \tag{5}$$

$$NPV_3 = \sum_{t=1}^{25} [(15,000 - 10,000)(1 + 0.03)^{-t}] = 87,065 \tag{6}$$

$$NPV_4 = \sum_{t=1}^{25} [(40,000 - 30,000)(1 + 0.03)^{-t}] = 174,132 \tag{7}$$

From the results obtained, it is determined that RCO 2 is the best option (from a cost-benefit point of view) and can be recommended for implementation.

The formal safety analysis can be further developed to make it more elaborate and complete by using the MCA/IMO type of FSA for a generic fishing vessel as more data is collected.

6. USE OF ADVANCES IN TECHNOLOGY FOR FACILITATING SAFETY ASSESSMENT

FSA is a rational and systematic methodology for assessing risks and evaluating the costs and benefits of different options for the reduction of those risks (Wang et al., 2004; Yang, 2006). The methodology is based on the principles of identifying hazards, evaluating risks and cost-benefit assessment, and has as its objective the development of a framework of safety requirements for shipping in which risks are addressed in a comprehensive and cost-effective manner (MCA, 1993). Use of FSA in ship design and operation may offer great potential incentives and lead to many attractive benefits (MCA, 1993). However, to obtain such benefits is not straightforward. The traditional FSA framework and the associated probabilistic risk analysis and decision-making techniques may not be well suited to modelling maritime system safety with a high level of uncertainty involved. Some arguments/problems such as the quantification of human elements, the availability and reliability of failure data, the feasibility and effectiveness of cost-benefit analysis and the treatment of system dependency have therefore arisen to challenge the qualification of the FSA methodology. It may become worse where the fact that the IMO guidelines do not explicitly address the issue on how to consolidate a decision-maker's confidence in both providing qualitative information and using the results and the recommendations produced from an FSA study, is concerned. Lack of reliable failure data and lack of confidence in safety assessment have been two major challenges in safety analyses of various engineering activities (Wang, 2001) including FSA of ship design and operation. Under this circumstance, one of the major concerns of marine safety analysts is to explore and exploit flexible and advanced risk-modelling and decision-making approaches using uncertainty treatment methods for producing detailed guidelines to facilitate the practical application of FSA.

In recent years, many research activities have taken place to tackle the uncertainties in maritime risk assessment. In the context of FSA of ship design and operation, the research has been carried out using the methods based on fuzzy possibilistic, Bayesian probabilistic, Dempster-Shafer theories and their combination, depending on the availability and completeness of failure data, the level of the analysis required and the degree of complexity of the inter-relationships of risk factors. Many relevant studies and their results have been observed and reported, including:

1. Approximate reasoning approach for dealing with risk analysis problems associated with a high level of uncertainty (Wang et al., 1995; Wang, 1997). It is extended to include subjective risk analysis methods (Wang et al., 1996), evidential reasoning techniques, fuzzy set modelling methods, and the Dempster-Shafer method for risk-modelling and decision making (Sii et al., 2001; Pillay and Wang, 2003).
2. Belief fuzzy rule-based evidential reasoning approach for risk estimation

(Liu et al., 2004; Yang et al., 2005a). It is extended to develop belief fuzzy link-based evidential reasoning method for safety-based multiple criteria decision making and to combine with a Bayesian reasoning mechanism for the generation of belief fuzzy rule-based Bayesian reasoning approach for both risk-modelling and decision making (Yang et al., 2007a).

3. Application of Bayesian network (BN) approach. It includes the use of traditional BN and fuzzy BN approaches for risk diagnosis and prediction (Eleye-Datubo et al., 2006; Eleye-Datubo, 2006) and the development of the hybrid of BN, fuzzy sets and entropy theory to handle multiple dynamic risk attribute decision making (Yang et al., 2007b).

It should be mentioned that the above is only a partial list that has been investigated by some selected researchers, and there are more techniques (i.e., Monte Carlo simulation, artificial neural network, fuzzy fault tree analysis, fuzzy TOPSIS and analytical hierarchy process, etc.) in general engineering and technology that have been/may be applied to facilitate the uncertainty treatment of risk-modelling and decision making in FSA of ship design and operation.

Apart from the uncertainty treatment, several research topics in the application of FSA to ship design and operation are currently under investigation in both academic and industrial areas. They include the introduction of individual ship safety cases; the collection and analysis of failure data; the definition of risk criteria acceptance; the consideration of human error; the standardisation of subjective judgement through the employment of effective expert assessment procedures; the qualification of the framework itself including the discussion related to the feasibility of adding new monitoring and verifying steps; the simplification of the techniques involved; and the exploration of appropriate computing software, etc. It is believed that through the research into such topic areas, more flexible and effective measures will be developed and applied towards the establishment of a safer shipping community.

7. DISCUSSIONS AND RECOMMENDATIONS

FSA can be feasibly applied to safety studies of many types of ships such as bulk carriers, containerships and fishing vessels, etc., provided that several areas, which may cause arguments, are further deliberated. These areas influence both the general principles of FSA and the specific requirements for their practical applications, either directly or indirectly. The most prominent ones are analysed and alternative suggestions are described as follows.

7.1 The brainstorming technique

Although the knowledge and expertise of the people involved in the brainstorming process is absolutely respectable, certain safety aspects may be overlooked as it might be considered "natural" from their point of view, while to a person outside the profession it might be something completely new, thus causing concern.

Since by definition the "brainstorming session" ought to be structured to encourage the unfettered thinking and participation of the people involved, the contribution by people with less expertise in the subject would be a positive one, as they might bring up safety issues, which otherwise would have been overlooked (Wang and Foinikis, 2001).

7.2 Need for interaction with other industries' safety and quality management systems

FSA for ships should develop the ability to interact with regulatory bodies responsible for port and land-based operations, especially with the fast development of container-based multi-model transportation. Sharing the relevant data of non-compliance with established safety and quality standards for the relevant industries would eliminate a considerable percentage of the uncertainty created in this direction.

7.3 Risk criteria

Risk criteria are standards that represent a view, usually that of a regulator, of how much risk is acceptable/tolerable (HSE, 1995). In the final step of FSA, the decision-making process, criteria may be used to determine if risks are acceptable, unacceptable or need to be reduced to an ALARP level. Large variations exist in the risk criteria in different industries by individual administrations. When quantitative risk assessment (QRA) is performed, numerical risk criteria are normally required. However, it may not always be appropriate to use risk criteria as inflexible rules, given uncertainties involved in risk assessment. The shipping industry has functioned reasonably well for a long time without consciously making use of risk criteria. In general, there are no quantitative criteria in FSA for a particular type of ship or a particular ship, although the MCA's trial applications have used QRA to a certain extent (Wang, 2002). As more QRA is conducted in maritime safety assessment, numerical risk criteria in the shipping industry need to be dealt with in more detail. Currently, the development of acceptable risk criteria for ships can be achieved through a compromise between qualitative and quantitative figures by following the general rules as (a) the activity should not impose any risk that can reasonably be avoided; (b) the risks should not be disproportionate to the benefits; (c) the risks should not be unduly concentrated on particular individuals; and (d) the risks of catastrophic accidents should be a small proportion of the total (Spouse, 1997; Wang, 2002). More specifically, a numerical value could be defined and agreed as the upper tolerable/acceptable limit, which should not be exceeded in any circumstances. For example, maximum tolerable risk for workers may be 10^{-6} per year according to the UK HSE industrial risk criteria. In the regions between the maximum tolerable and broadly acceptable levels, risks should be reduced to an ALARP level, taking costs and benefits of any further risk reduction into account (Wang, 2001).

7.4 Human element

Another important factor to be taken into consideration is human element. Problems like differences in language, education, training and mentality, etc., have increased over the past years, especially with the introduction of multi-national crews. Such problems largely contribute to marine casualties. On the other hand, crew reductions have increased the workload of operators, which in connection with the reduced opportunities for port stay and recreation equally increases the probabilities for errors.

It becomes apparent that FSA's success largely depends on two essential conditions. The first condition is the development of a safety culture at all levels of the industry's infrastructure, from company managers to vessel operators. The second one is the development of further guidance on how human factors would be integrated into the FSA framework in a feasible manner. To a large extent, the human error can be identified, dealt with and reduced by the application of effective human reliability methods to the FSA framework and adequate training of crews.

7.5 The availability and reliability of data/information

Primarily, great attention should be paid to the data resources, as the various databases do not always use the same platform for data analysis. This is attributable to the fact that different organisations look into safety issues from different perspectives, which facilitates their own interests. In order to overcome the problems related to the availability and reliability of failure data, international co-operation and coordination are required with the intention that a new global database will be established, controlled and updated by an international regulatory body (i.e., the IMO). Such a database should be easily accessible by both administrations and analysts/researchers providing reliable data with defined parameters upon which the incoming information has been processed.

As far as expert judgements used to compensate the lack of failure data are concerned: (a) scientific procedures that standardise a human being's performance; (b) analytical techniques that enable the reasonable aggregation of the estimations from multiple experts; and (c) logical approaches that maximally reduce their own limitation to the presentation of experts' judgements, should always be employed to support effective, consistent and informative decision making thus avoiding making costly inappropriate decisions.

7.6 Cost-benefit analysis

The use of cost-benefit analysis as a foundation on which a given option is finally selected for implementation is an appealing proposal. In practice, however, it can be quite complicated, especially in cases where human lives are involved. The fact that ships are manned with multi-national crews, usually officers from developed countries and other seafarers from developing ones, and obliged to trade in all parts of the world creates a difficulty in selecting the proper human life value for cost-benefit analysis. Furthermore, the use of different values on different nationalities would have an adverse and undesirable effect on both international relations and working conditions onboard ships.

A feasible solution to this problem would, once more, involve an international agreement on a reliable method of estimating the current value of human life. The international regulatory bodies should not only be responsible for the initial deliberations, but also for the constant follow up of the international economic, political and social trends which influence that value.

7.7 Risk-Based Verification

A Risk-Based Verification (RBV) scheme has been introduced recently to the offshore industry for the management of risks in design and operation. In the context of the offshore environment, verification of Safety Critical Elements (SCEs) is required to be undertaken by the operator for the life of an installation, from design and construction through to operation and ultimately decommissioning. The topic of RBV has recently attracted much attention from both the academic community and the industrial sector. To improve the efficiency of a verification scheme, a risk-based process can be employed in which the outcome may result in resources and attention being focused towards the high-risk areas. The risk associated with an asset or a system can be assessed in relation to different levels and the verification process can be used to manage such risk. The major steps in an RBV scheme are: (1) definition of asset hierarchy; (2) major accident hazard identification and screening; (3) identification of safety critical elements; (4) definition of performance standards; (5) identification of means of performance assurance; (6) assessment of criticality; (7) identification of means of verification; (8) documentation of the verification arrangements; and (9) execution of verification scheme.

RBV can appropriately ensure using available resources in a balanced way to control risks throughout the life cycle of an asset. In principle, through focusing on high-risk elements and prioritising verification efforts it should provide both time and cost savings compared with the traditional prescriptive verification or certification regime.

As more experience on the use of RBV is gathered in the offshore industry, it is likely and beneficial to apply it together with FSA to the marine industry for facilitating risk-based ship design and operation.

8. CONCLUSION

The main intention of FSA (during the development stages of the approach) was to be applied to the regulatory regime for shipping. However, over the years its potential has been recognised as a tool not only to develop safety rules and regulations but also to deal with safety problems associated with design and operation of ships. The necessity and benefits of adopting an FSA framework have been described, demonstrated and discussed.

The FSA philosophy has been approved by the IMO for reviewing the current safety and environmental protection regulations and justifying a new element proposal to the IMO by an individual administration. This chapter has described the current methodology in a five-step integrated framework as proposed by MCA to the IMO and also conducted a trial application of the proposed FSA method for a generic fishing vessel. As partially exposed in the trial application, several concerns regarding the application of the FSA are currently under debate, both at the IMO and by its member states, in terms of technical and regulatory considerations. Novel risk analysis and safety-based decision-making models have been developed to treat appropriately uncertainties involved in FSA for facilitating formal ship safety assessment. Other main technical concerns associated with the application of FSA and its future development have been addressed in this study by discussions and recommendations.

Among the possible regulation-related application options, questioning about the introduction of an individual ship approach may have the greatest impact on marine safety. It could change the nature of the safety regulations at sea as it may lead to deviation from traditional prescriptive requirements in the conventions towards performance-based criteria. However, due to many difficulties related to the safety evaluation by other administrations, it is in the near future unlikely to put in place a requirement for individual ship safety cases although its potential benefits have been well recognised.

It is also very important to take into account that with the employment of more novel uncertainty treatment methods, FSA may be used effectively to incorporate safety into the ship design process from the initial stages in order to reduce possible negative influence (i.e., unexpected costs and delays) due to late modifications. Finally, FSA could form the basis for further development of individual risk-modelling and decision-making tools to face the challenge imposed by the increasing technical standards and the growing complexity of modern ships.

CHAPTER 4

US SHIP ACCIDENT RESEARCH

Di Jin, Hauke Kite-Powell and Wayne K. Talley

1. INTRODUCTION

Accidents involving maritime vessels can lead to considerable economic losses that are borne by the shipping industry and by society. Accidents may be influenced by factors associated with human operators, vessel characteristics, weather conditions, local waterways, and economic conditions in the markets, among others. These factors influence both accident frequency and severity. Damages resulting from ship accidents include human injuries and loss of life, vessel damage, lost cargoes, environmental pollution and related economic impacts, and damage to other property. Government agencies have a recognised role in formulating and enforcing safety regulations that reduce the occurrence and effects of vessel accidents (Figure 4.1).

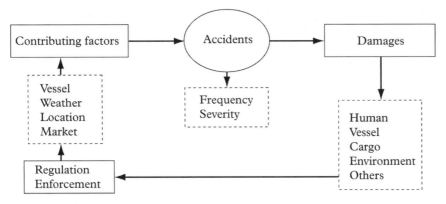

Figure 4.1 Ship accident analysis

This chapter reviews a series of prior studies of ship accidents in the United States and synthesises the results to present a comprehensive picture of vessel accident analysis using official data on maritime vessel accidents from the US Coast Guard. The review covers studies on accident severity and probability, the effectiveness of regulatory enforcement, the economics of alternative accident prevention technologies, and marine pollution liability.

Section 2 discusses ship accidents and their contributing factors, relevant data source, and research methods. Sections 3, 4, and 5 review research findings on crew and passenger injuries, vessel damages, and oil spills, respectively. Section 6 describes studies on accident probability. Reviews of analyses of marine safety enforcement programmes, accident and pollution prevention technologies, and oil pollution liability are presented in sections 7, 8, and 9, respectively. Section 10 summarises the key findings.

2. DATA AND METHODOLOGY

Most studies reviewed in the chapter utilize vessel casualty statistics compiled by the US Coast Guard. The Coast Guard database contains detailed records on vessel accidents in US waters, with each observation describing a vessel involved in an accident. A long list of variables describes the vessel, time and location of the accident, and other related information (e.g., vessel tonnage and flag).

The name and format of the Coast Guard database have changed over the years. Between 1981 and 1991, the vessel casualty database was called CAS-MAIN. From 1992–2001, vessel casualty records were incorporated into a larger database called the Marine Safety Information System (MSIS).

A central purpose of vessel accident analysis is to improve understanding of statistical relationships, and possible causal links, between accidents and contributing factors. Results of this type of study can help policymakers develop regulation and enforcement mechanisms to target key factors, and contribute to the effective reduction of vessel accidents.

The severity of a vessel accident may be measured as the damages to the vessel, cargo and other properties, the marine environment, and/or injuries to crew and passengers. This damage or injury severity associated with a vessel accident (Y) is hypothesised to be influenced by factors including vessel characteristics (including hull construction material, type of propulsion, etc.), vessel operations, weather and visibility conditions, waterway characteristics, and cause of vessel accident, i.e.:

$$Y = F \text{ (\textit{type of vessel accident, vessel characteristics, vessel operation phase, weather condition, type of waterway, type of vessel propulsion, type of vessel hull construction, cause of vessel accident, others})} \tag{1}$$

Table 4.1 Explanatory variables in ship accident analysis

Type of vessel	Type of vessel accident	Vessel characteristics	Vessel operation phase	Weather condition
Tanker Tank barge Freight ship Freight barge Passenger Tug boat Fishing vessel Recreational vessel	Allision Capsize Collision Equipment failure Explosion Fire Flood Sinking Grounding Number of vessels involved in the accident	Vessel size Vessel age US flag	Moored or docked Anchored Towed Underway or adrift	High winds Precipitation Cold temperature Poor visibility Night-time

Type of waterway	Type of vessel propulsion	Type of vessel hull construction	Cause of vessel accident	Coast Guard district
Harbour River Coastal Ocean Lake	Diesel Gasoline Turbine	Aluminium Fibreglass Steel Plastic Wood	Human Vessel Environmental	District 1 District 2 District 5 District 7 District 8 District 9 District 11 District 13 District 14 District 17

From the Coast Guard database, a set of variables can be extracted or constructed to quantify each contributing factor in equation (1). As shown in Table 4.1, "Type of vessel accident" includes allision, collision, equipment-failure, explosion, fire, flooding, grounding, capsize or sinking.[1] "Vessel characteristics" include vessel size, vessel age, and vessel flag (e.g., whether the vessel is a US flag vessel). "Vessel operation phase" distinguishes between vessels that were moored or docked, anchored, towed, underway, or adrift at the time of the accident. "Weather" describes whether high winds (greater than 20 knots), precipitation, and/or cold temperatures (less than 32°F) persisted at the time of the accident. Visibility differentiates between good and poor visibility at the time of the accident, and whether it occurred during night-time or daytime. "Type of waterway" includes harbour, river, coastal, ocean, lake, or bay. "Type of vessel propulsion" includes diesel, gasoline, and

---

1. An allision accident occurs when a vessel strikes a stationary object (not another vessel) on the water surface. A collision accident occurs when a vessel strikes or was struck by another vessel on the water surface. A grounding accident occurs when the vessel is in contact with the sea bottom or a bottom obstacle.

turbine. "Type of vessel hull construction" includes aluminium, fibreglass, steel, or wood.

"Cause of vessel accident" may be a human cause as opposed to an environmental or mechanical (vessel) cause.[2] The 10 US "Coast Guard districts" cover different regions of the country: the first Coast Guard District covers the New England and New York Atlantic coast; the second District covers the Midwest; the fifth District, the Mid-Atlantic coast (southern New Jersey to North Carolina); the seventh District, the Southern Atlantic coast (South Carolina to Florida); the eighth District, the Gulf coast; the ninth District, the Great Lakes; the 11th District, the California coast; the 13th District, the Pacific Northwest coast; the 14th District, Hawaii; and the 17th District, Alaska.

All the above variables are binary (0 or 1) except vessel size (measured in gross tons) and vessel age (years). In addition, variables on Coast Guard enforcement efforts (e.g., vessel inspection and port patrol hours) as well as market variables (e.g., price of oil) may be included to examine possible regulatory enforcement and market effects.

Using the explanatory variables (x_i) in Table 4.1, equation (1) may be written as a reduced-form equation:

$$Y = G(x_1, x_2, ..., x_n) + \varepsilon \tag{2}$$

where ε is an error term. The dependent variable (Y) may be estimated using different regression techniques, depending on the specific definition of Y.[3]

When Y represents counts of rare events such as crew injuries or deaths, equation (2) may be estimated using Poisson regression analysis. Typically, vessel accidents with injuries are infrequent; also, if injuries occur, they are few in number. The preponderance of zeros and the small values and discrete nature of accident crew injuries suggest that the estimation could be improved, relative to ordinary least squares (OLS), by using Poisson regression, which accounts for these characteristics.

However, the Poisson regression model has the restrictive assumption that the mean and variance of the dependent variable are equal. When this restriction is not met, equation (2) may be estimated using Negative Binomial regression, which is the most commonly used alternative to Poisson regression. The negative binomial regression model does not require the variance and mean of the dependent variable to be equal.

---

2. Examples of human causes of vessel accidents as classified by the US Coast Guard include stress, fatigue, carelessness, operator error, lack of training, error in judgement, lack of knowledge, inadequate supervision, psychological impairment and intoxication. Examples of environmental causes include adverse weather, debris, shoaling, submerged object and adverse current/sea condition. Examples of vessel causes include corrosion, dragging anchor, stress fracture, fouled propeller, steering failure, propulsion failure, auxiliary power failure and inadequate controls/displays/lighting (Millar, 1980).

3. For discussions of relevant regression models, see Greene (1997).

Given the absence of information on injury severity, Y may also be modelled as a latent variable with an observable ordinal injury severity variable S (e.g., $S = 0$, 1, and 2 denote no injury, non-fatal injuries, and fatal injuries, respectively). The probabilities of S can then be estimated using an ordered probit model.

When Y is binary (e.g., $Y = 1$ if the vessel is a total loss and 0 otherwise), equation (2) is estimated via Probit regression which restricts the predictions of Y to lie in the interval between zero and one. Logit analysis can also be used in this case.[4]

In modelling vessel damage severity, Y is typically defined as the value of vessel damage per gross ton. Given that a vessel accident does not necessarily incur damage, some of the observations of this parameter may be zero. If so, the distribution of Y observations will be left-censored. Consequently, parameter estimates for equation (2) obtained by using OLS, which ignores censoring, may be biased. Specifically, ordinary least squares fails to account for the qualitative difference between the limit (or zero) observations and the non-limit (or continuous) observations. Such bias is avoided by utilizing tobit regression analysis, which explicitly accounts for censored dependent variables.

3. CREW AND PASSENGER INJURIES

The determinants of crew injuries in vessel accidents were examined by Talley et al. (2005a). Separate equations for the number of non-fatal crew injuries, fatal crew injuries, and missing crew in freight ship, tanker and tugboat vessel accidents were estimated using individual vessel accidents data from the US Coast Guard for the 1991–2001 period and Poisson and negative binomial regressions. The results suggest that:

- conditions associated with non-fatal injuries include operations at a mooring or dock, high winds, and cold temperatures (for ships), and poor visibility (for tugboats);
- conditions associated with fatal injuries include higher vessel age (for freight ships), fires (for tankers), and capsize events (for tugboats); and
- conditions associated with missing crew events are higher vessel age (for freight ships) and fire and lake operations (for tugboats).

A similar analysis (Jin et al., 2001) was carried out on the determinants of the number of fatal and non-fatal crew injuries in commercial fishing vessel accidents, using negative binomial regressions. The results indicate that:

---

4. Probit is based on the cumulative normal probability function and Logit on the cumulative logistic probability function. Since these cumulative probability functions are quite similar, their estimation results, for a given model, are also quite similar. However, the Logit model is easier to use from a computational point of view and thus is often preferred. For further discussion, see Greene (1997).

- crew fatalities occur more often in the context of fires/explosions and capsizings than other types of accidents (3.5 and 3.8 fatalities for every 100 such accidents, respectively);
- the expected number of crew fatalities varies inversely with the price of fish, suggesting that fishermen may be less able to manage risks when the economics of commercial fishing are poor; and
- fishing vessel collisions result in non-fatal crew injuries at a rate of 2.1 crew injuries per 100 accidents.

A policy implication is that policies reducing fires/explosions and capsizings may be effective in reducing fatal injuries, whereas policies addressing collision risk may be more effective in reducing non-fatal injuries.

Talley et al. (2006) analyse determinants of the number of injuries, deaths, and missing person cases associated with passenger vessel accidents investigated by the US Coast Guard between 1991 and 2001. In this study, the different types of passenger vessels were included as explanatory variables.[5] Negative binomial regression estimates suggest that:

- the number of injuries incurred is greater for passenger-freight combination vessel accidents than for those involving other types of passenger vessels;
- accidents occurring in conditions of precipitation and poor visibility result in larger numbers of deaths; and
- capsize accidents and larger vessels are associated with larger numbers of missing person incidents.

A major conclusion of this study is that passenger vessel accidents resulting from human (as opposed to environmental and vessel/mechanical) causes result in increases in the number of injured, deceased and missing occupants.

Results of a closer analysis of cruise vessel[6] (Talley et al., 2008a) and ferry vessel (Talley et al., 2008b) accidents using ordered probit models suggest that:

- accident injury severity is greater for ocean cruise than for inland waterway and harbour/dinner cruise vessel accidents;
- accident injury severity is greater for both cruise and ferry vessel accidents associated with a human (as opposed to environmental or mechanical) cause; and
- in accidents caused by a human factor, the probabilities of non-fatal and fatal injuries increase by 0.088 and 0.008, respectively.

5. The type of passenger vessel includes ocean cruise, inland waterway cruise, harbour/dinner cruise, ferry, and passenger-freight combination vessel.
6. Including ocean cruise, inland waterway cruise, and harbour/dinner cruise.

Table 4.2 Factors affecting crew and passenger injury on ships

	Freight ship	Tanker	Tugboat	Fishing vessel	Passenger ship	Cruise ship	Ferry
Type of vessel accident							
Allision					⋆		
Capsize			⋆	⋆	⋆		
Collision				⋆	⋆		
Explosion				⋆			
Fire		⋆	⋆	⋆			
Sinking				⋆			
Number of vessels involved in the accident				⋆			
Vessel characteristics							
Vessel size			⋆		⋆		
Vessel age	⋆	⋆					
Vessel operation phase							
Moored or docked	⋆	⋆	⋆				
Anchored			⋆		⋆		
Towed		⋆					
Weather condition							
High winds	⋆	⋆					
Precipitation				⋆	⋆		
Cold temperature	⋆	⋆					
Poor visibility		⋆	⋆		⋆		
Type of waterway							
Ocean		⋆			⋆		
Lake			⋆				
Type of vessel propulsion							
Diesel					⋆		
Type of vessel hull construction							
Steel						⋆	
Cause of vessel accident							
Human					⋆	⋆	⋆
Coast Guard district							
District 2			⋆		⋆	⋆	
District 7		⋆			⋆		
District 8		⋆				⋆	
District 11		⋆					
District 13	⋆						
District 17					⋆		

Note: * denotes significance at or above 10% level.

Table 4.2 summarises results on key contributing factors to crew and passenger injuries across different vessel types. Among the types of accidents, fire, capsize, and collision are more likely to increase injury severity than others. Greater injury severity is associated with bad weather conditions, especially poor visibility. Injury severity is greater when cargo vessels and tugboats are moored or docked, than when they are underway. Accidents caused by human factors are highly significant for different passenger vessels. Injury severity appears to vary across geographic regions (Coast Guard Districts).

4. VESSEL DAMAGES

Talley (1999) examines determinants of the vessel, oil cargo spillage, and other-property damage costs of tanker accidents. Tobit estimation of a three-equation recursive model suggests that:

- fire/explosion accidents incur the largest vessel damage costs, but the smallest oil cargo spillage costs;
- grounding accidents incur the smallest vessel damage costs, but the largest oil cargo spillage costs, reflecting the difficulty of controlling oil cargo spillage subsequent to such accidents; and
- oil cargo spillage costs are lower for US flag tanker accidents than for those involving non-US flag tankers.

In a separate study (Talley, 2000) of the oil spillage, vessel damage, and other-property damage costs of US inland waterway tank barge accidents, tobit estimation of a three-equation recursive model suggests that type of accident, cause of accident, operating conditions, vessel characteristics, and regulation are significant determinants of damages:

- collision accidents incur the largest oil spillage and vessel damage costs; and
- fire/explosion accidents incur the largest other-property damage costs.

Talley (1996) examines determinants of the risk and severity of cargo damage associated with containership accidents, utilizing data on individual vessel accidents in US waters for the period 1981–1989. Results suggest that the propensity of a containership accident to incur cargo damage, and the monetary value of this cargo damage per ship gross ton, is:

- lower if the ship is manned by a licensed (versus an unlicensed) operator at the time of the accident;
- lower for larger-sized (versus smaller-sized) ships; and
- greater for collision and fires/explosion than for grounding accidents.

The results also suggest that the cargo damage per ship gross ton from a containership accident is greater if the vessel is adrift than if it is docked or moored.

Talley (2002) investigates whether there are accident vessel damage cost differentials among container, tanker and bulk vessels in US waters. Tobit estimates of accident vessel damage cost equations suggest that normalised vessel damage costs do not differ significantly between container and tanker vessels. However, the damage costs of bulk vessels differ significantly from those of the other two types of vessels. The vessel damage cost per vessel gross ton of a container ship accident is $33.37, and that of a tanker accident is $18.37, less than that of a bulk vessel accident, all else held constant. The damage cost differentials are associated mainly with fire/explosion accidents, and with those caused by human and environmental (as opposed to mechanical) factors. The author suggests that these accident vessel damage cost differentials might be compared with vessel hull insurance rates to investigate whether the latter reflect the former.

For bulk barge accidents on US inland waterways (Talley, 2001), tobit estimation suggests that:

- vessel damage cost is greater for collision, fire/explosion, and material/equipment failure accidents than for groundings;
- cargo damage cost is greater at night and during fog, and increases with barge age; and
- other property damage cost is greater for multi-vessel accidents, but decreases with barge size.

Jin et al. (2001) analyse determinants of vessel total losses resulting from commercial fishing vessel accidents, using probit regressions. Estimation results indicate that the probability of a total loss is greatest for a capsizing, followed by a sinking accident. The probability of a total loss varies inversely with the price of fish, suggesting that fishing vessels may take greater risks when they are under greater economic pressure.

Talley et al. examine determinants of the damage cost associated with passenger vessel accidents investigated by the US Coast Guard for the years 1991–2001 (2006) and of the property damage from cruise vessel accidents (2008a). The results suggest that:

- damage cost per vessel gross ton is less for ocean cruise and steel-hulled vessels than for other vessel types;
- cruise vessel damage cost per vessel gross ton is greater for allision, collision, equipment-failure, explosion, fire, flooding, and grounding accidents than for other types of accidents;
- cruise vessel damage cost per vessel gross ton is greater for accidents associated with a human, as opposed to environmental or mechanical, cause; and
- the unit damage cost of $207/vessel gross ton for explosion accidents is greater than that for other types of accidents.

Talley et al. (2008b) examine determinants of the property damage cost of ferry vessel accidents. Detailed data on individual ferry vessel accidents investigated by the US Coast Guard during the 11-year period of 1991–2001 are used to estimate ferry-vessel accident property damage cost, using tobit regression. Property damage costs include damage costs to the vessel itself, its cargo and contents, and other-property damage (e.g., damage to pier structures and waterfront facilities). The property damage estimation results suggest that allision, collision and fire accidents involving ferries incur more property damage cost per vessel gross ton than other types of accidents.

Table 4.3 Factors affecting vessel damages

	Tanker	Tank barge	Container ship	Bulk vessel	Bulk barge	Fishing vessel	Passenger ship	Cruise ship	Ferry
Type of vessel accident									
Allision							★	★	★
Capsize						★	★		
Collision	★	★	★	★	★		★	★	★
Equipment failure	★	★	★	★	★		★	★	
Explosion	★	★	★	★	★	★		★	
Fire	★	★	★	★	★	★	★	★	★
Flood							★	★	
Sinking						★			
Grounding							★	★	
Vessel characteristics									
Vessel size		★			★				
Vessel age	★				★	★			
Vessel operation phase									
Moored or docked		★					★		★
Underway or adrift	★		★				★		★
Weather condition									
Precipitation	★	★				★	★		
Night-time		★			★	★			
Type of waterway									
Harbour					★				
River					★				
Lake					★				
Type of vessel propulsion									
Gasoline						★			
Type of vessel hull construction									
Plastic						★			
Cause of vessel accident									
Human		★	★	★				★	
Vessel		★							
Environmental						★			
Coast Guard district									
District 11									★

Note: ★ denotes significance at or above 10% level.

Key factors affecting vessel damages are summarised in Table 4.3. Across all vessel types, greater economic damages are associated with fire and explosion, equipment failure, and collision than other types of accidents. Damages are greater when vessels are underway or adrift, during precipitation, and at night-time. Human factors, and both vessel size and age appear to have a significant effect on damage severity among different types of vessels. Unlike injury severity, damage severity does not appear to differ across regions (Coast Guard Districts).

5. OIL SPILLS

A number of studies have analysed vessel accident oil spills from oil-cargo vessels. Anderson and Talley (1995) investigate determinants of the oil cargo spill size (in terms of value of cargo spilled) for tanker and tank barge vessel accidents. Oil spillage from a tanker accident is greater when the tanker is adrift and when the accident occurs on a coastal waterway, but less for larger and for US flag tankers. For tank barge accidents, oil spillage is greater for collision and material/equipment failure accidents.

Tanker accident oil spillage per vessel gross ton is less for a US flag tanker, but increases with the vessel damage severity of the accident. Grounding accidents incur the smallest vessel damage costs, but the largest oil cargo spillage (Talley, 1999). For tank barges, spills are greater for accidents occurring on a river, at night-time, and with older barges (Talley, 2000).

The vessel accident oil-spillage literature has focused on oil-cargo vessels, tankers and tank barges, implicitly assuming that these vessels incur greater accident oil-spillage than other (i.e., non-oil-cargo) vessels that carry oil only in their fuel tanks. Talley et al. (2001) assess the validity of this assumption for the post-US Oil Pollution Act of 1990 (OPA-90) period by investigating determinants of vessel accident oil-spillage, where one of the hypothesised determinants is type of vessel (including both oil-cargo and non-oil-cargo vessels).[7] Tobit regression estimates of vessel accident oil-spillage (in gallons spilled) suggest that incidents involving tank barges have incurred greater in-water and out-of-water oil-spillage in the post OPA-90 period than non-oil-cargo vessels. They also indicate that tankers have not incurred greater out-of-water (in-water) oil-spillage than non-oil-cargo vessels (except for freight ships). The policy implication is that greater attention may need to be given to reducing tank barge accident oil-spillage.

Although oil spills from tanker accidents receive the most publicity, most vessel spills are not the result of accidents but of oil transfer activities.[8] Talley et al. (2005) examine determinants of the size of oil transfer spills. Out-of-water and in-water oil transfer spillage functions are estimated utilizing

7. Including tank barge, tank ship, fishing boat, passenger boat, freight barge, freight ship, and recreational boat.
8. Routine operations involve the movement (intentional or unintentional) of oil cargo and/or fuel oil to and from vessels. Such activities include loading and unloading of oil cargoes, fuelling, cleaning tanks, bilge pumping, and ballasting.

tobit regression and detailed data on individual vessel oil transfer data for the 1991–1995 period. The estimation results suggest that:

- in-water oil spillage is less for US flagged vessels;
- in-water oil spillage is greater for vessels being towed and when the spill incident occurs in the ocean as opposed to an inshore waterway;
- the in-water spillage is greater during cold temperatures, during precipitation, at night-time, and in times of higher oil prices.

Results also show that the in-water transfer oil spillage per vessel gross ton is greater for fishing, passenger, and recreational boats, and for older vessels. In-water oil spillage per vessel gross ton is greater in high winds, but less in cold temperatures.

Talley et al. (2004) develop a study of vessel oil spill differentials for transfer and vessel-accident spills for the post OPA-90 period. In-water and out-of-water transfer/vessel-accident oil spill equations are estimated, utilizing tobit regression analysis and data on individual vessel oil spills (of oil-cargo and non-oil-cargo vessels) investigated by the US Coast Guard for the 1991–1995 period. In the data, 47.5% of in-water and 94.1% of out-of-water gallons of oil spilled were from transfer spills; and non-oil-cargo vessels accounted for 44.2% of all gallons spilled. The estimation results suggest that for oil spilled out-of-water, transfer spills are larger in size than vessel-accident spills; but transfer and vessel-accident spills are similar in size for in-water spills. The policy implication of the results is that regulatory regimes may need to differentiate between transfer and vessel-accident spills and in-water and out-of-water spills.

Table 4.4 Factors affecting spill size (in water)

	Spill Size [a]	Unit Size [b]
Type of vessel		
Tanker	⋆	
Tank Barge	⋆	
Freight Ship		⋆
Freight Barge		⋆
Passenger vessel		⋆
Tug boat	⋆	
Fishing vessel		⋆
Recreational boat		⋆
Type of vessel accident		
Collision	⋆	
Equipment failure	⋆	
Grounding		⋆
Vessel characteristics		
Vessel size	⋆	
Vessel age		⋆
US flag	⋆(negative)	
Vessel operation phase		
Moored or docked	⋆	
Towed	⋆	
Underway or adrift	⋆	⋆
Weather condition		
High winds		⋆
Precipitation	⋆	
Cold temperature	⋆	
Night-time	⋆	⋆
Type of waterway		
River	⋆	
Coastal	⋆	
Ocean	⋆	
Coast Guard district		
District 8	⋆	

Notes: a. Volume or value spilled in gallons or dollars.
    b. Volume per vessel gross ton.
    * denotes significance at or above 10% level.

Table 4.4 summarises results of studies on oil spill size. Although the total spill volumes are greater when tankers, tank barges, and tugboats are involved, adjusted for vessel tonnage, other types of vessels are also significant contributors of oil spills. Collision, equipment failure, and grounding are three main accident types associated with large spills. Spill size is greater during bad weather and at night-time. When a vessel is underway or adrift, the expected spill size is larger at both the absolute and unit levels. US flag vessels are associated with smaller spills.

6. ACCIDENT PROBABILITY

The risk associated with vessel-accident related injuries, property damage, or oil spills depends on (a) the likelihood of the occurrence of a vessel accident (event probability) and (b) the severity of the event given that it has occurred (severity conditional probability). All the studies summarised above investigate accident severity. Since the severity of a vessel accident is conditioned upon its occurrence, a clear understanding of the event probability is of great importance. Investigating this probability requires data on both vessel accidents and on safe transits/trips; while the former are often available, comparable data on safe transits are often not readily available.

Kite-Powell et al. (1999) formulate a Bayesian model to estimate the probability of grounding during transits into and out of port as a function of potential risk factors. The study assembles and analyses information on factors surrounding groundings in three US ports between 1981 and 1995. Although the data are far from perfect, it is possible to establish associations between grounding risk and changes in factors such as vessel type and size, wind speed, and visibility. In particular, low visibility (less than 2 km) is associated with an increase of about one order of magnitude in the risk of grounding.

Commercial fishing is one of the least safe occupations. Fishing vessel accident probability and vessel trip probability for fishing areas off the northeastern United States have been modelled using logit regression and daily data from 1981 to 2000 (Jin and Thunberg, 2005; Jin et al., 2002). These studies found that:

- fishing vessel accident probability declined over the course of the study period;
- higher wind speeds are associated with greater accident probability;
- medium size vessels had the highest accident probability before 1994;
- accident probability was lower in southern New England and Mid-Atlantic waters than on Georges Bank and in the Gulf of Maine;
- accidents are more likely to occur closer to shore than offshore;
- accident probability is lower in spring and autumn;
- changes in fishery management put in place in 1994 did not lead to a general increase in accident probability; and
- although higher economic payoff (i.e., revenue from landings) induces more vessels to go fishing, this is not associated with an increase in accidents.

7. MARINE SAFETY ENFORCEMENT PROGRAMMES

In US waters, marine safety and environmental laws are enforced by the US Coast Guard. The effectiveness of Coast Guard enforcement efforts has been the subject of several studies. For example, Epple and Visscher (1984), Cohen (1987), and Grau and Groves (1997) examined oil transfer spills from oil-cargo vessels and the effectiveness of Coast Guard enforcement activities in reducing this spillage. In general, these studies conclude that enforcement activities have been effective in reducing vessel oil transfer spills. For 1973–1975 oil transfer spills, Epple and Visscher (1984) found a negative relationship between spill size and Coast Guard man-hours per oil transfer activity. For 1973–1977 spills, Cohen (1987) found negative relationships between spill size and both Coast Guard man-hours monitoring transfers and patrol man-hours per transfer activity. Based upon 1984–1987 spills, Grau and Groves (1997) found a negative relationship between spill size and the probability of oil transfer operations being monitored by the Coast Guard.

Anderson and Talley (1995) investigate determinants of the oil cargo spill size of tanker and tank barge vessel accidents. The effectiveness of various Coast Guard enforcement methods are examined, as well as the effects of vessel-related factors, the price of oil, and the price of vessel repair. The results suggest that Coast Guard pollution detection activity is effective at the margin in reducing tank barge (but not tanker) accident spill size, and that tanker accident spill size is less for US than for foreign flag tankers.

Talley et al. (2005) analyse determinants of the size of vessel oil transfer spills as well as the effectiveness of Coast Guard enforcement activities in reducing the size of these spills. The study examines spills from the post OPA-90 period, extending earlier empirical studies of similar spills in the 1970s and 1980s (Epple and Visscher, 1984; Grau and Groves, 1997). While previous studies have focused on oil-cargo vessels (i.e., tankers and barges), Talley's work considers transfer spills from non-oil-cargo vessels as well and explores spill size variation with respect to vessel type. Separate vessel out-of-water and in-water oil transfer spillage functions are estimated utilizing tobit regression on detailed data on individual vessel oil transfer spills, and Coast Guard safety/environmental enforcement activity data for the 1991–1995 period. The results suggest that Coast Guard hull (but not machinery) inspections are effective in reducing both out-of-water and in-water spills; and patrols by air (but not by boat) are effective in reducing out-of-water spills; but neither is effective in reducing in-water spills.

Talley et al. (2005) assess the probabilities of vessel safety and pollution inspections by the US Coast Guard based upon individual vessel inspections for the years 1992–2001. Probit estimates of vessel safety (versus pollution) inspection equations suggest that fishing, passenger, recreation and tug boats are less likely to be inspected for safety, but more likely to be inspected for pollution, whereas tank barges and US flag vessels are more likely to be inspected for safety and less likely for pollution. Also, vessel safety and pollution inspection probabilities vary by Coast Guard District and time. The probability of a US flag vessel being inspected for safety has increased over the period of the study. The results raise questions about the effectiveness of the

Coast Guard in reducing the oil-spill pollution of tank barges and improving the safety of fishing boats.

8. ACCIDENT AND POLLUTION PREVENTION TECHNOLOGIES

Marine pollution associated with shipping accidents can be prevented through the use of several alternative technologies, among them double hulls and electronic chart systems. Double hulls are effective in preventing oil spills or lessening their severity by reducing the volume of oil spilled compared with the single hull case. However, this design alternative requires substantial changes in ship construction, and in turn leads to large cost increases. Electronic charts and integrated, computer-based navigation systems are designed to increase safety and efficiency of navigation by automating traditional functions such as position plotting. Electronic chart systems have great potential for preventing maritime accidents.

Following the *Exxon Valdez* oil spill in 1989, the United States Congress mandated double hulls for oil tankers in US waters in the Oil Pollution Act of 1990 (OPA-90). To achieve maximum benefits from investments in pollution prevention, it is important to evaluate the economic efficiency of different marine pollution prevention technologies. Jin et al. (1994) formulate a social planner's problem using optimal control theory to examine the relative cost effectiveness of double hulls and alternative pollution prevention technologies, and the optimal installation strategy for such technologies. The model encompasses the costs and benefits associated with shipping operations, damage to the marine environment, and investment in each technology. A computer simulation of the model is used to evaluate investment strategies for two technological options: double hulls and electronic chart systems. Results indicate that electronic charts may be a far more cost-effective approach to marine pollution control.

Kite-Powell et al. (1997) present an assessment of the expected safety benefits associated with electronic charts, integrated navigation systems, and other technologies designed to reduce the damages of commercial maritime accidents in US waters. A model is developed to compare alternative policies consisting of combinations of onboard navigation systems, vessel traffic service systems, and double hulls in terms of benefits and costs. The analysis suggests that, when applied to tank vessels, electronic charts and integrated navigation systems compare favourably with vessel traffic service systems, and are clearly superior to double hulls, in terms of benefit-cost ratios.

9. OIL POLLUTION LIABILITY

The US imports over half of its total oil consumption and most of the imports are carried in foreign independent tankers. Marine transportation of crude oil and petroleum products creates risks to private property and the common environment. In US waters, environmental damages due to a single large spill in an environmentally sensitive area can amount to billions of dollars.[9] For the *Exxon Valdez* spill, Exxon paid $2.2 billion for clean-up, $1 billion to settle state and federal lawsuits, and $300 million for lost wages to 11,000 fishermen and business firms. The cost to the fisheries of south-central Alaska was estimated to be $108.1 million, the largest component being a $65.4 million reduction in the pink salmon fishery in the first year following the accident (Cohen 1995). In 1994 an Alaskan jury awarded an additional $5.3 billion in punitive and compensatory damages to those harmed by the spill.[10] The *Exxon Valdez* accident was the impetus for the US Congress to pass the OPA-90, which strengthened accountability for vessel oil spills in US waters.[11]

While liability rules can be useful in causing the oil transport industry to internalise the costs of oil pollution, unlimited liability combined with uncertainty in damage valuation can result in great costs to society. Economic theory suggests that some type of limit may be needed under certain conditions, and that such a limit should be set so that the marginal social benefit and cost are equal. However, it is unclear how a liability limit may be determined specifically in the case of tanker shipping in US waters.

Jin and Kite-Powell (1995 and 1999) develop a comprehensive review of the literature on environmental liability and marine insurance and formulate a model to determine an optimal level of risk-sharing for oil pollution damage between the public and the tanker industry. The model can be used to determine a socially optimal liability limit for oil pollution damage in US waters when a non-zero, finite liability limit is desirable. The model captures the trade-off between less expensive energy supply and more stringent protection of the marine environment. The study also examines conditions under which corner solutions (no liability or unlimited liability) are desirable.

10. SUMMARY

This review of studies on ship accidents in the US covers accident severity and probability, the effectiveness of regulatory enforcement, the economics of alternative accident prevention technologies, and marine pollution liability.

Among the types of accidents, fire, capsize, and collision are more likely to increase injury severity than others; fire and exploration, equipment failure, and collision are associated with greater vessel damages; and collision, equipment failure, and grounding are expected to cause large spills. Bad weather

---

9. Grigalunas et al. (1998) present an excellent discussion of relevant issues associated with liability for oil spill damages and a summary of representative cases.

10. Exxon appealed the ruling and the litigation process continues as of early 2008 (Wikipedia 2008).

11. For an assessment of OPA-90, see Kim (2002).

and visibility conditions affect both the probability and severity of ship accidents. Human factors are highly significant across different vessel types and damage measures.

In most cases, the findings from these studies of accident damage severity are not surprising and consistent with expectations about the causes and circumstances of maritime accidents. Together with models of ship accident probability, these quantitative models support understanding of the factors contributing to losses from maritime accidents, and are useful in the development of management mechanisms related to safety in the maritime industry.

The results of these studies also highlight the fact that maritime accidents and associated damages are complex events influenced by a range of factors that require more careful and multidisciplinary analyses. Policies to address maritime accidents and damages must address improvements in vessel design and operations as well as navigation infrastructure and human factors.

CHAPTER 5

SECURITY OF SHIPS AND SHIPPING OPERATIONS

Khalid Bichou

1. INTRODUCTION

The security of international shipping operations had first been formally recognised in the wake of the hijacking of the cruise vessel *Achille Lauro* in 1985. As a result, the IMO produced draft guidelines titled "Measures to prevent unlawful acts which threaten the safety of ships and the security of their passengers and crew". The guidelines became the first internationally approved formula which sets out what the shipping community had to do in order to provide proper protection against the threat of terrorism. However, it was not until the aftermath of the terrorist attacks of 11 September 2001 that the international shipping industry saw the introduction on 1 July 2004 of structured and targeted security legislation in the guise of the ISPS code. In 2005, the World Customs Organization (WCO) adopted the SAFE Framework of Standards to secure and facilitate global trade in co-operation with relevant intergovernmental organisations, notably the IMO.

A second set of ship-related security initiatives has been introduced at various national and regional levels, with the US-led security initiatives being the most significant. The US measures include core regulations such as the Maritime Transportation Act (MTSA) of 2002 as well as a set of security programmes that target specific types of shipping operations and facilities. Major initiatives in the latter category include the 24-hour advanced manifest rule (24-hour rule) and the Customs and Trade Partnership against Terrorism (C-TPAT). Initiatives have also emerged from the European Commission (EC) in the guise of the EC Regulation 725/2004 on enhancing ship and port facility security, Regulation 884/2005 laying down procedures for conducting Commission inspections in maritime security, and the Authorised Economic Operator (AEO) programme.

A third set of security initiatives consists of industry-led and voluntary programmes which often extend beyond the security of ships and shipping operations to include aspects such as trade and supply chain security. Examples of such programmes include the Smart and Secure Trade-lanes (SST), the ISO/PAS 28000: 2005 standard (Specification for security management systems for the supply chain), the Business Anti-Smuggling Coalition (BASC) scheme, and the Technology Asset Protection Association (TAPA) initiative.

With such plethora of maritime security programmes, much of the literature on the subject has focused on prescriptive details of the measures being put in place, the computation of their costs of compliance, and their *ex ante* economic evaluation. Nevertheless, little work has been undertaken to analyse the security risk in shipping both in terms of the perception of the risk and the assessment of costs and benefits of security investments. Following a critical review of risk and cost assessment models for maritime security, this chapter introduces a performance-based decision-making model through which ship operators can quantify their exposure to threats and assess the costs and benefits of various security investments.

2. CONVENTIONAL RISK ASSESSMENT FOR SHIPPING SECURITY: OVERVIEW AND CRITICAL ANALYSIS

The primary aim of maritime security assessment models is to assess the level of security within and across the international shipping network. When introducing the risk factor, the concept and measure of uncertainty must be considered. The conventional approach to risk defines it as being the chance, in quantifiable terms, of an adverse occurrence. It therefore combines a probabilistic measure of the occurrence of an event with a measure of the consequence, or impact, of that event. The process of risk assessment and management is generally based on three sets of sequenced and inter-related activities:

- the assessment of risk in terms of what can go wrong, the probability of it going wrong, and the possible consequences;
- the management of risk in terms of what can be done, the options and trade-offs available between the costs, the benefits and the risks; and
- the impact of risk-management decisions and policies on future options and undertakings.

Performing each set of activity requires multi-perspective analysis and modelling of all conceivable sources and impacts of risks as well as viable options for decision making and management. In engineering, traditional tools for risk assessment use the fault tree analysis (FTA) and the event tree analysis (ETA). Both are logical processes with the difference that the first examines all potential incidents leading up to a critical event while the second works the opposite way by focusing on events that could occur after a critical incident. In both models, risks are identified, estimated, assessed and prioritised through a combination of probability and impact. A simplified application of conventional risk assessment models to the ISPS code would be to categorise and grade scenario-risks according to their overall threat potentials using a rating scale system from (1) for minor to (3) for severe so as to fit into the ISPS provisions of maritime security (MARSEC) levels.

A widely-accepted methodology for security risk assessment in shipping is that which was published by the US Coast Guard Navigation in the Vessel Inspection Circular (NVIC) No. 11-02 "Recommended Security Guidelines for Facilities". Under this circular, the risk-based framework for security assessment and management is structured in terms of five steps as outlined in Figure 5.1 below.

Figure 5.1 The NVIC risk assessment model

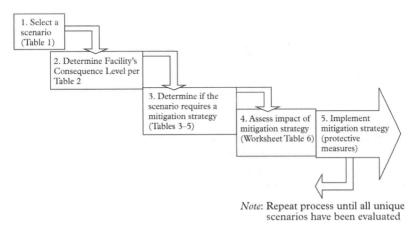

Note: Repeat process until all unique
scenarios have been evaluated

The NVIC model and other conventional risk models follow a safety-risk probabilistic approach, but the latter is based on the assumption of unintentional human and system behaviour to cause harm. However, this is not the case for security incidents stemming from terrorism and there is no awareness of the existence of any empirical risk model currently being applied to malicious acts in shipping. Another major problem with assessing security threats is that much of the assessment process is intelligence-based, which does not always follow the scrutiny of statistical reasoning.

In the following sections, some of the shortcomings of the current maritime security regime in view of security-risk assessment and management are briefly discussed.

2.1 Maritime security and the layered regulatory approach

In an effort to fill potential maritime security gaps, several researchers have advocated the use of a multi-layer regulatory system (Flynn, 2004; Willis and Ortiz, 2004; Bichou and Evans, 2007) through the introduction of a series of security regulations and initiatives.

One can argue, however, that the layered approach, as being currently implemented, has not yet materialised into an integrated and comprehensive system capable of overcoming existing and potential security gaps. For instance, the emphasis on goods' and passenger movements has diverted the attention away from non-physical movements such as financial and information flows. For instance, there exists no regulatory arrangement that ensures data and information security in the context of international shipping operations. Other security gaps include the exclusion from the current regulatory regime of fishing vessels, pleasure crafts and yachts, and other commercial ships of less than 500 GT. There is also a lack of harmonisation between the new maritime security regime and existing environmental and safety programmes in shipping, for instance the STCW convention, the ISM and IMDG codes.

2.2 Shipping security and reporting procedures

Among major changes brought about by maritime and shipping security are the requirements for additional documentation and screening for the cargo transported by sea. However, such requirements are not always consistent between regulations or countries. An instance of anomalies in maritime reporting systems is when ships and their cargoes become exempt from regular customs inspections when sailing between ports of countries belonging to the same trading or economic bloc such as the EU or NAFTA. In the EU, member states enjoy the freedom of moving goods within the Community, which means that as long as consignments originate within the EU, there are no controls concerning their movement. This gives rise to a range of anomalies in the reporting of cargoes since it is very likely that vessels plying EU ports may be carrying consignments under Community Transit Customs control, or sometimes cargo originating from outside the EU. Unless that cargo is individually reported as being in separate containers or trailers, or the vessel itself is registered within the EU, the cargo may not be declared and its content may be unclear. Vessels sailing in EU territorial waters may also be carrying consignments on a consolidated basis and for which there is only brief summary details referring to the consolidation and not necessarily for each individual grouped consignment.

To avoid such anomalies, countries such as the USA have introduced detailed documentation and reporting systems through regulations such as the 24-hour rule. However, the requirements of such levels of details raises another issue in that shipping lines and their agents are likely to fail at producing the detailed description and relevant documentation for all cargo consignments. A sample of potential errors that might occur in the work processes while satisfying the 24-hour rule is provided in Table 5.1.

Table 5.1 Potential errors from implementing the 24-hour rule (Bichou et al., 2007a)

Functional department	Potential errors
Marketing	Flagging the CSI cargo in business information system Booking data quality Booking confirmation to shipper CSI cut-off time
Administration (documentation and ICT)	Manifest data quality Transmission of manifest data to AMS timely Handling amendment Bill of lading issuance to shipper Rating the shipment Billing the CSI fee and amendment fee
Operations	Ship planning Release of empty container Coordination with container terminals and local customers for cargo inspection

2.3 Security incidents and precursor analysis

Precursors, also referred to as accident sequence precursors, may involve any internal or external condition, event, sequence, or any combination of these that precedes and ultimately leads to adverse events. More focused definitions reduce the range of precursors to specific conditions or limit their scope to a specified level of accident outcome. In either case, a quantitative threshold may be established for the conditional probability of an incident given a certain precursor, with events of lesser severity being considered either as non-precursors with no further analysis or as non-precursors that need categorisation and further investigation (Bier, 1993; Phimister et al., 2004).

Following the events of 11 September 2001, several formalised programmes have been developed for observing, analysing and managing accident precursors including comparison charts and reporting systems, with the most recognisable reporting system being the colour alert system used by the US Department of Homeland Security (DHS). Similar systems in maritime security include voluntary reporting initiatives for maritime safety, the IMB reports of piracy accidents, and the IMO reporting system for ISPS compliance.

A major drawback resulting from the combination of warning thresholds and security event-reporting is that the system may depict several flaws and errors. If, for instance, vulnerabilities are defined too precisely or the threshold is set too high, several risk-significant events may not be reported. On the other hand, setting the threshold for reporting too low may overwhelm the system by depicting many false alarms, which can ultimately lead to a loss of trust in the system. Table 5.2 shows the types of errors that may occur given these assumptions. Type I error refers to a false negative and occurs in situations of missed signals when an accident (e.g., terrorist attack) occurs with no warning being issued. Type II error refers to false positive whereby a false alert is issued, leading for instance to mass evacuation or a general disturbance of the system.

Table 5.2 Errors resulting from the interplay between threshold settings and event reporting

	Significant	Not significant
Event reported	True positive (Significant event)	False positive (Type II error)
Event not reported	False negative (Type I error)	True negative (Non-significant event)

Another issue arising from reporting security precursors under regulatory constraints relates to the fact that reported data remain in the hands of the regulator. This raises questions about (i) the reliability and validity of information since fears of regulatory actions may discourage organisations from reporting precursor events and (ii) the dissemination of reported information given that the regulator may restrict access to data which are considered too sensitive to be shared. The argument here is that the purpose of reporting must emphasise organisational learning along with a guarantee of privacy and immunity from penalties for those reporting the information.

A particular aspect of precursor analysis is the so-called "near miss" also referred to as the near hit, the close call, or simply the incident. A near miss is similar to an accident except that it does not necessarily result in an injury or damage. It is a particular kind of precursor with elements that can be observed in isolation without the occurrence of an accident. The advantage of the concept is that organisations with little or no history of major incidents can establish systems for reporting and analysing near misses.

In maritime security, implementing programmes of risk assessment based on precursor analysis would have a number of benefits including such aspects as identifying unknown failure modes and analysing the effectiveness of actions taken to reduce risk. Another opportunity from precursor analysis is the development of trends in reported data, which may be used for the purpose of risk management and mitigation. However, there is still no formal precursor programme being implemented in the context of maritime security, except for ongoing research into potential security hazards for liquid-bulk and specialised ships such as LNG and LPG vessels.

3. REVIEW OF COST AND OPERATIONAL IMPACT OF SHIPPING SECURITY

In order to comply with security initiatives, ship owning and operating companies have had to implement security measures and the route to compliance frequently requires investment in security equipment, procedures and the recruitment and training of security personnel. In addition to the cost of compliance, both shipping operators and users would incur extra costs stemming from the implementation of new procedural security and the provisions for additional inspections, detailed reporting and other operational requirements. The literature on cost impacts of port security may be classified into two main categories: the literature on compliance costs and the literature on procedural and operational costs.

3.1 Compliance cost of shipping security

3.1.1 Ex ante assessment

Even before the entry in force of the new security regulations, several studies have attempted to assess the compliance cost of port security, particularly for formal security regulations such as the ISPS code. *Ex ante* assessments of regulatory compliance are largely based on data and methods from national regulatory risk assessment models such as the US National Risk Assessment Tool (N-RAT) and the UK Risk Assessment Exercise (RAE). These are ad hoc programmes undertaken by governmental agencies in order to assess the costs and benefits of new regulatory initiatives. For instance, the US Coast Guard (USCG) has estimated the ISPS cost of compliance (including the installation of Automatic Identification System) for US-flag vessels to reach US$250 million for the first year and US$178 million each year up to 2012. Based on these estimates, the Organization for Economic Cooperation and Development (OECD, 2003) has produced a comprehensive report on the global economic impacts of maritime security measures. The OECD estimated that for ships and shipping companies alone, the cost of ISPS compliance would amount to US$1280 million on initial costs and US$716 million on recurrent costs.

3.1.2 Ex post assessment

Following the entry into force of the new security measures, a number of *ex post* assessments of the cost of compliance have been undertaken. In so doing, researchers have used a variety of approaches ranging from survey inquiries and economic impact studies to financial appraisal and insurance risk modelling.

Among major survey inquiries on the subject, it is worth mentioning the United Nations Conference on Trade and Development (UNCTAD) global survey on initial and annual costs of ISPS compliance (UNCTAD, 2007). However, the UNCTAD survey results are in contrast with the results of a recent survey by the World Bank on the subject (Kruk and Donner, 2008). Such contradictory findings may be explained by the variety of methods used to calculate the ISPS costs (unit versus average, initial versus running, etc.), but can also stem from the different interpretations of the Code across different types of ships and ship operating companies (Bichou, 2004).

Another problem with survey inquiries occurs when the findings of a case-specific survey are generalised to all stakeholders and/or security programmes. For instance, Thibault et al. (2006) found that small ocean carriers generally enjoy lesser initial compliance costs but incur higher recurrent costs because of the difficulty to spread fixed costs across a small business base. However, Brooks and Button (2006) found that the costs of enhanced maritime and supply chain security only accounts for 1% or less of shippers' total costs. Even when survey inquiries investigate a single security programme, their results may show inconsistent cost figures either over time or between participants. For example, when first enrolments in the C-TPAT programme began in 2004, the industry widely quoted Hasbo's figures of US$200,000 initial costs and US$113,000 annual operating costs as being the benchmark for C-TPAT average compliance cost for a multinational firm (Googley, 2004). However, in a recent survey of 1756 C-TPAT certified participants, Diop et al. (2007) report that C-TPAT implementation and operating costs only amount to US$38,471 and US$69,000, respectively. Furthermore, according to the same survey 33% of respondents said that the benefits of C-TPAT participation outweighed the costs while an additional 25% found that the C-TPAT costs and benefits were about the same.

- As with survey inquiries, economic impact studies on the cost of port and maritime security also depict inconsistent results. For example, Damas (2001) estimated that the new security measures introduced in the wake of the 9/11 terrorist attacks would cost the US economy as much as US$151 billion annually, of which US$65 billion just for logistical changes to supply chains. However, a study undertaken by the International Monetary Fund in the same year has estimated the increase to business costs due to higher security costs to cost around US$1.6 billion per year, with an extra financing burden of carrying 10% higher inventories at US$7.5 billion per year (IMF, 2001).
- Cost assessment of regulatory initiatives may also be undertaken through financial and insurance risk modelling. For the former, *ex post* costs are typically assessed by analysing market response to risk-return performance, for instance by translating security provisions into ship investments and analysing their *ex post* impact using models and techniques of financial appraisal and risk analysis. For the latter, researchers

typically use premium-price analysis whereby security costs and benefits are added to or subtracted from the price of port and shipping services; referring *inter alia* to the variations in freight rates and insurance premiums. For instance, Richardson (2004) reports that insurance premiums trebled for ships calling at Yemeni ports after the 2002 terrorist attack on the oil tanker *Limburg* off the Yemeni coast, which has also forced many ships to cut Yemen from their schedules or divert to ports in neighbouring states.

- Trade facilitation studies can also be used to analyse the *ex post* impacts of security such as by measuring the time factor (delay or speed-up) brought by security measures. Nevertheless, despite the rich literature on the interface between trade facilitation and economic development (Hummels, 2001; Wilson et al., 2003), few studies have investigated the role of the new security regime as either a barrier or an incentive to trade (Raven, 2001). For instance, the OECD (2002) reports that post 9/11 trade security measures would have cost from 1% to 3% of North American trade flows corresponding to a cost between US$60 billion and US$180 billion in 2001 figures. Another estimate places the global costs for trade of post 9/11 tighter security at about US$75 billion per year (Walkenhorst and Dihel, 2002).

- Another popular approach for analysing the cost-benefit of a regulatory change is to contrast transfer costs against efficiency costs. The former refer to the costs incurred and recovered by market players through transferring them to final customers (e.g., from ports to ocean carriers or from ocean carriers to shippers), while the latter represent net losses and benefits in consumer and producer surpluses. Compiled cost figures from industry and press reports suggest an average security charge of US$6 per shipped container, and up to US$40 per bill of lading for the 24-hour rule. Note that this approach is not without bias, including the common practice of cost spin-off and exponential computations of security expenses. In a highly disintegrated and fragmented maritime and logistics industry, there is no guarantee that additional security charges accurately reflect the true incremental costs incurred by each operator, including ports. Standard practices in the industry suggest that market players try to generate extra profits by transferring costs to each other (Evers and Johnson, 2000; Fung et al., 2003), and there is already evidence of similar practices in the recovering of security costs by the port industry (Bichou, 2005).

In evaluating the costs and benefits of regulatory decisions, Cost Benefit Analysis (CBA) is regarded as a fair and objective method of making assessments. While the costs of security compliance are possible to quantify either by direct surveys or through aggregate estimations, its benefits are very difficult to measure directly. Instead, most researchers assess the benefits of regulations by looking at the cost of non-compliance or failure, usually through the assessment of economic impacts of terrorist attacks and other similar events such as industrial actions and safety accidents. Cost-Efficiency Analysis (CEA) is an alternative method to CBA, and is usually applied when the output is fixed and the economic benefits cannot be expressed in monetary terms. However, both CBA and CEA make little consideration to cost-sharing and distribution of benefits. To correct this, Stakeholder Analysis (SHA) was introduced in the early 1980s with a view to identify the key players (stakeholders) of a project or a regulation and assess their interests and power differentials. CBA, CEA and SHA approaches have been extensively used in the field of shipping safety, but their empirical applications in the context of maritime security are difficult to undertake. Bichou and Evans (2007) provide a critical review of economic valuation methods and their applications in maritime security. In particular, they pointed out the difficulty to assess the cost of preventing principal losses in security incidents, much of which stems from economic losses and human casualties. Nevertheless, while economic losses can be measurable the value of human losses is difficult to observe in market transactions. Traditional safety methods such as the "Willingness to Pay" (WTP) approach are simply not suitable in a security context. A good discussion on the limitations of survey and economic costing approaches to port security is provided by Bichou (2004).

3.2 Procedural and operational impacts

The increasing interest into procedural and operational impacts of security has been fed largely by the continuing debate between those who anticipate productivity losses because of operational redundancies and those who advocate higher operational efficiency due to better procedural arrangements.

- On the one hand, many argue that procedural requirements of the new security regime act against operational and logistical efficiency. Proponents of this standpoint list a number of potential inefficiencies ranging from direct operational redundancies, such as lengthy procedures and further inspections, to derived supply chain disruptions such as in terms of longer lead times, higher inventory levels, and less reliable demand and supply scenarios. The 24-hour rule provides a typical example of procedural requirements with potential negative impacts on operational and logistics efficiencies. For example, the requirements of the 24-hour rule will result in ocean carriers declining any late shipment bookings but also bearing, under customary arrangements, the cost of at least one extra day of container idle time at ports. The latter may be extended to three days or more for carriers and forwarders that are not electronically hooked into the US CBP Automated Manifest System (AMS).

Shippers and receivers alike will then have to adjust their production, distribution and inventory management processes accordingly. Ports will also bear commercial and cost impacts of the 24-hour rule, including potential congestion problems and possible delays in both ships' departures and arrivals. Additional costs to shippers may also stem from the extra time and resources needed for carriers to compile and record detailed data information. In fact, shipping lines have already started transferring the cost of the 24-hour rule data filing and processing requirements to shippers and cargo owners who now have to pay an extra US$40 levying charge per bill of lading (*Lloyd's List*, 2003), plus any additional indirect costs from advanced cut-off times and changes in production and distribution processes. Ocean carriers and NVOCCs may also be faced with a violation fine of US$5,000 for the first time and US$10,000 thereafter in case they submit missing or inaccurate data to CBP. A detailed review of the 24-hour requirements, costs, and benefits is provided by Bichou et al. (2007a).

- On the other hand, proponents of new security measures argue that their implementation is not only necessary but can also be commercially rewarding. The main argument put forward is that measures such as the CSI, the 24-hour rule and the C-TPAT fundamentally shift the focus from inspection to prevention, the benefit of which offsets and ultimately outweighs initial and recurrent costs of implementation. Detailed data recording, electronic reporting and other procedural requirements brought about by the new security regulations would allow for pre-screening and deliberate targeting of "suspected" containers, which is proven as more cost-effective and less time-consuming than the traditional approach of random physical inspections. In addition to the benefits of access certification and fast-lane treatment, compliant participants would also benefit from reduced insurance costs, penalties and risk exposure. Other advantages that go beyond the intended security benefits include the protection of legitimate commerce, the exposure of revenue evasion, reduced risk of cargo theft and pilferage, real-time sharing of shipping and port intelligence, advanced cargo processing procedures, and improved lead-time predictability and supply chain visibility.

Nevertheless, both arguments are rarely supported by empirical analysis and much of analytical research on procedural security impacts uses either modelling techniques to predict the operational costs and benefits of security. Lee and Whang (2005) have developed a mathematical model to assess the benefits of reduced lead times and inspection levels in the context of SST. Using simulation, Babione et al. (2003) examined the impacts of selected security initiatives on import and export container traffic of the port of Seattle. Rabadi et al. (2007) used a discrete event simulation model to investigate the impact of security incidents on recovery cycle for the US container terminal of Virginia.

4. TOWARDS A NEW APPROACH FOR EFFICIENT INVESTMENT IN SHIPPING SECURITY

From the above review of both risk models and cost impact of shipping security, it is clear that there is a gap in linking risk exposure with cost assessment. Traditionally, the shipping and maritime industry has come from a compliance culture whereby both the perception of the risk and the response to it are defined to fit into the guidelines of regulatory frameworks and requirements. Furthermore, little work exists on how to identify and assess specific components of security investments and link them to industry and market performance. This chapter introduces a generic framework which allows the identification and assessment of individual security components in view of the costs and benefits of risk exposure.

As a guide for the shipping industry to embark on any security system, a general efficiency framework is proposed, which is also valid for implementing and managing maritime security regulations. The proposed framework translates various security regulations into a set of security components, the categorisation and prioritisation of which depend on their relative performance in reducing costs and risk exposure and optimising commercial rewards and competitive advantage. Shipping companies invest an S amount of security input (equipment, technology, labour, etc.) to produce a Y amount of security output (lower risk exposure, improved security, time-savings, reduced physical inspections, fast-lane treatment, etc.). Therefore, the assessment of a shipping line's security performance can be analysed by estimating an efficiency production frontier whereby the line seeks to maximise security rewards from a given amount of security investments.

Because of different operational and management features (type of trade, size of fleet, market coverage, agency system, etc.), shipping companies, which are referred to here as Decision Making Units (DMUs), will choose different bundles of security components in order to achieve the desired and/or required security output. The efficient frontier in Figure 5.2 represents the relationship between the input (S) and output (Y) of security. Moving along the efficiency frontier, it can be observed that DMUs A, B and C are all efficient in their security investments although each of them chooses a different bundle of security regulations. Conversely, DMU D is inefficient because it lies below the efficiency frontier. For DMU D to be efficient it has either to increase its security output to the level achieved by DMU C or decrease its security inputs to a level similar to that of DMU B.

Figure 5.2 Security investment efficiency frontier

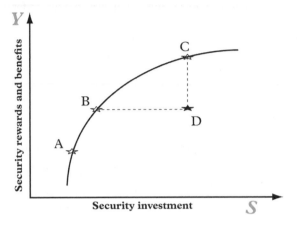

Assuming a set of security regulations and procedures, it is then possible to disaggregate them into a series of security components each with a different proportion of costs or investments ($S = s_0, s_1, . . ., s_m$) versus corresponding amounts of benefits or rewards ($Y = y_0, y_1, . . ., y_k$). Let ($S = \{s_1, s_2, s_3; . . ., s_n\}$ be the set of security components for a ship as shown in Table 5.3.

Table 5.3 Security components for Ship A

Security component	Description
S1	Install security alarms
S2	Company security officer
S3	Ship security officer
S4	Surface radar
S5	Auto CCTV ship
S6	Security patrol
S7	Auto CCTV cargo
S8	Security alarms – general
S9	Security alarms – ships stores
S10	Security patrol cargo areas
S11	Control access to ship
S12	Control – embarkation of persons
S13	Monitoring restricted areas
S14	Monitoring of deck areas
S15	Security training drills

Based on feedbacks from industry experts, a hypothetical simulation of Ship "A" security components' performance is shown in Table 5.4. The feedbacks were drawn from the results of Diop et al.'s (2007) survey as well as compiled responses from the author's informal discussions with 10 ship operating managers. The simulation shows that for a number of different prescribed potential security incidents, the access control to the ship was successful in deterring 45.8% of all on-board security incidents on average while the surface radar was only able to detect 12% of security incidents. Note that a detailed performance analysis integrating all aspects of security benefits (not just the deterrence of security incidents) is possible to undertake using such techniques as scenario-modelling, historical analysis, and/or survey-based risk assessment models.

Table 5.4 Simulation of ship's security components' performance

Security components	Y	
	Mean	Std. deviation
S1	.256	.264
S2	.340	.574
S3	.254	.535
S4	.121	.392
S5	.213	.217
S6	.283	.237
S7	.153	.134
S8	.216	.392
S9	.1875	.141
S10	.435	.185
S11	.458	.315
S12	.354	.371
S13	.138	.123
S14	.175	.154
S15	.341	.116

Using investment data on the different security investments by ship operators, it is possible to construct a frontier that shows the relationship between the cost and benefit of ship's security. This can be analysed empirically by using analytical frontier techniques such as Data Envelopment Analysis (DEA) or Stochastic Frontier Analysis (SFA). Both methods have been widely used for estimating production frontiers and measuring relative efficiencies of firms or DMUs. In the context of this paper, they can be used as a decision and management tool for evaluating the relative efficiency of shipping companies in investing in and/or implementing security initiatives and regulations.

5. CONCLUSION

This chapter is intended to provide a practical and critical analysis of risk and cost assessment models for the security of ships and shipping operations. In particular, it analyses the adequacy of the multi-layer approach, reviews the anomalies in cargo documentation and reporting procedures, and points out the problems related to precursor analysis in the context of maritime security. It also provides a structured and critical review of cost models for maritime security.

The chapter introduces a generic framework for assessing the cost and benefit of security investment. The model allows shipping companies to measure the gap between existing security performance and the risk-investment efficient frontier. It also allows them to prioritise and select the security components that best achieve their desired security output. This is particularly relevant to the current multi-layer maritime security framework where various regulations duplicate similar security requirements. The model can be applied to shipping lines in isolation or to a series of shipping lines in a multiple case study. The model is also relevant to situations where a shipping company has to select different security bundles for different ships or shipping markets.

CHAPTER 6

PIRACY IN SHIPPING

Wayne K. Talley and Ethan M. Rule

1. INTRODUCTION

Piracy in shipping is a current (as in the past) shipping problem. It is an act of boarding or an attempt to board a ship with the intent to commit theft or the intent or capability to use force in the furtherance of that act (IMO, 2005). Piracy in shipping includes the acts of armed robbery, theft and hijacking against a ship.[1] Unlike safety accidents which are unintentional, piracy incidents are intentional. Terrorist incidents are also intentional. However, piracy and terrorist incidents differ in that the focus of the former is theft, while that of the latter is damage to property and/or injury to individuals for political reasons.

Piracy in shipping may appear in many forms. It may, for example, involve petty thieves who look for quick and easy ship targets, taking money and other valuables (from the ship's safe) that can easily be fenced on the black market. Piracy may involve an organised-crime syndicate that seeks to hijack (or obtain possession of) ships and hold the crew hostage for ransom. In 2004 ransom money exceeding $1 million was paid to pirates from piracy acts in the Malacca Straits (Harris and Fiddler, 2005). Piracy in shipping is not central to any one region—it is a worldwide problem with higher concentrations in Southeast Asia and the waters between Somalia and Yemen.

The purpose of this chapter is to provide an overview of the current worldwide situation in piracy in shipping. Also, the chapter will investigate whether a time trend and seasonal variation exist in recent piracy attacks.

In the following section, ship boarding techniques utilized by pirates are discussed, followed by a discussion in section 3 of the regions of the world that are most likely to attract piracy attacks. Seafarer injuries, ship damage and environmental impacts of piracy attacks are presented in section 4. Securing

---

1. Piracy in article 101 of the 1982 United Nations Convention on the Law of the Sea (UNCLOS) is defined as follows: Piracy consists of any of the following acts: (a) any illegal acts of violence or detention, or any act of depredation, committed for private ends by the crew or the passengers of a private ship or a private aircraft, and directed: (i) on the high seas, against another ship or aircraft, or against persons or property on board such ship or aircraft and (ii) against a ship, aircraft, persons or property in a place outside the jurisdiction of any state; (b) any act of voluntary participation in the operation of a ship or an aircraft with knowledge of facts making it a pirate ship or aircraft; (c) any act inciting or of intentionally facilitating an act described in sub-paragraph (a) or (b).

ships from piracy attacks is discussed in section 5. In section 6 the reporting of piracy attacks is discussed. Estimates of the time trend and monthly variation in recent piracy attacks are presented in section 7. A summary of the discussion follows in section 8.

2. THE ACT

The majority of reported piracy attacks occur in port areas. In 2004, 146 of the 242 worldwide reported piracy attacks (or 60%) occurred in port areas. Among attempted piracy attacks, 31% (or 27 of 88 attempted attacks) occurred in port areas. However, for both reported and attempted piracy attacks, 52% occurred in port areas.[2]

Though the odds of a piracy attack are greater when a ship is in port, underway ships are also vulnerable. Pirates often linger in shipping lanes, waiting for unsuspecting ships to pass. They lurk in small, unlit boats that are less susceptible to detection by sailors on a ship's bridge (especially when heavy sea swells exist) and ship radar. Shipping lanes congested with small fishing boats are especially prime locations for pirates.

There are several common techniques utilized by pirates to board underway ships. For example, two small unlit boats on both sides of a shipping lane may raise a rope between them when a ship passes, catching the ship around her stern. This action brings the boats in along the sides of the ship, providing easy access to the ship via grappling hooks and bamboo poles. Another boarding practice is for a piracy boat to come up astern in the wake of a ship and board from its poop-deck (or fantail) that is often out of sight of the bridge and a few metres above the ship's waterline. The poop-deck is a blind spot in a ship's radar in that it is impossible for the radar to detect boarding pirates at this location from approximately 155 to 195 degrees relative. Once onboard, pirates often go unnoticed by the crew until they make their presence on the bridge.

On 5 November 2005, the cruise ship *Seabourn Spirit* was involved in an attempted piracy attack that occurred 100 miles off the coast of Somalia. The pirates used small but fast vessels in the attempted attack. Given the attack's significant distance from shore, it was expected that the pirates may have used a nearby "mother ship" from which the vessels were launched. It is somewhat surprising that this attempted attack occurred since cruise ships are not good targets for pirates—they are not easy to board and carry too many people.

---

2. If pirates see ports as soft targets, terrorists are likely to as well. In 2004 there were 17 terrorist attacks in port or anchorage in Indonesia's Tanjong Priok port and 13 at the port of Balikpapan (Hand, 2005a).

Pirates generally prefer to attack a ship with an easy access and few people to control.

Another technique used by pirates to gain access to an underway ship is to broadcast a phoney distress call. The Law of the Sea requires mariners to render assistance to ships in distress. Any ship operating in close proximity is expected to render assistance upon receipt of a distress call. Distress calls may be delivered by marine radio transmissions, Digital Selective Calling (DSC)—an automatic signal generated by an emergency beacon—and signal flares to attract the attention of nearby ships. A ship, in approaching the position of the distress call, slows and hence becomes vulnerable to a piracy attack.

In addition to commercial vessels, piracy is also a problem for recreational vessels. Sailboats are especially vulnerable to piracy attacks due to their relatively low-sail and power speeds. Further, there is little chance of combative confrontation from sailboats. In 2004, 18 documented cases of piracy against sailboats were recorded in the waters between Yemen and Somalia (IMO, 2005).

3. REGIONS AFFECTED

Regions of the world that are most likely to attract piracy attacks to ships are high volume in ship traffic, sheltered from high seas, low-economic regions and in political turmoil. The Malacca Straits (waterways surrounded by Indonesia, Malaysia and Singapore) have been subject to numerous ship piracy attacks each year. In 2004 there were 60 reported and attempted piracy attacks in the Malacca Straits by crime syndicates and local fishermen; this number declined to 22 in 2006 (see Table 6.1). The Straits are the busiest waterways in the world; 60,000 ships transit the Straits each year. Vessel traffic through the Straits has increased substantially in recent years with the increase in trade to and from China. The Malacca Straits are 621 nautical miles in length, connecting the Northern Indian Ocean with the China Sea. Alternative routes such as the Lombok and Sunda Straits add about three days to voyages. The many small islands, abundant coral reefs, calm waters and navigation widths measured in metres as opposed to miles are an ideal environment for using small boats in piracy attacks.

The South China Sea is another likely region for piracy attacks on ships. It is a large body of water bounded by Singapore, Hong Kong, Japan and the Philippines. It is one of the busiest shipping regions in the world. The South China Sea region has the highest number of ship piracy attacks in the world. In 2003 there were 152 reported and attempted piracy attacks in this region; followed by 113, 97 and 66 in 2004, 2005 and 2006, respectively (see Table 6.1). Most of these attacks are undertaken by crime syndicates and occur when ships cross into international waters. Fifty-seven piracy attacks were reported in 2004 in the coastal waters of West Africa, followed by 31 in 2006 (see Table 6.1).

In recent years there has been significant growth in the number of piracy kidnap attacks off the Somali coast. Rather than taking ships and their cargoes, Somalian pirates are taking crew members hostage and demanding ransom from vessel owners. On 7 November 2005 a Thai ship was hijacked off the Somali coast. The pirates demanded a ransom for the release of the ship and its crew. The ship's sugar cargo was worth an estimated $3.5 million.[3]

The IMB has advised vessels to keep 200 nautical miles from the Somali coast, adding one to two days of steaming times for ships using key shipping lanes linking the Mediterranean with the Indian Ocean. Recent piracy attacks off the Somali coast have led to the IMO requesting that the United Nations' Security Council take action on piracy in Somali waters. Also, Somalia has requested international assistance to combat the increasing problem of piracy in the waters off its coastline, e.g., neighbouring countries have been asked to use their navies to protect merchant shipping off the Somalia coastline. Somalia has no central government and no regular navy. The warlords who are in charge of much of the country are also thought to be behind the piracy attacks.

Even secluded island tourist destinations are subject to piracy. The waterways of the Caribbean and Eastern South America had 37 and 10 reported and attempted piracy attacks in 2004 and 2006, respectively (see Table 6.1). Brazil's Rio Grande, Haiti's Port Au Prince, Dominican Republic's Rio Haina, Kingston (Jamaica) and Callo (Peru) are areas with a high number of piracy attacks (International Chamber of Commerce, 2005). Chartered pleasure vessels in these areas are attractive targets for pirates, since those aboard are relatively inexperienced at sea and often carry large sums of money, jewellery and expensive electronics. Also, there is a relatively low threat of retaliation to the attackers by those onboard.

In 2003 the waterways of the Indian Ocean had 100 reported and attempted piracy attacks, followed by 53 in 2006 (see Table 6.1). In January 2006 an Indonesian soldier was arrested for piracy, supporting the claim by witnesses that pirates either appeared or purported to be Indonesian navy personnel. Small vessels such as fishing boats have also been subject to piracy attacks in Indonesian waters.

Piracy in shipping has been a concern of the IMO for a number of years. In 1998 the IMO implemented its anti-piracy project. It has conducted a number of regional seminars and workshops that have been attended by government officials in piracy-infested regions of the world. Also, anti-piracy experts have been sent to various regions to evaluate and assess measures for combating piracy.

---

3. It has been suggested that the IMO should improve security measures against piracy attacks via the ISPS Code (Hand, 2005d).

Table 6.1 Reported and attempted piracy attacks

Year	Malacca Straits	Indian Ocean	East Africa	Caribbean/ Eastern South America	South China	West Africa	Other	Total
1984	10	0	0	5	0	16	0	31
1988	6	3	0	3	7	10	0	29
1992	8	8	6	7	20	18	0	67
1996	12	30	8	35	120	20	5	230
2000	111	108	28	40	147	35	5	474
2001	53	75	22	15	120	55	2	342
2002	32	70	19	70	145	47	2	385
2003	27	100	18	75	152	72	3	447
2004	60	41	13	37	113	57	3	324
2005	20	51	49	14	97	23	12	266
2006	22	53	31	10	66	31	27	240

Source: International Maritime Organization (various years). *Reports on Acts of Piracy and Armed Robbery*, London: IMO.

4. IMPACTS

The estimated cost to US consumers, merchants and transportation industries from worldwide piracy attacks is reported to be US$16 billion per year (Harismo, 1999). The number of seafarers killed worldwide in these attacks were 70, 18, 5 and 15 for the years 2000 to 2003, respectively; in 2004, there were 30 deaths, 87 injuries, 140 hostages, 43 missing mariners, 7 hijacked ships and three ships declared total losses (IMO, 2005). Ships that suffer significant damage during an attack may founder and ultimately sink.

Sinking ships can create an environmental disaster, especially if they are carrying liquid petroleum cargoes. Today, Very Large Crude Carrier (VLCC) ships are in service; they may displace 300,000 long tons, have a small crew of 17 individuals and carry 84 million gallons of crude oil onboard. By comparison, *Exxon Valdez* had a carrying capacity of 53 million gallons of crude. If the hull of a VLCC is breached during a piracy attack, an environmental disaster is likely to occur. In 2004 there were 67 reported piracy attacks on ships carrying petroleum products (IMO, 2005). Hijacked petroleum-carrying ships can also be used as weapons of mass destruction.

During a piracy attack, a ship may be completely taken over and its crew gathered in a central location on the ship. If so, there would be no crew watch-stander on the bridge and no crew helmsman to steer the ship. Consequently, the ship would be vulnerable to a collision accident, especially with another ship—e.g., another ship believing it has the right of way. If two ships collide in a narrow waterway, vessel traffic in this waterway could be stopped for weeks while the wreckage is cleared. Narrow waterways such as the Straits of

Malacca, Hormuz, Bab el Mandeb and Gibraltar are susceptible to piracy attacks and subsequent ship collisions. Since 50% of the world's ship-transported oil passes through the Straits of Malacca, tanker accidents in the Straits and the subsequent losses of large quantities of oil could result in a significant increase in worldwide oil prices.

5. SECURITY

5.1 Patrols

The location of Liquid Petroleum Gas (LPG) and Liquid Natural Gas (LNG) ships are monitored worldwide by the US Navy and Coast Guard. The location of high interest ships that have or may have had a tie to crime syndicates or terrorist organisations are also monitored and tracked. In addition to LPG and LNG vessels, VLCC vessels bound for US ports are also tracked. A weekly-classified message is disseminated to all naval units, providing the last known position, heading, speed, flag, call sign, and last and next port of call for ships of interest. Frequently, US and foreign military ships escort commercial ships through the Straits of Bab el Mandeb, Gibraltar, Hormuz and Malacca. The escort services are used to ward off possible terrorist attacks as well as to deter potential criminal activity in these waterways.

In January 2006 the US ship, USS *Winston S. Churchill*, as part of the multinational taskforce patrolling the western Indian Ocean and the Horn of Africa region to thwart terrorist activity, boarded an Indian merchant ship that had been hijacked by pirates. The ship had 16 crew on board as well as 10 suspected Somali pirates. The suspects were handed over to Kenyan authorities and charged with hijacking the ship, threatening the lives of the crew and demanding a $450,000 ransom.

The territorial waters of a coastal state extend up to 12 nautical miles from its shore. A coastal state has no jurisdiction outside of its territorial waters to deter piracy, but is not precluded from rendering assistance in these waters to a ship that has been attacked by pirates. Coastal states have no obligation to ensure safe passage of ships passing through their territorial waters (with the exception of navigational marker maintenance), but do have an obligation to those who operate within their waters. Military and police ships of another country cannot enter a country's territorial waters without permission, but are allowed to patrol the high seas and waters outside of territorial waters.

Military ship patrols are viewed as one of the most effective deterrents to ship piracy. The Japanese Self-Defence Force (JSDF), for example, has conducted several anti-piracy drills with the Coast Guard agencies of Singapore, Malaysia, Indonesia and the Philippines. The Japanese Navy has conducted anti-piracy training for Japanese flagged ships that utilize the waters of the

South China Sea. This training is important in that much of the oil destined for Japan is transported through these waters.

Another approach for protecting the world's shipping lanes from piracy attacks is for coastal states to co-operate among themselves by allowing military and police ships of other states to enter their waters in the pursuit of pirates. Indonesia, Singapore and Malaysia, for example, are now coordinating joint piracy patrols in the Malacca Straits. Each country has agreed to give the other permission to cross into its waters in pursuit of pirates.

In October 2005 Malaysia, Indonesia and Singapore agreed to the Jakarta Statement—an agreement to ensure that the Malacca Straits are safe and open at all times to international shipping and to address the number of piracy incidents against ships and seafarers. The countries have agreed to fly aircraft over the Straits 24 hours a day to look for illegal activity. Malaysia has also announced plans to create the Coast Guard agency, the Malaysian Maritime Enforcement Agency, to patrol the Straits. The agency was to start operation on 30 November 2005 and to be equipped eventually with 72 vessels and 4,000 personnel. Furthermore, 34 countries have agreed to co-operate on ensuring safe navigation and security in the Straits. This would be done through security training programmes and joint co-operative exercises (Hand, 2005b).

In August 2005, Lloyd's and the London insurance market's Joint War Committee deemed the Malacca Straits as a shipping area to be at risk from "war, strikes, terrorism and related perils"; consequently, ships transiting the Straits would have to pay higher insurance premiums (Turner, 2005). The Committee noted that the failure of the regional governments of the Straits to successfully tackle piracy as well as the rising risk of maritime terrorism in the Straits led to its decision. In August 2005, Japan's main non-life insurance companies announced that the Malacca Straits is an area at risk from terrorism and a $250-a-voyage premium would be placed on Japanese vessels using the Straits (Grinter, 2005).

A memorandum of understanding was signed in September 2005 by Singapore, Malaysia, Indonesia and the IMO for World Bank funding of the Marine Electronic Highway—a regional information network to manage safe and efficient navigation, built around electronic charts, automatic identification systems, satellite-based positioning, ship-shore date communication and environmental mapping. This network will enhance navigational safety and security in the Malacca Straits.[4] Similar systems to the Marine Electronic Highway are found elsewhere in the world, e.g., the UK's Channel Navigation Information Service collects information from ships via AIS, radar and VHF and then broadcasts navigation difficulties and hazards back to ships every hour or every 30 minutes during low visibility times (Hand, 2005c).

---

4. For a discussion of the benefits and costs of the Marine Electronic Highway, see Marlow and Gardner (2006).

5.2 Security equipment

There are several means of communication by which ships can monitor and deter piracy attacks. The sounding of a ship's alarm, e.g., a whistle, notifies its crew of approaching danger from a piracy attack; the alarm may also deter potential attackers. The cruise ship, *Seabourn Spirit*, which was attacked by pirates off the coast of Somalia in November 2005 used a sonic (non-lethal) weapon, blasting earsplitting noise in a directed beam, to ward off the attackers. The sonic device, the Long Range Acoustic Device, was developed by the US military after the 2000 attack on *USS Cole* in Yemen as a way to keep operators of small boats from approaching US warships.

In addition, alarms may be placed in key areas within the ship to go off when there is a possible breach in ship security. If a suspicious boat is tailing a ship, the ship's alarm will alert both its crew and the crew of the tailing ship, possibly resulting in an aborted piracy attack. Another ship communicative signal is the pulsating red-over-red masthead light that indicates that an attack is in progress. Also, security lights may be installed that automatically illuminate the decks of a ship when an attack is in progress. Signals from flare guns are internationally recognised as distress calls.

A ship's radar is used to track nearby ships for contact avoidance. However, most ship radar units are equipped with the Automatic Radar Plotting Aid (ARPA), which allows the system to automatically track nearby ships with respect to their course, speed and closest point of approach. A ship's bridge crew can also use this equipment to determine if the nearby ship is steering an intercepting course.

Global Positioning Systems (GPS) allow shipowners to monitor their ships as well as provide cargo-tracking information to customers. These systems may also be equipped with a discreet alarm that can be activated to notify the ship's owner that his ship is in danger. The activated alarm will be routed automatically to the company's security officer and the flag state authority. The alarm's signal will transmit the ship's position, course and speed.

The IMO's Safety of Life at Sea Convention (SOLAS) requires that AIS systems be installed on ships exceeding 300 gross tons. These systems transmit a ship's speed, course, classification, call sign, registration and other information via VHF transmitters. The data are used for vessel contact avoidance and routing, e.g., by Vessel Traffic Systems (VTS) to monitor and control the movements of vessels while in port. This information may also be useful in preventing or aborting vessel piracy attacks.

Fire mains aboard ships usually consist of high-pressure water pumps and hoses. The water from high-pressure fire hoses is sufficiently strong to repel small boats and boarding pirates. The US Navy has used high-pressure fire hoses to deter unauthorised boarders in port and at sea. The fire hoses can also be flaked out and made ready for quick spraying when a ship enters a known piracy area. Some ships have gone as far as to set up fire-hose mannequins on their weather rails to fool pirates (Burnett, 2002, p. 131).

Closed Circuit Television systems (CCTV) have been installed throughout ships for monitoring the safety of their crew, equipment and cargo. However, these systems may also be used to abort piracy attacks. For example, areas of a ship susceptible to boarders such as the fantail and cargo decks can be easily monitored using these systems.

The IMO has recommended that electric fences be installed onboard ships as an anti-piracy defence mechanism. Intruders are shocked with a non-lethal voltage of 9,000 volts. Drawbacks to onboard electric fences include: (1) possible damage to the fences when loading or unloading the ship or in handling mooring lines and hoses, and (2) hindering sea rescue, i.e., they may be obstacles in recovering overboard seafarers.[5]

6. REPORTING

Piracy attacks worldwide are reported to the IMO's IMB. The IMB also provides reward money for information leading to the capture of missing ships and cargoes from piracy attacks and the apprehension of syndicate piracy members. Piracy reports are forwarded to flag countries (i.e., countries in which piracy attacks have occurred in their waters), shipping lines, insurance companies and appropriate security forces.

Since October 1992, the IMB has posted a daily piracy report. When the Bureau receives a report of piracy, the details of the incident, including the location, is sent out via telex and posted on the internet, making this information immediately available to ships at sea as well as shipping lines.

Piracy attacks may go unreported. Ship operators may be hesitant to report acts of piracy because of the lengthy investigation that follows an attack. When attacks occur in port, the ships involved may be required to stay in port for a number of days. The extra days in port will be costly to the ship's owner, i.e., in foregone revenue and time at sea. Some attacks may also go unreported due to the fear of rising insurance rates. Shipowners may prefer to absorb the cost of the attacks rather than chance an increase in insurance rates or the loss of their clients' confidence in avoiding piracy attacks. A client may be hesitant to use a particular shipping line in the future if the line has been the victim of multiple piracy attacks.

7. DATA AND ESTIMATION RESULTS

What has been the trend in worldwide piracy attacks in recent years? Have these attacks been declining, rising or remaining stable? Are the attacks higher during certain times of the year than at other times? These questions are

---

5. The IMO discourages the use of weapons as an anti-piracy defence.

answered by investigating the relationship between piracy attacks worldwide and the time trend and the monthly variation in these attacks, i.e.:[6]

Piracy Attacks = f(Time Trend, Time Trend Squared,
             Monthly Variation)   (1)

The variable Piracy Attacks is measured by the number of monthly world-wide piracy attacks (reported and attempted) taken from the monthly IMO "Reports on Acts of Piracy and Armed Robbery Against Ships" for the period April 2000 to August 2007. The Time Trend variable is assigned a 1 in April 2000 and consecutive integer values for subsequent months, finally assigning the value 89 for August 2007. If the sign of the estimated coefficient for Time Trend is negative (positive), this will suggest that there has been a declining (rising) linear trend in the monthly piracy attacks over the period of the data. If the estimated coefficient for the variable, Time Trend Squared, is significant, the inference is that the trend is non-linear.

The Monthly Variation variable is represented by the 12 monthly binary variables January, February, March, etc. Each monthly binary variable will be assigned a 1 or a 0. For example, the monthly binary variable January will be equal to one when the month of the piracy attack is January and zero when the month of the attack is other than January and similarly for the remaining 11 monthly binary variables. Substituting the month binary variables for the Monthly Variation variable in equation (1) and rewriting, the Piracy Attacks equation can be rewritten as,

Piracy Attacks = g(Time Trend, Time Trend Squared, January,
             February, March, April, May, June, July, August,
             September, October, November, December)   (2)

In order to avoid the estimation problem of perfect multicollinearity, the monthly binary variable February is dropped from the equation prior to estimation. As opposed to dropping the binary February, any one of the 12 monthly binary variables could have been dropped prior to the estimation of equation (2).

Estimation results for the Piracy Attacks equation are found in the second and third columns of Table 6.2. The Durbin-Watson (DW) statistic of 1.2444 in column two suggests the presence of serial correlation, indicating inflated "t" statistics for some or all coefficients. To correct for serial correlation, the Cochrane-Orcutt procedure is used, which assumes a linear relationship between error terms at time period t and time period t − 1 (see Greene, 1997). The results in the re-estimation of equation (2) using the Cochrane-Orcutt

6. As discussed above, piracy attacks are also affected by other explanatory variables not found in equation (1), e.g., shipping traffic and economic and political conditions. Data are not available for these variables. However, to the extent that these variables are correlated with the Time Trend, Time Trend Squared and Monthly Variation variables, they will be captured in the empirical analysis.

procedure are found in column three of Table 6.2. The Durbin-Watson statistic for this estimate is 2.1591 which suggests the absence of serial correlation. Thus, the estimate of equation (2) found in column three of Table 6.2 is used in making inferences from the estimation of equation (2).

The estimated coefficient on Time Trend and the monthly binary variables March, April, May, July and October are statistically significant at least at the .10 level. The −.3894 coefficient of the Time Trend variable indicates that for the period April 2000 to August 2007 there has been a declining trend in worldwide monthly piracy attacks; specifically, the coefficient indicates that attacks have declined by .39 attacks per month. With the coefficient on the Time Trend Squared variable being statistically insignificant, the estimation results with respect to the Time Trend and Time Trend Squared variables taken together suggest that the declining trend in monthly piracy attacks is a linear declining trend.

The positive signs for the statistically significant, monthly binary variables—March, April, May, July and October—suggest that more piracy attacks occurred in these months than in the month of February. In the ranking of the estimated coefficients of these binary variables from the largest to the smallest, it follows that one can infer that the month of May has the largest number of piracy attacks, followed by April, July, March and October, respectively. Specifically, the months of May, April, July, March and October are expected to have 11.3, 10.7, 10.3, 9.9 and 8.15 more attacks than the month of February.

Table 6.2 Estimated piracy attacks equation results

Variable	Estimate 1	Estimate 2
Time Trend	−.3261**	−.3894***
	(−2.18)	(−1.65)
Time Trend Squared	.0011	.0017
	(0.68)	(0.69)
January	4.7763	4.7736
	(1.01)	(1.27)
March	9.9358**	9.9391*
	(2.09)	(2.65)
April	9.8403**	10.7326**
	(2.13)	(2.43)
May	11.0706**	11.3307*
	(2.40)	(2.51)
June	4.9237	4.9477
	(1.07)	(1.08)
July	10.3996**	10.3376**
	(2.26)	(2.24)
August	7.1234	7.0316
	(1.55)	(1.52)
September	6.7166	6.9039
	(1.41)	(1.46)
October	8.0920***	8.1475***
	(1.70)	(1.73)
November	7.1794	7.1901
	(1.51)	(1.55)
December	5.8361	5.8343
	(1.23)	(1.32)
Constant	33.6882*	34.9416*
	(7.59)	(6.06)
R^2	.398	.398
$\overline{R}^2$	.293	.293
DW Statistic	1.2444	2.1591
# of Observations	89	89

*(**,***) significant at the (1, 5, 10) % level; t-statistics are in parentheses.

8. SUMMARY

This chapter has provided an overview of the current worldwide situation in piracy in shipping. The odds of a piracy attack are greater when a ship is in port, but ships that are underway are also vulnerable. Regions of the world that are most likely to attract ship piracy attacks are those that are high volume in ship traffic, sheltered from high seas, low-economic regions and in political turmoil. Such regions include those of the South China Sea and the Malacca

Straits. Piracy attacks result in crew deaths and injuries and cost consumers of shipped cargoes, shippers and transportation industries billions of dollars each year. Security against ship piracy attacks includes military and police vessel patrols of waterways that have high probabilities of piracy attacks as well as security equipment on ships for monitoring and deterring piracy attacks. Piracy attacks worldwide are reported to the IMO's IMB.

An investigation of the number of monthly piracy attacks (reported and attempted) worldwide reveals a declining trend in these attacks over the period April 2000 to August 2007. Specifically, the estimation results for a ship piracy-attack equation indicate that attacks have declined by .39 attacks per month. Further, more piracy attacks occur in the months of March, April, May, July and October, with the highest number of attacks occurring in the month of May.

CHAPTER 7

SHIP PIRACY: SHIP TYPE AND FLAG

Maximo Q. Mejia Jr., Pierre Cariou and Francois-Charles Wolff[1]

1. INTRODUCTION

Piracy in its various forms is undoubtedly the oldest threat to maritime security. Ancient accounts record piracy as having been a menace to the security and efficiency of the flourishing Minoan maritime commerce in the eastern Mediterranean as early as 4,000 years ago (Sestier, 1880; Dubner, 1980; Ormerod, 1997; Rubin, 1998; Sundberg, 1999). The most popular image of pirates, however, comes from a relatively more recent past. Mention of the word pirate to the non-maritime person evokes colourful images of swashbucklers from the eighteenth and nineteenth century Caribbean. This is a notion that regrettably endures due to a literary and cinematic tradition that portrays pirates as romantic and rebellious, if extinct, adventurers of a bygone era. Indeed, by the end of the nineteenth century, the global and regional threats of piracy were virtually eradicated "as a result of strong punitive action by legitimate users of the sea". (Brittin, 1986, p. 116). Unfortunately, this proved to be merely a short-lived respite. In the 1970s, less than a century after piracy's supposed demise, a steady rise in the number of attacks ushered in the present phenomenon of modern piracy.

Far from being an extinct phenomenon, piracy at sea is still very much alive today. More than 3,000 actual or attempted acts of piracy have been reported around the world from 1996 to 2005. During this period, a total of 340 persons were reported killed. In 2005 alone, 440 crew members were reported taken hostage, 24 were injured, and 12 were missing. During the same year, 182 ships were boarded and 19 were fired upon (ICC IMB, 2006). This violent phenomenon justifies the efforts of the international community through the IMO, the IMB of the International Chamber of Commerce, coastal states, and other maritime industry stakeholders[2] to identify, monitor, study, and implement preventive measures to combat piracy. One of the earliest practical measures implemented was to inform mariners of the location of piracy-prone areas through the establishment of the IMB Piracy Reporting Centre in Kuala Lumpur which is open 24 hours per day, 365 days a year. The IMB also endorses technology applications such as ShipLoc, a

---

1. The authors wish to acknowledge the assistance and co-operation of the IMB in providing the statistics used in this study.
2. Such as, *inter alia*, seafarers, ship owners, insurance companies, port authorities, etc.

satellite tracking system that allows ship operators to determine the exact location of their ships; Secure-Ship, a non-lethal electric fence installed around the ship; and Inventus UAV (unmanned aerial vehicle), "a state-of-the art reconnaissance system packaged in a highly efficient, highly stable flying wing form" (IMB, 2006, p. 29).

To address the policy aspects of combating piracy, IMO has collected international best practices and developed these into guidelines to aid maritime administrations as well as corporate boardrooms. These have taken the form of IMO Maritime Safety Committee (MSC) Circulars 622 and 623,[3] regularly updated through regional workshops and assessment missions conducted by IMO in the world's principal maritime areas. The workshops provide affected states with a venue for sharing piracy-related information, experience, and expertise that form the knowledge base for the formulation of policy and development of practical measures. This chapter aims to contribute to this knowledge base by inquiring whether an econometric analysis of the characteristics of vessels subjected to piracy attacks could reveal patterns or selection modes practised by pirates in targeting vessels. In other words, it seeks to discern whether pirates select randomly or not the vessels they plan to attack.

The chapter is organised as follows. The next section offers a review of selected literature on definitional aspects and typologies related to piracy. The third section presents results from reports and statistical analysis on acts of piracy. Section four uses a database assembled from information on reported acts of piracy and on the world merchant fleet to estimate four Probit models aiming at estimating the main characteristics of vessels subject to attacks. The final section draws conclusions and stresses how further research using a similar econometric approach could contribute to the knowledge base vital to formulating sound policies to eradicate or at least reduce the number of piracy cases.

2. DEFINITIONAL ASPECT AND PIRACY TYPOLOGY

Any study of piracy inevitably raises the issue of how the term is defined. The definition of piracy is relevant because any confusion in terminology invariably leads to debates between state sovereignty and universal jurisdiction over crimes. Rubin suggests that the numerous meanings of the word piracy include a vernacular usage with no direct legal implications; various international law meanings derived from, among others, international conventions; and various municipal law meanings defined by the statutes and practices of individual states (Rubin, 1988, pp. 1–2). As an example of the vernacular

---

3. MSC Circular 622 contains "Recommendations to governments for preventing and suppressing piracy and armed robbery against ships", whereas MSC Circ. 623 contains "Guidance to shipowners and ship operators, shipmasters and crews on preventing and suppressing acts of piracy and armed robbery against ships".

definition, the *Oxford Concise Dictionary* defines piracy as "the practice or crime of robbery and depredation on the sea or navigable rivers, etc., or by descent from the sea upon the coast, by persons not holding a commission from an established civilized state" (Oxford University, 1987, p. 1349).

The definition in international law is more precise and detailed. Article 15 of the Convention on the High Seas (Geneva High Seas Convention, 1958) and Article 101 of the United Nations Convention on the Law of the Sea (UNCLOS, 1982) are generally recognised as providing the definition of piracy in international law. These two articles define piracy as consisting of any of the following acts:

> "(a) any illegal acts of violence or detention, or any act of depredation, committed for private ends by the crew or the passengers of a private ship or a private aircraft, and directed:
>> (i) on the high seas, against another ship or aircraft, or against persons or property on board such ship or aircraft;
>> (ii) against a ship, aircraft, persons or property in a place outside the jurisdiction of any State;
> (b) any act of voluntary participation in the operation of a ship or of an aircraft with knowledge of facts making it a pirate ship or aircraft;
> (c) any act of inciting or of intentionally facilitating an act described in subparagraph (a) or (b)."

Halberstam's review (1988) of the *travaux préparatoires* to the Geneva High Seas Convention and UNCLOS makes it clear that the definition of piracy was not updated to take into account the development of the modern regime of maritime zones and remains trapped in a period where the high seas were only three miles from shore. Mejia (2003) likens this asynchronous situation to a gerrymandering of the oceans that effectively legislated piracy away to areas far beyond its traditional locus. The international convention definition of piracy is seen as being highly restrictive particularly because it requires the act to be motivated by private ends involving two ships located on the high seas. According to the IMB's annual piracy reports and a study conducted by Farley (1993), the majority of acts reported today take place in waters within the jurisdiction of states. This causes a potential inconsistency in the case of many coastal states where the crime of piracy may not carry the same definition in municipal law or, as in some cases, where it might not even be defined at all. Birnie (1987) rightfully notes that in theory the number of definitions of piracy in municipal law is limited only by the number of states enacting laws against the crime.

To ensure that all crimes against shipping that resemble piracy are addressed in its documents and deliberations, IMO uses the term "piracy and armed robbery against ships". IMO defines armed robbery against ships as "any unlawful act of violence or detention or any act of depredation, or threat thereof, other than an act of piracy (as defined in Article 101 of UNCLOS), directed against a ship or against persons or property on board such a ship, within a State's jurisdiction over such offences" (IMO, 2002, p. 4). On the other hand, IMB (2006) defines piracy and armed robbery as "an act of boarding or attempting to board any ship anywhere with the apparent intent to commit theft or any other crime and with the apparent intent or capability to use force in the furtherance of that act". IMB's definition is intentionally broad and is designed to capture all reports of violence against ships. The IMB definition has no standing in international law and is used for statistical purposes only.

The confusion as to what constitutes piracy in international law is compounded further by its occasional use as a political or journalistic pejorative, particularly in high profile cases that strictly speaking would not readily meet the UNCLOS criteria. Menefee (1999) writes, "international lawyers have come to expect, whenever there is an act of violence or lawlessness on or above the sea which involves community sensibilities, that the Press will describe the act as piracy". Brown (1994) presents the following as examples of the use of the term piracy as a political pejorative: the submarine attacks against neutral merchant vessels during the Spanish Civil War, the seizure of *Santa Maria* in 1961, the Cambodian seizure of *Mayaguez* in 1975, and the hijacking of *Achille Lauro* in 1985.

When publishing articles or broadcasting reports, most news magazines, newspapers, news services, and non-maritime journals generally refer to piracy in its vernacular sense. In academic writing, however, particularly in the maritime journals, authors are more careful in the usage of terminology and normally specify which meaning of piracy and/or armed robbery against ships is being adopted in their paper. The present study covers all the possible threats of maritime violence, not from a strategic perspective, but from the practical point of view of threats to the personal security of seafarers or passengers. The term "piracy and armed robbery against ships" is, therefore, used throughout this chapter. When referring to the individuals carrying out the attacks, however, this chapter shall restrict itself to using the label "pirate".

A sound understanding of the nature of attacks or piracy typology is essential to the formulation of effective policies to combat piracy and armed robbery against ships. There are a number of studies that attempt to characterise modern piracy and the behaviour of pirates through different typologies. The typologies take into account *modus operandi*, level of violence, level of sophistication in planning and execution, target victims, and prevailing geopolitical phenomenon. Birnie's 1987 study, for instance, describes piracy not only in the context of customary international law but also coastal piracy, yacht piracy, piracy against boat people, and piracy for political purposes. Beckman (2002), on the other hand, characterises attacks "according to their seriousness and the level of interest of the international community" and takes into consideration the types of weapons employed, treatment of crew, value of property stolen, and level of threat to safety of maritime navigation. Beckman's typology includes piracy under UNCLOS, offences under the Suppression of Unlawful Acts (SUA) Convention, major criminal hijacks, attacks on vessels in international straits, attacks on vessels in major international shipping lanes in Indonesia, and attacks on vessels in ports.

Dillon (2005, pp. 155–165) writes, "current definitions of piracy are inadequate as a tool for policymakers and need to change". The classification proposed by Dillon—extortion by government functionaries, sea robbery, piracy, and maritime terrorism—emphasises varying levels of action required to combat different types of attacks. For instance, because agents of the government commit the first category mentioned above, the most effective means of eliminating it is through an anti-corruption programme. According to Dillon's typology, since sea robbery takes place within the coastal area, it is best addressed by local police and coast guard agencies; piracy on the high seas is ideally curbed by national navies; and the transnational nature of maritime terrorism requires a multinational approach to combating and information-sharing (Dillon, 2005, p. 157).

In describing the types of piracy (Abhyankar, 2005, pp. 201–243), IMB focuses mainly on the behaviour and *modus operandi* of pirates. First is the "Asian" type of piracy where the ship is boarded, cash is stolen from the safe, and valuables taken from the crew. This type of piracy normally involves only a minimum level of violence from the attackers and is particularly prevalent in the Port of Phillip Channel, Malacca Straits, and in Indonesian waters. In contrast, the "South American" and "West African" types of piracy usually involve more violence and are usually attacks made by armed gangs that mainly target cash, cargo, personal effects and equipment while ships are berthed or at anchor. The third type has a military or political feature. This type is particularly prevalent off the Somali coast but has also been reported at different times in the South China Sea as well as in waters off the Philippines and Indonesia. The fourth type involves the hijacking of vessels (23 out of 276 acts of piracy in 2005) where the entire ship is stolen and its cargo diverted. Many occurrences of this last type have been reported in Southeast Asian waters.

3. STATISTICAL STUDIES ON PIRACY

A number of papers and reports have presented statistical analyses of incidents of piracy and armed robbery against ships. One of the earlier studies was Farley's (1993, p. iii) "data-based analysis of worldwide maritime piracy incidents against commercial merchant shipping from January 1989 to September 1993". Farley's study begins with a brief description of the global impact of piracy and armed robbery against ships and then proceeds with an analysis and characterisation of incidents on a regional basis. The regions selected for analysis (South/East Asia, Northeast Asia, Indonesia, West Africa, and South America) represented 88% of all the attacks reported during the period covered. Drawing on a database containing 523 reported cases, Farley (1993, p. 27) analyses the different regions in terms of the identity of the typical attack using the following characteristics: type of vessel, target items/objects, time of day, boarding success rate, location, status of vessel during attack, number of attackers. The database was constructed by Farley using a wide variety of reporting sources on pirate attacks worldwide. Having been a pioneering effort in piracy data collection, the database and corresponding analysis suffers from gaps in the detailed information relating to attacks. Nevertheless, it represents an important early attempt into determining where piracy occurs and how pirate attacks are carried out. Table 7.1 below presents a summary of the statistics presented by Farley.

Table 7.1 Selected descriptive statistics relating to attacks reported, 1989–1993

		South/East Asia	North-east Asia	Indo-nesia	West Africa	South America	Other regions	Inter-national totals
Total number of attacks reported		284	31	65	40	42	61	523
Number of attacks according to time of day	Day	33	9	6	3	2	9	62
	Night	127	10	44	31	28	32	272
	Not indicated	124	12	15	6	12	20	189
Number of attacks according to location	International waters	114	23	34	1	0	11	183
	Territorial seas	138	5	31	37	42	45	298
	Not indicated	32	3	0	2	0	5	42
Ship status during attack	Number of ships underway	124	22	18	1	3	20	188
	Number of ships stationary	13	4	10	36	34	32	129
	Not indicated	147	5	37	3	5	9	206
Number of persons killed as a result of attacks		11	0	1	0	1	13	15
Number of persons injured as a result of attacks		21	1	6	3	7	38	43
Boarding by pirates	Number of successful boardings	149	14	34	33	34	46	310
	Number of unsuccessful boardings	50	10	11	3	4	8	86
	Not indicated	85	7	20	4	4	7	127
Detection of pirates	Number of attacks in which pirates were detected before boarding	70	16	13	6	3	19	127
	Number of attacks in which pirates were not detected before boarding	16	0	8	2	11	3	40
	Not indicated	198	15	44	32	28	39	356
Success in boarding by pirates in spite of detection	Number of attacks in which pirates boarded successfully in spite of detection	11	7	1	2	0	7	28
	Number of attacks in which pirate boarding was unsuccessful as a result of detection	46	7	10	3	3	8	77
	Not indicated	227	17	54	35	39	46	418
Mean number of pirates involved in attack		7.32	9.5	9.42	9.45	7.67	8.03	7.98

Source: M. C. Farley, "International and Regional Trends in Maritime Piracy 1989–1993" (Master's diss., Naval Postgraduate School, 1993).

Another statistical study, conducted by Mak (2002), examines IMB reports on piracy and armed robbery against ships for the years 1995–2000 and disaggregates the data in order to determine the nature of attacks in five locations in Southeast Asia, namely Indonesia, Malaysia, Malacca Straits, Singapore

Straits, and South China Sea. Using his statistical analysis, Mak questions some of the reasoning behind IMB's methodology, draws attention to the exaggeration of the problem of piracy in Southeast Asia in the popular press, and highlights the positive effects of national and regional anti-piracy programmes.

The only regularly recurring statistical analysis of reported incidents of piracy and armed robbery against ships thus far is the annual report published by IMB.[4] The results of the analysis of all attacks, both actual and attempted, documented during the year are presented in tabular form in each annual report. The analysis of the data gathered during the year for which the report is generated is also compared with those of past years.

It must be noted that the IMB database is not comprehensive as it reflects only incidents that were reported to the Bureau. It is widely acknowledged that there is an under-reporting of cases due to, among others, the daunting and complex reporting procedures imposed on ship captains, mistrust in the integrity of local authorities, concerns about commercial reputations, and the substantial financial implications of further delays in port that can be brought about by lengthy investigations (Johnson, Pladdet and Valencia, 2005; Abhyankar, 2002; Menefee, 2005; Farley, 1993, p. 15). Another limitation comes from incomplete reports submitted to IMB. For instance, when looking at statistics on the status of vessels when attacks occurred from 1996 to 2005, 49.53% were categorised as "not stated" as opposed to 24.34% "anchored", 20.64% "steaming", and 5.40% "at berth". Figure 7.1, Figure 7.2 and Table 7.2 below present some descriptive statistics from the 2005 report.

4. It should also be noted that IMB compiles quarterly interim reports complete with statistical analyses for the first three quarters of each year.

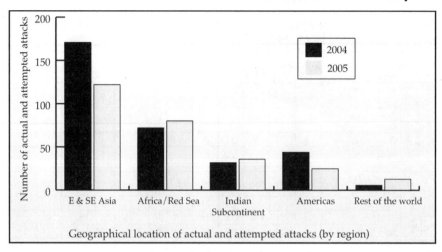

Source: ICC IMB, "Piracy and Armed Robbery Against Ships Annual Report 1 January–31 December 2005" (London: ICC IMB, 2006).

Figure 7.1 Location of actual and attempted attacks reported, 2004–2005

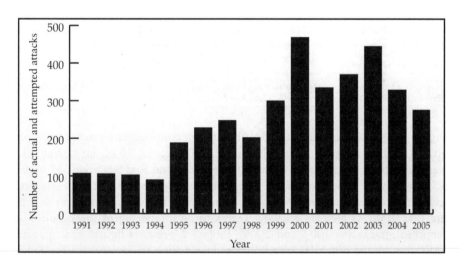

Source: ICC IMB, "Piracy and Armed Robbery Against Ships Annual Report 1 January–31 December 2005" (London: ICC IMB, 2006).

Figure 7.2 Number of actual and attempted attacks reported, 1992–2005

Table 7.2 Types of weapons during attacks, type of attacks, and types of violence employed, 1994–2005

	Types	1994	1995	1996	1997	1998	1999	2000	2001	2002	2003	2004	2005
Weapon employed during attack (number of attacks)	Pirates with guns	17	39	32	71	48	54	51	73	68	100	89	80
	Pirates with knives	13	9	23	31	40	85	132	105	136	143	95	80
	Other weapons	6	34	54	24	18	24	40	39	49	34	15	13
	Weapon not stated	54	106	119	12	96	137	246	118	117	168	130	103
Type of attack (number of attacks)	Boarding of ship attempted	22	27	36	18	25	46	143	83	71	93	77	52
	Ship fired upon	–	9	6	24	11	12	8	14	13	20	13	19
	Ship boarded	54	129	180	174	145	227	307	219	257	311	228	182
	Ship hijacked	5	12	5	17	17	10	8	16	25	19	11	23
	Ship detained	6	11	–	8	4	1	2	1	–	–	–	–
	Ship missing	–	–	–	–	–	4	1	2	4	2	–	–
	Type of attack not stated	3	–	1	7	–	–	–	–	–	–	–	–
Type of violence (number of persons affected)	Taken hostage	11	320	193	419	244	402	202	210	191	359	148	440
	Kidnap/ransom	–	–	–	–	–	–	–	–	–	–	86	13
	Threatened	8	59	56	119	68	21	72	45	55	65	34	14
	Assaulted	–	2	9	23	58	22	9	16	9	40	12	6
	Injured	10	3	9	31	37	24	99	39	38	88	59	24
	Killed	–	26	26	51	78	3	72	21	10	21	32	–
	Missing	–	–	–	–	–	1	26	–	24	71	30	12
Total reported number of attacks for the year		90	188	228	248	202	300	469	335	370	445	329	276

Source: ICC International Maritime Bureau, "Piracy and Armed Robbery Against Ships Annual Report 1 January–31 December 2005" (London: ICC International Maritime Bureau, 2006).

Figure 7.1 shows that East and Southeast Asia continue to bear the brunt of attacks against shipping. According to the 2005 report, 79 of the 122 attacks were reported in Indonesian waters. In the Africa and Red Sea areas, 35 of the 80 attacks were reported off the Somali coast. Figure 7.2 exhibits the rising trend in actual and attempted attacks from 1992 to 2003, peaking at 469 in the year 2000. It also shows what seems to be a tapering of the number of reported attacks for 2004 and 2005. Table 7.2 presents figures that give an indication for the potential for armed violence during attacks, types of violence employed, and the type of attack.

The analysis contained in the reports issued by the IMB are extremely useful in understanding the phenomenon of piracy in terms of typology, location, trend, level of violence, vessel details, *modus operandi*, etc. However, it can be argued that the application of more advanced statistical tools in analysing the IMB data could lead to a deeper understanding of the nature of piracy and armed robbery against ships and thus contribute to more effective preventive measures and policies. The next section applies such tools in inquiring whether pirates consider ship type and flag of registry in selecting the vessel they plan to attack. Additionally, since most of the attacks reported during the period covered in this study took place in Southeast Asia, the next section tries to estimate if specific characteristics for acts of piracy on Asian flagged vessels can be detected.

4. AN ECONOMETRIC ANALYSIS ON ACTS OF PIRACY

The sample used in this study is assembled from two databases. The first one comprises 3,164 actual or attempted attacks against ships that have taken place from 1996 to 2005, as reported to and documented by IMB.[5] The second database consists of statistics from the Institute of Shipping and Logistics of Bremen (ISL) on the total world merchant fleet for ships of 300 gross tonnage and comprises 350,376 vessels from 1996 to 2005. A comparison of the two databases led to the elimination of 565 vessels from the IMB database that did not appear in the ISL database. Among the vessels eliminated were 126 fishing boats, 91 tugs, and 69 yachts.

The final sample is derived from 350,376 observations in which 2,599 vessels (3,164 – 565) were subjected to actual or attempted attacks from 1996 to 2005. For the 2,599 observations, information is available on the year of the attack (from 1996 to 2005), the ship type (of which there are seven[6]) and the flag of registry (of which there are 10[7]). The selection of the various vessel types and flags of registry was made according to their relative ranking in the statistics on piracy and armed robbery against ships. Information from the IMB database as to the location of the attack was not considered since, for purposes of comparison, it is impossible to determine a location for vessels that were not attacked. This study looked at all attacks, whether attempted or actual, and made no distinction as to the severity of the attack. The only factor considered was whether the ship was attacked or at least targeted for attack by pirates. Table 7.3 and Figure 7.3 below are descriptive statistics relating to the proportion of the world sea-going fleet that reported actual and attempted attacks according to year of occurrence, type of ship, and flag or registry.

---

5. The statistics compiled by IMB are widely recognised as being "the only consistent source of region-wide time series data" on piracy and armed robbery against ships. See Mak (2002).

6. 1. bulk carrier; 2. general cargo including general cargo, multipurpose, reefer and RoRo; 3. container ship; 4. tankers; 5. chemical and product carriers; 6. liquid gas carriers including LPG and LNG; and 7. others.

7. 1. Panama; 2. Singapore; 3. Liberia; 4. Malaysia, 5. Cyprus; 6. Malta; 7. Bahamas; 8. India; 9. Hong Kong; and 10. all other flags.

Table 7.3 Descriptive statistics of the sample

Variables	Actual and attempted attacks (number) (1)	Observations (number) (2)	Actual and attempted attacks (%)	Number of vessels (%)	Actual and attempted attacks (%) (1)/(2)
Ship type					
Bulk carrier	741	59,760	28.51	17.06	1.24
General Cargo	654	106,967	25.16	30.53	0.61
Containership	418	25,103	16.08	7.16	1.67
Tanker	408	71,932	15.7	20.53	0.57
Chemical/product carrier	275	75,940	10.58	21.67	0.36
Liquid Gas	103	10,674	3.96	3.05	0.96
All types	**2,599**	**350,376**	**100**	**100**	**0.74**
Flag					
Panama	444	48,159	17.05	13.74	0.92
Singapore	225	9,297	8.66	2.65	2.42
Liberia	203	14,701	7.81	4.2	1.38
Malaysia	130	4,390	5	1.25	2.96
Cyprus	178	13,175	6.85	3.76	1.35
Malta	137	12,571	5.27	3.59	1.09
Bahamas	116	9,597	4.46	2.74	1.21
India	86	3,627	3.31	1.04	2.37
Hong Kong	87	4,166	3.35	1.19	2.09
Others	993	230,693	38.25	65.84	0.43
All flags	**2,599**	**350,376**	**100**	**100**	**0.74**

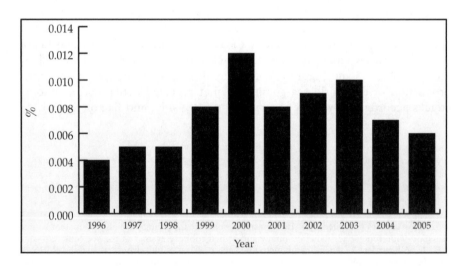

Figure 7.3 Proportion of the world sea-going fleet that reported actual and attempted attacks

The highest proportion of attacks occurred in 2000 (414 attacks or 12% of total attacks on the whole period) followed by 2003 (358 attacks or 10%) and 2002 (305 attacks or 9%). The descriptive statistics reveal that among the world merchant fleet in operation from 1996 to 2005, 0.74% was subjected to actual or attempted attacks. In absolute values, the vessel types that were subjected to the greatest number of attacks were bulk carriers (741 attacks) followed by general cargo vessels (654 attacks), container ships (418), tankers (408), chemical and products carriers (275) and liquid gas carriers (103). As a percentage of the total fleet for each ship type during the period studied, the number of container ships attacked represents 1.6% of the container fleet, while the corresponding percentage for bulk carriers is 1.2%, and 0.9% for liquid gas carriers.

In absolute terms, the flag of registry victimised by the greatest number of attacks is Panama (444 attacks or 17.0% of the attacks), followed by Singapore (225 attacks or 8.6% of the attacks) and Liberia (203 attacks or 7.8% of the attacks). Looking at the number of attacks as a percentage of the total fleet registered under a flag, however, Malaysia is the flag with the highest proportion of attempted or actual attacks (2.9% of the fleet), followed by Singapore (2.4%), India (2.3%), and Hong Kong (2.0%).

An econometric analysis for potential factors that influence a ship's probability to be attacked was then done, followed by a study of whether there are differences between Asian and non-Asian flags. For that purpose, it is estimated that several Probit models applied to different sets of data.

Table 7.4 Econometric analysis of the probability of being attacked

Variables	(1) All		(2) Asian flag versus non-Asian flag		(3) Non-Asian flag		(4) Asian flag	
	coef	marginal prob.	coef	marginal prob.	coef	marginal prob.	coef	marginal prob.
Constant	−2.693***		−2.423***		−2.439***		−2.058***	
Year 1997	0.068*	0.12%	0.103*	0.32%	0.158**	0.46%	−0.040	−0.19%
Year 1998	0.033	0.05%	0.015	0.04%	0.035	0.09%	−0.035	−0.16%
Year 1999	0.198***	0.39%	0.310***	1.17%	0.331***	1.14%	0.263***	1.57%
Year 2000	0.365***	0.87%	0.485***	2.17%	0.488***	1.96%	0.482***	3.46%
Year 2001	0.251***	0.53%	0.326***	1.25%	0.350***	1.23%	0.264***	1.57%
Year 2002	0.273***	0.59%	0.245***	0.87%	0.298***	0.99%	0.102	0.53%
Year 2003	0.323***	0.73%	0.364***	1.45%	0.374***	1.34%	0.331***	2.07%
Year 2004	0.196***	0.39%	0.231***	0.81%	0.327***	1.12%	−0.039	−0.18%
Year 2005	0.139***	0.26%	0.168***	0.55%	0.225***	0.70%	0.023	0.11%
Bulk carrier	0.052	0.09%	−0.033	−0.09%	−0.044	−0.11%	−0.010	−0.05%
General cargo	−0.153***	−0.23%	−0.337***	−0.87%	−0.345***	−0.80%	−0.332***	−1.37%
Container ship	0.153***	0.29%	0.042	0.12%	0.037	0.09%	0.053	0.26%
Tanker	−0.227***	−0.31%	−0.252***	−0.61%	−0.252**	−0.53%	−0.241**	−1.06%
Chemical/ product carrier	−0.274***	−0.37%	0.517***	2.57%	0.374***	1.42%	0.875***	9.49%
Panama	0.189***	0.37%						
Singapore	0.604***	2.05%						
Liberia	0.345***	0.84%						
Malaysia	0.702***	2.75%						
Cyprus	0.325***	0.77%						
Malta	0.266***	0.59%						
Bahamas	0.342***	0.84%						
India	0.597***	2.05%						
Hong Kong	0.444***	1.26%						
Asia			0.320***	1.16%				
Predicted prob.	0.57%		1.07%		0.93%		1.97%	
Observations	350,376		119,683		98,203		21,480	

Estimates from Probit models. Marginal probabilities are expressed in percentage. Significance levels are respectively 1% (***), 5% (**) and 1% (*).

The first Probit estimation considers the complete sample of 350,376 observations (first column in Table 7.4). It appears that all variables are statistically significant at 1% except for years 1997 and 1998 and for the bulk carrier category. Estimations also confirm that the probability to be attacked was higher in 2000 (0.87%/0.57% equal to 153% higher compared to the reference year 1996) and in 2003 (129.3% higher). Furthermore, general cargo vessels (− 40.6%), tankers (− 55.3%) and chemical and products carriers (− 65.2%) face less attacks compared to the reference category (liquid gas) while container ships (51.8%) are statistically subject to more attacks. Finally, it appears that the flag of registry also affects in the highest proportions the probability for a vessel to be attacked, with vessels flying the Malaysian (484.6%), Singaporean (362%), and Indian (361.5%) flags leading in this respect.

The proportion of Asian flags among those shown in the initial results exhibiting the highest probability of being attacked led to a focus on two groups of vessels: the principal Asian registries (Singapore, Malaysia, India, and Hong Kong) and the principal non-Asian registries (Panama, Liberia, Cyprus, Malta, and Bahamas). Vessels that belonged to the "other flag" category and that could not come under any of the two groups were deleted from the initial sample. This resulted in a final sample of 119,683 observations.

The second estimation introduces into the regression a dummy variable which is equal to one when the vessel is under Asian flag (column 2 in Table 7.4). The estimation confirms that this variable is statistically significant at 1%, with a t-value of 14.24.

The comparison between the Probit estimations for Asian flags (column 4, Table 7.4, with 21,480 observations) and non-Asian flags (column 3, Table 7.4 with 98,203 observations) suggests that the flag registration (Asian or not) does not change the main determinants on the probability to be attacked, apart from some years that are no longer significant such as 2002, 2004 and 2005 for Asian flags. Results stress that the main difference comes from the impact of the explanatory variables, which is different in both groups of vessels.

For instance, in the case of a general cargo vessel, the probability to be attacked reduces in a quite similar proportion regardless of the flag group to which they belong, i.e., − 85.8% for non-Asian and − 69.7% for Asian compared to the reference category liquid gas. However, such is not the case for chemical and product carriers. The probability to be attacked increased for both these categories, but with a higher impact for vessels under Asian flags (+481.4%) than for non-Asian flags (+153.1%) and could be explained by a potential connection between vessel flag and location of attacks.

This analysis suggests that the vessel type is not affected in the same proportion as the probability to be attacked according to where the vessel is registered (coefficients effect). To further understand the observed differences between the two groups of countries, some decomposition analysis is performed. The aim is to determine whether the gap between Asian and non-Asian flags stems from differences in the composition of each group (characteristics effect) or from differences in the returns of the covariates for each group (coefficients effect). For that purpose, the method described in Yun (2004) which generalises the Oaxaca-Blinder decomposition to the case of non-linear dependent variables is relied on. The idea is then to decompose the mean probabilities of attack for each group obtained through the use of Probit models.

Table 7.5 Results from the non-linear decomposition method

Decomposition		Endowments effect	Coefficients effects
Total decomposition			
	Difference	−0.42	2.13%
	Absolute t-value	(5.24)	(3.99)
Detailed decomposition			
Year	1997	0.00%	−0.03%
	1998	0.00%	−0.02%
	1999	−0.01%	0.12%
	2000	−0.01%	0.27%
	2001	0.00%	0.09%
	2002	0.00%	−0.03%
	2003	0.02%	0.12%
	2004	0.00%	−0.08%
	2005	0.00%	−0.03%
Ship type	Bulk carrier	0.00%	−0.03%
	General cargo	0.05%	−0.38%
	Container ship	0.01%	−0.01%
	Tanker	−0.12%	−0.15%
	Chemical/product carrier	−1.92%	2.30%
	Liquid gas	−1.98%	2.13%

When turning to the data, performing the non-linear decomposition leads to the following conclusions. First, differences between the two groups are not particularly associated with differences in characteristic effects (differences in constant being included), but they are instead due to differences in coefficients. Second, results from a detailed decomposition which evidences the weight of each explanatory variable to the gap between the two groups indicate that the type of vessel plays the most influential role. It therefore confirms that pirates distinguish between flags of registry not in selecting a vessel type instead of another according to its flag of registry but rather in giving more focus on a specific vessel type. In the Asian flag group, for instance, more focus is given to chemical and product carriers.

5. DISCUSSION AND CONCLUSIONS

The nature of the link between flag of registry and type of vessel on the one hand and probability to be attacked on the other hand, is possibly related to the type of piracy or armed robbery attack a vessel is facing. The study's findings may help confirm (Mukundan, 2005) that the Asian type of piracy or armed robbery against ships, which implies the boarding of vessels, focuses on fully laden chemical and product carriers that are relatively easy to board because of their low freeboard. The findings also suggest how future studies may explore factors beyond the scope of earlier piracy and armed robbery typologies, by giving a focus on specific ship types targeted.

The fact that most attacks are reported in Asia where a high proportion of vessels registered in Asian flags operate is a likely explanation why the probability for Asian vessels to be attacked is higher. In 2005, 79 attacks were reported within Indonesian waters (29% of all reported attacks) and 12 in the Malacca Straits (4%) according to IMB (2006). However, it is important to examine the figures presented in this study in a balanced context, and not to dramatise any interpretations. For instance, calculations (see Table 7.3) indicate that 5% of vessels attacked are registered under the Singaporean flag when it represents 1.25% of the world fleet. These values should be taken in light of the fact that in the absence of accurate information as to the duration of the attack, each reported attack does not mean, for instance, that the ship is taken out of service each time it is victimised. The duration is variable—an attack could take as little as half an hour or last a number of days or weeks. The absence of information on the cost/damage also represents an important limitation of the present study.

Furthermore, it is difficult to acquire data on the frequency that vessels navigate through a given waterway. Another issue is the fact that both attempted and actual attacks are considered in the data. Finally, data consists of reports made voluntarily to the IMB and that under-reporting is a widespread phenomenon.

Notwithstanding the above limitations, the findings of this study can contribute to the existing knowledge base on which international organisations and national governments may draw when formulating policy and developing practical measures against piracy and armed robbery against ships. Indeed, MSC Circ. 622 calls upon states to "assess the nature of the attacks with special emphasis on types of attack, accurate geographical location and *modus operandi* of the wrongdoers and to disseminate or publish these statistics to all interested parties in a format that is understandable and usable" (IMO, 1999a, p. 1). This study's findings certainly add to a deeper understanding of the nature of attacks, within the context of flag of registry and type of ship.

MSc Circ. 622 also urges states flag and coastal states to develop detailed action plans to prevent pirate attacks as well as mitigate or dampen the negative effects in the event that such attacks succeed. In particular, states are exhorted to take into account the possibility of an environmental disaster arising from piracy and armed robbery against ships in areas of restricted navigation. The potential for such accidents to occur in the narrow waters of the Malacca and Singapore Straits is enormous. For instance, in 1999 fully-laden VLCC *Chaumont* was seized in the narrow waters of the Phillip Channel by pirates who threatened the chief officer with a machete on the back of his neck. Another recorded incident in the Straits involved a ship whose bridge was unmanned for a period of 70 minutes "due to the fact that when the attackers left the ship the crew could not immediately free themselves" (Abhyankar, 2002, p. 21).

This study's findings can also assist shipowners who operate particular types of ships in preparing appropriate ship security plans. These would complement the guidance in MSC Circ. 623, emphasising the need to develop preventive and deterrent measures that can be modified and updated to take into account different types of ship (IMO, 1999b, p. 3). It is reasonable to assume that many shipowners weigh the costs related to implementing measures to prevent such attacks against any potential savings or benefits. More information such as the findings of this study can serve as input in any corporate risk-based decision-making process looking to identify the most effective ways to combat piracy and armed robbery against ships.

One of the main advantages of the approach taken in this study is in trying to identify which flags of registry and types of vessels are statistically subject to more attacks instead of providing only general statistics on acts of piracy and armed robbery against ships. In so doing, it sheds light on some specific segments of the market for which combating piratical attacks should be a priority. These elements could be relevant not only to international organisations, national governments, and shipowners but also to other actors in the maritime industry such as insurance companies, P&I clubs, classification societies, seafarers unions, etc., all of which could benefit from a better understanding of the phenomena.

It is in this vein that further research using similar approaches could be implemented and focused on potential regional similarities and differences in vessel selection by pirates. For instance, are Latin American flags targeted more in Latin America than non-Latin American flags? How about the Indian subcontinent? Are there similarities in pattern and experience? Different types of piracy and armed robbery against ships require different approaches, methods, and resources. Without accurate insight into the planning and decision-making processes among pirates, states and shipowners might end up merely "targeting resources and dispersing efforts to unrelated and inconsequential issues" (Dillon, 2005, p. 155).

PART II
PORTS

CHAPTER 8

PORT SAFETY AND WORKERS

Sara E. Russell

1. INTRODUCTION

From ocean shipping's early origins to the present, daily operations at seaports represent potentially dangerous worksites. In an industry where time equates to money, port management forfeited safety protocols in favour of faster operations to improve profit margins. The result yielded work environments that placed dockworkers at risk for respiratory disease, occupational injury and in extreme cases, death. Today's terminal operations depend more upon the synchronisation of complex cargo stowage manoeuvres coupled with the simultaneous use of oversized handling equipment. Although worker safety has always been a cornerstone of domestic and international union platforms, port authorities, governmental agencies, and member-state organisations reactively have created safety programmes in response to maritime tragedies.

Traditionally, management viewed safety programmes as non-complementary hindrances affecting desired performance levels and infringements upon expected earnings. Higher insurance premiums, workers' compensation claims, penalties and hefty fines, however, are far more costly than the design, implementation and control of safety and health plans.

Safety and health plans are vital in today's global economy. With increasing globalisation, levels of importing and exporting are estimated to reach record highs. More cargo entering port facilities necessitates more handling equipment on-terminal and cargo movements to deliver it to its next stage in the intermodal process thus increasing the chances for worker accidents.

Examples of industry responses that have improved working conditions include safety-training programmes, environmentally friendly initiatives and the introduction of automated machinery such as electric-powered handling equipment, automatic guided vehicles, and optical character recognition devices.

This chapter will review the historical and current terminal worksite conditions, identify union forces supporting the creation of safety programmes, examine various safety programmes around the globe that mitigate risks, and highlight industry and government-sponsored plans to improve port worker safety and health. As evidenced in the proceeding discussion, associated costs and benefits to the plans continue to drive their creation and acceptance.

Management strives to achieve operational proficiency and reduce accident rates with limited resources.

2. EARLY CARGO HANDLING AND SAFETY

2.1 Dock work—the early years

Early cargo handling equipment was relatively primitive utilizing the long-shoremen hook (Goldblatt, 1963) as well as systems of ropes and slings. The hook, a curved piece of iron or steel attached to a handle, allowed the men to grab onto bags of breakbulk cargoes like coffee and cocoa beans and bales of cotton. These labour-intensive operations were tiring for labourers, both quay and dockside. For example, in 1942, a 10,000-ton vessel loaded with bags of sugar from Hawaii took Californian labourers 6,650 man-hours to unload. Utilizing five gangs of longshoremen on seven shifts, 10 hours each, the men moved the cargo, sack by sack (Goldblatt, 1963). These physically demanding work conditions led to workers routinely suffering accidents and sustaining personal injuries.

In conjunction with the hook, slings and early forms of winches eased the tension on the dockers' backs. Workers tied ropes, creating a stopper knot, now known as the stevedore knot (Warde, 1989), around the cargo and hoisted the loads out of ships' holds using a system of pulleys. In the late 1700s, hand-operated cranes were introduced. London dockworkers, however, opposed the use of cranes (Alderton, 2005). Although working conditions and operational efficiency improved with such innovations, they conversely reduced the number of men necessary per ship. Fewer dockers potentially threatened the union's perceived dominance along the waterfront.

Following World War II, heavier load-bearing winches replaced winches that could only move cargoes of one ton or less at the Port of New York. Now equipment handled loads of increased volume and tonnage in a single movement. Although this innovation improved operational efficiency, due to the lack of safety measures, poorly maintained equipment such as frayed lines, and an increased demand on worker productivity, dockers continued to suffer worksite injuries, including hernias, falls and cuts from the collapse of the slings and falling cargo (Winslow, 1998).

Similarly, dangers existed within the vessels as well as quayside. Holdmen, individuals working and manipulating the cargo inside the vessel from the wings to the centre of the hold, communicated with winch operators via a system of signals. Holdmen's hand gestures informed winch operators where to move the cargo within the ships' confined spaces (Davis, 2003). An unnoticed or incomprehensible signal could lead to disastrous results for individuals stationed below the heavy cargo. Since holdmen performed their duties mostly in the square, also known as the opening of the hold, they had little space or time to escape falling cargo, ranging from lumber products to steel pipes if a sling were to hit a beam or rupture.

Inhaling dust, a second work hazard for holdmen, occurred because of the inherent vice of bulk cargoes—cement, talcum powder, and cocoa. Due to the poorly ventilated spaces, holdmen were unable to avoid the suffocating particulate matter, which led to long-term breathing disorders. Other hazardous products included asbestos, poisons, acids, and fertilizers. While dockers complained to supervisors about handling products with skull and cross bone markings, management maintained their position that cargoes were safe to handle and workers continued to suffer injuries and develop chronic diseases (Davis, 2003).

Reports by the US Department of Labor from 1940–1950 highlighted the severity of worker injury rates, disclosing it as the most dangerous form of labour in the United States (Bureau of Labor Statistics, 1944). The 1942 report attributed the injuries and accidents to three causes: casual nature of the workforce, the need for speedy unloading and loading operations, and the lack of training in forms of equipment and handling procedures.

2.2 Casual labour

On any given day, dependent upon the number of vessel calls, members of gangs shuffled within and among the terminals and management hired different men on various days to handle diverse cargoes, hence fostering the casual nature of the workforce. For example, at the United Kingdom docks from 1947 until 1967, men arrived outside the docks for a chance to receive a ticket 7.45 am and 12.45 pm, guaranteeing a day of work (McNamara and Tarver, 1999). Accordingly, individuals selected and assigned to various gangs one day could be completely different from those chosen the following day. Because it took time to learn one another's strengths and weaknesses in the loading and unloading operations, gangs' work expertise and capabilities changed daily affecting the rhythm of daily operations. These differences created conditions for accidents among inexperienced workers.

During World War II, the UK abolished the use of casual labour and instituted the National Dock Labour Scheme (NDLS) to maintain a more stable civilian workforce. The reversal of NDLS in 1989 reintroduced casual labour and allowed stevedore companies to compete for business at UK docks. In an attempt to reduce operating costs and effectively compete among more companies, stevedore organisations decreased the amount of training and welfare benefits workers received. As might have been predicted, the number of accidents among port workers increased (McNamara and Tarver, 1999).

2.3 Speed of operations

In addition to casual labour, the rapidity which ships required for loading and discharging contributed to high accident rates. The monetary factor influenced both worker and shipowners. First, workers received payment by a piece rate system and second, ships needed to achieve quick turn around in the trade lanes. The piece rate system entitled dockers to be paid based on the number of break-bulk products they handled, such as per bag of coffee or drum of cargo unloaded. Because the more cargo handled would yield greater pay per day, labourers concentrated solely on the speed of their movements. More movements equating to more pay was the driving force. Consequently, all parties ignored safety protocol, if it existed, and concern for others.

Second, vessels do not make money while berthed. Shipowners earn profit on the number of turns their vessels make annually. If the vessel waits in port, achieves fewer turns, and accrues higher mooring costs (those costs charged by the terminal to use berth space), then the shipowner achieves lower profit margins. Ship productivity necessitated efficient functionality at each port of call with minimal interruption. Accordingly, a shipowner sought such ports. As a result, terminal operators demanded workers perform proficiently to assure repeat vessel calls. Again, such hastened operations created an environment where safety measures were largely ignored.

2.4 Training

The lack of dockworker training contributed to high accident rates among dockworkers. Few ports created training programmes emphasising safety protocols. And for those ports that did have policies, they were rarely enforced (Davis, 2003). Training was not a new concept, apprenticeship programmes date back to ancient times when master craftsmen shared their talents and techniques with younger, unskilled labourers. However, during periods of industrialisation, training was overlooked in favour of reduced costs and quick-paced operations. Safety protocols, then as today, were expensive to create, institute and monitor. In addition, conducting on-the-job training slows down port operations while labourers learn hands-on safety processes. The actual job takes longer to complete, thereby, potentially reducing revenue for all stakeholders from dockworker to shipowner.

During its existence, registered workers within NDLS participated in a required port training which consisted of a four week college safety course. With the elimination of the NDLS, terminals hired fewer employees and colleges trained fewer employees. The economies of scale for teaching larger groups of dockworker-students eroded, thus increasing the price of training per dockworker (McNamara and Tarver, 1999). Eventually, port authorities and terminal managers deemed extensive training as an ancillary cost and replaced the training courses with the adoption of the UK Health and Safety at Work Act of 1974. Among the criticisms of this act is the lack of required safety training courses and specific skills for dockers. Currently, standards in training vary from port to port.

2.5 Advent of the container and changes to cargo handling equipment

To ensure speedier movements at terminals, more mechanised forms of handling equipment replaced the antiquated methods of pulleys and winches. Forklifts and mobile cranes became common pierside equipment around the 1960s (Cargo Handling, 2007). Newer and more modern forms of equipment speed up loading and unloading operations, yet original techniques still exist and are used throughout terminals. For example, a flagman's role on terminal includes the use of hand signals among crane operators, and individuals in the holds and quayside (Hensel, 2001), much like the handling operations of the 1800s. Moreover, with the introduction of the container, traditional breakbulk cargoes were consolidated into bulk operations or even into containerised operations. To the dismay of labour organisations, the loading and unloading operations required fewer labourers onsite. Consider the sugar cargoes moving from Hawaii to California. When bagged, 10,000 tons of sugar took 80 men 6,650 man-hours to unload; when moved via a belt operation the same 10,000 tons took eight men only 1,000 man-hours (Goldblatt, 1963).

As gang sizes changed, so did terminal operations; yard layouts now included large, empty parcels of land to handle containers rather than rows of warehouses to accommodate individual pieces of cargo. With the increased use of mechanical equipment, worker accidents and illnesses decreased (Spielman, 2007). However, even with the introduction of new types of cargo-handling equipment, dock work remained incredibly dangerous and the severity of the accidents intensified (Harrison, 2008). With the introduction of gantry cranes, straddle carriers, and hustlers, new accidents emerged in the form of equipment collisions, falling containers and hatch covers, and slips from cranes.

A 1987 Bureau of Labor Statistics survey analysed injuries and illnesses among dockworkers (Lettman, 1989). The Bureau compared the number of days lost for longshore work as compared to traditional work; on average 41 days per case were lost to disabling injuries as compared to the national average of 18 days[1] (see Table 8.1).

The transportation and warehousing industry retains its classification as an industry with the highest recorded injuries and fatalities, lagging slightly behind construction trades (see Figure 8.1). In 2005, the US Bureau of Labor Statistics reported 15 fatalities in the marine cargo industry (Bureau of Labor Statistics, 2007).

---

1. A more recent comprehensive breakdown of longshore accidents has not been republished by the Bureau of Labor Statistics.

Table 8.1 Injuries involving longshore operations, selected characteristics, 1985–1986

Characteristics	% of total cases	Characteristics	% of total cases
Job category at time of accident		**Activity at time of accident continued:**	
Clerk, checker	7	Climbing or coming down ladder, gangway, vehicle and so forth	9
Deckman	5	Checking cargo	6
Dockman	12	Fixing or repairing gear, equipment, or container	6
Driver: forklift, tractor	15	Other	15
Holdman	29		
Maintenance, mechanic, gearman	7	**Personal protective equipment worn:**[1]	
Warehouse or shedworker	6	Dust mask	3
Other	19	Gloves	59
		Hardhat	77
Nature of injury:[1]		Reflective vest or jacket	3
Cut, laceration, puncture	19	Safety goggles	5
Bruise or contusion	28	Steel-toed safety boots or shoes	61
Muscle sprain or strain, torn ligament	48	Other	4
Hernia	1	Not wearing any safety gear	9
Fracture	18	**Worksite conditions contributing to the accident:**[1]	
Object in eye(s)	4	Too noisy	2
Other	9	Poor weather conditions	6
		Cluttered work area	8
Part of body affected:		Slippery work services	17
Head, including neck	9	Uneven work surfaces	19
Upper extremities	19	Equipment broke or did not work properly	16
Trunk	28	Working in too small or tight an area	13
Lower extremities	28	Hard to see or bad lighting	9
Multiple parts[2]	14	Work area not properly safeguarded	5
		Other work site condition	8
Activity at time of accident:		None	29
Handling cargo/ equipment by hand	31		
Helping crane or winch operator to load or unload cargo	19		
Drive yard tractor, lift truck or other mobile equipment	10		
Using hand tools	3		

1. Because more than one response is possible, the sum of the percentages exceeds 100.
2. Applies when more than one major body part has been affected, such as an arm and a leg.
Source: A Comprehensive Report, Injuries Involving Longshore Operations, Bulletin 2326. Superintendent of Documents, Government Printing Office, Washington, D.C. 20402. Bureau of Labor Statistics.

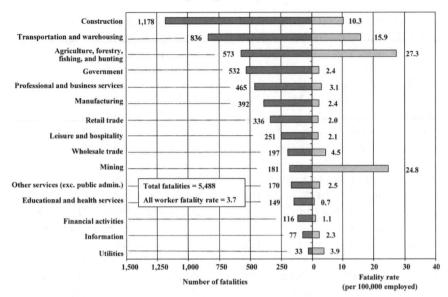

Source: US Bureau of Labor Statisics, US Department of Labor, 2008.

Figure 8.1 Number and rate of fatal occupational injuries, by industry sector, 2007

3. FIGHTING FOR IMPROVED CONDITIONS—UNIONS

3.1 Impact of US unions

Although port workers united in haphazard groups along the docks, poor working conditions and paltry compensation characterised the United States' waterfront throughout the mid 1800s and into the 1930s. The informal assemblies prevented the men from mounting more effective protests to demand improved working conditions. Early formations led the way to a blending of the East Coast dockworkers into the already established Great Lake Association of Lumber Handlers in the late 1800s, the precursor to the International Longshoremen Association (ILA, 2006).

Once united, among the chief concerns for dockworkers were improved wages and working conditions. New locals joined the efforts on a regular basis for several decades. By 1911, 306 locals existed, encompassing ports along the Great Lakes, the East, the Gulf and even West Coasts, as well as Puerto Rico. However, by the late 1920s, with the Great Depression influencing the economy, wages decreased while intense competition for work filled the waterfront. Dockworkers' needs went unnoticed as economic strife dominated. Despite organised labour's continued efforts, a safety guideline for dockworkers had yet to be realised during this period.

The Pacific Coast ILA maintained loose ties with their East Coast brothers in the ILA throughout the 1930s (ILWU, 2005). Similar to the situation on the East Coast, West Coast labourers' demands and interests were overlooked due to the Depression. As part of an economic stimulant, Congress passed the National Industrial Recovery Act (NIRA) to improve employment among various industries throughout the country (Finlay, 1988). Aided by President Franklin D. Roosevelt's newly formed National Recovery Administration (NRA), components included reducing hours of labour, increasing wages, and eliminating unfair trade practices. Industry leaders were asked to submit proposals anticipated to stimulate growth in their respected vocations. Plausible suggestions would be included in the Act.

In the summer of 1933, under the guidance of West Coast ILA officials Jack Bjorklund and Paddy Morris, delegates from the Pacific Coast ILA designed and sent a maritime industry policy to Washington, D.C. to be included within the Shipping Code of the NIRA. Concurrently, West Coast waterfront employers created and submitted a code to the NRA. Despite the NIRA's attempt to create a working group, the West Coast employers refused to combine efforts with labour to jointly present an employer/employee code. The immediate dismissal and unilateral stance regarding policy-making ardently reinforced the union's platform and strengthened their solidarity.

Unrelenting, the West Coast ILA submitted deadlines to waterfront employers in hopes of working together to establish a coast-wide contract outlining the request for a six-hour working day, a basic wage for all dockers at West Coast ports, and a union-controlled hiring hall. West Coast employers disregarded the labour union and its deadlines and, instead, sparked a flame that led to an industry-wide strike (ILWU 19, 2008).

Dockworkers, along with seafarer unions and other maritime workers, maintained their position into July of 1934, but events became critical when employers tried to break the strike and force the labourers back to work. Unrelenting, the West Coast members of ILA stood firm under the guidance of a San Francisco longshoreman and eventual International Longshore and Warehouse Union (ILWU)[2] leader, Harry Bridges. In the commotion, six persons lost their lives in the events of 5 July 1934, known as Bloody Thursday (ILWU, 2005). Unyielding, other US industry unions and global unions joined the protest and mounted a general strike in the pursuit of worker rights.

Eventually, President Roosevelt appointed the National Longshoremen's Board to handle the disagreements. In October 1934, the board issued its award in favour of the union workers. The award included a six-hour workday; established that any work performed beyond the six hours was to be paid at an

2. In 1936, the Pacific Coast ILA petitioned for the unification of all US maritime unions, the proposal was dismissed by the East Coast ILA, inciting intense tension between the two groups. In response, the West Coast ILA voted to separate from the East Coast ILA and receive a Congress of Industrial Organizations charter, forming the International Longshore and Warehouse Union. Harry Bridges was elected President of the newly formed ILWU (ILWU, 2005).

overtime rate and increased the basic wage by $0.10. A central hiring hall and ILA-selected dispatcher was reinstated in each creation port to be managed by the ILA, the Pacific Coast District. Overall, the outcome represented a pro-union award, which satisfied the workers. Work stoppages and slowdowns remained prevalent occurrences at the ports throughout the 1930s and 1940s. Workers sought enforcement of minimum manning policies that included limitations concerning heavily-weighted cargo slings. Occupational health and safety now dominated operations (Finlay, 1988).

Future West Coast contracts further supported occupational safety initiatives and included detailed weights and measures of specific cargoes allowed in slings per individual lifts. Slings were limited to no more than 2,100 pounds when previously workers handled loads weighing in excess of 3,000 pounds. By the 1937 labour contract, a newly-created union and management task force began work on a longshoremen safety protocol. With passage of the 1940 labour contract, labourers now had the right to stop all work in response to unsafe working conditions. Unions exerted this newfound power to stop operations and wait until the situation could be resolved, repaired or alleviated—many times at significant cost to dock employers. The economic burden for employers was particularly great if stoppage occurred during off hours when dockworkers earned overtime compensation.

However, in the 1940s, as cargo handling evolved and new forms of mechanisation were adopted along the waterfront, cargo-handling styles changed. Pallets and forklift trucks replaced slings and hand trucks. Safety protocols established post-1934 became outdated. Previous policies concerning sling loads were no longer applicable. These policies were redesigned in the 1960 Mechanization and Modernization Agreement and adopted by the West Coast unions (Finlay, 1998). Thus presents the challenge—as management introduces new forms of terminal operations and cargo handling, so too exists the need for dockworkers to be protected by relevant safety measures.

3.2 Unions and safety—around the globe

The International Labour Organisation (ILO), a United Nations group headquartered in Geneva, Switzerland, comprised of governments, employers and employees, creates and supports decent working conditions for labourers around the world (ILO, 2008). The ILO's doctrine, Occupational Safety and Health (Dock Work) Convention, 1979, addresses safe working conditions among dockworkers. Still applicable today, the doctrine details safe operating procedures for handling different types of cargoes; proper stacking and storage of cargoes; and general safe operating procedures for dockworkers along the berths and throughout marine terminals.

Similarly, the International Dockworker's Council (IDC) has also taken a stance on safety and health at work in their support of a unified European Port Policy. Founded in 2000 by dockworker trade unions, the IDC is comprised of over 55,000 dockworkers from around the globe. The IDC promotes safe working conditions for its dockworker members including proactive measures to decrease accident rates and worker health problems (IDC, 2007). One key component to their platform is the creation of a European Port Policy that includes a "European code for the prevention of occupational hazards in the stevedoring sector", encompassing all European Ports to eliminate varying and disjointed standards currently in existence.

A third global union, the International Transport Workers Federation (ITWF), a collection of over 600 transportation unions from around the globe, also includes worker protection and promotion among its core objectives. Member unions of the ITWF in conjunction with the Maritime Union of Australia (MUA) are petitioning the International Transport Workers Federation to explore and adopt safety guidelines for the creation of a universal safety code, to be eventually incorporated into an ILO convention (MUA, 2007). Following several fatal accidents at various Australian ports, the union's campaign requires support from terminal operators around the globe and the recognition that safety supersedes productivity measures.

An integral component of the international unions is the fact that they monitor workplace operations in both rich, developed nations, and developing nations, which have yet to establish occupational safety organisations. The World Health Organization estimates that only 10–15% of the global workforce has access to occupational health services (WHO, 2008). Globalisation is primarily fuelled by capitalistic organisations seeking out underdeveloped areas for purely monetary savings, which in turn exploit workers in locales lacking in protective legislation. For these activities such as the handling of hazardous wastes and ship dismantling, to be performed in developed nations, organisations would be required to spend large sums of money to abide by not only occupational health and safety guidelines but also environmental protection guidelines. Thus, a cheap and easy alternative exists in the off-shoring of such activities. However, the ILO, the IDC, and the ITWF rally to combat these underhanded manoeuvres in effect to protecting workers around the globe.

For example, in the late 1990s, a Greenpeace report stated that Indian ports reluctantly received hazardous waste imports on a routine basis; the products were shipped under the pretext of "recycling". Transportation of hazardous materials from the Organization for Economic Cooperation and Development (OECD) nations to non-OECD nations is illegal under the Basel Convention of the Transboundary Movement of Hazardous Wastes and their Disposal (Basel Convention, 2005). Despite existing regulations, exporters in developed nations continued the practice and smaller ports lacking dockworker guidelines accepted the cargo. Alarmed by the exploitation, Greenpeace joined efforts with the ITF. And, in 1999 with the assistance of the ILO's Bureau for Worker's Activities (ACTRAV) guided hazardous material policy creation and training sessions for Indian union representatives (O'Neill, 2002).

Unions are important partners in the creation and execution of effective safety and health plans. To these individuals, workplace safety is the number one priority of the job—to ensure that the healthy workers are able to return day-after-day. Herbert Abrams wrote that it was labour's dissent in the workplace and eventual organised strikes and litigation that led to policy creation (2001). And this tenet remains true in today's workplace.

3.4 Link between unions and safety

Numerous studies have highlighted the negative link between unions and workplace accidents. Dating back to the late nineteenth century, research and work conducted by Sidney and Beatrice Webb highlighted European trade unions and their significant impact upon workplace injuries (1897). As a collective entity not only did the unions have the capability to highlight safety discrepancies, but formal grievance procedures protected the workers from management retaliation and led to timely remedies. More recent research conducted by Adam Seth Litwin and his review of health and safety of workplaces in the UK concluded that unions successfully reduce workplace injury rates (2004). For example, he estimates that a non-union, assembly-line worker is 13 times more likely to suffer an injury than was a union worker. Moreover, he concluded that facilities without formal union presence will proactively create and institute safety plans as incentive to attract workers while and at the same time deter the creation of formal trade unions.

Additionally, observations and research conducted by Conway and Svenson and their analysis of occupational injury and illness reductions from 1992–1996 highlights how the impact of unions and insurance companies translates into a reduction in workplace hazards as well as the creation of workplace safety standards (1998). Their research found that 29.4% of industrial union collective bargaining agreements contained clauses requiring safety and health committees. Twenty years ago, 26.5% of agreements included such clauses.

4. SAFETY PLANS

4.1 Port authority plans

Most plans stem from accidents that have occurred on terminal property. After thorough inspections, safety plans are created and administered. In Hong Kong, from 2000–2004, 420 container yard accidents were reported at various yards (Hong Kong News, 2005). Hong Kong, like other Asian ports have limited land for container storage, thus, stacking containers eight high is a normal port practice and makes the safety of container stacking a challenge. Subsequent accidents for workers include falls from heights and object collisions.

For example, among its "Code of Practice on Mechanical Handling Safety in Container Yards", the Hong Kong Department of Labour created new standards for container stacking following accidents in 2005 due to strong wind conditions, which can cause empty containers to fall into the yard (Hong Kong News, 2005). The Department not only amended the original document, but also created and offered safety seminars detailing precautionary measures during inclement weather conditions. In addition, safe storage practices of containers in terminal yards are detailed in Hong Kong's Factories and Industrial Undertakings Regulations and the Department of Labour's Factories and Industrial Undertakings Ordinance. Hong Kong's Labour Department routinely inspects container yards and issues warnings regarding non-compliance activities every six to 12 months. Monetary fines are issued to those terminals that fail to comply with guidelines while extreme cases of nonconformity warrant jail time.

In addition, Hong Kong International Terminals created a Safety and Health Policy that focuses on high risk operations; fire safety, and procedures for the handling, storing and transporting of dangerous goods. With the introduction of these measures, the terminal safety record improved. Between 1997 and 2004, the number of accidents per TEUs handled has decreased by 54%. The terminal's focus extends beyond its employees to other port stakeholders including stevedores. Recognition awards are given to those organisations that achieve accident-free records (Hong Kong International Terminals, 2007).

In contrast, Saudi Arabian ports took a proactive approach to dockworker safety in the 1980s. During 1987, 70 million tons of commercial and industrial goods moved through its ports on the Red Sea and the Arabian Gulf (Martens, 1989). The Saudi Ports Authority, formerly Saudi Seaports Authority (SEAPA) under the control of the Prime Minister, worked with each port to create safety departments and guidelines encompassing occupational and fire safety standards. SEAPA also conducted routine inspections and worked with the ports to establish and implement accident-reporting procedures. Not only did each port manage its own safety department but also a first-aid clinic and an outfitted fire station. All facilities provide service 24 hours a day, 7 days a week. Moreover, SEAPA designed and distributed safety manuals and handbooks, including the 1980 "Rules and Regulations for Saudi Arabian Seaports" and guidelines in 1986 detailing proper forklift operating procedures. With these measures in place, the accident rates decreased from 28.1 per 1,000 men employed in 1985 to 9.9 per 1,000 men employed in 1987, and no fatal accidents occurred in 1987.

Similar to Saudi Arabia's proactive approach, Westport Malaysia emphasises its role in adopting international standards for marine security and safety. The port takes a proactive stance regarding all measures of safety, security and emergency protocols. Westport's Safety Department identified six key areas: equipment safety; safety of port infrastructure and operational sites; human safety; accident prevention; traffic flow; and root-cause analysis to ensure that operations at its site are in accordance with international marine security and safety (*New Strait Times*, 2005).

A unique focus for the port is its root-cause analysis component designed to prevent future accidents and fatalities. Following on-site port accidents, the port analyses the problem, assesses its origin and studies the cause to prevent future occurrences. The iterative process allows for evaluation of current practices and design of new policies to avoid a similar result.

4.2 Industry plans

Ironically, with shipping being one of the oldest forms of commerce and the first step to globalisation, an international convention on port safety does not exist (Secretariat of the Pacific, 2002). Today numerous programmes exist nationally and internationally to address worker and stevedore safety that span from the proper use of equipment to fire safety guidelines. Plans have been created by industry representative groups, as in the case of the Regional Maritime Programme of the Secretariat of the Pacific Community and the UK's Ports Skills and Safety Limited (PSSL) and by federal governments as with the United States Department of Labor—Occupational Safety and Health Administration's Marine Terminal plan.

These plans analyse the risk of accidents, identify potential hazards and create guidelines focusing on accident and illness prevention. However, port safety protocols differ from port to port and local factors contribute to the disparities. These factors include individual jurisdiction of terminal property and the types of cargo handled, which in turn influence the activities performed on terminal property. Core elements addressed by all safety procedures include the responsibilities of the port authorities, the terminal operators, and the employees with regard to air pollution; transportation, storage and handling of harmful goods; proper equipment usage; maintenance and training policies; emergency and first aid plans; and general yard operations.

4.3 US Occupational Safety and Health Administration (OSHA)

The United States' Department of Labor instituted the Occupational Health and Safety Act in 1970, creating national workplace safety standards for the millions of US workers throughout every industry. Since 1970 more than 271,704 workers' lives have been saved due to the introduction of OSHA standards (AFL-CIO, 2003). A three-pronged approach to workplace safety characterises the Act, including the creation of standards regarding workplace safety and health; a reporting system for on-the-job accidents and injuries; and finally, inspectors to enforce the guidelines in the workplace. Also, in accordance with the Act, the Occupational Safety and Health Administration was

created to administer the guidelines (MacLaury, 1984). Concerns over operation costs, the capability of inspectors, as well as reporting requirements have
contributed to organisational reluctance to adopt the Act. However, organised
labour, a strong proponent for the Act, worked with the federal government
throughout its creation and implementation.

Throughout the 1970s and 1980s, a proposal to remove the focus from
workplace safety to workplace health as well as an introduction of employer
economic incentives to complement workers' compensation strategies were
included in OSHA restructuring plans (MacLaury, 1984). An attempt to
ignore workplace safety ignited dissent among organised labour including
members of the United Auto Workers (UAW) and the American Federation of
Labor and the Congress Industrial Organizations (AFL-CIO). As an alternative, OSHA, under President Jimmy Carter's administration began to offer
and supplement the safety aspects with workplace training and economic
incentives for the employers. Championing for the maritime industry was
Joseph Leonard, whose role as Safety Director for the ILA spanned 40
years.

Directives addressing maritime workplace hazards originate via the Office of
Maritime Standards and Guidance, a subset of OSHA. Title 29 Code of
Federal Regulations (CFR) Parts 1910, 1917 and 1918 pertain to general
industry standards, federal health and safety standards of longshore and
marine terminal operations, respectively. The Marine Terminal guidelines
identify hazardous situations common to marine terminals and provide proper
operations within those areas from handling of hazardous cargo, to manning
of lines, and the use of conveyors and winches. The Longshoring guidelines
specifically address: gangway use; accessing barges; handling of hatches; and
crane operations. Finally, the Gear Certification governs the ship equipment
as well as landside operations including certification for those workers manning the equipment.

In June 2006, the National Maritime Safety Association (NMSA), a group
representing the marine cargo handling industry in the US, signed a partnership agreement with OSHA in effect creating an alliance and reinforcing each
party's commitment to worker health and safety. As part of the two year
agreement, OSHA will promote NMSA's Best Practices concerning marine
cargo handling procedures and the groups will discuss current issues impacting the work environments from container lashing to marine terminal traffic
(NMSA, 2006).

Alliances and proposed working groups are evident in the current operations of OSHA, to ensure that individuals familiar with the industry are a part
of policy creation as well as a constant emphasis on updating OSHA safety
rules. The last overhaul of the safety rules occurred in 1997 to reflect the
changes within the shipping industry. For example, post-1960 guidelines
concentrated on pre-mechanisation work injuries including back strain from
over-exertion and lifting. New safety guidelines focus on slips and falls from

containers, accidents with mechanical forms of equipment (e.g., forklifts, straddle carriers, gantry cranes), and terminal traffic in container yards as well as ergonomic standards that focus on matching job designs to worker tools, thus eliminating musculoskeletal disorders and leading to greater levels of productivity. In addition, OSHA estimated that with the implementation of new guidelines along with increased outreach and training programmes, five lives would be saved annually along with avoiding over 1,300 accidents and preventing 30,000 lost workdays, with an estimated $18 million annual savings (Sansbury, 1997).

4.4 Cost of worker injuries

Direct and indirect costs resulting from worker injuries account for an economic loss nearing 4 to 5% of Gross Domestic Product (WHO, 2008). Direct costs include medical expenses for hospitals, physicians, drugs, health insurance administration and worker compensation costs, whereas indirect costs include loss of wages, costs of fringe benefits, employer retraining, workplace disruption costs (damages to equipment, tools and materials and required overtime), increased insurance premiums and loss of company goodwill.

The American Society of Safety Engineers (ASSE) states that the indirect costs associated with safety failures can continue to impact organisations and are potentially 20 times greater than direct costs (ASSE, 2002). Negative publicity is the automatic result from workplace accidents and health scares, thus manifesting a cost associated with the inability to attract potential employees. Other costs include a worker's inability to reach productivity levels following a traumatic event, or the costs of counselling stemming from traumatic events. Therefore, by instituting a plan, the organisation not only saves and improves productivity, but it is perceived as a well-respected corporate citizen.

According to the National Health Accounts data (traces expenditures in the health care systems), "injury-related medical expenditures were estimated to cost Americans $117 billion every year"; this cost does not take into account the costs to the organisations' loss of productivity (CDC, 2006). According to the National Institute for Occupational Safety and Health (NIOSH), each day US workers suffer injury, disability, and death from workplace incidents. On average, nearly 16 workers die each day from traumatic injuries. Overall, 5,734 workers died in 2005 from an occupational injury and more than 4 million workers had a non-fatal injury or illness. On a global scale, Leigh estimates that approximately 100,000,000 occupational injuries occur every year resulting in 100,000 deaths (Leigh et al., 1999).[3]

---

3. Due to inconsistencies in reporting mechanisms between developing and developed nations, estimation of occupational injuries is required and crude estimates are given.

According to the Liberty Mutual Research Institute for Safety, a component of the Liberty Mutual Insurance Company, worker compensation claims in 2005 totalled $48.3 billion (Liberty Mutual Group, 2008). Within the maritime industry, the Longshore and Harbor Workers' Compensation Act (LHWCA) covering US longshoremen, shipbuilders and marine construction workers is the most expensive workers' compensation programme, other medical costs and claims are higher than state workers' compensation programmes.[4]

In 2003, the Office of Workers' Compensation reported a total benefits payout (see Table 8.2) from both private and public funds, including insured and self-insured employers under the LHWCA to be $716 million (Sengupta, 2005). In 2004, claims paid by the private maritime sector totalled $595 million (see Figures 8.2 and 8.3). The National Council on Compensation Insurance Inc. (NCCI) states from 1993 to 2002 total cost per claim under the LHWCA increased 72%, hence significantly increasing the costs to employers despite increased OSHA standards and diminishing on-the-job injuries. For example, employers of two freight handlers in Georgia performing the same duties, one covered under the Georgia workers' compensation programme and one covered under the LHWCA will pay entirely different compensation costs. The employer of the LHWCA worker pays $18.46 per $100 of payroll, while the non-union employer pays $5.48 per $100 of payroll in compensation. The cost differential is significant, average LHWCA claims are 221% higher than state workers' compensation claims (NCCI, 2007; CLAR, 2007).

4. Salaries for maritime workers are on average higher than traditional workers (i.e., emergency responders, truck drivers), therefore the compensation claims are under a higher benefit scheme as compared to state workers.

Table 8.2 Longshore and Harbor Workers' Compensation Act, Benefits and Costs, 1997–2003 (in thousands)

	1997	1998	1999	2000	2001	2002	2003
Total Benefits	$617,927	$642,321	$659,800	$671,991	$689,065	$696,450	$716,218
Insurance Carriers	219,352	238,464	232,778	249,671	236,726	242,491	262,753
Self-Insured Employers	263,255	261,559	283,991	278,952	307,708	310,939	309,843
LHWCA Special Fund	123,772	129,777	131,152	131,564	133,374	131,684	132,504
DCCA Special Fund	11,548	12,521	11,879	11,804	11,341	11,336	11,118
Total Annual Assessments	121,300	122,000	141,300	145,700	145,000	136,000	135,800
LHWCA	110,000	111,000	130,000	133,000	133,000	125,000	125,000
DCCA	11,300	11,000	11,300	12,700	12,000	11,000	10,800
Administrative Expenses[1]	9,356	9,821	10,822	11,144	11,713	11,970	12,314
General Revenue	8,378	8,596	8,947	9,373	9,807	9,988	10,297
Trust Fund	978	1,225	1,875	1,771	1,906	1,982	2,017
Indirect Administrative Costs[2]	1,799	2,107	2,247	1,787	2,207	2,514	2,347

1. Longshore program administrative funding is divided between two sources. Industry oversight and claims activities are funded from general tax revenues. The program also exercises fiduciary responsibility for a Special Fund, which draws its revenue primarily from annual industry assessments based on anticipated benefit liabilities. This fund makes direct benefits payments for certain categories of claims and provides funding for the program's rehabilitation staff and Special Fund oversight activities.
2. Includes legal and investigative support from the Office of the Solicitor and the Office of the Inspector General. Funded by General Revenues.

Source: U.S. DOL 2005b.

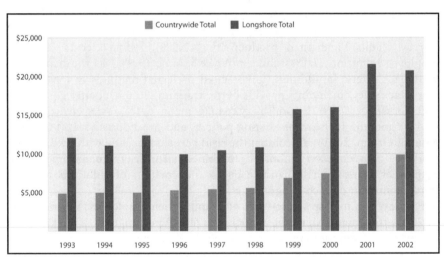

Source: Annual Statistical Bulletin, the National Council on Compensation Insurance, Inc.

Figure 8.2 Average cost per lost-time claim

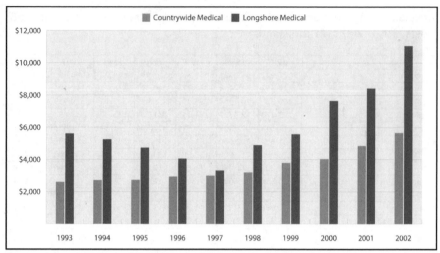

Source: Annual Statistical Bulletin, the National Council on Compensation Insurance, Inc.

Figure 8.3 Average medical costs for lost-time claims

To reduce the financial impact of such claims, organisations must understand where their employees are injured on the job and how to prevent these injuries. According to the Liberty Mutual Chief Financial Officer (CFO) Survey,[5] company CFOs realise the benefit to an improved focus on workplace safety. Survey results highlighted productivity (42.5%), reduced costs (28.3%), employee retention (7.1%) and employee morale (5.8%) as the benefits to workplace safety. In addition, CFOs cited preferred methods to maximising workplace safety including: provide better training (26.6%), better equipment and workspace (7.4%), more safety management (6.9%), safer environments (6.4%) and enforcement of existing policies and procedures (6.4%) (Liberty Mutual Group, 2008). To combat the rising costs associated with medical and workers' compensation claims, a combined effort from management and employees identifies risks and leads to the creation of solutions and the implementation of such programmes.

Employers must assess the costs of training their employees. For example, in 2005, the Pacific Maritime Association (PMA) estimated training costs of a new casual longshoreman to be $2,900 (Kearney, 2005). The incentive exists to hire individuals committed to the organisation and who plan on staying with the corporation. Port-related employers relying on casual forms of labour are at a disadvantage when workers fail to show up for work regularly.

5. The Liberty Mutual Chief Financial Officer Survey includes responses from 231 senior financial executives of large and mid-size corporations.

PMA estimated that between 1997 and 2001, 13.7% of their casual workforce failed to report to work[6] and retain their status as casual labourers. As a result, the organisation incurs costs associated with lost training and a shortage of employees that impact terminal productivity (Kearney, 2005).

5. MANAGEMENT

5.1 Terminal management

Management organisations realise the negative impact of ignoring worker safety which often translates into costly downtimes and high fines. Additionally, equipment malfunctions can not only lead to worker accidents but they can result in delayed vessels and fewer vessel calls. For example, in January 2008, the Southampton Container Terminal experienced such delays and reduced productivity when a crane collapsed onto a berthed ship (Porter, 2008). As a result, five cranes of similar design were pulled from quayside operations for inspection, thus necessitating over a dozen ships to reroute their cargo. The port experienced a 40% decline in business due to the down cranes. As investigations continue into the cause of the accident, the terminal loses business as ships and cargo are rerouted to neighbouring ports.

In an attempt to lessen the impact of such instances, many ports are proactively creating and monitoring safety plans for on-site operations. For example, APM Terminals, a division of the A.P. Moeller-Maersk Group, created plans addressing safety at their facilities. In response to its need for improved efficiency at all facilities, the organisation launched its Global Terminal Development Programme in 2004 (*Lloyd's List*, 2006). Although safety is a priority in Western ports, it is often overlooked at the ports in developing nations. Therefore, the policy guidelines, enforceable from Malaysia to Rotterdam, ensure the terminal's role in a carefully designed supply chain does not become the bottleneck. Moreover, the policy supports APM's primary focus that reducing accidents leads to fewer work disruptions and ultimately improves the terminal's efficiency, consequently creating a competitive advantage, and ultimately leading to improved profits (APM Terminals, 2007). Lloyd's Maritime Academy worked with APM to create and offer tailored programmes for port personnel and workers regarding health and safety.

APM's 2006 Virtual Safety Organization (VSO) serves as a guiding framework for safe terminal operations using information technology to advance port operations into the twenty-first century. VSO prioritises safety throughout daily operating procedures stressing zero-tolerance for those who divert

---

6. Pacific Maritime Association casual workers are required to show for one shift every six months in order to retain casual status.

from the policy. In addition, all APM Terminal employees participate in a terminal safety workshop prior to working on-site. To further support APM Terminal's focus on employee safety, on 24 October 2007, every terminal ceased operations for one half-hour to discuss safety issues (Quay Words, 2007).

5.2 Industry management

The Hampton Roads Shipping Association (HRSA) located in Norfolk, Virginia also takes a proactive approach to worker safety and training. Through a committed relationship among the OSHA, ILA and Virginia International Terminals Inc., and its many member organisations, the HRSA provides a central location for dissemination of safety information and administration of training courses as well as collection and analysis of dock worker data. Training schedules and updates are maintained in a database and, at any time, a worker's record can be accessed. The immediate retrieval of data allows for hiring halls to prevent workers in need of updated training to work until appropriate training is completed. In turn, member organisations hiring ILA workers rest assured that these workers have undergone extensive training with HRSA.

For all new longshore workers, HRSA requires a 40-hour training programme, which includes 12 hours of classroom time and 28 hours on-terminal work experience. Classroom sessions are devoted to explanations and discussions of proper working procedures with various forms of equipment and analysis of worker accident prevention aided by the use of graphic and videoed scenarios. Throughout the on-terminal training portion of the course, retired longshoremen guide and assist new workers with actual forklift and hustler operations. As workers achieve competency, training progresses to traditional dock-side movements with containers and chassis.

HRSA offers additional forms of training including hazardous materials training, homeland security training, updated re-certification training for Powered Industrial Truck drivers, and drug and alcohol prevention programmes. In the 1980s, HRSA designed and instituted a drug and alcohol prevention programme that ILA President, John Bowers, endorsed and was eventually adopted by the ILA.

HRSA works to follow the guidelines established by OSHA under 29 CFR 1917, 1918 standards; however, they continue to strive beyond these directives. "There is nothing that says we can't do more than what is required by OSHA", states Dan Harrison, Director of Safety, HRSA. "We work to constantly improve our screening process and educate new people working in our terminals" (Harrison, 2008). And the results are significant for the ports in the Hampton Roads communities, since 1984 accident rates have dropped significantly, even with increases in the amount of cargo and the number of workers employed (see Table 8.3).

Table 8.3 Hampton Roads Shipping Association, 1984–2006

Accident/Injury Statistics No. of Injuries x 200,000/No. of man hours worked (200,000 = base for 100 equivalent full time workers, working 40 hours per week, 50 weeks per year)			
Year	Man hours	Injuries	Rate
2006	2,539,718	55*	4.33119
2005	3,443,705	82	4.762313
2004	3,369,652	93	5.519858
2003	2,911,153	106	7.282338
2002	2,202,652	93	8.444366
2001	2,352,241	109	9.267758
2000	2,674,717	124	9.272009
1999	2,580,584	133	10.30774
1998	2,662,097	152	11.41957
1997	2,514,950	130	10.33818
1996	2,384,904	148	12.4114
1995	2,425,525	111	9.152658
1994	2,060,172	145	14.07649
1993	2,006,902	163	16.24394
1992	2,058,504	142	13.79643
1991	2,260,350	243	21.50109
1990	2,079,191	200	19.23825
1989	1,983,341	268	27.02511
1988	1,776,196	327	36.82026
1987	1,338,490	325	48.56219
1986	1,431,477	323	45.12821
1985	1,843,448	348	37.75534
1984	1,662,523	366	44.02947

* Total includes date from January–September 2006.

6. MODERN SAFETY MECHANISMS

By 1986, only 14% of US occupational injuries were the result of accidents involving machinery, included in these totals is traditional port equipment such as cranes, forklifts and lifting machinery. The decrease is attributable to machine guards, fail-safe devices and automated safety mechanisms (Baker et al., 1992). One effective solution to improving worker safety at ports involves the adoption of automated systems. These forms of cargo operations range from automatic guided vehicles (AGVs) to the use of optical character recognition devices and RFID tags. Implementation of these instruments reduces the number of workers necessary on-terminal, thereby reducing the chance for accidents. As with any asset procurement, consideration must be given to the performance capabilities as well as the financial outlay. Port operators must assess the environment and financial situation and research options that exist for environmentally-friendly equipment, while assuring decisions align with organisational operating goals. Once equipment is purchased, effective handling and training programmes need to be instituted to ensure safe handling.

6.1 Automatic Guided Vehicles

As early adopters in the 1990s, European sites such as the Rotterdam Delta Terminal and Thamesport Intermodal port facility introduced Automated Guided Vehicles (AGVs) and Automated Lifting Vehicles (ALVs) (Higgins, 1999; Vis, 2004). AGVs, programmemed and enabled by Global Positioning Systems (GPS), position an empty chassis or cassette under a ship-to-shore crane, where the crane operator unloads the container from the ship and places it onto the chassis or cassette. Upon receiving the box, the AGV moves to a specified yard address, much like a traditional yard hustler and chassis operation, minus the driver. A second piece of equipment, either a manually operated lift truck or an ALV removes the container from the chassis and positions it within the stacks. Then the AGV locates the next empty chassis or cassette and repeats the operation.

Although capital outlay for new generation cargo-handling equipment far exceeds the cost of traditional equipment, these unmanned systems require fewer labourers on quay and in yard operations. Downtimes rarely extend beyond maintenance or technological problems, and unlike labour, AGVs do not break for meals or at the conclusion of a day. A continuous operating schedule is achievable, increasing terminal productivity. The advantages to management might well be the savings realised by the elimination of salaries, benefits, training programme costs, and so forth. From labour's perspective, the new environment eliminates driver fatigue and stresses (Lou and Goh, 2003) and reduces worker peril.[7]

Although mechanised forms of cargo handling are continuously being designed to improve on-terminal operational efficiency, the costs associated with such improvements are still beyond the reach of many port operators. Due to either the costs of automation or the dominance by union workforces, the industry will maintain its reliance on men and women and employ them throughout the many processes of cargo operations. Safety plans are therefore necessary and management support is instrumental in their successful creation and implementation.

6.2 Twist locks

Automatic twist lock devices further improve worker safety during the loading and unloading operations of containers. During the loading process of a

7. More in-depth analysis regarding the potential link between automated forms of terminal equipment and worker safety have not been published.

container onto a vessel, a twist lock is inserted by a quayside employee into each of the four corners of the container, thus enabling it to secure itself onto the container below. Once the container has been positioned onto the vessel, another stevedore inserts cones into the slots for the next container that will be stacked. With the use of cell guides, this cone activity has been eliminated, yet the twist locks still must be placed on the container prior to their delivery on board the ship (Besco, 2001). This activity places the dockside worker at risk of a falling container in the event of crane malfunction and places the shipside worker at risk of falling from the container due to a slippery surface, lack of a protective railing, or harnesses. OSHA estimates that with the use of automatic twist locks, it will lessen the need by 90% for labourers to go on top of containers, thereby reducing the chance of a fall.

The National Maritime Advisory Committee on Safety (MACOSH), a workgroup under the OSHA umbrella tasked with identifying safety issues within the industry as they pertain to containers, traffic safety and worker health, has highlighted fully-automatic twist locks (FATL) as an issue for OSHA to review. MACOSH strongly recommended OSHA join with the IMO to create international standards for shipside safety issues (Witt, 2005).

Unions around the globe also support the use of FATLs. For example, since 2004, the Maritime Union of Australia has campaigned for the elimination of manually-operated twist locks and the denial of ships to berths that continue to use manual locks, due to the numerous perils facing workers when having to install the twist locks—such as standing below a loaded container, or on top of a container to insert the twist locks (MUA, 2004). OSHA advocated the use of semi-automatic twist locks in container hoisting operations and incorporated the directive into the marine terminal regulations concerning containerised cargo (29 CFR 1918.85(j)(1)(ii)) (OSHA, 2000).

6.3 Mooring

A third automated system capable of reducing accidents among port workers is the automatic mooring system. The mooring operation consists of a single worker to man the system as a directional vacuum pad attaches to the side of the vessel and adjusts to the ship's movements alongside the berth. This operation reduces the need for crews to tie down lines on incoming vessels. By eliminating the need for line handlers upon vessel arrivals, port authorities are able to reduce the chances for accidents quayside, and lessen the time needed to tie down ropes. Costs involved in adopting such technology include the redesign and retrofitting of the docks; but the cost reductions come in the form of reduced manpower quayside and the reduced need for tug power. The engineering design firm, Moffatt & Nichol, estimated that throughout a 20 year period, the costs for the operation of a Vessel Mooring System (VMS) programme would be somewhat higher than the costs of line operations (Allen, 2007). Additional capital is required to purchase the equipment and to continuously maintain its operational capabilities; however, the reduction in manpower reduces labour costs.

6.4 Radio Frequency and Optical Character Recognition

Other measures to reduce the risk of terminal worker costs include the use of remote operations. This alternative does not eliminate worker roles on port property, only redesigns the positions, but does require employees who possess more advanced and technical job skills. For example, firms like APM Terminals are instituting Optical Character Recognition (OCR) and RFID technologies allowing checkers to be moved to inside locations rather than located at the gates of entry to the ports. Trucks entering the APM-VA Terminal in Portsmouth, Virginia are given an RFID tag which is placed in the cab's front window. As the trucker departs the interstate, enroute to the terminal, the RFID signal is captured, alerting the terminal which trucker and, if loaded, which container is coming onto port property. Upon arrival, the OCR captures the container number and through various imaging techniques examines the container (Swedberg, 2006). The technologically-advanced operation allows for the segregation of the person and the activity which eliminates the chances of worker peril in the midst of incoming and outgoing trucks. Also, a speedier process allows for check-ins to be uniform, enabling drivers to make more turns per day at the facilities.

In addition to the use of RFID tags on incoming trucks, RFID tags are also used on the containers, enabling a container's physical location to be tracked anywhere on port property. Tags eliminate the need to search and scour port property for lost or mis-addressed containers, increasing port productivity and eliminating the chance for a worker, shadowed amongst rows and columns of containers, to step into the path of an oncoming vehicle. Thus, yard productivity is not the sole benefit to RFID, decreases in the number of worker accidents is also a benefit to the terminal.

7. EARLY WORKER HEALTH PROGRAMMES

7.1 Docker hospitals and clinics

Due to the dangerous nature of terminal operations and frequency of injuries, on-site medical care would be a natural complement to the terminal. Yet, with cost reduction as the prevailing focus within the industry, such units do not exist. It took the initiative of philanthropists to highlight and fund such a project. Samuel Gurney, a UK banker and philanthropist and William Money Wigram, a shipbuilder and liner owner, championed the cause of dockworker health following the death of a worker en route to the hospital. With their financial support, the first dock hospital opened in 1858, the Poplar Hospital for Accidents. The strategic location, across from the East and West India Docks allowed workers to be quickly treated, ultimately reducing the number of fatalities resulting from terminal operation accidents. The original hospital operated until 1941 when it was destroyed during a German second world war airstrike (PORTCities London, 2008). It was later rebuilt and remained in operation until 1982.

Immediate medical attention was also the driving force behind the creation of industrial health clinics at several New Zealand ports. In the late 1940s, the New Zealand Health Department established an occupational health nursing service to treat dockworkers, labourers in nearby factories and industries, and local citizens of the surrounding communities at the ports of Auckland, Lyttelton, Dunedin, and Wellington (Walker, 1959). The nurses cared for minor cuts and scrapes to more serious wounds resulting from terminal operations. On-site clinics allowed the dock workers to seek immediate treatment and reduced travel time to and from local hospitals. Workers were able to return quickly to the job without significant delay to port operations.

In addition to the on-site medical care and treatment, the nurses also worked with the New Zealand Port Authorities to teach workers about occupational safety through the screening of safety films and discussions. The nurses also provided insight to the terminal regarding workplace safety and accident prevention.

7.2 Spread of epidemics

Not only were goods traded among nations, but also infectious diseases. Travellers and traders spread diseases around the globe from smallpox and syphilis to the Black Death plague. All moved and spread via trade routes and ports of entry. To combat these epidemics, various forms of sanitary authorities were introduced to the London docks. In 1872, the Port of London Sanitary Authority (PSA) opened (Maglen, 2002). Infectious disease control officers inspected newly arrived vessels and passengers in an attempt to mitigate the spread of new forms of bacteria and diseases. Medical examinations were performed on passengers to help prevent the spread of diseases and suspected cases were monitored for developments. Through the PSA's efforts, the prevalence of various infectious diseases declined.

8. CURRENT OCCUPATIONAL HEALTH PROGRAMMES

Worker safety also encompasses healthy working conditions; conditions free of dust, particulate matter, and noxious fumes. Marine terminal operations utilizing diesel-powered cargo handling devices and fumigation services that emit hazardous fumes and particulate matter into the environment impact not only workers' health, but the health of those citizens living and working in the region of the terminal property. Many port authorities and terminal operators are turning to electric and/or low-sulphur diesel fuel powered cargo handling equipment as well as various on-terminal operations to reduce emissions, including reduction in truck idling times.

8.1 Emissions

The California Air Resources Board (CARB) identified health risks including premature death, cancer risk, respiratory disease and increased risk of heart disease among the effects of air pollution stemming from international trade. CARB estimated that of the 9,000 premature deaths in California, 750 were the consequence of trade-related pollution; and residents of West Oakland, California are exposed to nearly five times more diesel particles than neighbouring communities (Raine, 2006). Based upon these data, the ILWU supports efforts by environmental policy organisations, terminal operators and port authorities to explore ways to reduce emissions stemming from international trade.

A health hazard evaluation conducted at the request of the Joint Pacific Maritime Safety Code Committee (JPMSCC) in April 2003 at terminals in Long Beach and Oakland, California and Tacoma, Washington showed that persons in specific jobs across the terminals were exposed to high levels of diesel exhaust and carbon monoxide (CO) (NIOSH, 2006). The study included a collection of samples from 168 personal breathing zones across 15 job titles, and findings showed average diesel exhaust and CO did not exceed California Department of Health Services recommended exposure limits of 20 micrograms per cubic metre (see Table 8.4). However, Side Pick operators (container handling equipment) exposed to the equipment's diesel stacks and diesel engine repair workers were exposed to levels exceeding the standard. NIOSH recommendations for these specific jobs included the re-positioning of the diesel stack away from driver's cabs as well as increased ventilation systems in the work shops.

Table 8.4 Summary statistics for diesel particulate personal breathing zone air samples

						Mean value was significantly different* than other job title ID numbers
Job title ID	*Job title*	*Number of samples*	*Mean*	*Std Dev*	*Range*	

Table header:

	Summary Statistics for Diesel Particulate Personal Breathing Zone Air Samples – All Terminals Combined Joint Pacific Marine Safety Code Committee, San Francisco, California (HETA 2003-0246-3013) Concentrations shown in micrograms/cubic meter (μg/m³)					
Job title ID	*Job title*	*Number of samples*	*Mean*	*Std Dev*	*Range*	*Mean value was significantly different* than other job title ID numbers*
1	Shop man	18	12.0	9.0	2.1–42	6–9, 11–15
2	Side picker	8	14.0	8.7	12–22	12–15
3	Ship tractor driver	17	7.3	7.3	1.7-33	14–15
4	Transtainer mechanic	2	6.4	3.0	4.3–8.5	
5	Yard tractor driver	13	6.2	3.1	1.6–14	14–15
6	Dockman	14	5.1	2.6	1.6–11	1
7	Top picker	17	5.0	2.2	2.4–9.0	1
8	Hatch clerk	12	4.6	2.9	1.8–12	1
9	Lane clerk	9	4.5	2.2	1.5–7.6	1
10	Transtainer operator	5	4.4	2.7	2.5–9.0	
11	Walking boss/ yard supervisor	7	3.7	0.9	2.4–5.1	1
12	Guard	14	3.2	1.3	1.3–5.4	1, 2
13	Rail man	8	3.0	1.7	1.0–5.0	1, 2
14	Hatch boss	10	2.6	2.2	0.8–8.1	1–3, 5
15	Crane operator	14	2.5	1.2	1.0–5.2	1–3, 5

* Indicates mean concentration for a specific job title was compared to the mean for each other job title using the Tukey-Kramer Multiple Comparison Test at a significance level of $p < 0.05$.

Ports along the West Coast of the United States and Canada are tackling clean air initiatives to encompass not only on-site workers, but also citizens of the surrounding communities. Although their approaches are drastically different, ports from the Pacific Northwest to the Southern Coast of California are working to improve the air quality, thus improving the lives for citizens living and working within these areas.

The "Northwest Ports Clean Air Strategy" designed by the US ports of Seattle and Tacoma in Washington and Vancouver, British Columbia's Fraser Port Authority focuses on voluntary compliance and collaborative working relationships among all parties involved in marine operations, terminal operators, over-the-road trucking firms, and rail operators. The proposed plan is designed to reduce diesel and greenhouse gas emissions along the coast (Dibenedetto, 2008).

This shared approach facilitated by the US Environmental Protection Agency, the Washington Department of Ecology, the Puget Sound Clean Air

Agency and Environment Canada consist of plans for both shore and shipside activities to be implemented in 2010 and 2015. The plans include a change from diesel-powered equipment to equipment using cleaner fuels or electricity, engine retrofits, and studies to evaluate the effect of emission-reduction technologies. Similarly, plans recommend cleaner fuels for ships that include reduced sulphur content with a maximum content of 0.5% for auxiliary engines and 1.5% for main engines. Long-term measures coincide with the proposed IMO regulations of using 0.1% sulphur fuel and an 80% reduction in nitrous oxide emissions along the coasts.

The Clean Air Action Plan (CAAP) proposed by the Ports of Los Angeles (LA) and Long Beach in 2006 also attempts to curb the emissions from diesel-powered cargo handling equipment, ships, and trucks, and provide training. Studies by CARB estimate that diesel exhaust contributes to 2,400 deaths annually in California, half of those within the South Coast Air Basin, where the ports of LA and Long Beach are situated. Due to high instances of respiratory illness around these ports, CAAP aims to reduce emissions by 44% in the next five years; a much stricter and costly goal for port stakeholders as compared to Pacific Northwest's plan. However, with a unified front regarding emissions issues, the ports intend to eliminate users who abandon ports with emissions policies in favour of ports with lax emissions protocols.

A component plan of CAAP, the Clean Trucks Program, attempts to reduce the number of diesel-spewing trucks entering port property and travelling on neighbouring roads, thus lessening truck pollution by more than 80% (Mongelluzzo, 2007). The programme intends to decrease the number of pre-2007 year model trucks entering the terminal. Through a grant subsidy, owner operators will be given over $200 million to replace pre-2007 model year trucks and replace them with newer, cleaner trucks including Liquefied Natural Gas (LNG) powered trucks and clean diesel-powered trucks or retrofit old truck models because 2007 model year trucks are 90% cleaner than their predecessors (Government Technology, 2007). Older trucks entering the port will be assessed an impact fee. Estimates indicate that the plans will reduce diesel emission particulates by 45% and nitrogen oxides by 30% by 2011 (Gallagher, 2007). In February 2008, Long Beach's plan was approved. The Port of Los Angeles' approval of the proposal is expected in the near future.

8.2 Dust

Dust, another occupational air-borne hazard common on marine terminals, has many origins. Sources of dust include construction projects, abrasive blasting, or handling (bagging, transferring. or transporting) of powdered chemicals, pesticides or soils. Workers routinely exposed to such operations breathe in the dust particles. The particles enter the bloodstream and attach to internal organs, leading to lung and respiratory diseases. The WHO's 1999 "Hazard Prevention and Control in the Work Environment: Dust" outlines the numerous causes of dust and provides examples of many organisational control processes from ventilation to the use of containment mechanisms (WHO, 1999). In addition, preventative measures are detailed for those individuals that are exposed including the proper use of personal protective equipment and respirators.

A number of organisations are now reeling from the long-term effects of particulate matter exposures. High insurance costs and worker compensation claims stemming from asbestos and lead exposure plague these organisations. Therefore, to prevent future cases and lower costs, many organisations are researching and investing in cargo handling devices designed to control dust during loading and unloading. Grab cranes and conveyor belts have been replaced with mobile grab hoppers that incorporate air flows and flap devices, preventing dust from escaping upwards during the discharging process (Landon, 2007). Additionally, organisations are pressured and challenged by localities to become good corporate citizens and reduce the environmental impact of their operations.

In 2005, the port city of Thessaloniki, Greece faced such a challenge and confronted the issue of dust emissions. Dust from bulk cargoes was determined to be a major source of air pollution to the neighbouring community; the area's air quality level fell far below acceptable standards (Koutitas et al, 2005). As a result, the Thessaloniki Port Authority, aided by the city, developed various policies and procedures to control, minimise, and monitor the offending dust.

The port discovered that managing the dust was necessary not only to comply with legislated standards in the European Union, but also to improve the health and safety of its workers and the surrounding communities. The port created various models measuring the wind direction and speed, incorporated the findings into a dust dispersion model, and tracked the dust movements on terminal. Following the analysis of the dust movements, the port instituted plans to further prevent the spread of dust. Concrete walls were erected to surround bulk cargoes storage areas, dusty cargoes were covered with tarpaulin during storage and transportation, and the port instituted the use of hoppers and pneumatic vacuum conveyors to lessen the dust on terminal.

Air quality remains a prime consideration for the Port of Thessaloniki, and the port was recognised for their commitment to sustainability programmes with the environmental certification, Port Environmental Review System, PERS/2003 (Koutitas et al., 2005). PERS, an environmental-focused management plan created and managed by EcoPorts Foundation, combines the recommended Best Practices from the European Seaports Organization's 2003 Environmental Code of Practice into operational plans (EcoPorts Foundation, 2008). Certificate recipients are recognised for their creation and implementation of environmental management plans that are in accordance with legislative measures and achieve operational success with little environmental impact.

9. CONCLUSION

Prior to the 1940s, cargo handling at marine terminals consisted of labour-intensive operations. Large gangs utilized hand carts, pulley and winch systems to physically handle individual pieces of cargo. Automated forms of technology have transformed these labour-intensive operations. Today, container terminals have adopted container cranes and stacking equipment. With the introduction of such technologies, accidents have shifted to back strains and falls to more severe accidents involving equipment malfunctions and collisions. However, through the combined efforts of occupational health and safety organisations—including: the US federal government programme and OSHA; global maritime management organisations such as the IMO; regional organisations such as the Pacific Maritime Administration and the Hampton Roads Shipping Organization; and regional and local labour unions—the number of worker accidents has declined. The influence of these groups on terminal management has led to the creation of safety standards as well as the adoption of safety programmes.

Together stakeholders identify terminal areas and operations that are potentially dangerous to workers and strive to mitigate the consequences. The impact of dangerous conditions include not only worker injuries and associated medical costs but also increased port operational costs such as lost productivity, increased insurance premiums and loss of goodwill. As identified by insurers and industry occupational groups, the severity of both indirect and direct costs can be further lessened with the investment and adoption of safety programmes. OSHA's Office of Regulatory Analysis states that the creation and implementation of workplace safety plans can realise a reduction in workplace accidents of 20% or more, and for every $1 invested, organisations should see a return of $4–6, attributable to higher productivity levels and fewer downtimes (ASSE, 2002).

With globalisation, port and terminal operators will see an ever-increasing amount of cargo arriving at their terminals. Inevitably, new yard layouts will be designed to maximise storage space and automated forms of handling equipment will be introduced to improve productivity levels and allow for the increases in cargo. Consequently, each of these improvements will ultimately have an effect on dockworker safety, either through the increased use of mechanised handling equipment or via the elimination of labourers on terminal from the introduction of automated handling.

Since the devastating effects to chronic disease manifestation exceed 25 years, the impact of port air pollution has yet to be totally realised. Proactive approaches to lessen emissions such as the use of low-sulphur diesel, electric equipment and containment mechanisms are potential steps to mitigate future healthcare cost increases and workmen's compensation claims.

CHAPTER 9

PORT STATE CONTROL INSPECTION AND VESSEL DETENTION

Pierre Cariou, Maximo Q. Mejia Jr. and Francois-Charles Wolff[1]

1. INTRODUCTION

The regime of port state control (PSC) was created more than 30 years ago (Kasoulides, 1993)[2] and is defined by the IMO as "the inspection of foreign ships in national ports to verify that the condition of the ship and its equipment comply with the requirements of international regulations and that the ship is manned and operated in compliance with these rules".[3] These regulations are under the provisions of the International Convention for the Safety of Life at Sea, 1974, as amended (SOLAS), the International Convention on Standards of Training, Certification and Watchkeeping for Seafarers, 1978, as amended (STCW), the International Convention for the Prevention of Pollution from Ships, 1973, as amended (MARPOL), the International Convention on Load Lines, 1966 (Load Lines), and the International Convention on Tonnage Measurement of Ships, 1969 (Tonnage 69).

PSCs are mainly justified by the limited resources available for some flags of registry and the necessity, at the same time and for most sovereign states, to have a better control over foreign vessels calling at their port and sailing through their territorial waters. This necessity is even higher nowadays when maritime safety and security issues are under the scrutiny of public opinion. Sovereign states, with limited control over these issues, are the first ones usually blamed by public opinion when accidents, incidents or marine pollution occur.

Within this general framework, detention rates and records from PSC for vessels, shipowner, and flag of registry . . . are under the scrutiny of regulators and of the industry. This chapter deals with this issue. It presents in the next section elements relative to the use of detention records to determine which vessels to inspect during a PSC (section 2). The third section offers a methodology in order to identify vessels that could be subject to detention as well as

1. The authors wish to express their gratitude to the Indian Ocean MoU Secretary Mr. Ganguli who allowed us to have access to the data used in this study.
2. The present regime of PSC traces its origins from a memorandum of understanding signed in The Hague between eight North Sea states in 1978.
3. www.imo.org

an application on 26,515 inspections that took place within the Indian Ocean PSC region from 2002 to 2006. The last section offers some conclusions.

2. PSC INSPECTION AND DETENTION RECORDS

Most PSC MoUs[4] consider their effectiveness through their ability to target vessels that might be detained, meaning vessels for which inspections will lead to the identification of deficiencies that are "clearly hazardous to safety, health and environment". However, this pragmatic approach is mainly justified by the limited number of inspectors and the need to avoid unnecessary inspections but is subject to interrogations for several reasons.

The first interrogation is related to the use of different targeting systems when one would expect that the factors to consider should be similar. Depending on the priorities of the various authorities, each state has developed its own criteria; criteria that may be compatible or not. The same remark holds within the nine regional agreements on port state control that cover virtually all of the world's seas and aim at coordinating the controls within a region.

The second interrogation is on the focus on vessels that might be detained. This makes sense as long as the implicit assumption that vessels detained are substandard ships that represent a risk in terms of safety holds. Unfortunately, the causal relationship between casualties and detentions is not so direct and was for instance challenged in a working paper[5] submitted by Turkey during the Maritime Safety Committee 82/10/9 and then completed during the last Flag State Implementation sub-committee of IMO (2007). The paper stresses for instance that using data from Paris MoU and Tokyo MoU (1998 to 2002), no clear significant relationship exists between the detention rate for a particular flag of registry and its respective weighted casualty ratio.[6] It would be particularly true within the Paris MoU area where a negative relationship is even found.[7]

---

4. These different MoUs are: Paris MoU—Europe and the North Atlantic; Tokyo MoU—Asia and the Pacific; Acuerdo de Viña del Mar—Latin America; Caribbean MoU—Caribbean Sea region; Abuja MoU—West and Central Africa; Black Sea MoU—Black Sea region; Mediterranean MoU—Mediterranean Sea region; Indian Ocean MoU—Indian Ocean region; Gulf Cooperation Council (GCC) MoU—Arab States of the Gulf.

5. The document was initially motivated by the use by some MoUs such as Paris and Tokyo MoUs of Black/Grey/White list of flags to define unsafe ships.

6. The Weight Casualty Rate considers different degrees of severity (1 for very serious, 0.5 for serious and 0.25 for less serious casualties) and is calculated as:

$$\text{Weight Casualty Rate} = \frac{\Sigma \text{Weight Coef} \times \text{Number of casualties over 5 years}}{\text{Number of ship years}}$$

7. Their findings are in line with previous studies focusing on casualties such as Alderton and Winchester (2002), Li and Wonham (1999) and Li (1999).

This conclusion was, however, challenged by two documents submitted respectively by New Zealand (FSI 15/3/1) and by Australia/New Zealand (FSI 15/3/2). In the first document, although New Zealand recognised the interest of introducing casualty data within existing targeting systems, it stresses that a wide range of factors might determine a ship to be substandard and that casualties are very often explained by factors outside the scope of PSC inspections (human element for instance).[8] Furthermore, and conversely to the Turkish study, New Zealand joint document with Australia (FSI 15/3/2), based on former studies by Knapp (2007) stresses that the probability of very serious casualties would decrease by 5% for vessels that have been inspected previously and that, for black listed flag States, the probability of a very serious casualty is higher than for those who are not. In the same vein, Degré (2008) advocates for a multivariate approach to consider casualties instead of detentions in order to establish a Black Grey White (BGW) list which will be applied to category of vessels instead of flag of registry as done presently.

However, and apart from a problem with the compatibility of PSC and casualties datasets, two main issues remain. First, the initial objective of PSC is not to avoid casualties, but to prevent non-conformity with international regulations. It would therefore mean that the definition of PSC should be enlarged. Secondly, earlier approaches ignore the ability for PSCs to reduce the consequences from casualties. For instance, compliance for life-boats equipment aboard a vessel will not avoid the accident happening, but limits its foreseen consequences.

A third main interrogation related to the use of detention records in PSC and target system is on the methodology used to identify vessels that might be detained. If a relative consensus exists on the main factors to consider, a disparity still exists on the weight that should be given to these various factors.[9] Usually, three main categories of information are considered:

- first, related to the vessel's characteristics such as the type of vessels and their age;
- secondly, to the performance of the flag of registry, the classification society, and the shipowner; and
- thirdly, to records from previous inspections for a specific vessel.

For instance, the Paris MoU (2007)[10] calculates at the end of each day generic and historical factors for a specific ship to reach an overall target factor (see Appendix 1).[11] Generic factors are based on the past performances of the ship's flag of registry, vessel type, age at inspection, and the performance of its

---

8. A correspondence group was set up by IMO during last FSI 15 to examine these issues.
9. See Knapp (2007) for an overview of the various target systems.
10. See www.parismou.org for additional information.
11. If the overall target factor is more than 50 points, the inspection becomes mandatory.

class society. Historical factors are related to whether the vessel is entering the region for the first time, has been inspected during the last six months, has been detained, the number of deficiencies recorded during last inspection, and actions taken to correct outstanding deficiencies.[12]

The target system used by the Indian MoU[13] created in 1998 is representative of practices used by more recent MoUs that cannot rely on a comprehensive dataset such as the Paris MoU. Its secretariat[14] states that members of the Indian MoU should inspect 10% of foreign vessels calling at their ports and that focus should be given to: ships that enter for the first time or that have not entered during the last 12 months in the region; ships with deficiencies noted during former inspections that still need to be rectified; ships that have been reported by pilots or port authorities as having deficiencies which may prejudice their safe navigation; ships whose statutory certificates on the ship's construction and equipment have not been issued in accordance with the relevant instruments; ships carrying dangerous goods or pollutants which have failed to report to the competent authority of the port and coastal State all relevant information concerning the ship's particulars, the ship's movements, details concerning the dangerous goods cargo being carried; and ships which have been suspended from their class for safety reasons in the last six months. Finally, the Indian MoU stresses that in selecting vessels to inspect, authorities should seek to avoid inspecting ships that have been inspected by other authorities within the previous six months, unless clear grounds for inspection exist.

A last example is the target system used by the Australian Maritime Safety Authority (AMSA).[15] AMSA has developed its own targeting system since 2001[16] using a generalised additive modelling to identify factors to consider and to offer a hierarchy amongst the various factors. It relies on a dataset of 29,500 inspections that took place in Australia from 1996 to 2005 to identify the factors that explain the probability for a vessel to be detained and to rank

---

12. Within the Paris MoU, a new inspection regime (NIR) is expected to replace the current system to consider two main issues. First, the targeting system does not set criteria on the total percentage of vessels to be inspected within the Paris MoU region (only 25% of foreign vessels calling for each member). Consequently and secondly, multiple inspections exist for vessels having fairly good records. The NIR sets a goal for 100% of vessels entering the region to be inspected and a hierarchy to be developed amongst High Risk Ships (HRS) inspected every 5–6 months, standard/Medium Risk Ships (MRS—every 10–12 months) and Low Risk Ships (LRS—every 24–36 months).

13. The members of the Indian MoU in 2007 are: Australia, Bangladesh, Djibouti, Eritrea, Ethiopia (observer), India, Iran, Kenya, Maldives, Mauritius, Mozambique, Myanmar, Oman, Seychelles, South Africa, Sri Lanka, Sudan, Tanzania, and Yemen.

14. See www.iomou.org for additional information.

15. Although Australia is part of two distinct MoUs (Indian MoU and Tokyo MoU), it still uses its own criteria to select vessels to inspect. See www.amsa.gov.au/Shipping_Safety/Port_State_Control/ for additional information.

16. The system was implemented in co-operation with the Commonwealth Scientific and Industrial Research Organisation (CSIRO).

them according to their relative influence (from important, 1, to marginal, 4, see Appendix 2). Results suggest that for bulk carriers (around 60% of foreign vessels calling at Australian ports), the age of the vessel is the most important factor, followed by the number of deficiencies at the previous inspection and the time elapsed since the previous inspection, the recognised organisation and the flag the vessel is flying. On the other hand, the fact that the ship is undergoing its first inspection plays only a marginal role. For the other ship types, age still represents the most important factor, followed by the type of ship and the gross tonnage, the number of deficiencies at previous inspection, the time since previous inspection and the flag of registry, while the recognised organisation and the fact that the ship is undergoing its first inspection play significant, but marginal, roles.

To conclude, it appears that the current PSC system leads to issues related to their harmonisation, to their focus on detention and not on casualties, and to the identification and weight of factors explaining detention. For the latter, which is the focus of the next section, while the factors retained by various MoUs to target vessels are fairly similar (age at inspection, vessel type, previous records, etc.), the weight that should be given (none in the Indian MoU for instance) or the reasons for the weight that has been given (Paris MoU for instance) to the various factors is still unclear. AMSA represents here a notable exception. The next section offers a methodology to estimate such factors and their respective weight using 26,515 inspection results carried out by countries belonging to the Indian Ocean MoU.

3. AN ESTIMATION OF FACTORS INFLUENCING THE DETENTION RATE

As stated in the previous section, if a relative consensus exists amongst various MoUs on the factors to be considered to select vessels for inspection (Knapp, 2007; Knapp and Franses, 2007), few studies (AMSA 2001; Cariou et al., 2007, 2008) have offered a methodology to estimate the weight that should be given to these various factors. This second section contributes to this issue using a sample from 26,515 PSC inspections carried out within the Indian MoU region from 1 January 2002 to 31 December 2006. The 26,515 inspections correspond to 10,236 vessels as a vessel can be inspected several times.

Every PSC boarding generates a detailed inspection report containing the following information: ship's name, IMO vessel number, flag of registry, recognised organisation, vessel type, gross tonnage, deadweight tonnage, year built, type of inspection, date of inspection, date of detention, date of release from detention, place of inspection, inspecting authority, and nature of deficiencies. In this section, the focus will be on detention records (Table 9.1).

Table 9.1 Vessel inspection sample

Variables (in %)		Distribution of characteristics			Rate of detention
		No detention	Detention	All	
Age of ship at PSC inspection	0–4	16.4	3.2	15.4	1.6
	5–9	21.7	7.5	20.6	2.8
	10–14	15.7	10.4	15.3	5.2
	15–19	15.7	15.6	15.7	7.6
	20–24	18.8	28.3	19.5	11.1
	25+	11.6	35.0	13.4	20.0
Inspecting authority	Australia	58.0	40.6	56.6	5.5
	Iran	11.5	25.6	12.6	15.6
	India	17.3	29.7	18.2	12.5
	South Africa	9.5	1.7	8.9	1.5
	Others	3.8	2.4	3.7	4.9
Flag of registry	Panama	26.8	25.5	26.7	7.3
	Liberia	6.8	4.1	6.6	4.7
	Hong Kong/China	6.2	2.6	5.9	3.4
	Bahamas	5.1	3.2	4.9	5.0
	Cyprus	4.6	5.3	4.7	8.7
	Singapore	4.6	4.0	4.6	6.8
	Russian Federation	4.6	2.7	4.4	4.7
	Malta	4.4	4.2	4.4	7.4
	Greece	3.5	2.0	3.3	4.5
	Others	33.5	46.4	34.5	10.3
Type of ship	Bulk carrier	47.1	36.7	46.3	6.1
	General cargo/multi-purpose ship	17.3	32.1	18.4	13.3
	Oil tanker	10.2	11.1	10.3	8.3
	Containership	8.4	5.9	8.2	5.5
	Chemical tanker	3.1	4.3	3.2	10.2
	Vehicle carrier	3.1	1.1	2.9	2.8
	Woodchip carrier	1.6	0.8	1.5	3.9
	Refrigerated cargo carrier	1.3	0.9	1.3	5.7
	Ro-Ro cargo ship	1.3	1.0	1.3	6.3
	Gas carrier	11.3	5.9	11.0	2.2
	Others	22.5	23.4	22.6	8.3
Recognised organisation	Nippon Kaiji Kyokai	31.0	17.1	30.0	4.4
	Lloyd's Register	15.0	14.4	14.9	7.4
	Det Norske Veritas	9.9	6.4	9.7	5.0
	American Bureau of Shipping	8.8	7.7	8.7	6.8
	Germanischer Lloyd	8.0	7.2	7.9	7.0
	Bureau Veritas	7.6	10.2	7.8	10.0
	Russian Maritime Register of Shipping	6.0	7.1	6.1	9.0
	China Classification Society	3.8	2.2	3.7	4.5
	Korean Register of Shipping	3.6	2.6	3.6	5.6
	Others	6.3	25.1	7.7	25.0
Number of observations – Mean		24,484	2,031	26,515	7.7

Source: Indian MOU (2007).

The sample concerns 10,236 vessels, the average number of inspections by vessel being equal to 2.59. The average age of vessels subject to inspection is 14.43 years old with a fairly equal distribution amongst various age categories (15.4% of vessels are between 0 and 4 years old, 20.6% between 5 and 9, 15.3% between 10 and 14, 15.7% between 15 and 19, 19.5% between 20 and 24 and 13.4% are more than 25 years). Australia carried out the majority of controls (56.6%) followed by India (18.2%) and Iran (12.6%). Panama is the first flag of registry subject to inspection (26.7%) followed by Liberia (6.6%) and Hong Kong/China (5.9%). Bulk carriers represent 46.3% of vessels inspected followed by general cargo/multi-purpose ships (18.4%) and oil tankers (10.3%). Finally, the Nippon Kaiji Kyokai classification society is the first recognised organisation inspected (30%) followed by Lloyd's Register (14.9%) and Det Norske Veritas (9.7%).

A dependent binary variable is constructed which takes the value of 1 when the vessel is detained and 0 otherwise. The number of controls leading to detention is 7.7%, ranging from 5.6% in 2002 to a maximum of 9.1% in 2003. In columns (2) and (3) of Table 9.1, the occurrence of detention by vessel's characteristics are described.

Turning first to age at inspection (last column in Table 9.1), statistics show as expected a constant increase in the average number of detentions with vessel's age (from 1.6% of controls leading to detention for vessels less than five years old to 20.0% for vessels older than 25 years old). Regarding the inspecting authority, Iran is the country for which the average number of detentions is the highest (15.6% deficiencies on average) followed by India (12.5%) and Australia (5.5%). Concerning the flag of registry, a high number of detentions is detected for Cyprus (8.7%) and Panama (7.3%), the highest proportion being for flags belonging to the "other flag" category[17] (10.3% of controls). Turning to the type of vessels, general cargo/multi-purpose ships are the most subject to detentions (13.3%) followed by chemical carriers (10.2%) and oil tankers (8.3%). Finally, regarding recognised organisations, the other category[18]

17. Other Flags of Registry are Saint Vincent and the Grenadines; China; Marshall Islands; Norway; Korea, Republic of; Philippines; Antigua and Barbuda; Malaysia; Isle of Man (UK); India; Netherlands; Japan; Thailand; United Kingdom (UK); Turkey; Korea, Democratic People's Republic; Denmark; Italy; Taiwan, China; Azerbaijan; Bermuda (UK); Vanuatu; Germany; Cayman Islands (UK); Iran; Cambodia; Indonesia; France; Sweden; Bangladesh; Belize; United Arab Emirates (UAE); Sri Lanka; Papua New Guinea; Saudi Arabia; Vietnam; Egypt; Croatia; Georgia; Switzerland; Myanmar; Comoros; Kuwait; Netherlands Antilles; Tonga; Jordan; Qatar; Belgium; Syrian Arab Republic; Gibraltar (UK); Turkmenistan; Mongolia; Ethiopia; Pakistan; Bolivia; Lebanon; United States of America; São Tomé and Príncipe; New Zealand; Bahrain; Ukraine; Dominica; Saint Kitts and Nevis; Honduras; Algeria; Sudan; Barbados; Luxembourg; Mauritius; Ireland; Portugal; Samoa; Seychelles; Ghana; Sierra Leone; Slovakia; Bulgaria; Maldives; Fiji; Eritrea; Brazil; Morocco; Tuvalu; Jamaica; South Africa; Tunisia; Spain; Lithuania; Chile; Colombia; Cook Islands; Tanzania; Dominican Republic; Kiribati; Namibia; Somalia; Costa Rica; and Nigeria. This category also includes vessels listed as being registered under unspecified "other" flags.

18. Other Recognised Organisations are Registro Italiano Navale; Indian Register of Shipping; China Corporation Register of Shipping; International Register of Shipping; Korea Classification Society; International Naval Survey Bureau; Hellenic Register of Shipping; Polski Rejestr Statkow; Croatian Register of Shipping; Biro Klasifikasi Indonesia; Turkish Lloyd; Viet Nam Register of Shipping; Register of Shipping, Albania; Isthmus Bureau of Shipping; Honduras International Surveying and Inspection Bureau; Panama Register Corporation; Panama Maritime Documentation Services; Panama Shipping Registrar Inc.; Global Marine Bureau; Panama Maritime Surveyors Bureau Inc; RINAVE Portuguesa; Bulgarski Koraben Registar; Shipping Register of Ukraine; INCLAMAR; Honduras Maritime Inspection; Panama Bureau of Shipping; Belize Register Corporation; Ceskoslovensky Lodin Register; Seefartsaht Helsinki; Honduras Bureau of Shipping; Russian River Register; Marconi International Marine Company Ltd; Registro Internacional Naval S.A.; Compania Nacional de Registro e Inspeccion de Naves. This category also includes vessels listed under "Other", "No Class", and "Class Withdrawn".

contains the highest proportion of vessels detained (25% of detentions), followed by Bureau Veritas (10%) and the Russian Maritime Register of Shipping (9%).

An explanation would then be sought as to how the characteristics of the vessels influence the probability for a ship to be detained. As the dependent variable is binary, the appropriate specification is a Probit model. The choice is then made to correct the standard errors using a clustering method at the vessel level, since a given ship may have recorded former detentions. Denoting by D the detention outcome, it is thus estimated $\Pr(D=1)=\Phi(\beta'X)$, where $\Phi(.)$ is the univariate distribution function, X is a set of explanatory variable and β is the vector of associated coefficients. In Table 9.2, the choice is made to report the marginal effects of the different explanatory variables, which are given by $\beta\phi(\beta'X)$, where ϕ is the normal density function.

Table 9.2 Econometric analysis of the probability of detention—marginal effects

Variables		(1)	(2)
		Marginal effects	Marginal effects
Age of ship at PSC inspection	0–4	Ref	Ref
	5–9	2.6%***	1.9%***
	10–14	7.4%***	5.8%***
	15–19	11.7%***	9.3%***
	20–24	14.4%***	11.2%***
	25+	22.3%***	17.9%***
Inspecting authority	Australia	7.8%***	8.2%***
	Iran	16.0%***	16.4%***
	India	14.9%***	20.9%***
	South Africa	−1.3%	−0.8%
	Others	Ref	Ref
Flag of registry	Panama	1.0%***	1.4%***
	Liberia	−0.5%	−0.2%
	Hong Kong, China	−1.7%***	−1.2%
	Bahamas	−1.2%*	−0.4%
	Cyprus	0.3%	0.3%
	Singapore	0.7%	0.1%
	Russian Federation	−4.8%***	−4.7%***
	Malta	−1.6%***	−1.4%*
	Greece	−1.3%*	−0.2%
	Others	Ref	Ref
Type of ship	Bulk carrier	2.1%***	3.0%***
	General cargo/multi-purpose ship	4.0%***	5.0%***
	Oil tanker	1.0%	2.7%**
	Containership	0.7%	2.7%**
	Chemical tanker	4.8%***	6.1%***
	Vehicle carrier	−2.1%**	−1.0%
	Woodchip carrier	1.1%	2.3%
	Refrigerated cargo carrier	0.7%	−0.9%
	Ro-Ro cargo ship	0.2%	2.0%
	Gas carrier	−2.3%	−0.7%
	Others	Ref	Ref
Recognised organisation	Nippon Kaiji Kyokai	−5.7%***	−5.0%***
	Lloyd's Register	−4.3%***	−3.8%***
	Det Norske Veritas	−4.5%***	−3.8%***
	American Bureau of Shipping	−3.6%***	−3.4%***
	Germanischer Lloyd	−3.2%***	−2.1%***
	Bureau Veritas	−3.1%***	−1.9%***
	Russian Maritime Register	−2.4%***	−1.9%**
	China Classification Society	−4.8%***	−4.3%***
	Korean Register of Shipping	−4.3%***	−4.1%***
	Others	Ref	Ref
Nb of deficiencies during previous inspection			0.3%***
Number of observations		26,515	16,279

Source: Indian MOU (2007)
Marginal effects obtained from Probit models. Absolute values of t statistics are in parentheses. Significance levels are respectively 1% (***), 5% (**) and 10% (*). Standard errors are corrected for clustering at the vessel level.

As shown in column 1, results evidence the strong positive effect of age at inspection. The probability for a vessel to be detained increases by 14.4 points of percentage when the vessel is between 20 and 24 years at inspection and even 22.3 points of percentage for vessels older than 25 years, the predicted probability of detention being equal to 4.9 points (at the mean of the sample). Iran, India, and Australia record higher detentions than other inspecting authorities. Furthermore, vessels flying the Russian Federation flag have relatively good records when it comes to detentions, while general cargo/multipurpose ships and chemical carriers are subject to more detentions. Finally, all recognised organisations have good records compared to the other category, a conclusion particularly true for Nippon Kaiji Kyokai, China Classification Society, Det Norske Veritas and Korean Register of Shipping.

In column 2 of Table 9.2, the number of deficiencies recorded during the previous inspection was taken into consideration. A positive coefficient for that covariate is found, meaning that vessels with many deficiencies recorded in the past are more likely to be detained. Different types of deficiencies are used and a grouping of the various deficiencies code in eight categories (see Cariou et al., 2008) are also accounted for.[19] Estimations (not reported here) suggest that deficiencies related to management, safety and fire appliances and certificates play a more influential role when explaining the probability of detention. Similar results are reported in Knapp and Franses (2007), who underline these last two elements (safety and fire appliances and certificates) as the first two contributors to the probability of detention.

An interesting feature is to estimate the contribution of the selected explanatory variables when explaining detentions. A decomposition method originally proposed in Fields (2003) in the case of a linear model is applied. While it could be tempting to use changes in the value of the R^2 as a measure of the explanatory power of each covariate, the *ceteris paribus* condition is unfortunately not respected in that case so that the more complex procedure described in Fields is relied on.

A difficulty in the context is that the dependent variable is not continuous. As there is no decomposition method for a binary variable, the following procedure was chosen. First, the re-estimation of the probability for a vessel to be detained using an OLS regression. The coefficients then provide the marginal effects for each covariate. Then, as the results were very similar under both the Probit and the OLS estimations, it was decided to proceed as if the detention outcome was continuous and so the decomposition methodology described in Fields (2003) was applied.

---

19. The deficiencies related to safety and fire appliances are the first category of deficiencies recorded during inspections (29.3% of the cases), followed by deficiencies related to stability and structure (20.5%), navigation and communication (16.6%) and ship and cargo operations (11.5%). The four other categories (certificates, working and living conditions, equipment and machinery, and management) are less frequent. Cariou, P., Mejia, M.Q. Jr., Wolff, F.C. (2008), "Evidence on target factors used for Port State Control inspections/WMU working paper".

Table 9.3 Decomposition analysis of the factors contributing to detentions

Variables	All		Inspecting authority			
			Australia		Other countries	
	%	Rank	%	Rank	%	Rank
Age of ship at PSC inspection	40.4%	1	64.2%	1	42.5%	1
Inspecting authority	16.6%	3	–	–	–	–
Flag of registry	4.2%	5	3.5%	4	6.2%	4
Type of ship	5.9%	4	6.3%	2	8.1%	2
Classification society	31.1%	2	25.1%	3	39.1%	3
Year of inspection	1.8%	6	1.0%	5	4.1%	5
Total	100%		100%		100%	

Source: Indian MOU (2007).

As shown in Table 9.3, the first factor to explain the probability to be detained would be the age of the vessel at inspection (40.4%) followed by the recognised organisation (31.1%), the inspecting authority (16.6%) and the type of ship (5.9%). Although the variables retained by the Australian Maritime Safety Authority in their analysis are not exactly the same (see Appendix 2), the results similarly point out the age of vessel at inspection as the first factor to explain detentions.

That the inspecting authority plays a role in understanding both the number of deficiencies detected during an inspection and the probability for a vessel to be detained is striking from a policy viewpoint. Since PSC regimes aim at setting uniform or harmonised standards and procedures worldwide, this result could be used by shipowners to question the fairness of PSC inspections. This question was partially tackled by Knapp and Franses (2007), who identified the background of inspectors (engineer, nautical, naval architect or radio) as an element explaining the type of deficiencies detected, but did not conclude on discrepancy across various PSC regimes.

The differences that can be found at a country level on detentions are then attempted to be understood. For that purpose, records from the Australian authority (56.6% of the inspections) and other inspecting authorities (43.4%) were compared. The relative weights of the covariates for both groups (columns 2 and 3, Table 9.3) were then calculated.

The results show first that age at inspection is by far the first factor to explain detentions records in Australia. Age at inspection explains 64.2% of the detention outcome, a result once again in line with the AMSA study. Age is still the first explanatory factor for the other group of countries, but with a lower weight (42.5%). Another major factor when explaining detentions is the type of ship (39.1% for other countries, but 25.1% for Australia). It therefore seems that the split done by AMSA between bulk carriers (60% of vessels calling at Australian ports) and other types of ships would make sense as different target factors should apply to the various types of vessels. Furthermore, the recognised organisation and the flag of registry matter less to understand the probability of detention.

Table 9.4: Additional findings from decomposition analysis

Variables	Flag		Ship types		Classification societies	
	Panama	Others	Bulk carriers	Others	Lloyd's register	Other
Age of ship at PSC inspection	40.5%	43.2%	61.1%	33.9%	57.2%	58.8%
	(2)	(1)	(1)	(2)	(1)	(1)
Inspecting authority	9.6%	19.7%	14.4%	23.0%	24.1%	22.2%
	(3)	(3)	(3)	(3)	(2)	(2)
Flag of registry	–	–	0.4%	4.4%	7.7%	6.7%
	–	–	(5)	(4)	(3)	(4)
Type of ship	7.6%	5.7%	–	–	6.4%	10.5%
	(4)	(4)	–	–	(4)	(3)
Classification society	40.7%	29.5%	22.7%	36.6%	–	–
	(1)	(2)	(2)	(1)	–	–
Year of inspection	1.6%	2.0%	1.5%	2.0%	4.6%	1.8%
	(5)	(5)	(4)	(5)	(5)	(5)
Total	100%	100%	100%	100%	100%	100%

Source: Indian MOU (2007)
Ranks are in parentheses under the percentage contribution.

Finally, using similar decomposition method, investigations into whether the results differ significantly from former results for vessels flying the Panamanian flag, for Bulk Carriers and for vessels registered under Lloyd's Register (Table 9.4) were undertaken. Results suggest that the ranking in the main factors is fairly similar with age at inspection and ship type always remaining the two main contributors.

4. CONCLUSION

This chapter aims to investigate the weights that should be given to factors explaining detention records within the target systems. It appears that most of the conclusions do not contradict the current targeting factors used by most of MoU or individual states. For instance, the age of vessel at inspection, records from previous inspections, the classification society, and type of vessel proved to be significant factors in predicting detention. In line with the study of AMSA, analysing the contribution of the various factors to detentions also stresses the major role played by the age of the vessel at inspection. Another interesting finding was to point out the inspecting authority as an important element to explain detentions. Keeping in mind that one of the objectives of PSC regimes is to apply uniform standards across various states, the conclusion that the ranking of the selected covariates is the same in the two groups of countries is, in that sense, a positive result.

Finally, a main issue concerning more specifically the Indian MoU region is the adoption of a more elaborate and harmonised targeting system instead of the current list of criteria to consider.[20] It might do well to take the cue from recent developments within the Paris MoU that led its Secretariat to propose a New Inspection Regime system to increase the proportion of vessels controlled within the region. With multiple inspections at a regional level, the fact that each inspecting authority within the Indian MoU uses its own criteria might be counterproductive.

20. The objective set by the Indian MoU secretariat is for each authority to achieve a target inspection rate of 10% of the estimated number of individual foreign vessels entering ports under their national jurisdiction during the previous calendar year.

APPENDIX 1

Paris MoU[1] Target factor
Signed in 1982
Belgium, Bulgaria, Canada, Croatia, Cyprus, Denmark, Estonia, Finland, France, Germany, Greece, Iceland, Ireland, Italy, Latvia, Lithuania, Malta, Netherlands, Norway, Poland, Portugal, Romania, Russian Federation, Slovenia, Spain, Sweden, United Kingdom
Number of inspections: 25% of vessel entering for each individual state
Total Target Factor = Generic Factor (GF) + Historical Factor (HF) If TF>50 points then the control is mandatory. The overall target factor is calculated at the end of each day.
GF-Flag. If detention during last 3 years is • More than 10% then TF = +4 • More than 13% then TF = +8 • More than 16% then TF = +14 • More than 18% then TF = +20
GF-Vessel type. TF = +5 • for Bulk carrier > 12 years old • for Gas carriers > 10 years old • for Chemical carriers > 10 years old • for Oil tanker GT > 3000 & > 15 years old • Passenger ship/Ro-Ro ferry > 15 years old[2]
GF-Non-EU RO. If Non-EU recognised classification society then TF =+3
GF=Age • 25 years old then TF = +3 • 21–24 years old then TF = +2 • 13–20 years old then TF = +1
GF=Flag state. TF = +1 if Flag has not ratified main conventions
GF=Targeted class. Class with a 3-yr average record of detentions above the average class detention value. A classification society with class related deficiencies in the last 3 years exceeds the average class detention rate by: • 0% then TF = 0 • 0–2% then TF = +1 • 2–4% then TF = +2 • >4% then TF = +3

HF-New. If entering a region port for the first time in the last 12 months then TF = +20
HF-Inspected. If not inspected in the last 6 months then TF = +10
HF-Detained. If detained in the previous 12 months then TF = +15
HF-Deficiencies If last control 0 then TF = −15 If last control 1–5 then TF = 0 If last control 6–10 then TF = +5 If last control 11–20 then TF = +10 If last control 21+ then TF = +15
HF-Outstanding deficiencies. For latest inspection if action taken "rectify deficiency at next port" or "Master instructed to rectify deficiency before departure" & for every two listed actions taken "rectify deficiency within 14 days and/or other" then TF = +1 For latest inspection in case "all deficiencies rectified" then TF = −2

1. Does not consider the new inspection regime that should replace the current system.

2. Other than Ro-Ro ferries and HS passenger craft operating in regular service under the provision of Council Dir. 1999/35/EC.

APPENDIX 2

Australian Maritime Safety Authority target factors (based on data from 2001–2005)

	Bulk carriers (17,520 observations)	Other ships* (11,658 observations)
Age of ship	1	1
Number of deficiencies at the previous inspection	2	3
Time since previous inspection	2	3
Recognised organisation	3	4
Flag	3	3
Ship is undergoing first inspection	4	4
Type of ship	–	2
Gross tonnage	–	2

* Passenger ships were excluded due to their specific regime
Source: AMSA (2007)

CHAPTER 10

PORT SHIP ACCIDENTS AND RISKS[1]

Tsz Leung Yip

1. INTRODUCTION

The aim of this chapter is to analyse the ship accidents and risks that exist in ports in order to seek ways to manage these risks. Safety awareness in ports is growing among local and international regulators.

Maritime operations are an essential component of port safety. Collision is the dominant maritime accident in ports, with groundings contributing to approximately one-third of maritime accidents around the world. In addition to explanatory factors such as ship age, flags of registration, which are significant in ship accidents, traffic and port layout are also critical in terms of ship accidents in ports. These additional factors are often port-related, and include such factors as the specifics of channel design, navigational aids configuration and tidal currents.

Many studies have been conducted into ship accidents and risks at sea but little attention has been paid to the risks in ports. The ability to measure port risks is hampered by the data available. Despite ports being a key component of waterborne transportation, data on marine accidents in ports are generally not available to the general public. One reason for this is because a port policy is often designed specifically to fit local situations. Another reason is because the port state jurisdiction over ships is limited within the territorial sea, with flag states having greater jurisdiction. A ship's "Flag of Registry" is its nationality, and each ship has only one nationality. Nevertheless, the globalisation of trade has led to a rapid increase in ship movements in ports. As this trade continues to grow, many ports will soon face an increasing number of ship accident-related risks akin to those observed in the busiest ports of today.

This chapter investigates ship risks in ports by discussing accidents of note in several ports. It presents an overview of ship accidents in ports, then discusses the efficiency of the current management system in ports, finally suggesting additional measures that can be adopted in ports to manage dense marine traffic.

1. The author thanks Dr Wayne K. Talley, the book editor, for his valuable comments and helpful suggestions on earlier versions of this paper. The author owes a great deal to the anonymous referee for his stimulating comments and insightful suggestions.

2. THE SOURCES OF RISK TO SHIPS IN PORTS

The term "risk" is typically defined as either the product or a composite of (1) the probability or likelihood that any accident leading to unwanted consequences (such as human fatalities, environmental damage, loss of property and financial expenditures) and (2) the resulting consequences.

$$Risk = (Consequence) \times (Probability\ of\ occurrence) \tag{1}$$

The assessment of ship risk in ports can be conducted in the Formal Safety Assessment (FSA) methodology (IMO, 2002). Recent developments in the UK's Port Marine Safety Code also adopted the application of FSA to address port safety issues at a strategic level (Dft, 2006). The FSA has five principal steps:

1. *Identification of Hazards* (What is the distribution of hazards?);
2. *Assessment of Risks* (How bad and how likely is the risk and hazard to life?);
3. *Risk Control Options* (How can matters be improved?);
4. *Cost Benefit Assessment* (What would be the likely cost/improvement?); and
5. *Recommendations* (What actions should be taken?).

In the design and operation of the port traffic systems, a number of hazards must be well managed. Ship risks in ports may be broadly classified into the five port hazards (basic causes and/or immediate causes).

I. *Natural hazards*—strong winds, high waves, strong currents, low visibility, storms, shallow waters and other natural phenomena;
II. *Nautical hazards*—unfavourable port layouts, insufficient channel width, shallow water depths, and narrow tidal windows;
III. *Marine traffic hazards*—incompatible ship types, high traffic volume, speeding, insufficient navigation aids, and inappropriate traffic control;
IV. *Human hazards*—insufficient training, errors or violations by the ship masters, pilots, or crew, and acts of sabotage or terrorism; and
V. *Technical hazards*—loss of navigation aids, loss of power or equipment failures, outdated admiralty charts and obsolete equipment.

Among the five port hazards above, nautical hazards and marine traffic hazards are relatively local and not usually considered in ship accidents at sea. Actually, there are no consistent criteria across ports for determining local hazards. A common approach is to determine the acceptable limits on the basis of FN evaluation criteria (e.g., Trbojevic and Carr, 2000; Darbra and Casal, 2004; SAFEDOR, 2005; Wang, 2006).

3. STATISTICAL OVERVIEW OF SHIP ACCIDENTS IN PORTS

The contributing factors to the seriousness of marine accidents are many and complex (Talley, 2002). Table 10.1 lists the factors in a structural manner.

$$Port\ accident\ (Damage) = f(Type\ of\ accident,\ Vessel\ characteristics,\ Operating\ conditions)$$

(2)

$$Number\ (Port\ accident) = Number\ (Port\ traffic) \times f(Type\ of\ accident,\ Vessel\ characteristics,\ Operating\ conditions)$$

(3)

"Port traffic" are usually "ship transits". However, sometimes it is not possible to have ship transit data and "ship arrivals" used as similar measures.

The combination of probability (number per movement) and severity (damage) defines the level of risk, see equation (1), while the combination of number and damage indicates the level of potential losses. Ship damages can be caused by a variety of means (e.g., by collision) and may involve more than one means (e.g., collision and then sinking). Therefore, it is common practice that ship accidents are classified according to the so-called "first event" (e.g., a ship is materially damaged by weather, a ship running to ground, etc.) rather than root/immediate causes (e.g., human error or poor maintenance).

Table 10.1 Parameters of maritime accidents

	Parameters	*Numeric Example*[1]
Type of accident	Collision	54%
	Contact	12%
	Grounding/stranding	9%
	Foundering/sinking	8%
	Fire/explosion	7%
	Capsized/list	2%
	Machinery failure	2%
	Damage to equipment	1%
	Heavy weather damage	0.2%
	Structural failure	0.1%
	Missing vessel	0.0%
	Others (e.g. flooding)	4%
		Subtotal = 100%
Vessel	Port of registry	–
characteristics	Gross tonnage	–
	Length overall	–
	Date of construction	–
	Type of vessel (subtotal = 134%[2])	
	Bulk carrier	3%
	Cargo ship	47%
	Tanker	3%
	High speed craft/ passenger ship	10%
	Barge	19%
	Warship	0.0%
	Tug	11%
	Fishing vessel	16%
	Government vessel	9%
	Motor sampan	2%
	Pleasure vessel	10%
	Miscellaneous vessels	4%
Operating conditions	Type of waterway	Channel, fairway, anchorage, typhoon shelter or port shelters
	Underway	–
	State of weather	–
	Wind direction and force	–
	Visibility	–
Damage	Number of deaths	0 to 25
	Number of injuries	0 to 102
	Vessel damage cost	–
	Cargo damage cost	–
	Environmental cost	–

1. Source: Yip (2008).
2. An accident may involve one or multiple vessels.

Maritime accidents have primarily been investigated at the national government level. Some accident investigation authorities and bodies are listed in Table 10.2. However, in the port domain, there is no standardised accident reporting system. The reporting of port accidents is generally not comprehensive enough for analysis, which poses a problem when determining causal relationships from accident data.

Table 10.2 Examples of safety boards and authorities

International	
Global	IMO Maritime Safety Committee
	Marine Accident Investigators International Forum (*MAIIF*)
	International Transportation Safety Association (*ITSA*)
Europe	European Maritime Safety Agency
National/local	
Australia	Australian Transport Safety Bureau (*ATSB*)
Canada	Transportation Safety Board (*TSB*) of Canada
China	China Maritime Safety Administration (*CMSA*)
	Marine Accident Investigation Branch, Hong Kong
Denmark	Dutch Transport Safety Board (*DTSB*)
Finland	Accident Investigation Board of Finland (*AIB*)
Germany	Federal Bureau of Maritime Casualty Investigation
Japan	Japan Marine Accident Inquiry Agency (*MAIA*)
New Zealand	Maritime New Zealand (*MNZ*)
Sweden	Maritime Casualty Investigation Division
United Kingdom	Marine Accident Investigation Branch (*MAIB*)
USA	US Coastguard (*USCG*)
	National Transportation Safety Board (*NTSB*)

While most databases of maritime accidents are nation-based and include all national territorial waters, port accidents only account for a portion of all reported accidents in national databases. For example, as illustrated in Figure 10.1, port accidents share approximately 30% of all reported accidents in Japan, which stayed constant from 2002 to 2004. Thus, most databases of ship accidents do not reflect the risks of ship accidents in ports.

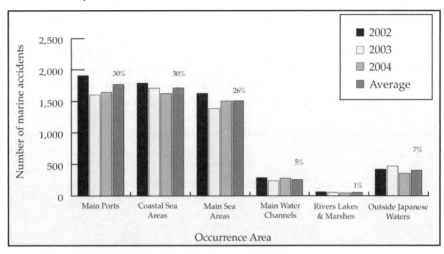

Source: Japan Marine Accident Inquiry Agency (MAIA).

Figure 10.1 Number of marine accidents by occurrence area (Japan, 2002–2004)

3.1 Average distribution

The annual distribution of ship accidents in ports illustrated in Figure 10.2 is an example. In Hong Kong port, almost 68% of all accidents recorded in 2001–2005 were "Collision" and "Contact", with "Stranding/Grounding" accounting for approximately 8%. "Foundering/Sinking" (7%) and "Fire/Explosion" (7%) are significant hazards, accounting for over half of the remaining accidents.

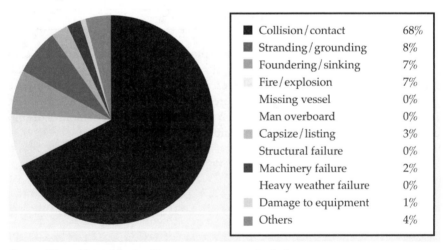

■ Collision / contact	68%
■ Stranding / grounding	8%
■ Foundering / sinking	7%
Fire / explosion	7%
Missing vessel	0%
Man overboard	0%
■ Capsize / listing	3%
Structural failure	0%
■ Machinery failure	2%
Heavy weather failure	0%
■ Damage to equipment	1%
■ Others	4%

Source: Hong Kong Marine Department, own calculations.

Figure 10.2 Distribution of ship accidents in ports (Hong Kong, 2001–2005)

Figure 10.3 shows the yearly data of accidents in ports, 1984–2007. This shows that the occurrence distribution (e.g., percentage) of each accident type is nearly constant over the report years. Among the types of port accidents reported, "Collision", "Contact", "Grounding" and "Stranding" are viewed as being closely related to nautical hazards and marine traffic hazards. Repeated groundings along a fairway implies the design depth of the fairway is insufficient for the draft of ships. Repeated collisions at a particular location suggests the sea-room is insufficient for the volume of traffic. As these four types of accidents are more port-related, extra attention will be given to them.

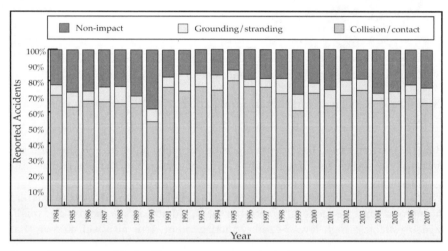

Source: Hong Kong Marine Department, own calculations

Figure 10.3 Distribution of ship accidents in ports (Hong Kong, 1984–2007)

The relative importance of ship accidents at sea is different (Figure 10.4) from those at port. "Grounding" (20%) and "Foundering" (43%) dominate in terms of total ship casualties (ISL 2006, Table 1.3.4). Foundering may be the result of a wide range of root causes, e.g., extreme weather conditions and hull material fatigue. The higher percentage of "collision" and "contact" accidents in ports has been explained by operation in congested coastal waters, relatively high-speed operation and a mix of international and local operational practices. Another "sea" example is the Strait of Istanbul, and along this seaway "Grounding" and "Collision" shared 55% and 30% of marine accidents in 1994–2002, respectively (Akten, 2004). At sea, as the traffic is low, "collision" is not the leading accident.

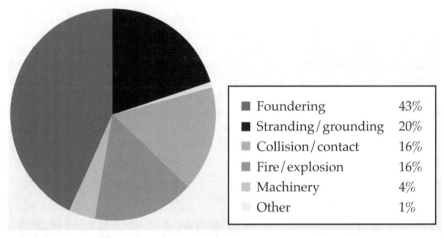

■ Foundering	43%
■ Stranding/grounding	20%
■ Collision/contact	16%
■ Fire/explosion	16%
■ Machinery	4%
■ Other	1%

Source: ISL (2006) Shipping Statistics and Market Review, Table 1.3.4.

Figure 10.4 Reported world total losses (2001–2006) by frequency (> or =500gt)

The proportion of total accidents reported by each ship type and their annual arrivals are shown in Figure 10.5. Container ships are the class most frequently involved in accidents, which reflects the active movements of that ship type in Hong Kong. For high-speed craft (HSC), although movements are numerous and frequent, the number of accidents is comparatively small, which reflects a high level of safety management. It is also well known that smaller ships operating in coastal waters are more prone to maritime accidents than large ships operating across seas (Table 10.3), as indicated by the number of incidents per ship arrival. This conventional wisdom is indirectly confirmed by accident occurrences versus ship registry, with injury rates lower in Hong Kong and International Registries (ocean-going ships) than regional/local licences (coastal ships), possibly reflecting a greater level of safety training received in large ships (Yip, 2008).

Table 10.3 Consequences of ship accidents in ports (Hong Kong, 2001–2005)

Trade of ships	Incident	Injury	Fatality	Incidents per ship arrival[1]	Injury per incident	Fatality per incident
Ocean-going	342	9	38	1.9×10^{-3}	0.03	**0.11**
Coastal	1,340	347	23	2.3×10^{-3}	**0.26**	0.02
Local	1,639	300	65	N.A.	**0.18**	0.04

1. Number of Ship arrivals = 181,800 (ocean-going) and 590,220 (coastal) in 2001–2005.
An incident may involve more than one vessel, and the numbers of injury and fatality may be multiple counted in this table.
Source: Hong Kong Marine Department, own calculations.

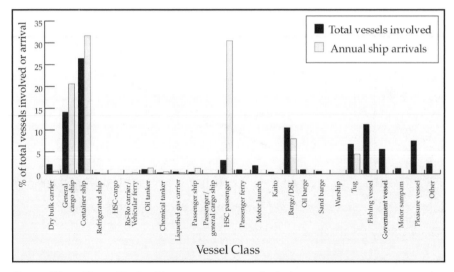

Source: Hong Kong Marine Department, own calculations.

Figure 10.5 Types of ships reporting accidents (Hong Kong, 2001–2005)

The density of port traffic is believed to be second to human error as a contributing factor for traffic-related accidents, particularly in restricted areas such as approach channels and harbour basins, where sea-room is relatively narrow. A general correlation between ship transit statistics and associated port accidents for all major US ports was found, as shown in Figure 10.6 (USCG 1999, Table 9). Approximately one more accident would be observed if 317 more ship transits occurred. Kite-Powell, et al. (1999) studied the factors of groundings in US ports (Figure 10.7). On average, one more grounding would be reported if 81 more ship transits occurred. By comparing accident rates in five US ports, a strong correlation between groundings and the number of transits is found. Data for the average and annual hourly distribution of accidents are presented in Figure 10.8 in Hong Kong (Yip, 2008). It is likely that most accidents occurred during daytime and this peak is related to ship activity occurring during daylight hours, particularly for passenger ships. New Zealand data showed a similar observation that 70% of accidents in 2003/04 occurred between 6 am to 6 pm, which is related to ship activity occurring primarily during daylight hours (MaritimeNZ, 2006).

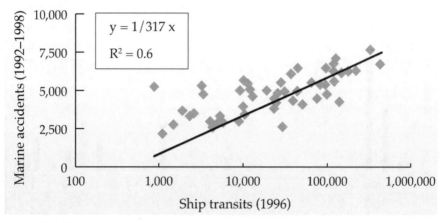

Source: USCG 1999, Table 9.

Figure 10.6 Maritime accidents versus ship transits in US ports

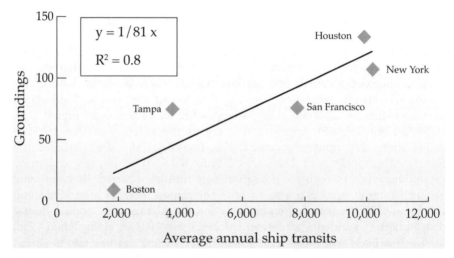

Source: Powell, et al. (1999).

Figure 10.7 Groundings versus ship transits in five US ports, 1981–1995

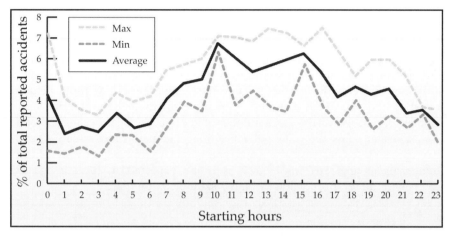

Source: Hong Kong Marine Department, own calculations.

Figure 10.8 Reported accidents by time of reporting

When types of waterway are considered in the analysis, risks are likely to be higher in a restricted area. Should an accident occur in a channel or a limited waterspace, the port traffic is relatively dense, the sea-room relatively insufficient and depth of water is rather restricted, and an accident is likely to result. However, human beings are less likely to be injured within this restricted area where, for instance, ship speed is low in typhoon shelters.

There is no comprehensive data source of ship accidents in ports, but Liu, et al. (2006) has produced a similar picture of Taiwanese ports' ship accidents and similar distribution, excluding "Collisions" and "Others" (Figure 10.9). "Collision" and "Contact" shared 23% of marine accidents in Taiwanese ports in 1992–2003.

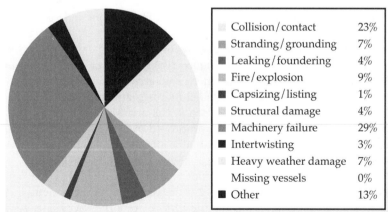

Collision / contact	23%
Stranding / grounding	7%
Leaking / foundering	4%
Fire / explosion	9%
Capsizing / listing	1%
Structural damage	4%
Machinery failure	29%
Intertwisting	3%
Heavy weather damage	7%
Missing vessels	0%
Other	13%

Source: Liu, et al. (2006).

Figure 10.9 Distribution of ship accidents in Taiwanese ports, 1992–2003

3.2 Long-term trends

The historic pattern of marine risk in Hong Kong waters is illustrated in Figure 10.10, following analysis of average distribution. It is apparent that after a strong surge in incidents in the early 1990s, the number of collisions and other incidents has decreased and may be levelling off. Without data on reporting and survey coverage, it is difficult to guarantee the integrity of the apparent trends. Nevertheless, a number of key issues appear to suggest a shift from collision being the principal cause of accidents to more widely distributed causes. Local waters have significantly greater frequency of collision and foundering/sinking/capsizing, which is to be expected in local congested waters with a high proportion of highly loaded coastal craft.

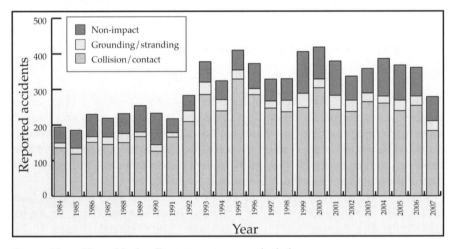

Source: Hong Kong Marine Department, own calculations.

Figure 10.10 Distribution of ship accidents in Hong Kong, 1984–2007

It is instructive to review the number of reported accidents with respect to the port traffic over a long time span. Figure 10.11 plots this relationship of the accident rates versus port traffic (namely, ship arrivals, cargo throughput, and TEU throughput) for the period 1990–2006. It is apparent that regardless of whether a comparison is made between vessel arrivals, cargo or TEUs, that safety in Hong Kong port waters has improved over the last decade, with an accident rate approximately half that of a decade ago. The time trend of reported accidents to TEU throughput shows the highest R^2 number, which may be because Hong Kong port traffic is highly related to TEU movements. On the other hand, the value $R^2=0.9294$ suggests that the exponential decay model is a good approximation for the ratio of reported accidents to TEU throughput.

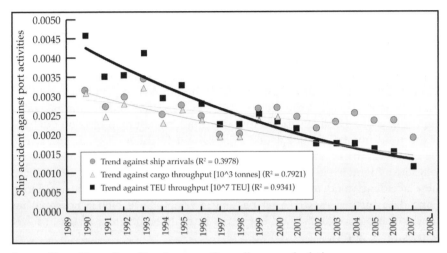

Source: Hong Kong Port Development Council, own calculations.

Figure 10.11 Ship accident trends in Hong Kong, 1984–2007

Figure 10.10 and Figure 10.11, which collate data for marine risks in 1984–2007, illustrate the key characteristics of the local marine risk profile. When reviewing any data it is necessary to identify the nature of the data and manner of collection. A review of the time series suggests that, in comparison with other incident types, collisions have increased proportionately (Figure 10.10). It may be argued that the collisions should in fact have decreased over time. While collisions have always been well reported, often firstly by the aggrieved party, a decade ago incidents such as fires and contacts were less well represented. Without data on reporting and survey coverage it is difficult to guarantee the integrity of the apparent trends. However, there are a number of key issues which appear to be dominated by a shift from collision being the principal cause of incident to more widely distributed causes.

The principal driver behind the general reduction of accident occurrence rate, observed in Figure 10.11, is the action of external forces (such as the port authority and IMO) in improving the safety of the water area. Improved VTS, navigation aids (e.g., ECDIS), ship specifications, advanced technologies (e.g., AIS) and training requirements (e.g., ISM Code) have also all reduced collision rates. The improvements made in this respect are a credit to the vigilance of local port authorities. In contrast, stranding/grounding, foundering/sinking, capsized/listing and fire/explosion are principally dependent on the safety culture of mariners. Given that the immediate cause of these incidents is associated with ship managements and maintenance outside the jurisdiction of port authorities, the ability of port states to directly improve safety in these non-impact type accidents is more limited. More frequent inspections (such as information posters on ship overloading, and parallel enforcement actions) targeted against regional-trade ships are clearly addressing the key risk issues, and will hopefully bear fruit in future years.

3.3 Human risk

Having identified the distribution of marine accidents, it is also important to review the consequences of incidents when they occur. Fatality risks in port shipping vary considerably among the accident types. Theoretically, the maximum number of fatalities of port traffic is the number of people aboard (and at the waterfront) and in the order of 10^2 for cargo ships and 10^3 for passenger ships. Figure 10.12 shows the relative distribution of human risks on the basis of the total number of accidents, injuries and fatalities. As can be seen in Figure 10.12, the accident types leading to the highest number of fatalities are collisions, foundering and capsized. Although there are many groundings, these accidents tend to result in relatively few fatalities and injuries. Hong Kong data further showed that passenger vessels have higher potential for injuries during accidents, and accidents in typhoon shelters result in fewer injuries (Yip, 2008).

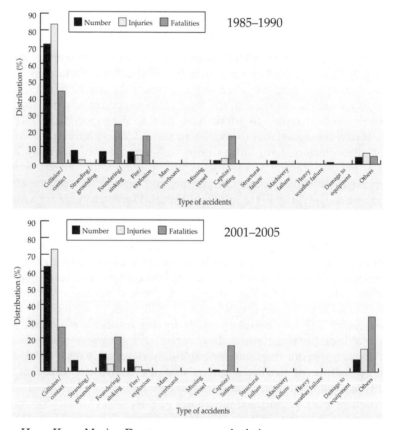

Source: Hong Kong Marine Department, own calculations.

Figure 10.12 Distribution of ship accidents, injuries and fatalities

Table 10.4 identifies an injury rate of 0.16 per accident and a fatality rate of 0.02 per accident, given a collision. For both, there is no suggestion of an increasing number of injuries per accident. In other words, there is no evidence from the data presented that increasing vessel size induces more injuries or fatalities in an accident on average. However, because the accident severity may be a function of increased vessel size, speed and crew/passengers potentially at risk, accidents may be less frequent but will be more serious with remarkably high numbers of injuries and fatalities.

Table 10.4 Consequences of ship accidents in ports (Hong Kong, 1984–2007)

Type of accident	Collision/contact					Groundings					All others				
	Incident	Injury	Fatality	Injury per collision	Fatality per collision	Incident	Injury	Fatality	Injury per incident	Fatality per incident	Incident	Injury	Fatality	Injury per incident	Fatality per incident
1984	136	0	3	0.00	0.02	13	0	0	0.00	0.00	45	0	3	0.00	0.07
1985	116	14	1	0.12	0.01	18	4	0	0.22	0.00	52	2	1	0.04	0.02
1986	151	12	2	0.08	0.01	15	0	0	0.00	0.00	63	10	9	0.16	0.14
1987	145	47	1	0.32	0.01	21	1	0	0.05	0.00	54	11	5	0.20	0.09
1988	150	8	2	0.05	0.01	25	1	0	0.04	0.00	56	12	12	0.21	0.21
1989	165	42	9	0.25	0.05	13	0	0	0.00	0.00	77	8	6	0.10	0.08
1990	126	53	1	0.42	0.01	16	1	0	0.06	0.00	90	14	9	0.16	0.10
1991	163	13	3	0.08	0.02	14	1	0	0.07	0.00	39	3	1	0.08	0.03
1992	209	36	2	0.17	0.01	29	0	0	0.00	0.00	46	1	0	0.02	0.00
1993	286	44	6	0.15	0.02	34	0	0	0.00	0.00	58	4	2	0.07	0.03
1994	239	18	2	0.08	0.01	31	0	0	0.00	0.00	54	0	2	0.00	0.04
1995	327	25	0	0.08	0.00	27	1	1	0.04	0.04	56	5	9	0.09	0.16
1996	283	20	2	0.07	0.01	18	0	0	0.00	0.00	72	19	7	0.26	0.10
1997	246	38	5	0.15	0.02	19	0	0	0.00	0.00	62	3	2	0.05	0.03
1998	236	15	6	0.06	0.03	32	0	0	0.00	0.00	62	7	3	0.11	0.05
1999	246	34	12	0.14	0.05	42	2	0	0.05	0.00	119	30	23	0.25	0.19
2000	302	48	0	0.16	0.00	26	0	0	0.00	0.00	92	7	2	0.08	0.02
2001	242	33	1	0.14	0.00	38	0	0	0.00	0.00	98	14	6	0.14	0.06
2002	237	27	14	0.11	0.06	32	2	0	0.06	0.00	67	8	4	0.12	0.06
2003	263	56	0	0.21	0.00	25	2	0	0.08	0.00	70	7	6	0.10	0.09
2004	259	27	0	0.10	0.00	20	3	0	0.15	0.00	109	8	4	0.07	0.04
2005	239	148	3	0.62	0.01	29	2	0	0.07	0.00	100	29	6	0.29	0.06
2006	253	7	2	0.03	0.01	25	2	0	0.08	0.00	83	6	0	0.07	0.00
2007	181	20	1	0.11	0.01	27	0	0	0.00	0.00	70	13	4	0.19	0.06
Total	5,200	785	78			589	22	1			1,694	221	126		
Ave	216.7	32.71	3.25	0.16	0.02	24.5	0.92	0.04	0.04	0.00	70.6	9.21	5.25	0.12	0.07

Source: Hong Kong Marine Department, own calculations.

Table 10.4 shows that over the long term (1984–2007) there was an average of 311.8 (=216.7+24.5+70.6) ship accidents in ports and 8.54 (=3.25+0.04+5.25) fatalities per year. It should be noted that the frequency of ship accidents in Hong Kong port has slightly increased over the long term. Table 10.4 further shows that the great majority of fatalities occurred in non-traffic-related type accidents (annual ratio of 0.07 fatalities per accident and 0.12 injuries per accident), while traffic-related type accidents more likely resulted in injuries (annual ratio of 0.02 fatalities per collision and 0.16 injuries per collision; and 0.00 fatalities per grounding and 0.04 injuries per grounding). This reflects the fact that on average traffic-related type accidents are more frequent but less severe in ports, perhaps because speed controls are often placed within port water areas. An important fact should be noted from Figure 10.2—the average number of traffic-related accidents per year is twice that of the non-traffic-related accidents. Distribution remains essentially unchanged in recent reports.

However, the increase in ship size to achieve economies of transport scales may result in more serious ship accidents, when they occur. Table 10.3 shows a 0.11 total average fatality per incident for ocean-going ships, which is the highest, while the highest total average injury per incident of 0.26 is found for coastal ships. This suggests that average fatalities are greater for ocean-going ships or larger ships. Figure 10.13 shows that average vessel capacity in the container trade has increased significantly, driven by technological advancement and economic demand.

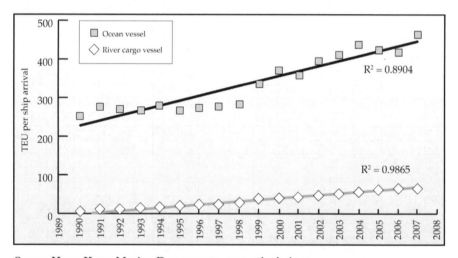

Source: Hong Kong Marine Department, own calculations.

Figure 10.13 The trend of ship size in terms of TEU to vessel arrivals

While the number of vessels calling at ports grows, there has also been an ongoing increase in container ship size. Although the width of the fairways in the harbour has not been reduced, these developments of ship design contribute to the high traffic density inside ports and diminish synergies to the existing fairway system. The continuing growth of container ports in the world, together with availability of water depth, means that the busiest ports are liable to receive some of the largest container vessels in the foreseeable future. There will be a technical limit to ship size at some stage, but the trend for larger and larger ships will continue for several years. As a result, if the capacity projections for ships are realistic, these projections should be adopted in the forecast model.

A weakness of the Hong Kong data on ship accidents in ports is that the number of high-fatality accidents is relatively small. This means that high fatality accidents can only be roughly estimated.

4. ASSESSMENT FOR SHIP RISKS IN PORTS

There are a number of ways to quantify ship risk in ports. Darbra and Casal (2004) used a FN curve to illustrate the societal risk level. They conducted a study on 471 port accidents in the period 1941 to 2002. They observed that 57% of port accidents occurred during transport (moving ships) and 44% of accidents in ports were caused by impact (i.e., collision). Although port operations are often considered dangerous, they found that the likelihood of loss of life in an accident in a port is lower than in a natural disaster (e.g., earthquakes, floods etc.). Christou (1999) also used FN curves to investigate 617 port accidents over the period 1934–1995. Ronza, et al. (2003) used the event tree model to collate 828 historical accidents that have occurred since the beginning of the twentieth century to predict accident frequency. Akten (2004) provided simple statistical analysis of the 82 shipping casualties in the Strait of Istanbul. Liu et al. (2006) applied the Grey relational analysis to investigate 3,428 marine accidents in four Taiwanese ports from 1992–2003. Yip (2008) applied the count data model to study the port traffic risk issues by discussing 2,012 historic accidents in Hong Kong port in the years 2001–2005.

Three assessment models are introduced in the following paragraphs.

4.1 Count model

A negative binomial and a Poisson regression model have been developed to study traffic safety and predict accident frequency and damage (e.g., Talley, 2002; Yip, 2008).

It is assumed that the port accident count data can be approximated well by a negative binomial process; the simultaneity of the accidents (i.e., ship accidents, human injuries and fatalities) is modelled by using simultaneous model estimation techniques. The advantage of using a negative binomial model is that there is no restriction on the ratio of the mean to the variance of data (Greene, 2008). The negative binomial model has the expression:

$$Prob[Y = y_j \mid \varepsilon] = \frac{exp[-\lambda_j \, exp(\varepsilon)](\lambda_j)^{y_j}}{y_j!}, \; y_j = 0,1,2,\dots \tag{4}$$

$$\lambda_j = exp(x_j\beta] + \varepsilon_j) \qquad \text{for the } j\text{-th observation,} \tag{5}$$

where λ_j is the expected mean, β is a vector of estimable parameters, x_j is the explanatory variables, and $exp(\varepsilon_j)$ is a gamma-distributed error term with mean 1.0 and variance α^2. The addition of this term allows the variance to differ from the mean:

$$Var[y_j] = E[y_j]\{1+\alpha E[y_j]\} = E[y_j] + \alpha E[y_j]^2 \tag{6}$$

The variable α, or alpha, is the dispersion parameter. If α is equal to zero, the model reduces to a Poisson regression model.

Parameters of Table 10.1 can then be tested by collating data in the hypothesised equation (2), e.g., in the expression of negative binomial model, equation (4) and (5). The determinants of maritime accident consequences together with statistically significant estimation results will then be used for policy design. For example, Yip (2008) using the negative binomial model, found that the port of registration, the vessel type and the accident type are critical to the number of injuries and fatalities. Accidents involving passenger-type vessels are more likely to result in injuries, whereas accidents in typhoon shelters have a lower probability of causing injuries. The marginal effects of the estimated negative binomial regression analysis indicate that accidents with passenger type ships result in a relatively high number of injuries, with each port accident involving passenger ships expected to result in more than one injury.

4.2 Exponential decay model

In order to have some idea about the safety improvement over a long period, a simple exponential decay function is used to describe the general trend. The exponential decay model assumes the ship accident ratio should steadily decrease each year by a fixed percentage, finally to zero for time t approaching infinity. This is so-called exponential "learning curve" effect. The exponential decay function is defined as follows:

$$N(t) = N_0 \, exp(-\alpha t) \tag{7}$$

where t is an index for time, and α is a parameter to be determined.

In particular, the possible effect of the increase in ship arrival and port throughputs to accidents are tested in the exponential decay function, equation (7), in the ratio of the number of ship accidents to port traffic. The results are illustrated in Figure 10.11 and show satisfactory correlation ($R^2=0.9294$). Further from Figure 10.11, the exponential decay function is expressed as:

$$\ln N = -\alpha t + \ln N_0 = -0.0641t + \ln N_0 \tag{8}$$

The model further quantifies that it takes about half-life $T_{\frac{1}{2}}$ for the accident ratio to fall to one half of its initial value.

$$T_{\frac{1}{2}} = \frac{\ln 2}{\alpha} = \frac{\ln 2}{0.0641} = 10.8 \ years \tag{9}$$

This means that port safety improves in the last 24 years when the accident occurrence rate falls by approximately 50% in 10 years. It is found that ship accidents in ports related to port activity is on a consistent downward trend, reflecting improvements in port management and vessel traffic services (VTS) operation. However, since the explanatory variable in the exponential decay model (ship arrivals and port throughputs) increases over time owing to the growth in world trade and associated port activities, further research is needed into the predictability of the exponential decay model across the different ports.

4.3 Traffic-based simulation model

The discussion has centred on how to estimate the probability of an accident based on historical accident numbers. However, such a statistical approach may only describe the average risk of a large number of ships and not reflect variation in explanatory factors (e.g., traffic density). In ports, the analysis of risk is commonly undertaken for certain waters or fairways. Based on a traffic model, the probability of a collision accident can be estimated for a specified waterway of specified alignment. It is to be expected that the probability of collision given an encounter varies with the nature of encounter (how the ships approach each other), whether overtaking, crossing, or head-on (Figure 10.14).

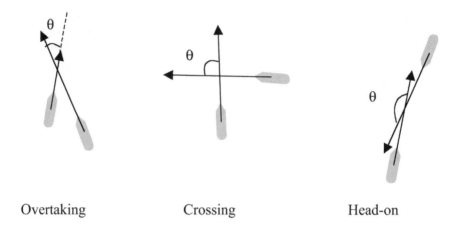

Overtaking   Crossing   Head-on

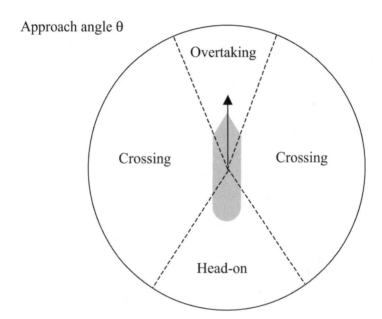

Figure 10.14 Definition of encounter

An encounter is defined as a vessel being required to make a corrective steering or speed change in order to avoid a close quarter situation arising with another vessel. Given that the principal cause of vessel collision is human error, it is inferred that a higher number of encounters is consistent with an increased level of incidents. Analysis and "expert group" consensus reported by the USCG (1999) have proposed that different types of encounters should have different relative weightings. Validation of the model identified that best agreement of model with historic incidents occurred when factors of 0.80, 0.15 and 0.05 are adopted for crossing, heading-on and overtaking encounters, respectively. These encounters are then converted into "risk-adjusted encounters" to take account of the different hazards posed by different collision avoidance actions.

$$N(Risk\text{-}adjusted\ encounters) = Sum\ of\ [Weighting\ factor \times N(Encounter)] \quad (10)$$

Table 10.5 Weighting factors of risk-adjusted encounter

Type of encounter	USCG (1999) Weighting factor	Fujii (1982) Collisions per traffic distance	Fujii (1982) Weighting factor	Lewison (1978) Collisions per encounter	Lewison (1978) Weighting factor
Head-on	0.15	2.9×10^{-5} nm	0.66	2.7×10^{-5}	0.50
Overtaking	0.05	1.5×10^{-5} nm	0.34	1.4×10^{-5}	0.25
Crossing	0.80		–	1.3×10^{-5}	0.25

Table 10.5 summarises the weighting factors to develop "risk-adjusted encounters" (RAE) from three different types of "encounter". These validations were developed on the premise that collisions are solely a function of risk-adjusted encounters and the distribution of crossing, heading and overtaking events:

$$N(Collisions) = (Ratio\ of\ Collisions\ to\ RAE)\ N(Ship\ transits)$$
$$N(Risk\text{-}adjusted\ encounters\ per\ transit)$$
$$f(Distribution\ of\ encounter\ types) \quad (11)$$

The above relationship assumes that in an open waterspace the encounter between two vessels has the same probability of collision regardless of traffic density or vessel size. While the majority of traffic within port waters is with vessels of consistent size and density (across large waterspaces), validation of the encounter model across different waterspaces may not provide the same level of accuracy in predicting collisions. Thus, when modelling smaller waterspaces in detail it is necessary to account for the distribution of ship sizes and traffic density:

$$N(Collisions) = (Ratio\ of\ Collisions\ to\ RAE)\ N(Ship\ transits)$$
$$N(Risk\text{-}adjusted\ encounters\ per\ transit)$$
$$f(Distribution\ of\ encounter\ types)$$
$$f(Distribution\ of\ vessel\ size)$$
$$f(Distribution\ of\ traffic\ density) \quad (12)$$

It should be noted that simulation studies help to evaluate the different port design/layouts and operational measures within a given port environment and a given traffic distribution. This is a viable and powerful tool for the assessment of the feasibility of a port design on the operational level. However, for a total risk level, other factors (e.g., the variation of traffic distribution) needs to be further evaluated.

5. RISK CONTROL MEASURES

In port traffic management, the key areas where control is available are:

- speed controls;
- vessel routing/fairway alignment/traffic separation;
- reallocation of anchorage and other specific waterspaces;
- advancement of vessel traffic services (VTS);
- provisioning of navigation aids.

Figure 10.15 presents the terms necessary to describe the entire accident as a process. The development of accidents follows an "incident chain" of events developed from root causes to local consequences. The qualitative and quantitative risk analyses are formulated along this discrete event approach (e.g., Harrad et al., 1998, Figure 1; Ronza et al., 2006, Figure 1).

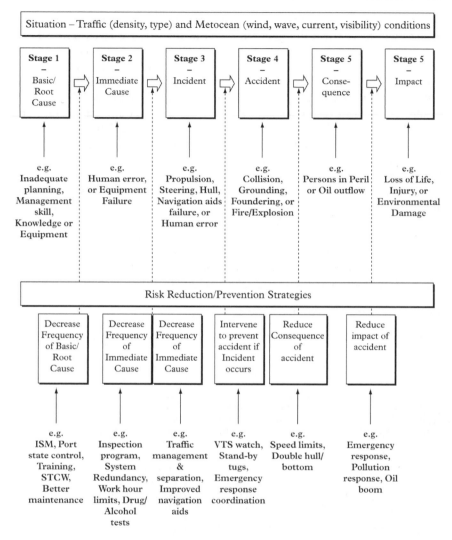

Note: modified on the basis of Harrald et al., 1998.

Figure 10.15 Incident chain

It is apparent from Figure 10.15 that there are many areas in which improvements may be made in reduction and prevention strategies at an international and local level to improve the future safety of ship traffic in ports. For example, with respect to international control, the IMO required the mandatory installation and deployment of Automatic Identification of Ships (AIS) on all ships of at least 10,000 gross registered tonnes by July 2005. This system will be progressively rolled out to include smaller coastal vessels. Such systems will enhance the control of ocean-going and coastal ships throughout port waterspaces. The provision of better information on vessel positions and courses will help break the incident chain at the Stage 2 level. The STCW training of mariners and ship masters, assisted by greater contacts among port authorities, also acts to reduce incident chains at the Stage 2 level.

It has been identified in Figure 10.13 that ships are increasing in size and that operations are being consolidated into larger port ventures. This advance in ship design and technology is expected to reduce equipment failure and assist the reduction in Stage 2 and Stage 3 along the incident chain (Wang, 2002). Continual improvement of local VTS systems and navigation aids will also assist in decreasing the exposure of mariners to hazardous procedures (e.g., Lam and Yip, 2008).

It should be stressed that the risk control measures should also be developed in accordance with historical data so as to define the highly relevant parameters of the model. This would enable the risk control measures to be made applicable and effective to local port issues across a wide range of risks. For particular types of accidents, key parameters of risk control measures are summarised in Table 10.6 (e.g., Trbojevic & Carr, 2000; Yip et al., 2002; SAFEDOR, 2005; Kristiansen, 2005; Yip, 2008).

Table 10.6 Parameters of maritime accidents

Accident	*Example scenario*	*Key parameters*
Collision (ship-to-ship)	Striking or being struck by any self propelled ships whilst at sea whether the ship is in transit or anchored.	Route positions, visibility, encounter angle, VTS areas, vessel type and size, vessel speed, and number of vessels on route.
Grounding (powered & drifting)	Grounding, bumping over sandbars, striking underwater wrecks and ships, reported hard and fast for an appreciable period of time, and cases reported as touching bottom when the reporting ship is under power or adrift due to loss of power, steering or due to adverse weather conditions.	Number of vessels on route, proximity of route to coastline, vessel size, VTS areas, sea state, vessel type, geometrical probabilities, navigational error probabilities, sea-conditions, self-repair probabilities, mechanical failure probabilities, drift speeds.
Contact (impact with structure)	Ships striking navigation marks or other buoyage and severe impact on jetty structure.	Vessel type and size, fairway alignment, metocean conditions, tug provision.
Foundering & structural failure	Ships which sank or were damaged as a result of full failure, heavy weather damage, springing leaks, breaking in two, etc., and not as a consequence of the other defined causalities.	Vessel type, size and age, probability of severe weather in different geographical locations.
Fire and explosion	Accidents where fire and/or explosion is the first event reported.	Vessel type and size, traffic densities.

Examples: Trbojevic & Carr, 2000; SAFEDOR, 2005; Kristiansen, 2005; Yip, 2008.

It is clear that there are a number of ways in which risks have been reduced and Figure 10.11 shows that safety levels are improving with a consistent reduction of incidents per vessel arrival. In order to thrive, a port must provide well-marked navigation channels, water of sufficient depth for the expected traffic, safe anchorages and vessel traffic management services, so that ships can navigate safely to their berths for cargo or passengers. The approach channels and fairway systems within the harbour may be considered hardware, whereas the VTS is the software part. It is difficult not to argue that the improvements that have seen risk levels fall by over 50% in 10 years, as Figure 10.11 shows, will not continue, to some degree, into the future.

Lastly, it is expected the number of traffic-related accidents will further increase in ports, as the port traffic inevitably increases with growing trade activities. Traffic level is one of the main indicators for improvements in the efficiency and service of ports (De and Ghosh, 2003). An efficient port often implies a shorter waiting time for ships and then attracts more traffic (e.g., Alderton, 2004, p. 290). As the container port market continues to emphasise faster and more reliable handling in ports and terminals, there is a need for Hong Kong and other busy ports to continue to deploy better and more effective traffic control systems to match the increasing volume of vessel and cargo movements. The major obstacle to the improvement of port traffic control is the lack of a comprehensive database of port accidents. Nevertheless, both the port authority and the private sector are making efforts to resolve this issue by developing value-added information platforms, such as the marine information system (MIS) of San Diego port in California (see Pillich, Pearlman and Chase, 2003) and marine electronic highway (MEH) proposed for the Straits of Malacca (see Marlow and Gardner, 2006).

6. SUMMARY

Recently there has been an increased interest in ship accidents and risks in ports, because rapid growth of traffic needs to be accompanied by additional efforts to improve port safety. Overall, port traffic activity, while busy, is efficiently regulated and generally safe. Ship accidents in ports are well within acceptable limits on the basis of FN evaluation criteria (e.g., SAFEDOR 2005, Annex B; Darbra and Casal, 2004).

A review of the ship risks in ports (as it impacts shipping) and their associated historic port traffic levels has been conducted to assist the development of a strategic risk management for ship risks in ports. Port traffic risks follow a certain pattern over a period and collision accidents are the most common incidents when port traffic is dense.

It is identified that maritime accident frequency, as a result of port traffic, is on a consistent downward trend—possibly reflecting improvements in shipping management and operation. There is no apparent trend of increasing numbers of injury and fatality given an accident. However, while ship accidents versus ship movements will be less frequent, the consequence of accidents may be more serious, due to function of increased ship size, speed and number of crew/passengers at risk. In general, the risk in ports has the potential to fall in the presence of a societal learning curve effect.

Future management measures against ship risks in ports are focused on large ships. It is believed that ports will face a requirement to provide safe access to the increasing size of ships and volume increases of traffic transiting through ports, owing to the increasing trade activities. While the inevitable increases in ship size will ensure a consolidation of cargo in large ships (e.g., ultra large container ships or ULCS), water depths in many ports limit the passage of the largest container ships; and container ship volumes have the opportunity to multiple fold on the hub ports. The future impacts of this multi-folding of ship movements cannot be quantified easily.

The improvement of port traffic safety is an on-going process, and it is important that the local port planning issues are effectively addressed. Further research is needed to compare port traffic risks across the world and to explore the impact of various traffic control philosophies. This study should be extended to consider the evolution of the adoption of information technology in port traffic control and how the adoption is affecting port risks. This is important because any future framework of port traffic management should result in reducing port accidents and consequently enhancing port efficiency.

CHAPTER 11

PORT SECURITY: A RISK BASED PERSPECTIVE[1]

Mary R. Brooks and Ronald Pelot

1. INTRODUCTION

Ports have always been concerned about the safety of their personnel, the cargo they transfer and the ships that call. Risk assessment and risk management, therefore, traditionally focused on the potential for criminal activity and man-made or natural disasters. Just as the hijacking of *Achille Lauro* and the rising tide of piracy in various hot spots around the world have opened the eyes of port authorities to the spectre of vessel hijacking as a threat to be considered, the *USS Cole* incident awakened port authorities to the potential for small boat interference. Perhaps most important in sparking global re-examination of port security against terrorism, however, was the September 2001 attack on the World Trade Centre, New York, buildings owned by the Port Authority of New York New Jersey and its headquarters. Seven years later, the assessment and management of risk are still important primary concerns for port authorities.

The philosophy of risk management and its application have become pervasive in many domains, and port security is no exception. The basic risk framework is essentially invariant across applications, but the details and implementation vary considerably. The purpose of this chapter therefore is to provide an overview of fundamental risk concepts and approaches, discuss what types of issues are particular to maritime security applications, and discuss how this methodology has been, and can be, applied to port security. This foundation provides a context for the following chapters that explore the state of many port security initiatives across a wide range of issues and jurisdiction.

2. GENERAL RISK MANAGEMENT ELEMENTS

In common parlance, the term "risk" typically refers to the possibility of some uncertain event occurring, one which could result in an undesirable outcome.

---

1. The assistance of Kim MacInnis, Dalhousie MBA/MLIS 2008 graduate, and David Wootton, CS 2004 graduate, in the research for this chapter is much appreciated.

Risk analysis, the cornerstone of many risk mitigation strategies, can be very specific as, when possible, an attempt is made to quantify the degree of risk. There are several key elements in performing a risk assessment, which comprises only part of a broader risk management strategy, as discussed later. Hazard or threat identification and characterisation is primary, considering for example the possibility of an attack on a port by a bomb hidden in a container. The potential target(s) must be identified, such as the port infrastructure or ships berthed in the port, in order to plan both defensive and responsive strategies and their implementation.

The two principal measures in a risk model are the probability of an event occurring, and the consequences once it does. The probability of a defined threat causing adverse impacts depends on many factors, such as the likelihood of initiation of an attack, the confluence of numerous antecedents, and the effectiveness of any shielding mechanisms. Concepts like exposure and vulnerability play a role here. Exposure is a quantification of the degree of interaction between potential threats and defined targets. For example, if any individual on port property can be considered a potential threat, then the number of people at the facility per unit time reflects the amount of exposure. Vulnerability (of an asset or a system) is a set or measure of weaknesses that can be exploited, such as a port facility that has no intrusion detection system. The consequences considered in a risk model can be wide-ranging—from property damage and harm to humans, to environmental and financial impacts.

In the classic risk model formulation, therefore, the risk associated with a given event j is:

$$Risk\,(j) = likelihood\,(j) * \; consequence\,(j) \tag{1}$$

As part of a comprehensive strategy to enhance supply chain security, the US Department of Homeland Security (2007) prescribes risk-based approaches to several aspects of the problem. Therein, they deviate somewhat from this standard risk equation as follows:

$$Threat\;Risk = likelihood * vulnerability * consequence \tag{2}$$

This variation serves two useful purposes. Typically, the vulnerability of the system at risk is subsumed in the equation (1) variables, as a more vulnerable system will either increase the likelihood and/or the amount of damage from an attack. However, isolating the vulnerability as a distinct factor emphasises that complementary security strategies should be pursued to address all three of the elements in equation (2), as discussed later in this chapter. Furthermore, if likelihood of attacks and resulting consequences are deemed to be similar across several ports, their relative vulnerabilities may be the primary differentiator for prioritising funding and actions.

While actual risk models are much more complex, and some embellishments are discussed below, this elemental relationship provides the basis for the discussion of port security. In some circumstances, an overall risk index can be calculated, which it serves to rank the alternative options; in other cases, the likelihood and consequences estimates are kept separate for more effective decision making. In that case, alternative plans to improve security can be compared using a risk matrix (Figure 11.1). Evidently, potentially high impact, very likely events (upper right) must be addressed with intensive efforts to prevent them and to mitigate the consequences should prevention fail. Conversely, relatively low probability minor impact events (lower left) do not command the same attention for prevention plans.

For example, an event of type E1, considered to be somewhat probable with moderate consequences, is obviously dominated by event E3 which is both worse and more likely, and E1 thus should be ranked as a lower priority. However, the challenge of setting strategic priorities to deal with potential security threats E2 versus E3 illustrates the crux of risk modelling. One is more likely while the other is expected to have greater adverse consequences. Therefore, introducing measures to deal with both E2 and E3 is preferable but, as a key aim of risk analysis is to set priorities in order to allocate scarce resources effectively, choices may have to be made. A single risk index subsumes both these measures (likelihood and consequence) into a single value, thus achieving simplicity at the expense of masking the contributing factors to the risk index.

As shown later, and in subsequent chapters, some measures are formed primarily to deal with high consequence unlikely events (generally referred to as rare events) while other strategies focus on frequent, low consequence occurrences. The choice made between allocating resources to address events of type E2 versus events of type E3 will reflect the relative importance of the consequences to the decision maker(s). In some cases, the (political) risk in the consequences is simply too high to ignore the rare event while, in other decision-making situations, the relative merit of addressing those with a higher probability but lower consequences will be preferred. Understanding the decision-making context, therefore, becomes important when dealing with events reflecting similar risk scores but divergent probabilities and consequences, as illustrated here.

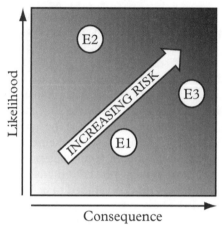

Figure 11.1 Schema for evaluating risks

The above approach assumed that the total consequences can be estimated as a single value for the impact of that event. What is more common is that different possible types and levels of consequence are considered, and the risk for an event *j* is calculated by summing over the *n* different estimated levels of impact as follows:

$$Risk_j = likelihood_j \ast \left[\sum_{i=1}^{n} prob_{ij} \ast consequence_i \right] \tag{3}$$

This illustrates another general principle regarding the scope of a risk analysis. There are always multiple consequences to an event, and many of them are not easily quantified. Furthermore, some are immediate, like the destruction of a berth or navigable channel, while others are derivative, like the disruption to the supply chain(s) of a port's customer(s), who may then be faced with consequential losses arising from cargo delay causing production shutdown, for example. Thus, a systems view must be adopted to clearly identify which aspects are to be incorporated explicitly in a particular risk model, and which other ones should be considered in terms of their eventual downstream impacts.

These elements comprise the basic foundation for a risk model. There are many strategies and procedures that have been, and could be, implemented to improve port security, and a risk model serves as a decision aid in many ways. At the very least, it is a formulation exercise that facilitates better under-standing of the scope and nature of the security uncertainties that a port faces. It helps to prioritise actions by categorising the risks by type, likelihood and potential severity. This also allows cost-effectiveness evaluations to be con-ducted in the face of these uncertainties, as limited resources should be applied where the most benefit will accrue given that not all risks can be foreseen nor addressed.

The need for a risk-based approach is expressed in several port security policies and strategies, including the International Ship and Port Facility Security Code (IMO, 2002), the Maritime Transportation Security Act (Public Law 107–295), the SAFE Port Act (2006), and the C-TPAT programme (Customs and Border Protection, 2004). Following the introduction of the ISPS Code, Bichou (2004) prescribed several approaches to developing robust quantitative methods to assist with risk management at all levels, from port security to supply chain integrity. A more recent report by UNCTAD (2006) provides an overview of relevant regulatory frameworks, and recommends how risk-based processes could be more actively pursued to achieve their goals. In fact, risk-based approaches have recently been applied to several specific aspects of maritime security. The US Coast Guard incorporates many elements of a comprehensive risk model in its custom-designed software for assessing threats and determining the need for action (Adler and Fuller, 2007). Likewise, the US Department of Homeland Security has worked diligently, holding consultations with supply chain participants globally, to model risk in supply chain processes in the absence of secondary data (US Department of Homeland Security, 2007).

Despite well-developed risk modelling approaches, there remain significant limitations to applying risk assessment in practice. Reliable data, whether based on historical information or expert opinion, are often hard to acquire. The number of variables that would comprise a comprehensive port security risk model is daunting, and the relationships between factors driving the event—from attack initiation to post-event consequences—are often complex. Nevertheless, it is arguably the only framework that adequately incorporates all of the essential ingredients to evaluate and counter these threats.

Although a risk assessment is the core component of a risk management approach, as mentioned earlier it forms only part of an holistic approach to working effectively in uncertain environments. One of the earliest and best-known risk frameworks is the AS/NZS 4360 standard, which provides broad guidance for risk management, as shown in Figure 11.2. Strategies that are developed for port risk security do not always infer that quantitative risk modelling is essential (or even feasible), but that the entire spectrum of risk aspects be explored and understood to ensure effective communication, preparedness, and indeed to establish a mindset that is aware and wary (Thibault et al., 2006). Heightened risk awareness will go a long way towards dealing with these new threats by discouraging complacency.

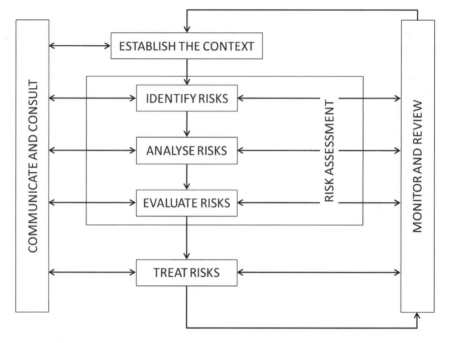

Source: AS/NZS 4360:2004:Risk Management Standard, Standards Australia.

Reproduced with permission under SAI Global Copyright SAIG Ref: 0808-C106. An electronic copy of the complete Standard online can be ordered at www.saiglobal.com

Figure 11.2 Risk management framework

   This general preamble serves to present the terminology and the basic overall concept of risk assessment, so that the balance of the chapter can illustrate the application of this risk management framework specifically to port security initiatives. While the examples used may be specific to one particular jurisdiction, the principles of the approach should be geographically unbounded, that is, applicable generally wherever the port may be located.

   The next section provides an overview of the port risk issues and then explains, in detail, each of the risk components. The section develops a framework for looking at the sequence of events and, therefore, the strategies that could result from using a risk-based approach, and is divided into pre-event and post-event components. Using examples that would be applicable to port security in some regions, this chapter sets the scene for the three following chapters that discuss current security strategies in three jurisdictions—the US, Europe and Asia. The intent is to frame the elements that need to be addressed in an holistic approach to assessing port security risks. The chapter then draws conclusions about current issues hampering the implementation of a comprehensive port security programme, discussing a number of gaps that present themselves, including the issue of measuring the performance of port security programmes.

3. RISK ISSUES FOR PORT SECURITY

Having laid the risk groundwork, the port security context will be described next. There are certain features that differentiate port security from other risk management problems, including maritime safety. Three primal aspects distinguish security risk analysis: (1) the deliberate intent to cause harm; (2) the unpredictable and unique nature of the threats; and (3) the adaptability of the enemy to attempt to circumvent new security measures. While seemingly intractable, the menace must still be addressed, and risk management approaches tailored to deal with these challenges. An argument has been made that security planning is not suited to risk analysis at all because the threats are unquantifiable and practically unknowable (Brooks and Button, 2006). Although this perhaps holds from an actuarial perspective for insurance purposes, for security planning this view can be countered by noting that this limitation also applies to many "extreme event" risk analyses (Nott, 2006). Expert estimates of terrorists' possible actions can provide a reasonable basis for relative worthiness of possible strategies, even if the absolute values of likelihood are indefensible. Security strategies aimed at prevention can be better targeted with such modelling.

These challenges also induce authorities to concentrate much of their effort on preparedness (for response and recovery), and on strengthening the systems that are at risk, by understanding and fortifying vulnerable assets, and improving the resiliency of the system through adaptability and/or redundancy. In other words, despite intensive efforts to prevent attacks, it is highly likely that some will succeed; without knowing their nature in advance, preparation for all eventualities is a sound strategy when using risk management practices to ascertain how to best direct efforts and allocate limited resources.

Safety and security initiatives are often complementary, but one significant difference that derives from the peculiarities of terrorist actions concerns the control of information. In general, it behoves agencies to collect and share a lot of information to improve safety practices and responses. Conversely, in the security realm, rigid protocols must be in place to prevent sensitive information about systems and security strategies from being accessible to the enemy while, at the same time, not imposing excessive barriers amongst stakeholders so as to preclude effective counter-terrorist collaboration. (It is this control of information that makes scholarly research in this area difficult; scholars may conclude erroneously "nothing is being done" when the reality might be the opposite.)

In order to provide the context for elaborating on security risk model aspects, it is useful to provide an illustration of the approaches that can be considered for addressing security threats. If they are placed in a logical decision process, they can be evaluated in sequence. This process is illustrated in Figure 11.3, highlighting the various phases of security incidents that must be dealt with, and the range of strategic options to address the problem at different levels. The diagram illustrates the timeline of an event, from the initial conception of an attack, through the actual attack, immediate and consequential impacts, to the final "steady-state" of the assaulted system. It also presents the types of strategies developed to deal with different phases of security threats.

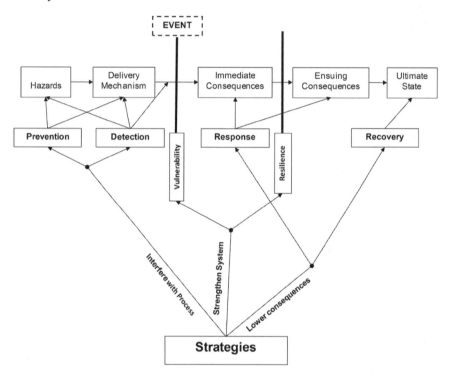

Source: created by authors.

Figure 11.3 The risk management framework

3.1. Situation analysis: hazards

As noted by the OECD (2004), the threat to transport security is not uniform; the first question it poses is: who are the terrorists and how might they execute their plans? In other words, what is the nature of the threat? The list of potential security hazards threatening ports is practically endless, but salient threats include the use of weapons of mass destruction (WMD), whether chemical, biological, radiological, or nuclear (CBRN); use of a vessel itself as a ram; conventional explosive devices; and cyber attacks by stealing, corrupting or destroying port or supply chain information or communication equipment (Kshetri, 2005). Furthermore, ports can serve as access points for transferring materials for terrorist purposes, such as guns or weapons-grade materials.

3.2. Situation analysis: delivery mechanism

The threat delivery mechanism, or platform, is discussed as a separate event phase as it is the focus of many security detection and deterrence measures. The mechanisms can be grouped into goods, people, and vehicles. Possible means of access are by air, land, water, underwater, electronic, and satellite, and the transport mechanisms include by foot, car, truck, ship, the cargo itself, small boats and aircraft. In the case of marine containers, a primary focus of US security initiatives, the OECD (2004) divides threats into "Trojan horses" (otherwise known as "weapon-in-a-box") and "Hijacked containers". The need to track vessels has resulted in several initiatives, the most broad-reaching being the Automatic Identification System (AIS) providing position and attribute information on international voyaging ships of 300 GT or more (Regulation 19 of SOLAS Chapter V, IMO, 2002). In the US, the requirement to track people engendered the Transportation Worker Identification Card (TWIC), discussed in more detail later. Of course, the goal is to identify people with bad intentions by performing background checks, excluding those who are deemed higher risk based on certain criteria (US House of Representatives, Committee on Transportation and Infrastructure, 2008), and limiting access to certain sensitive facilities to those with appropriate clearance.

One perspective is to conceive of the port as a system encapsulated in a hypothetical dome, with the aim of monitoring and checking everything and everyone crossing the boundary in efforts to keep undesirable elements out. Notably, the further away this threshold is from the target, the more time there is to respond effectively to a threat, hence resulting in several programmes geared to inspect and control the movements of goods closer to origin, and throughout the supply chain. For example, the OECD (2004) noted several weaknesses in supply chain protection, including at the periphery of the maritime transport system:

> "Addressing the security of the container transport chain requires a comprehensive inter-modal framework integrating measures across the entire container transport chain. Whereas such a framework may exist at the centre of the chain covering ports and maritime transport, as codified in SOLAS and the International Ship and Port Facility Security Code (ISPS), there is not yet an analogous framework for inland transport on the outer edges of the chain."

3.3. Situation analysis: consequences and impacts

The consequences and impacts of port security failure fall into six key areas: the destruction of port property, consequential supply chain impacts, economic impact (e.g., financial ones), environmental damage, people impacts, and damage to the port's reputation. These can be categorised by timeframe into immediate impacts in the target area, those arising in the immediate aftermath and further afield, and the eventual state of the system after the shock (see Figure 11.3).

The traditional view of port protection focuses on the destruction of port property (i.e., physical damage that changes the capability and capacity of the port to handle its business). Thus, conventional approaches for Critical Infrastructure Protection and Emergency Response have been, and continue to be, the linchpins for port security (GAO, 2006). However, an impaired port almost invariably leads to consequential supply chain impacts, and increasingly attention has turned to estimating the risks at a much broader level in order to better protect the entire system, and to allocate resources accordingly (US Department of Homeland Security, 2007).

While not so in the port management literature, there is an extensive literature in the area of corporate reputation more generally. No company wants to find itself subject to enduring scrutiny as the one that allowed a "bomb in a box" to happen on its watch. AON's Global Risk Management Survey 2007 found that "damage to reputation" is the most frequently expressed concern of companies, as it can result in costly litigation, negative publicity and reduced earnings to name a few of its consequences. The second highest risk to a company was found to be business interruption (AON, 2007). Both of these are mission critical factors in port security consequences for cargo owners and carriers alike.

3.4. Situation analysis: vulnerability and resilience

Holistic risk management for port security must also deal with the vulnerability and resilience of the threatened systems and assets. Barnes (2004:1) points out that: "Security concerns and systemic vulnerability within trading systems are critical factors in international business success." Although definitions of vulnerability vary (Peck, 2006), it generally denotes the degree of susceptibility of an asset or system to damage, and protective mechanisms include fortifying the structure itself and/or introducing barriers that shield the asset from threats. Vulnerability assessments can range from very general considerations like the weakness of a port's defences resulting from a lack of effective perimeter fencing (or the degree of reliance of the supply chain on a particular port's operation) to more detailed appraisals of the strengths of specific assets to withstand severe physical or cyber shocks, for example. The Transportation Security Administration developed a vulnerability self-assessment tool called TMSARM[2] (Havemen et al., 2004).

2. TSA Maritime Self-Assessment Risk Module.

The broader concept of resilience connotes the ability of the threatened system to recover quickly from an adverse event, or to adapt to its impacts. Governments today are concerned about system resiliency, and view this to be a public benefit arising from proactive port security activities. Strategies enhancing resilience include maintaining the ability of a compromised system to achieve its purpose. Many studies have been conducted to demonstrate the importance of improving resilience in parallel with port protection measures (Sarathy, 2006). In Figure 11.3, the degree of vulnerability is shown as a buffer between the threat and the system under attack, thus ultimately having a major influence on the level of consequences resulting from an event. The system resilience is likewise a moderating factor that affects the degree to which the damage radiates outwards from the immediate target in time and space.

4. STRATEGIES AND ACTIONS FOR MITIGATING RISKS

Strategies in the model serve one or more of three main purposes: (a) to lower the probability of an event or incident occurring in future; this includes strategies to interfere with the process (thereby making it more difficult to execute the event) or to detect the plan for a future event (resulting in faster interdiction); (b) developing plans to respond to the event, and lower the consequences; this second one includes strategies aimed at remediation and recovery in the case of an event; and (c) strategies aimed at strengthening the system, which includes vulnerability assessment, and system redesign to promote system resiliency in the case of an event.

The majority of port security programmes currently in place are aimed at reducing the probabilities of an event, that is, they focus on pre-event analysis and planning. This agrees with the approach by Sarathy (2006) who argues that it is better to build security into supply chains than to deal with the consequences of poor risk management. Prevention strategies focus on pre-event issues to attempt to preclude certain threats from being realised. An attack progresses through a series of steps, regardless of whether the time-frame from inception to completion is short or long. The perpetrators first develop the intent to do harm, formulate a plan, and acquire the required resources to carry out the plan: before they perform they prepare to initiate the attack, expecting to carry it out to fruition. The goal of the port security personnel is to detect trouble as early in this sequence as possible, but in general the difficulty of doing so reliably grows significantly before visible manifestations of the scheme appear. However, detection at the preparation phase, such as bomb materials being acquired by a potential attacker, or during the initial stages of execution, such as placing a bomb in a container to be delivered to a port, are preferable to sensing the threat just prior to the event occurring.

Many governments conduct covert and overt operations to address all of these stages of threat development, and, in particular, seek to better examine and control goods and people in advance through numerous strategies, as described below.

The key international programmes are identified in Appendix 1 (with US domestic programmes presented briefly in Appendix 2). For example, the International Ship and Port Facility Security Code (ISPS, Appendix 1) is a multilateral programme, under the IMO umbrella, intended to meet the strategic purpose of letting supply chain participants know the level of threat assessment that has been identified by government security officers and, therefore, the strategy (plan) that should be implemented to deal with the threat. Commonalities in strategies have occurred with those measures implemented for cargo through the World Customs Organization and the International Standards Organization, and for ships and ports via the ISPS Code. Likewise, the Container Security Initiative (CSI, Appendix 1), while a US programme, is classified as an international programme because it has negotiated extra-territorial rights for US customs officers in foreign ports; the implementation to common principles occurs because it is a US national strategy rolled out internationally for US-destined cargoes. However, it is not a global strategy of benefit to other countries, except in a political sense. On the other hand, the TWIC is a US national strategy to deal with personnel threats across a variety of modes, but it is not harmonised with similar programmes in other jurisdictions—something that would enhance its effectiveness as a risk management strategy—and so it is classified as a national strategy. The Secure Freight Initiative provides another example of a strategy focused on pre-event minimisation of risk, intended to reduce the vulnerability of US ports by moving the detection activity offshore (Appendix 2).

Some of the programmes developed by governments act as mirrors to US programmes, while others exhibit their own unique approach. For example, the Canadian Government's Partners in Protection programme is a mirror of the US Customs-Trade Partnership against Terrorism programme, a "known shipper" programme that reduces the probability of an event by enabling security officials in customs and border protection to allocate investigative resources to identified non-members. On the other hand, there are considerable divergences between strategies in Europe, Asia and North America, as will be seen in this and forthcoming chapters.

5. THE THREE Rs: RESPONSE, REMEDIATION AND RECOVERY

Response strategies most commonly refer to actions taken during and after the initiation of an event, defined as the beginning of an impact on the target. One key strategy here is preparedness, which refers to steps taken in advance to have available resources and personnel to address defined or unforeseen threats, which often involves detailed communication, command and control plans, as well as training of general skills and simulations exercises (Malak,

2007). Port Authorities in North America have already established a set of guidelines for Emergency Preparedness (American Association of Port Authorities, 2008). Further action to restore an attacked system, once the event is over, is generally referred to as the recovery phase. This is dealt with separately for planning purposes, as the goals, parties involved, and time imperatives are very different from the reaction to an unfolding event.

As the purpose of this chapter is to establish a framework for thinking about risk-based management and to examine strategies that would interfere with the activities of those seeking to disrupt secure ports, the reader is referred to the following three chapters that focus on programmes that deliver both the strategies to interfere with the process, and those designed for response and recovery by strengthening the system and lowering the consequences when an event occurs.

6. THINKING AHEAD: CHALLENGES IN PORT RISK MANAGEMENT

It has become clear throughout the course of developing this framework for thinking about risk-based management that the issue of port security is a somewhat disjointed one from a global perspective. Strategies have focused primarily on the external activities, the identification of hazards and threats for example, and on system vulnerability; there has been much less emphasis on the end of the process, that is dealing with a problem when it occurs. While cost-effective risk-based management would seem to imply that this is the right order, what is not clear is: why has there been, in current programmes and policies, a higher priority placed on goods management and much less on the management of people? After all, it is "bad people" who create the security problem and "good people" who see it and take action. Is it because the people management issues are much more difficult to resolve?

These issues and several other challenges remain, to achieve balanced, effective and affordable security measures. The remainder of this section discusses seven key difficulties that confront the authorities as they attempt to grapple with this matter.

6.1. Port security involves multiple jurisdictions

Jurisdictional discrepancies will become very clear over the next three chapters. Pinto et al. (2009) examines programmes in the US and it is clear that the US took the lead in raising port security standards. Pallis and Vaggelas (2009) detailed US rules as setting the standards for a risk-based approach with the Europeans and Asians as followers. In fact, Ng and Gujar (2009) used the phrase "half-hearted" to describe the Asian approach to port security and "stagnant" to describe the enforcement of compliance processes. It would be fair comment that the Asians have followed a minimalist, but pro-trade approach to port security.

Furthermore, Pallis and Vaggelas (2009) note that jurisdictional issues are critical as European ports want to be more integrated with their adjacent cities and accessible to citizens, while the North American approach of establishing fences and gates between ports and communities is entrenched and Asian ports approach port security with a "minimalist" approach (Ng and Gujar, 2009). The net impact is that there is little harmonisation across jurisdictions except that afforded by the intent (if not the execution) of ISPS Code and the US-imposed Container Security Initiative.

Within the US, a critical challenge ports face is that multiple parties are involved in delivering port services, and there is only so much that can be imposed nationally. As noted by Newman and Walder (2003), the planning, development and operation of landside infrastructure rests with the state or local governments and the imposition of federal requirements are strictly prescribed. Furthermore, as many American ports operate as landlords, leasing terminals and facilities to private companies, the Maritime Transportation Security Act of 2002 (MTSA), by which the US implemented the ISPS Code, limits the amount of security oversight that any US port authority may exercise, as security compliance is primarily a matter between the US government and the private terminal operating companies.

Not only is the jurisdictional problem in US ports an issue with the rights of ports versus those of their tenants, as noted above, but there also remains the tension between tenants and their, in many cases, unionised workforce. This underscores the challenge of introducing the TWIC in a timely manner (noted in Appendix 2).

6.2. Port security is part of a larger supply chain

While the threat of Chemical, Biological, Radiological or Nuclear (CBRN) weapons in a box (the "Trojan Horse" scenario) drives current security measures from a US government perspective, Brooks and Button (2007) found that most cargo interests believe that by the time the box arrives in the port, it is too late if either the container or the ship is the weapon. While cargo owners are generally supportive of measures that push back the border nearer to the location where the box is stuffed, the US companies they interviewed are much more concerned about incident management and remediation than further investment in prevention. They also noted the OECD (2004: 16) finding that ports are only one of the 23 actors in a marine container supply chain that can affect the security of the cargo. Furthermore, private ownership of many of these actors complicates what public officials may be able to do to address security issues in such complex chains (Peck, 2005).

From the port security perspective, on the landside, a very few shipping and rail companies have considerable power and influence through their security programmes while the trucking industry presents a more fragmented and vulnerable picture. Vulnerabilities are often considered highest at the nodes, the transfer points in the chain, where there are more players and a greater number of "touch points" that can expose the cargo to the perceived threats. Brooks and Button (2007) illustrated this (see Figure 11.4).

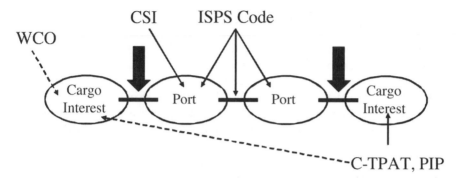

Note: Downward arrows reflect the weakest links in the chain.
Source: Brooks and Button (2007: 223).

Figure 11.4 Brooks and Button (2007), Cargo Security Programs

Brooks and Button (2007: 231) concluded:

> *"There is general acceptance of the necessity to have a layered and targeted risk management approach as companies believe that to inspect every maritime container would be too costly. The question is how much security is enough. The two weakest links for the US-bound maritime containers are: the US domestic trucking link as the Oklahoma bombing revealed the "enemy within"; and foreign domestic trucking still provides the Trojan Horse opportunity. Terrorists have imagination; the next incident is highly unlikely to reflect similar patterns to the last."*

So far, efforts in maritime and port security have focused on the cargo, the port, the ship and the landside carriers as different focal points of the risk assessment. Yet the security systems that have evolved in these domains have evolved differently. Only the ISPS Code (IMO, 2002) has similarities between systems applicable to ships and to ports. Both involve a common three-level threat assessment and procedures for preventing threats at each level. In sum, however, programmes and strategies to date have effectively tackled the low-lying fruit. The Transport Workers' Identification Credential is proving to be a little further up the tree.

Finally, heightened port security may be one cause of growing road congestion. Both Brooks et al. (2006) and Cambridge Systematics Inc. (2007) have concluded that security considerations are a significant impediment to the development of short sea shipping alternatives to trucking on the coastal north-south corridors of North America, respectively. The former also found that the advance notification requirements found in the existing legislation governing US imports are particularly onerous for marine containers originating on the continent. Well-managed port security is only one piece of an holistic security programme.

6.3. Programme disparity and complexity

The US considered that the primary focus of their efforts was internationally arriving vessels and that they saw the threat in the chain as coming from foreign source. Pallis and Vaggelas (2009), however, point out that the threat in Europe was seen more broadly and therefore as also coming from intra-European trade and so their port security programme was designed to include cabotage trades and ports that only might occasionally serve international cargoes.

Currently, the truckers that serve US ports have to comply with four separate security processes: a Transportation Worker Identification Credential, a Free and Secure Trade endorsement, a Hazmat endorsement, and US Visit credential (if the driver is also transporting goods from Canada or Mexico). These could be streamlined, and only one credential required for all supply chain partners who are involved. Perhaps that fruit remains firmly lodged on the top branches and seemingly difficult to reach.

6.4. Information sharing and privacy

As already noted, information sharing has its own risks. Share too much about the risk approach used and the strategies followed, and "the enemy" knows too much; share too little and, to use a phrase used by Flynn (2007), you create "more shadows for bad people to hide". Poor sharing of information between executing agencies creates its own set of problems; GAO (2007b) noted that information planning and sharing is "spotty at best" between the various US authorities responsible for disaster coordination and recovery; an all-hazards approach is called for by stakeholders, which is an effective way to prepare effectively regardless of the threat (US Department of Homeland Security, 2006). One year after the implementation of the SAFE Port Act, the GAO concluded that communication efforts have improved but that the implementation continues to be slow (GAO, 2008a). Like the US Department of Homeland Security, the Office of the Inspector General (2007) has been critical of the information system more generally as well.

6.5. The timing challenge

While the Smart Border Accord between Canada and the US was signed a mere three months after 11 September 2001, most security programmes have taken a considerable length of time to implement. For example, in 2002, the C-TPAT programme, which focused on cargo security, was implemented in the US (as was its Canadian equivalent Partners in Protection), but its rollout was slower than expected. It has become obvious that this is true of most port security programmes and many remain incompletely executed years after their introduction.

The Automated Targeting System for the US has been in place since 2004, and the subject of review on its effectiveness since the GAO report of 2005 (GAO, 2005). The European system of cargo threat assessment (Community Customs code and advanced cargo notification system), according to Pallis and Vaggelas (2009), will not be fully implemented until 2009.

The US Government Accountability Office, which has been monitoring US implementation of the port security system, continues to report concerns from delays resulting from testing of equipment for TWIC cards (GAO, 2008a) to problems with improving the communications needed to make ports resilient (GAO, 2007b). Timing continues to be a problem at the time of writing.

6.6. The costs of port security

In the seven years since September 2001, it is clear that the costs of increased security at ports have been severely under-estimated. The delays in introducing the TWIC have been traced to this issue. The requirements to put in place port security programmes in the US have prompted a tussle between port authorities, the US Department of Homeland Security, and terminal operators about who will pay. The US Government Accountability Office (2007a) noted that the US Coast Guard will be hard pressed to find and train an adequate number of inspectors, let alone meet other requirements of the SAFE Port Act 2006. The implementation of C-TPAT has been noted to be less than complete due to problems in auditing the member companies (Ojah, 2005).

The CSI programme's aim to scan 100% of inbound containers can incur inordinate costs. A detailed quantitative analysis, by Bennett and Chin (2008), of the benefits and drawbacks of 100% container scanning highlights the severity of the impacts on costs, delays and security. As noted by the GAO (2008b:18), such scanning raises questions from a risk-based management perspective:

> " . . . *some European customs officials have told us that the 100 percent scanning requirement is in contrast to the risk-based strategy behind CSI and C-TPAT, and the WCO has stated that implementation of 100 percent scanning would be 'tantamount to abandonment of risk management'.*"

6.7. Measuring the performance of the security strategy

The tool of benchmarking is often used to evaluate the implementation of processes in any organisation, and to determine their success measured against objectives. To examine the implementation of port security as a benchmarked process, a bibliography of the major articles on measuring port performance in key transport journal publications of the last seven years was developed. A content analysis of these was undertaken, and based on this analysis, it is clear that there is very little performance benchmarking of port security discussed in the literature. The port performance literature contains limited discussion of security indicators. A content analysis of 69 port performance articles over the past 10 years confirms this; port safety and security is mentioned but undefined in four, and only two articles mentioned measures to assess the performance of security in ports—Lirn et al. (2004) and Pantouvakis (2006).

Lirn et al. (2004), using the analytic hierarchy process technique to determine the importance of various criteria in the transhipment port selection decision-making process in Taiwan, found that "port security" was a relevant factor in the choice. How "port security" was defined, however, was unclear. Pantouvakis (2006), in his study of ferry passengers in Greece, found that one of the criteria for choosing a particular port was the "feeling of security and surveillance inside the port". Both studies fall short of introducing measures to evaluate port security. More generally, advanced information systems and cargo tracking are listed in a further five papers in the set. These are, however, activities not measures.

In addition, Drewry (2004) suggested that a port must satisfy a shipping line that the port security meets an "acceptable security" level in terms of ship, cargo and both direct and indirect employee security measures as well as be ISPS code-compliant in order to be chosen by the line. How the "acceptable" is measured by a line is unclear but appears to be a subjective criterion. While it might be said that ISPS-compliant is a minimum acceptable level, most ports today are certified by their respective governments as compliant even if they are not. As Flynn (2006) noted, port security can be seen as a "house of cards", that is, it is fragile.

Bichou (2004) was not included in the performance benchmarking literature review (as it was not a benchmarking article) and so was not considered in the discussion above. However, he suggested that risk management is one of three models required to achieve superior security, the other two being channel design and process mapping, and cost control and performance monitoring.

This then raises the question about how security in the absence of an existing port performance measurement system for security can be measured. Some suggestions that we would make based on work in progress are:

- existence of disaster recovery plan (yes/no);
- number of months since last update;
- number of personnel with security clearance as a percentage of total personnel granted access;
- evaluation of number and type of security training sessions and/or exercises;
- percentage of inbound containers scanned;
- percentage of ports assessed (US DHS 2007: 82);

- number of false positives and false negatives (where possible) for scanned containers;
- improvements in vulnerability as measured by TMSARM (Havemen et al., 2004).

The Department of Homeland Security (2007) includes a discussion of the importance of performance measures in security preparations, and tabulates a number of key metrics, although this performance measurement activity does not appear in the academic literature already mentioned.

7. SUMMARY

It has now been seven years since the fateful events of 11 September 2001 that created a tectonic shift in thinking about security. The signs were there well before that date—*Achille Lauro* was more than 20 years earlier—yet it does not appear that the challenges of port security have been resolved. Several reasons have been identified for this failure: (1) port security involves multiple jurisdictions; (2) port security is part of larger supply chain security challenges; (3) there is considerable programme disparity and complexity internationally; (4) there is a significant problem with privacy issues in information sharing; (5) there is the ever-present issue of timing of initiatives; (6) the costs of port security; and finally (7) the measurement of port security for effectiveness and continuous improvement. All of these conspire to leave port security strategies in doubt seven years after security efforts moved to the front burner for most ports and governments.

The US approach is generally a risk-based one, as evidenced by the notable legislative changes, and level of budget commitment. As information sharing is perforce incomplete, it is not possible to assess all elements as being risk-based. The conclusion is that any person can instigate a terrorist attack, and so therefore inclusive personnel screening programmes, like the US TWIC, are appropriate. However, it remains to be questioned as to whether scan-all elements of US container screening programmes are the optimal risk-based approaches, or have been implemented merely because a partial approach to these risks is not deemed politically acceptable. The risk-based approach has a number of difficulties in its execution, but if it is not taken, there is an even greater risk that trade and economic security will be adversely impacted.

APPENDIX 1: INTERNATIONAL SECURITY PROGRAMMES (STRATEGIES)

International Ship and Port Facility Code

The ISPS Code was finalised in December 2002, as amendments to the UN Safety of Life at Sea Convention (IMO, 2002). The US implemented the ISPS Code by passing the Maritime Transportation Security Act of 2002, with effect on 1 July 2004, the same day the Code took effect. The ISPS Code sets mandatory security requirements to be taken by a number of actors—governments, ports, shipping companies, and terminal operators—to enhance the security of the world's shipping network. Each signatory nation is required to establish a three-tier security system and assess the risks its ports face—Level 1 is a normal level of security threats, Level 2 medium, and Level 3 is a high threat level. The Code also mandates that ports establish corresponding three-tier security plans that will identify both physical and operational measures to be implemented according to the threat assessment level. Each port is also required to designate a security officer who will be responsible for ensuring compliance with the requirements.

Container Security Initiative

The CSI places US Customs and Border Protection personnel in foreign ports and enables them to optimise the use of the Department of Homeland Security Automated Targeting System. Examining the *Journal of Commerce* list of the Top 50 container ports in the world as of July 2007, a majority of the largest container ports were members of the Container Security Initiative (Anonymous, 2007). However, some of the largest ports in China (Qingdao, Ningbo-Zhoushan, Guangzhou, Tianjin, Xiamen and Dalian) do not belong; other key ports are also missing when this list is cross-referenced against the list of members: Jawaharia Nehru (India), Tanjung Priok (Indonesia), Manila (the Philippines), Port Said (Egypt), Ho Chi Minh (Vietnam), Jeddah (Saudi Arabia) and Osaka (Japan). However, CSI ports account for 85% of all traffic bound for the US (US Customs and Border Protection, 2008), and this raises a second issue about the benefits of further investment for a higher probability of marginal return.

APPENDIX 2: US NATIONAL SECURITY PROGRAMMES (STRATEGIES)

Advanced Notification Rules

In addition to implementing the ISPS Code, the Maritime Transportation Security Act instituted new security requirements, such as 96- and 24-hour rules, to further reduce the vulnerability of American ports and supply chains.

Over the years, there have been a number of refinements to the initial requirements since implementation (GAO, 2005). The 96-hour rule is intended to
protect ports and American interests by requiring all vessels calling into
American ports to provide the US government with advance notice of arrival
96 hours before the estimated arrival time, ensuring that the US government
has time to determine if the vessel poses a threat and to prepare for action.

The 24-hour rule requires that container shipping companies and non-
vessel operating common carriers provide notice in advance of loading, of the
contents and characteristics of containers bound for US ports. This rule
allows the US government to use its Automated Targeting System to identify
particular marine containers for inspection prior to being loaded, in keeping
with the notion that the container may contain a threat or the components to
create a threat. (The advanced notification rules are an integral component of
the broader Container Security Initiative.)

The Transport Workers Identification Credential (TWIC)

In addition to the notification rules and the establishment of port security
threat assessment levels, under the Maritime Transportation Security Act,
ports were also to introduce port worker security controls through the introduction of a Transportation Workers Identification Credential. This was
delayed significantly and was still not implemented four years after the passage
of the MTSA. Congress reinforced the requirement with the passage of the
Security and Accountability For Every (SAFE) Port Act of 2006. However,
the enrolment process did not begin until October 2007 (recall that the
passage of the MTSA was in 2002) and by January 2008 only about 110,000
of the more than one million workers (estimated by the US House of Representatives Committee on Transportation and Infrastructure, 2008) had pre-
enrolled and "almost 12,000 cards activated" (Fanguy, 2008). The
Transportation Security Administration, by January 2008, had not issued
regulations for when the TWIC would be mandatory at ports, nor had it
provided a timeline for when approved TWIC readers would be installed
(Cummings, 2008). By May 2008, the implementation of the programme was
proceeding sufficiently slowly that its full implementation target date was
moved on 2 May 2008 to 15 April 2009 (US House of Representatives
Committee on Homeland Security, 2008).

Secure Freight Initiative

The Department of Homeland Security established another programme
focused on freight screening in foreign ports in December 2006 (Department
of Homeland Security, 2006). Called the Secure Freight Initiative, the programme's initial phase deploys nuclear detection devices to six foreign ports,
some deemed high risk—Port Qasim (Pakistan), Puerto Cortes (Honduras),
and Port Salalah (Oman)—and others in significant originating markets

—Southampton (UK), the Gamman Terminal at the Port of Busan (Korea), and Singapore. Marine containers at these ports will be scanned for radiation before loading for the United States. Unlike the Automated Targeting System, in the case where an alarm is sounded, both host country officials and the Department of Homeland Security will be simultaneously notified. The programme funding is US but the programme is another of extra-territorial nature.

CHAPTER 12

US PORT SECURITY

C. Ariel Pinto, Ghaith Rabadi and Wayne K. Talley

1. INTRODUCTION

Each year, 7,500 commercial vessels make 51,000 calls at 361 US ports (Makrinos, 2004). In 2002 approximately 7 million containers arrived at US ports, carrying more than 95% of the nation's non-North American trade by weight and 75% by value (Government Accountability Office, 2003). While US ports are engines for growing the US economy, their cargoes are also vulnerable targets for terrorists (Cooperman, 2004). A single US import transaction typically involves 30 different documents and at least 25 parties, e.g., shipowners, truckers, freight forwarders and third-party logistics providers.

After the terrorist attacks of 11 September 2001, it became clear that US ports were at high risk for terrorist activities. Since the 11 September attacks, US port security has gone through considerable evolution. This chapter presents the current state of US port security.

The following section discusses US port security legislation and programmes that have evolved since the 11 September attacks: the 2001 Aviation and Transportation Security Act, the 2002 Maritime Transportation Security Act, the establishment of Department of Homeland Security (DHS) in 2003, the development of the Coast Guard's maritime security programme, the development of the Bureau of Customs and Border Protection's (CBP's) maritime security programme, and the Security and Accountability for Every (SAFE) Port Act of 2006. The next section describes the CBP's maritime security programme within the context of port security risk management. A discussion of DHS's financing of port security follows. Then, a theoretical discussion regarding how to allocate port security resources at a given port is presented. Finally, concluding discussions are presented in the Summary section.

2. PORT SECURITY LEGISLATION AND PROGRAMMES

Since 11 September 2001, the US has created barriers to deny terrorist plans and events. The US Congress passed the Aviation and Transportation Security Act on 19 November 2001 which established the Transportation Security

Administration (TSA). TSA's initial emphasis was on aviation security; today, its mission is to ensure the security of the transportation of people and goods on all modes of the US transportation system. An important component of TSA's port security programme is to improve the access control to the US. Port access-control measures include alarm systems, perimeter fencing, employee background checks, security patrols, terminal lighting, closed circuit television systems and port access/egress controls on trucks and rail cars (i.e., vehicle checks).

The US Maritime Transportation Security Act (MTSA), designed to protect US ports and waterways from terrorist attacks, was signed into law on 25 November 2002. The MTSA seeks to prevent security incidents in the maritime supply chain, in particular the port link in this chain. The MTSA also incorporated the international security requirements found in the International Ship and Port Security (ISPS) Code that was ratified earlier in 2002 by the IMO.

The ISPS Code is a risk management code for securing ships and ports, e.g., monitoring the access and control of people and cargo to ships and ports and ensuring the availability of security communications. The Code requires ports and marine terminals, serving seagoing vessels of 500 gross tonnage and upwards, to have security plans, officers and certain equipment in place (i.e., in order to comply with the Code) by 1 July 2004. Port security plans include access control, responses to security threats and drills to train staff (Staff, 2004).

On 1 March 2003, the US DHS was established. The DHS has federal responsibility for funding, standards and strategies (to do so) for the security of ports and other transportation infrastructures. Further, the US Coast Guard was removed from the US Department of Transportation and placed under the authority of the DHS.

The US Coast Guard's maritime security programme includes, for example, the deployment of Coast Guard personnel as "Sea Marshals" aboard certain ships entering and leaving ports, the creation of the High Interest Vessel Boarding Program and the establishment of port security zones around ships and high-risk port facilities (to prevent sabotage or other subversive acts). Sea Marshals provide security to a vessel's pilot and crew during its transit while in port, thereby diminishing the potential for vessel hijacking. Security zones protect port waterways, vessels and facilities from security incidents. The Coast Guard has also established the Maritime Security Level (MARSEC) system to indicate the severity of a security threat: level 1—a threat is possible, but not likely; level 2—terrorists are likely active in an area; and level 3—a threat is imminent to a given target.

The DHS unit, the US Bureau of Customs and Border Protection (CBP), has established voluntary international security programmes that are designed to provide point-of-origin to final destination visibility and control over containerised freight movements. These voluntary programmes include: (1) the

Container Security Initiative (CSI), in which CBP works with foreign ports to identify potentially dangerous shipments before they arrive in the US; and (2) the Customs-Trade Partnership Against Terrorism (C-TPAT), through which CBP provides streamlined clearance of cargo to shippers that establish appropriate security procedures. The CSI is a bilateral agreement between the US and a foreign port, whereby the foreign port is to identify high risk containerised cargo and work with deployed CBP officers (at the foreign port) to target such cargo. Under CSI, foreign ports are asked to pre-screen containers (for dangerous cargo) before they are loaded onto US-bound ships. As of the first quarter of 2007, 50 foreign ports that handled 85% of the container volume destined for the US were designated as CSI ports. Benefits of the CSI programme to CSI ports include the reduction in: (1) delay times in the departure of export cargoes to the US; and (2) inspection times for US export cargoes.

C-TPAT is a joint government-business initiative to build co-operative security relationships, i.e., to reduce the vulnerability of the US international supply chains to terrorism. Businesses seeking to become C-TPAT companies are required to: (1) submit a security profile of their international business practices to the CBP; (2) conduct a self-assessment of their security practices; (3) develop a security plan that incorporates C-TPAT guidelines; and (4) work towards the promotion of C-TPAT guidelines with other global firms (Thibault, Brooks, and Button, 2006). The primary benefit to C-TPAT companies includes accelerated customs clearances at US ports. By the end of 2004, C-TPAT companies included: 9,083 US importing companies, 2,208 carriers, 1,412 brokers, 393 foreign manufacturers and vendors and a small number of port authorities and marine terminal operators (Keane, 2005).

The CBP is also seeking mutual recognition C-TPAT status with other countries. If a company receives C-TPAT status (or its equivalent) for exports to the US (or a mutually recognised country), it will receive C-TPAT status (or its equivalent) for exports to the mutually recognised country (or the US). In November 2007, the US and the EU announced that they would begin extending reciprocal fast-lane customs clearances by 2009 for shippers that meet joint security standards. The mutual recognition status is a means by which the CBP is seeking to provide security to international supply chains.

Another major US maritime cargo security programme, though involuntary, is the 24-Hour Advance Manifest Rule (24-hour rule). This programme requires container shipping lines to provide information electronically to the CBP about container cargo on board their ships at foreign ports, but destined for US ports, at least 24 hours prior to the departure of these ships from foreign ports. The submitted information allows for the pre-screening and targeting of suspected containers.

A DHS rule that is similar to the 24-hour rule but relates to ships rather than cargo is the 96-hour rule which requires that all ships that are to call at US ports provide the US government with a 96-hour advance notice of arrival.

This rule provides the US government with the opportunity to target particular ships for which it has security concerns.

On 13 October 2006, President Bush signed into law the Security and Accountability for Every (SAFE) Port Act. Its purpose is to strengthen port security by enacting technology initiatives and better data-collection programmes. One such technology initiative is the Transportation Worker Identification Credential (TWIC) programme that requires background security checks and biometric-based credentials (that require the unique physical characteristics of an individual to be known) for all those working in or around US ports. TWIC credentials will ensure that only authorised persons will have access to US ports. TWIC cards are expected to be issued to more than 750,000 US maritime employees (Natter, 2007).

The SAFE Port Act also requires the DHS to establish at least three pilot overseas scanning programmes to test the feasibility of 100% domestic screening of containerised cargo and 100% scanning of high-risk containerised cargo destined for US ports. The pilot programmes involving high-risk containerised cargo destined for US ports are to have this cargo 100% scanned with both non-intrusive radiographic imaging and passive radiation detection equipment placed at the terminal arrival gates of foreign ports. The ports of Singapore, Puerto Cortes (Honduras), Southampton (UK), Salalah (Oman), Qasim (Pakistan), Busan (Korea) and Hong Kong agreed in 2007 to participate in the DHS pilot overseas scanning programme. The results of the overseas programme will also be used to evaluate the effectiveness of the new radiation scanning technology for 100% scanning for radiation of all shipping containers that enter US ports by the end of 2008.

The SAFE Port Act also requires improvements in the collection and analysis of container cargo data for the targeting of high-risk cargo, i.e., improvements in the US automatic targeting system programme. Data gathered on US import containers will be encrypted and transmitted in near real time to the CBP's National Target Center, where it will be combined with other data, e.g., manifest submissions, to improve the risk scoring for targeting high-risk containers.

The Act further instructs the DHS to obtain better data from US importers for container security screening and targeting efforts. In response, the CBP has established the "10 plus 2" Initiative for Containerized Cargo programme that seeks data on US imported containerised cargo (prior to the loading of this cargo on ships at foreign ports) for 10 additional variables and information on ship stowage plans and container status messages from shipping lines. Also, the Act requires the development of a Post-Incident Trade Resumption and Supply Chain Security Strategic Plan and the promotion of International Container Security Standards.

In January 2008, the DHS released the National Response Framework (NRF), which focuses on response and short-term recovery, articulates the doctrine, principles and architecture by which the US prepares for and responds to all-hazard disasters, across all levels of government and all sectors of communities (US Department of Homeland Security, 2008). The NRF is intended for elected and appointed leaders, such as federal department and agency heads, state governors, mayors, city managers, emergency management practitioners at all levels of government and the private sector. The NRF is meant to be a "living system" that can be revised and updated as necessary to reflect real-world events and lessons learned, and be scalable, flexible and adaptable; and articulates clear roles and responsibilities among local, state, and federal officials.

3. FINANCING PORT SECURITY

US federal homeland security grants are primarily meant to enhance emergency preparedness and response capabilities. Since 2002, the DHS has distributed over $19 billion in federal funding for planning, equipment, and training to enhance the nation's capabilities to respond to terrorist attacks. Part of the funding includes funds for port security and natural and accidental disasters (Government Accountability Office, 2008, p. 1). The Post-Katrina Emergency Management Reform Act requires DHS grants to be allocated to the Federal Emergency Management Agency (US Department of Homeland Security, 2007a). The DHS grants allow US ports to respond to MTSA requirements for securing their facilities against terrorist attacks, but fall short of what is requested by ports.

In its purest sense, risk is highly abstract. Even if it is quantitatively defined, whether with respect to damage and probability, or using utility concepts, risk is still often represented as a mere number without a physical representation. The DHS uses a risk-based methodology to identify urban areas that are eligible for grants. The methodology is designed to measure the relative risk of states and urban areas to terrorist attacks. A risk analysis model utilizes information from each state and urban area. Two primary pieces of information considered by the model are population and population density. Information used and how it is used to measure relative risks to states/territories and urban areas to terrorist attacks have evolved over recent years (Government Accountability Office, 2008, p. 4).

The DHS model for allocating security grants consists of three phases: (1) risk analysis phase—determine the potential risk of a given state/territory or urban area to terrorist attacks relative to that of other states/territories and urban areas using empirical analytical methods and policy judgements; (2) effectiveness assessment phase—assess the effectiveness of the proposed investments submitted by the eligible applicants; and (3) final allocation phase—allocate security grants. Figure 12.1 is an adaptation from a figure appearing in a Government Accountability Office (2008, p. 7) report that presents these three steps in a schematic diagram.

During the risk analysis phase, risk scores are determined for states/territories and urban areas that are under consideration for DHS security grants. The formulas for determining the risk scores are:

$$R = (T + V\&C) \qquad (1)$$

$$V\&C = P + E + I + N) \qquad (2)$$

Where R represents a risk score index, T represents a threat index and V&C represents a vulnerability and consequence index. The V&C index is the sum of four indices, P, E, I and N, representing population status, economic status, national infrastructure status and national security status, respectively.

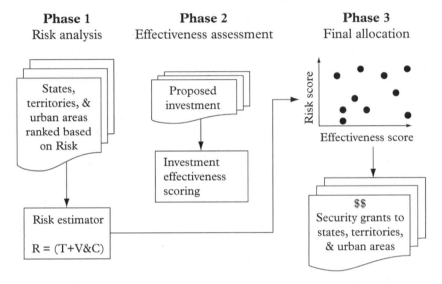

| **Phase 1** | **Phase 2** | **Phase 3** |
| Risk analysis | Effectiveness assessment | Final allocation |

Figure 12.1 The DHS model for allocating security grants to states/territories and urban areas

Threat (T) which accounts for 20% of the total risk score (R) in equation (1) is based upon threat information for multiple years. The value of T for each state/territory and urban area is reviewed and approved by a number of offices in the federal intelligence community—including the Federal Bureau of Investigation, Central Intelligence Agency, National Counter-Terrorism Center, Defense Intelligence Agency, DHS Under-Secretary for Intelligence and Analysis, and the Secretary of DHS. The threat values are then used to categorise states/territories and urban areas into four tiers—from highest relative threat with respect to other areas (Tier I) to the lowest relative threat with respect to other areas (Tier IV).

Vulnerability and consequence (V&C) make up the remaining 80% of the risk score (R) in equation (1). The indices that are summed to obtain V&C in equation (2) for a given state/territory or urban area and their percentage weights to do so (see Figure 12.2) are the:

- Population Index (40% weight), which is based on the night-time and military dependent populations, population density, number of commuters, and number of visitors.
- Economic Index (20% weight), which considers the economic value of the goods and services produced.
- National Infrastructure Index (15% weight), which considers the relative importance of a critical infrastructure or key resource asset which if attacked could trigger major national or regional impacts similar to those experienced during Hurricane Katrina or 9/11.
- National Security Index (5% weight), which considers the presence of three key national security factors: the number of military bases; the number of critical defence industrial base facilities; and the number of people traversing international borders.

Risk = Threat Index (T) + Vulnerability and Consequence Index (V&C)

T – threat index (20%)	**V&C = (P+E+I+N)**
Data: plot scenarios, investigation reports, threat information	**P – population index (40%)** **E – economic index (20%)** **I – national infrastructure index (15%)** **N – national security index (15%)**
Sources: DHS intelligence officer, wider intelligence community	**Data:** population (total and density), gross metropolitan product, percent GDP, infrastructure asset tiers, presence of military bases and international borders
	Sources: DHS intelligence officer, wider intelligence community, census, commerce and economic statistics

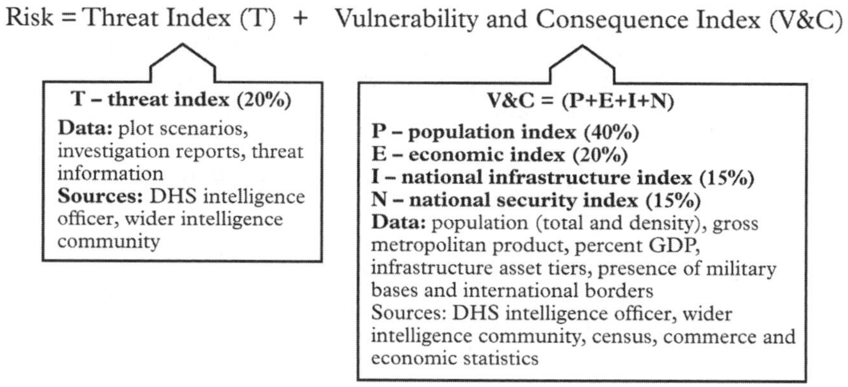

Figure 12.2 The DHS model for determining risk scores to be used in allocating security grants to states/territories and urban areas

During the effectiveness assessment phase, urban areas with risk scores higher than a stated cut-off score are eligible to submit investment proposals with accompanying justifications.[1] The DHS then uses expert peer reviewers from fire, rescue, and emergency services and law enforcement to assess the effectiveness of the investment proposals. The effectiveness is based upon (Government Accountability Office, 2007):

- How well does the result of the investment relate to its purpose?
- How well does the state/urban area organising regional partnerships implement this investment and address duplication of efforts?

1. According to the Government Accountability Office (2008, p. 7), there is a statutory per state minimum allocation of the total funds appropriated, e.g., 0.375% for fiscal year 2008, 0.75% for fiscal years 2006 and 2007.

- How rational is the investment in decreasing or mitigating risk?
- What are the potential barriers to the effective implementation of this investment?

Based upon the responses to these questions and other information, the DHS determines an effectiveness assessment score for each proposing urban area.

Those urban areas scoring high on both risk and effectiveness will be given higher priority for receiving DHS grants.

Unlike the calculation of risk scores during phase 1, the effectiveness assessment and final allocation phases are less defined and highly evolving. For example, the weights to be assigned to the risk and assessment scores for the succeeding year are not necessarily the same from the preceding years. The Secretary of Homeland Security makes the final decision on the allocation of DHS grants, but the DHS does not "provide additional details about the information presented to the Secretary to inform his decision", nor "other goals or data [that] may have factored into the allocation decision" (Government Accountability Office, 2007, p. 45).

Consider the following hypothetical example for determining the risk score indices for the three urban areas A, B and C. The values for the urban areas' Population, Economics, National Infrastructure, National Security, and Threat indices and their percentage weights are found in Table 12.1(a). The risk score indices for the three urban areas found by multiplying their indices in Table 12.1(a) by their percentage weights and then summing are found in Table 12.1(b).

Table 12.1(a) Urban areas, indices and weights

Urban area	Population score	Economic score	National infrastructure score	National Security score	Threat score
Weights	40%	20%	15%	5%	20%
A	80	55	65	75	30
B	40	40	80	30	55
C	65	45	50	50	75

Table 12.1(b) Urban areas, weighted indices and risk score indices

Urban area	Population index (P)	Economic index (E)	National infrastructure index (I)	National Security index (N)	Threat index (T)	Risk Score R=T+P+E+I+N
A	32	11	9.75	3.75	6	62.5
B	16	8	12	1.5	11	48.5
C	26	9	7.5	2.5	15	60

The risk score indices in Table 12.1(b) reveal that urban area A has the highest risk score of 62.5, followed by risk scores in urban areas C and B of 60 and

48.5, respectively. The calculation of the risk scores is the first phase of the process in the allocation of DHS security grants to the three urban areas (recall Figure 12.1). For Phase 2, the security investment proposals submitted by the three urban areas are assessed (Phase 2). Finally, DHS security grants are allocated to the three urban areas (Phase 3) based upon their calculated risk scores (Phase 1) and the assessments of their security investment proposals (Phase 2).

In Table 12.2 the 20 largest US ports with respect to cargo tonnage handled for the years 2002–2007 are found as well as the amounts of DHS security grants that they have received over these years. It is interesting to note that the Port of New York/New Jersey with less than half of the cargo tonnage handled by the Port of New Orleans received considerably more DHS security funds than the Port of New Orleans. This is likely explained by higher values for the threat, population, economic and national infrastructure indices for the New York/New Jersey urban area than for the New Orleans urban area.

Table 12.2 The 20 largest US ports in cargo tonnage handled and DHS security grants, 2002–2007

US location	Rank (tonnage)	Rank (security grant) grant)	Tonnage* (millions)	Security grant received 2002–2007** ($ millions)
New Orleans, LA	1	4	385	79
Houston-Galveston, TX	2	2	277	118
New York/New Jersey	3	1	152	119
Los Angeles-Long Beach, CA	4	3	134	114
Delaware Bay, PA/NJ/DE	5	8	112	47
Sabine-Neches River, TX	6	6	105	52
Huntington, WV	7	18	83	3
Corpus Christi, TX	8	10	77	28
Puget Sound, WA	9	5	74	66
Mobile, AL	10	16	57	7
Lake Charles, LA	11	9	52	29
Columbia-Willamette River System	12	15	49	9
Tampa, FL	13	13	49	15
Hampton Roads, VA	14	11	49	27
Bay Area, CA	15	7	46	48
Duluth-Superior, MN/WI	16	20	44	1
Valdez, AK	17	19	44	2
Baltimore, MD	18	12	44	20
Pittsburgh, PA	19	17	43	4
Freeport, TX	20	14	33	10

Sources: *US Army Corps of Engineers Waterborne Commerce Statistics Center (2005). *Waterborne Commerce of the United States (WCUS) for Waterways and Harbors (5

Parts). Washington, D.C.: US Government Printing Office; **US Department of Homeland Security (2007b). Port Security Grant Programme—Award Comparison by Port Area, www.dhs.gov/xgovt/grants/gc1178831744366.shtm, Retrieved 10 March 2008.

The authors would like to acknowledge John Joeckel of SEA Consulting for compiling Table 12.2.

4. PORT SECURITY INCIDENT CYCLE

A port security incident is an intentional port event resulting in a significant loss of life, environmental damage, economic disruption or transportation system disruption that affects the maritime transportation system. A port security incident cycle is the life cycle of a security incident at a port. There are four stages in the cycle (Pinto and Talley, 2006): (1) prevention of the incident; (2) detection of a possible incident; (3) response to the occurrence of an incident; and (4) recovery from an incident. Prevention and detection are *ex ante* efforts to secure a port from a security incident, and response and recovery are *ex post* efforts to secure a port once a security incident has occurred.

4.1 Prevention

Port security can be improved by concentrating on reducing vulnerabilities, thus diminishing the potential of threats. A terrorist attack can be engineered by the application of criminal intent. "The most prevalent threat to port security in the Western Hemisphere remains drug smuggling, followed by cargo threat, stowaways and alien smuggling, and sea robbery in the port or harbor" (US Maritime Administration, 2002, p. 7).

US ports have a layered security defence that consists of four zones: foreign port, offshore, coastal and dockside zones (Pinto and Talley, 2006). Layer 1, the foreign port zone, is the far-out-to-sea-as-possible security defence for US ports. For a vessel arriving at a US port from a foreign port for which there are security concerns, the US Coast Guard may deny entry or prescribe conditions for entry. Layer 2, the offshore zone, includes US waters inside the 200-mile exclusive economic zone but beyond the 12-mile territorial sea. Ships in this zone bound for US ports are required to provide Advanced Notice of Arrival of at least 96 hours prior to entering a US port. Layer 3, the coastal zone, includes US waters that extend inward from the 12-mile territorial sea to the docks and piers of a US port. In this zone, high-interest vessels may be escorted into port by armed Sea Marshals on board. Layer 4, the dockside zone is the port itself and the focus of US port security legislation that was discussed in section 2 of this chapter.

4.2 Detection

Procedures for detecting possible port security incidents include—inspection, tracking, monitoring and intelligence. Many US ports inspect containers for radiation. Specifically, many ports utilize Radiation Portal Monitors (RPMs) to screen departing containers and vehicles at departure gates for radiation. These RPMs can detect radiation emanating from nuclear devices, natural sources, dirty bombs, special nuclear materials and isotopes commonly used in medicine and industry.

Devices for tracking containers include electronic seals and radio frequency identification (RFID) tags attached to containers to detect tampering. However, container doors can be removed and replaced without breaking the seal and RFID seals can be reset after unauthorised openings. The contents of containers can be monitored with radiological, chemical and atmospheric sensors with global positioning capabilities. Data on container movements can also be used to detect possible security incidents.

4.3 Response and recovery

The ISPS Code and the MTSA require that US ports revise their security plans to include response actions to security incidents. Specifically, the MTSA requires a National Maritime Transportation Security Plan to deter and minimise the damage from a security incident. The US Homeland Security Presidential Directive 13 (HSPD-13) of December 2004 states that "expediting recovery and response from attacks within the maritime domain" is one of six core elements of US policy for enhancing the security of this domain (US House of Representatives Homeland Security Committee, 2008, p. 74). If a major security incident occurs at a port, the likely initial response is to shutdown the port. If the port is shutdown for a significant length of time, the economic loss to the port, e.g., the opportunity cost of cargo revenue foregone, may be greater than the damage cost from the security incident itself.

Once the Coast Guard's Captain of the Port who is responsible for the security of the port announces that the port is secure from terrorist attacks and secondary security incident impacts (e.g., explosions and fires), the security incident recovery phase begins. The recovery phase ends when the port has resumed normal operations. In the recovery phase, the FBI is a major decision maker. It may require that the port remains shut down until it finishes its investigation of the crime scene. Once finished, it will so inform the Captain of the Port.

5. PORT OPERATING OBJECTIVES AND SECURITY

Consider a container port that has an operating objective of maximising its annual container throughput subject to a minimum profit constraint, i.e.,

Maximise Q subject to Minimum Π = TR − TC   (3)

Where, Q = Port Container Throughput

  TR = Port Total Revenue

  TC = Port Total Cost

  Π = Profit

The means by which the port can vary the quality of its service are its operating options (Talley, 2006). Since these operating options are largely under the control of the port, they are also the port's choice variables for optimising the above operating objective.

A change in the port's operating options will lead to changes in the port's throughput production, total revenue, total cost and resource functions, i.e.:

  Q = Q(Port Resources)   (4)

  TR = TR(Q)

  TC = TC(Q)

Port Resources = h (Port Operating Options; TEUs Provided by Carriers to the Port)

  Where, Q(Port Resources) relates the maximum port container throughput (provided by the port) to the port's resources, e.g., dockworkers, dock cranes and yard cranes, utilized by the port; TR(Q) relates the revenue (received by the port) to the port's container throughput; TC(Q) relates the minimum total cost incurred by the port for a given container throughput; and h(Port Operating Options; TEUs Provided by Carriers to the Port) relates the minimum amounts of resources employed by the port given the levels of its operating options and the number of TEUs provided by carriers, e.g., shipping lines, truck carriers and railroads, to the port. TEUs is the number of twenty-foot equivalent units or containers that are twenty feet in length (Talley, 2006). A list of a container port's operating options appears in Table 12.3.

Table 12.3 Port operating option variables

Probability of damage to cargo in port
Probability of loss of cargo in port
Departure gate reliability—the average daily percentage of time during the year that the port's departure gate is open for vehicles
Entrance gate reliability—the average daily percent of time during the year that the port's entrance gate is open for vehicles
Berth accessibility—the average daily percent of time during the year that the port's berth adheres to authorised depth and width dimensions

Berth reliability—the average daily percent of time during the year that the port's berth is open to the berthing of ships

Channel accessibility—the average daily percent of time during the year that the port's channel adheres to authorised depth and width dimensions

Channel reliability—the average daily percent of time during the year that the port's channel is open to navigation

Probability of damage to containerships in port

Average loading service rate for containerships

Probability of loss of container ship property in port

Average unloading service rate for containerships

Probability of damage to vehicles in port

Average loading service rate for vehicles

Probability of loss of vehicle property in port

Average unloading service rate for port vehicles

Source: Talley, W.K. (2006), "An Economic Theory of the Port", in Cullinane, K. and Talley, W.K., eds. *Port Economics: Research in Transportation Economics*, 16, Amsterdam: Elsevier Ltd., 43–65.

Based upon the above discussion, the container port's operating objective (3) can be rewritten as follows:

Maximise Q subject to (5)

Minimum Π = TR − TC

$Q = Q$(Port Resources)

$TR = TR(Q)$

$TC = TC(Q)$

Port Resources = h (Port Operating Options; TEUs Provided by Carriers to the Port)

Now assume that the port incorporates port security into its operations. The maximum level of security that a container port can provide is a function of its level of security resources, i.e., its port security production function may be expressed as:

Port Security = PS(Port Security Resources) (6)

The port's security resource function may be expressed as:

Port Security Resources = hs (Port Operating Options; (7) TEUs Provided by Carriers to the Port)

This resource function relates the minimum amounts of security resources to be employed by the port given the levels of its operating options and the number of TEUs provided to the port by carriers.

If port security, for example, includes conducting radiation inspections on all import containers, the inspection activity will require the use of such port security resources as security personnel and equipment. Also, changes in port operating options can affect the port's level of security, negatively or positively. For example, an increase in the operating option, probability of loss of cargo in port, with respect to a security incident has a negative effect on port security, while a decrease has a positive effect on port security.

Subsequent to the terrorist attacks of 11 September 2001, port security regulations by government and international agencies require that ports utilize certain security resources, e.g., the ISPS Code requires that certain equipment be in place at a port in order for the port to comply with the Code. A resource function with respect to ISPS Code Port Security Resources may be expressed as:

$$\text{ISPS Code Port Security Resources} = \text{hisps (Port Operating Options;} \quad (8)$$
$$\text{TEUs Provided by Carriers}$$
$$\text{to the Port)}$$

For other port security regulations, their required security resources may be expressed as similar functions.

The container port's operating objective (5) after incorporating the above port security functions with some adaptations may be expressed as:

Maximise Q subject to   (9)

Minimum $\Pi = \text{TR} - \text{TC}$

$\qquad Q = Q \text{ (Port Resources)}$

$\qquad \text{TR} = \text{TR}(Q)$

$\qquad \text{TC} = \text{TC'}(Q, \text{Port Security})$

Port Resources = h (Port Operating Options; TEUs Provided by
$\qquad$ Carriers to the Port)

Port Security = PS' (Non-ISPS Code Port Security Resources,
$\qquad$ ISPS Code Port Security Resources)

Non-ISPS Code Port Security Resources = hs' (Port Operating
$\qquad$ Options; TEUs Provided
$\qquad$ by Carriers to the Port)

ISPS Code Port Security Resources = hisps (Port Operating Options;
$\qquad$ TEUs Provided by Carriers to the
$\qquad$ Port)

Note that port security resources are either described as Non-ISPA Code or

ISPS Code port security resources and the port security production function is a function of the amounts of both types of port security resources.

Assuming that the provision of port security has a negative impact on a port's throughput, throughput will be highest when no security activities are conducted and lowest when security is extremely tight. In between these two extreme levels of port security, a negative correlation will exist between port throughput and security levels, i.e., higher the security level, less the throughput. Alternatively, the existence of a securitised port might be a competitive advantage for the port and thus attract more cargo than its competitors.

6. PORT DISRUPTIONS FROM SECURITY BREACHES

Disruptions in port throughput can arise not only from security breaches that result in port security incidents, but also from detection of security breaches that do not result in port security incidents. There are three possible scenarios involving a security breach at a port for which disruptions in the port's throughput will occur:

- Detection of a security breach, but no security incident occurs, a false positive (FP).
- Detection of a security breach, and a security incident occurs, a true positive (TP).
- No detection of a security breach, but a security incident occurs, a false negative (FN).

It could also happen that there is no detection of a security breach, but no security incident occurs. However, in this case, there will be no disruption to the port's throughput.

The false-positive (FP) security breach is expected to be the most common of the above three scenarios of security-breach disruptions at a port. The detection of a security breach (even though there is no security incident) will still result in disruptions to the port's throughput from heightened security activity at the port. For example, an increase in the port's inspection of containers may take place, thereby negatively affecting the unloading/loading service rates of containerships and inland vehicles.

The true-positive (TP) security breach is expected to be more disruptive to the port's throughput given that a security incident has occurred than the FP security breach. The false-negative (FN) security breach is expected to be the worst case scenario, since the port has no time to prepare for the security incident prior to its happening. Although prevention and detection have failed, the response and recovery stages of the port's security incident cycle, however, may be able to limit the security incident's disruptions to the port.

The impact of the above security breach disruptions on a port's productivity (or throughput) over time is shown in Figure 12.3. Over time, the port will seek to minimise the total area under the normal operation productivity (dashed) line by either a minimal drop in productivity and/or a minimal time to return back to normal operations. Specifically, the port operator will change the values of its operating options in magnitude and/or directionally in order to minimise port losses in productivity over time.

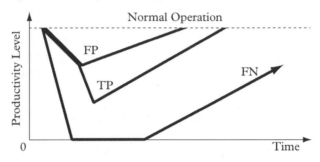

Figure 12.3 Port productivity and security breach disruptions

The impact of changes in the port's operating options on its security and operating objectives may be investigated with the aid of a simulation model. An example of such a simulation model is found in Rabadi et al. (2007), where knowledge of port facilities and operation with a simulation model are used to investigate the impact of various port security disruptions on the productivity of a container port.

7. SUMMARY

In this chapter, US port security legislation and programmes were discussed. The three major US maritime cargo security initiatives are—two voluntary security programmes and the 24-Hour Advance Manifest Rule (24-hour rule). The voluntary programmes include the Container Security Initiative (CSI) and the Customs-Trade Partnership Against Terrorism (C-TPAT) pro-grammes. The Security and Accountability for Every (SAFE) Port Act of 2006 requires the US Department of Homeland Security (DHS) to establish at least three pilot overseas scanning programmes to test the feasibility of 100% domestic screening of containerised cargo and 100% scanning of high-risk containerised cargo destined for US ports. The US Bureau of Customs and Border Protection (CBP) has established the "10 plus 2" Initiative for Con-tainerized Cargo programme that seeks data on US imported containerised cargo (prior to its loading on ships at foreign ports) for 10 additional variables and information on ship stowage plans and container status messages from shipping lines.

Critical to securing US ports effectively is the disbursement of federal port security grants among these ports. The DHS allocates these security grants based upon risk criteria. Specifically, risks to US states, territories, and urban areas are based on threat, vulnerability, and consequence indices. A port security incident cycle is the life cycle of a security incident at a port. There are four stages in the cycle: (1) prevention of the incident; (2) detection of a possible incident; (3) response to the occurrence of an incident; and (4) recovery from an incident. Assuming that the provision of port security has a negative impact on a port's throughput, throughput will be highest when no security activities are conducted and lowest when security is extremely tight. Disruptions in port throughput can arise not only from security breaches that result in port security incidents, but also from detection of security breaches that do not result in port security incidents.

CHAPTER 13

EU PORT AND SHIPPING SECURITY

Athanasios A. Pallis and George K. Vaggelas

1. INTRODUCTION

In the beginning of the twenty-first century the formation of transport policies at almost every international, peripheral, national and local level focused on the competitiveness and the effectiveness of transport systems and modes. It was only sporadically that security-related initiatives (i.e., measures intending to minimise the possibility of successful unlawful acts against transport means and nodes) were part of the policy agendas. A series of events, foremost the 11 September attacks in New York, fostered an increasing awareness on security issues. Incidents such as the attacks to the Madrid commuter trains (2004) and the London public transport system (2005) increased public unease. Security awareness expanded and policy transport regimes developed, aiming to minimise relevant risks in every transport system and mode and supply-chain operations.

Maritime transport, in particular container terminals, is among the transport sectors that have drawn most of the attention. This is not least because the transportation of containers is characterised by multiple actors and complex interactions, whereas international transport is subject to multiple legal frameworks. Modern terminals are industrial complexes with high economic values and areas where international trade takes place. Vessels and unitised (containerised) cargoes might be used as weapons, or be used to carry weapons. A maritime-related security incident might not only cause human casualties, but also produce an economic shock by interrupting trade and resulting in an economic loss for the entire society (Johnston, 2004). For example, the incident involving *M/V Limburg* (October 2002) resulted in a short-term collapse of shipping businesses in Aden, a tripling of war risk premiums levied on vessels calling at Aden, the Yemeni economy losing an estimated \$3.8 million in port revenues per month, and an increase in crude oil price by \$0.48 per barrel (Greenberg et al., 2006).

Due to the characteristics of the maritime transport system, however, security enhancement cannot be addressed by minimising the risk in isolated port facilities only. The extensive use of combined transport results in the integration of ports in supply-chains. As a result, any security breach at any transport node or/and link might jeopardise the security of the entire chain (Lee & Wang, 2005). Moreover, the consequent spatial and functional regionalisation of ports (Notteboom & Rodrigue, 2005) expands the port-related hinterland and requires an appropriate security policy that covers a broader geographical area. Hinterland expansion also increases the number of stakeholders involved. Security policies ought to recognise the specialised needs of the different participants in this complex trans(port) system (cf. Brooks & Button, 2007). The costs for securing transportation increase, along with the number of interactions between stakeholders. All these demand an holistic approach which takes into account the total of the system, i.e. actors, facilities, broader entities like ports, and the entire supply-chains.

International organisations have strived to develop initiatives that respond to this need. The major ones are the ISPS Code, as endorsed by the IMO, and the Code of Practice on Security in Ports, as collectively agreed by the IMO and International Labor Organization (ILO) in 2003. Other major policies are the new port-related ISO standards, like the ISO 20858 and the ISO 28000 (ISO, 2004; 2005), the ILO's (2003) Revised Seafarer's Identity Documents and the 2004 World Customs Organization's (WCO, 2004) Resolution on security and facilitation measures concerning the international trade supply chain. These measures are associated with different degrees of enforceability and target multiple security goals at different parts of the supply chain.

The adoption of international rules has been followed by regional policy regimes. The US led this trend by endorsing national-level initiatives with a global impact. The US was also among those advocating the need for endorsing similar measures within the international maritime rule-making organisations, and exercised its capacity to influence these organisations to move towards this direction. The EU, as well as other regions (i.e. Asia) and/or countries of the world followed this policy approach. Progressively, however, European policymakers and stakeholders became uneasy with the US initiatives and focused on a more flexible approach.

This chapter provides a comparative assessment of the EU and US maritime and port security policies, the initiatives under discussion, the stakeholders' approaches vis-à-vis the potential policies and the advocacy of a distinctive EU security policy regime. It also compares the relevant schemes of policy-making and implementation processes that are in place on both sides of the Atlantic. The analysis indicates the progressive divergence of attitudes and concludes on the reasons that motivate the search for a distinctive European approach in addressing the different security issues.

2. THE US APPROACH

Following the 11 September attacks, the US government moved decisively towards filling what was assessed to be, a "security policy gap" and developed policies that cover an extensive range of activities throughout the transport system. In the case of maritime transport, these policies focus mainly on the transportation of containers, including vessels, containers, terminals and facilities hosting containers, without, however, ignoring cargoes per se and passengers. Initially, the US government adopted measures largely supplementary to the ISPS Code (which is based on risk assessment), as had been agreed within the IMO and the emphasis was on the most extended application of the Code possible. Gradually, and in response to its own analysis of the vulnerabilities of the system, the US regime expanded well beyond the scope of the IMO initiatives.

Chronologically, the first relevant US security policy was the so-called 96-hour rule. A few weeks after the 11 September attacks, the US developed a rule which requires that every vessel intending to enter the US territorial waters sends an advanced notice of arrival to the US Coast Guard (USCG) 96 hours prior to her arrival. The notice includes detailed information on the crew, the passengers or/and the cargo, and the vessel herself. The rule aims at minimising the security risk at the final stage of the supply chain, i.e., before the vessel arrives at the US. It does not, however, safeguard the transportation process from the cargo/passenger origin to the loading port. In its early implementation days this was thought to be a temporary reaction to the events that had taken place. It turned to a permanent regime enforced by the USCG, which comes under the Department of Homeland Security (DHS).

This rule was followed by the Coast Guard and Maritime Transportation Security Act (MTSA; adopted November 2002). This is the US equivalent to the ISPS Code. The Act, which was developed by the DHS and the Maritime Administration (MARAD), and is enforced by the USCG, requests the development of a security plan by all the US ports and US flagged vessels as well as the implementation of all the requirements of the ISPS Code. The ISPS Code applies not only to the international trade to and from the US, as the IMO decision requests, but it also covers the transactions between those participating in intra-US trade as well. This policy concentrates mainly on the sea part of the supply chain and on the interaction points between the vessels and the land transport modes, i.e. between the vessels and port areas.

Another major US initiative is the so-called 24-hour rule. Adopted in 2002 (in force since February 2003) this rule obliges all ocean carriers or non-vessel operating common carriers (NVOCC) departing from a foreign port to reach the US, to send cargo manifest information to the US Customs and Border Protection (CBP) 24 hours before the loading of the cargo onto the vessel heading directly to a US port. The enforcement of the 24-hour rule is a responsibility of the CBP which operates under the DHS. This is a stricter version of the 96-hour rule, as it prohibits high risk cargoes from being loaded onto the vessel, rather than targeting the identification of high risk cargoes a few hours before a vessel enters the US territorial waters.

The 24-hour rule is related to the Container Security Initiative (CSI) that was also adopted in 2002 (in force since February 2003). CSI focuses explicitly on security gaps in port facilities and has a major global impact as it aims to increase the security of the US trade by a process that broadens the US borders far away from the actual ones. This target is fulfilled by inspection controls in containers which bound to US at foreign ports. These inspections are carried out by assigned personnel of the CBP that is the responsible agent for the CSI application in co-operation with the custom authorities of the foreign countries. The implementation is based on a risk management approach, as the US officials inspect only the high risk containers based on intelligence. It is also implemented on a reciprocal basis so that custom personnel from foreign countries can also perform security controls in the US ports and in containers bounding to their country (CBP, 2007). Until now, 58 foreign ports (13 ports in the Americas, 23 in Europe, 20 in Asia and the Middle East and 2 in Africa) that account for 85% of the container traffic bound for the USA participate in the CSI.[1] Notably, the importance of the CSI on the US-EU trade impelled the two trade partners to sign a bilateral agreement (CEU, 2004) which defines a joint customs co-operation framework. The long-term target is to progressively include all foreign ports which load containers to be transported to the US.

The Security and Accountability For Every (SAFE) Port Act (endorsed in 2006; implemented since August 2007; fully in force in 2012) is part of the broader framework defined by the MTSA and, as described in following sections, one of the most controversial US policy developments. This act requires the DHS to develop operational standards for scanning systems to be used in order to conduct scanning for nuclear and radiological materials in all the containers (100%) departing from foreign ports with destination to the US. This programme differs from the CSI and the C-TPAT (Customs-Trade Partnership Against Terrorism, described in following paragraphs), as scanning should take place regardless of the prior assessed risk of each container (GAO, 2007a). If a container does not pass through this scanning process it is not allowed to be transported to the US. Another major difference between this rule and the CSI is that the latter works on a reciprocal base, while the former is a unilateral policy that is not based on the co-operation between US and other countries.

The Transportation Worker Identification Credential (TWIC) further broadens the MTSA and the SAFE Port Act. This proposal, quite sensitive in terms of data demanded, requires that every trans(port) worker who has access to security sensitive areas of vessels and port facilities should provide biometric information (such as fingerprints) to the US government. An estimated one million individuals are required to obtain a TWIC and this includes Coast Guard-credentialled merchant mariners, port facility employees, long-shoremen, truck drivers, and others requiring unescorted access to secure areas of maritime facilities and vessels regulated by the MTSA. Facility and vessel owners/operators are required to inform employees of their responsibility to possess a TWIC and what parts of the facility and vessel will require a TWIC for unescorted access. The scope is to enhance security of port areas by

1. Source: www.dhs.gov. Accessed: June 2008.

requiring security threat assessments of persons and by improved access-control measures in order to prevent those who may pose a security threat from gaining unescorted access to secure areas of ports. Even though there are no regulatory requirements pertaining to the use of TWIC readers yet, TWIC enrolment began in October 2007 and has been phased in at both small and large ports over the course of 2008.

All these policies aim to avert the entry of high risk and dangerous cargoes to the US and they do so via inspections taking place either in US or foreign ports. With ports, however, being only an "embedded" (Robinson, 2002) part of the supply chains, policies focusing on the port-related leg of transportation have to be implemented in conjunction with initiatives aiming to secure the rest of the transport modes and nodes of the supply chain. On the one hand, the intention of the US government has been for some of the above initiatives to expand progressively towards that direction. For example, the application of TWIC in ports constitutes a pretesting of its effectiveness and its capability to ensure labour securitisation. This capability would provide the background for the potential application of the rule in cases of employees working in other parts of the supply chain as well. On the other hand, there are some additional rules aiming precisely to secure the entire supply chain.

In a direct response to the 11 September events, the US Customs Service, renamed CBP, challenged the trade community to partner with it in order to design a new approach to enhance supply-chain security while speeding the flow of compliant cargo and conveyances. The result is the voluntary C-TPAT adopted in 2002. The scope of the C-TPAT is to secure the landside part of the supply chain via a risk management approach. In particular, the C-TPAT calls US exporters and importers to develop security requirements on themselves and their partners. Those participants that develop a well-defined security framework receive the Green Lane award and experience fewer customs inspections. In the absence of an international rule aiming to enhance the security level of the landside part of the transport chain, the C-TPAT has been considered by some as the base for a future international initiative (OECD, 2004).

A number of other US programmes deal with specific maritime issues and situations as well. The National Infrastructure Protection Plan (NIPP) of 2006 is the most significant one. The NIPP aims at securing every public or private infrastructure in the US that is assessed as crucial. It does so by providing sectoral plans for a coordinated approach by all, public and private, actors involved in each sector. This plan is used to establish national priorities, goals, and requirements for infrastructure protection so that funding and resources are effectively applied and every state is leading, integrating and co-ordinating the security of its critical infrastructures in the most effective manner. The programme explicitly mentions 17 crucial infrastructures and key resources, with transportation systems being one of them. Once more, this is an initiative based on a risk-assessment management strategy, including the setting and prioritising of security goals and an assessment of risks on critical (transportation) assets, systems, networks, and functions. Other illustrative examples of relevant programmes are the pilot project Operation Safe Commerce (developed by the Transportation Security Administration (TSA) and the CBP), and Megaport (developed by the Department of Energy). The former intends to verify the contents of containers at the port of loading, ensure the physical integrity of containers in transit, and track their movement through the transport chain from the origin to the final destination (Frittelli, 2005). The latter facilitates, since 2003, the scanning of containers in foreign ports for radioactive materials. For this reason, radiation detection equipment has been placed in some foreign ports[2] as well as in US border crossings (rail crossings, vehicle crossing, and small seaports). Based on the experience of the Megaport and the CSI programmes, the Department of Energy and CBP launched the Secure Freight Initiative (SFI). Aiming to advance the feasibility of the 100% scanning procedure, this initiative resulted in the installation of relevant equipment in six foreign ports.[3] This pilot implementation will report by the end of 2008 and, if a success, it will be expanded to every CSI port.

The primary goal of the US approach is to safeguard the entire supply chain. The established regime has not, however, been able to guarantee a significantly higher security level for all the relevant flows. Cargo, labour, services and information flows remain in certain respects exposed to the same security risks as before.[4] Issues of security during the collection and the distribution of cargoes in the hinterland, or those related to the several services offered during the landside part of transportation have still to be addressed as the C-TPAT programme works on a voluntary basis only. The promise that by securing cargoes prior to their arrival at the US ports is a means to secure all the different phases of the transportation chain is rather doubtful. Similarly, whereas the TWIC focuses on the employees in the port industry, it is the extension of its application to other industrial and transport employees that would enhance security. Yet, this development would result in further demands for sharing sensitive personal data and stakeholders' reactions. Finally, the flow of information is only partially secured by the 24-hour and the 96-hour rules, as these rules are not relevant during inland transport operations. Whereas the various initiatives have resulted in an overregulated policy framework, the achievement of a satisfactory security level at every part of the supply chain remains questionable.

2. The list of foreign ports that participate in the Megaport programme include the ports of Algeciras, Bahamas, Colombo, Rotterdam, Singapore and Piraeus.

3. Port Qasim (Pakistan), Puerto Cortes (Honduras) and Southampton (UK) deploying scanning equipment to capture data on all containers bound to USA. Port Salalah (Oman), Port of Singapore and Busan—Gamman terminal (South Korea) have an initial limited deployment in order to learn how to integrate the new technology with port operations and commerce flow. Data from DHS: www.dhs.gov/xprevprot/programmes/gc_1166037389664.shtm. Accessed: 10 July 2008.

4. Flows of payments and relevant economic transactions are also involved; they are not though crucial elements within the context under discussion.

3. THE EUROPEAN PATH TOWARDS MARITIME SECURITY

The EU reacted to the new "securitised" trans(port) environment by formatting its own legislative framework. Reversing a period of inertia in the specific policy sub-field (cf. Power, 1992; Pallis, 2002) the EU developed a rather comprehensive regional regulatory framework in order to secure the about 9,500 flagged vessels (over 500 gt), 4,300 maritime companies, 1,250 ports and over 4,100 port facilities that exist in the 27 EU member states (Dupont, 2007). This has been done via an evolutionary process reflecting the concept that the realities of the market make a big-bang approach unrealistic.

Coincidentally, the European Commission published a White Paper detailing the EU transport policy to 2010 (CEU, 2001) only one day after the events of 9/11. This report had a broad reference on the security of passengers onboard cruise vessels and ferries, as well as on the transportation of nuclear goods. Those concerns that had led to these general observations were fuelled by the combination of an increasing global awareness regarding security, and of an assessed need to be in line with relevant initiatives endorsed by the international fora or developed by one of the region's geopolitical allies and trading partner, the US. The latter acted as the locomotive for such developments, with researchers observing that the first ever prepared EU security legislations relied primarily on (existing or already published) rules that had been developed elsewhere (Schilk et al., 2007).

In fact, the first endorsed relevant EU policy was one having a reference to international rule-making. Regulation 725/2004 (in force since 2004) targets the enhancement of ship and port facilities security, via the enforcement of the major IMO relevant decision, which is the ISPS Code.[5] By transforming the latter to EU legislation, the Regulation demands that ship security plans (SSPs) and port facility security plans (PFSPs) specify a range of security measures to be maintained by ships and port facilities respectively. Ports have to identify restricted areas and monitor them in order to prevent unauthorised access. They also have to implement measures to prevent weapons, dangerous substances and devices being taken onto ships or into port facilities. Each of the 27 EU member states is responsible for enforcing this policy in its national territory and, in particular, the national administration identifies and evaluates the transport assets and infrastructures that are important to protect and develop practices that minimise risks of unlawful acts. The primary concern of this process is to avoid any human casualties. The secondary concern is to figure out how the port facility, structure, or installation can rapidly re-establish a normal functioning following the threat or occurrence of a security incident. Member states might also determine security measures for the vessels and ports that are not covered by the specific regulation.

5. Regulation 725/2004, of 31 March 2004, on enhancing ship and port facility security, OJ L. 129/6, 29 April 2004.

Via this rule, the EU introduced stricter security measures than those of the respective IMO decision. While the ISPS Code covers ships engaged in international voyages and those ports that accommodate them, the EU rule includes provisions that extend these measures to the ships engaged in national voyages within the EU, as well as to the related port facilities that serve them. The application of the Regulation goes beyond the international extra-EU trade to cover intra-EU (between EU member states) trade and transport as well. It has also expanded the policy agenda, by extending the application of the rule to those ports that might only occasionally serve international transport (see Thai & Grewal, 2007). This expanded application has been deemed as necessary in order to minimise risks in ports serving vessels engaged in domestic voyages.

Following the adoption of a policy dealing only with the port area where an interaction between the port and maritime carriers takes place, the EU moved towards an integrated security framework for the European port industry. It did so by endorsing Directive 65/2005 (in force since June 2007) that applies to every port in which Regulation 725/2004 applies and enacts security practices in the port area that is not covered by the latter Regulation.[6] This non-"ship/port interface" port area is designated by the member states. The Directive designates three security levels, namely normal, heightened and exceptional, respectively. These levels reflect differences in the risk profile of different sub-areas in the port and demand different measures by the key actors. Such measures are the creation of a port security plan that contains the necessary procedures and actions to be undertaken in the event of a security incident, and the designation of a port security officer. The enforcement of the directive is a responsibility of the port authority, but the monitoring of the compliance (for all ports in an EU member state territory) is the responsibility of a national lever port security authority. The port security officer acts as the contact person between the port authority and the port security authority. The whole process is periodically under review, while member states ensure the presence of a focal point for port security as the contact point between them and the European Commission.

The implementation of the Directive is well underway with reported difficulties such as the additional work and thus costs for port authorities. These difficulties are mainly observed in the case of ports which have no clear natural borders. Especially for those ports which are characterised by a far-reaching integration of maritime and/or more industrial activities and a functional regionalisation that expands well beyond national borders (a phenomenon extensively observed in North Europe), the implementation of the Directive seems to cause a lot of additional work. The same is true in the case of those ports which are stretched out over a wide area and the relevant maritime cluster is associated with a mixture of broader port-related activities. Due to

---

6. Directive 2005/65, of 26 October, on enhancing port security, OJ L. 310/28, 25 November 2005.

these problems, European port authorities argue that this policy initiative entails an overload of assessments whilst additional security measures might seem rather abundant.

These two rules are part of the EU move to minimise security risks throughout the entire transport chain. A first step towards this direction was the endorsement of a revised Community Customs Code, to be fully in force in 2009. The relevant Regulation 648/2005 sets up a common EU secure custom system based on the electronic exchange of advance information between traders and customs authorities on all goods entering or leaving the EU.[7] The most important provision of this measure is the introduction of the Authorised Economic Operator (AEO) status, which is a core element of the EU strategy. Any transport operator can enjoy the AEO status when it fulfils four interrelated criteria:

- an appropriate record of compliance with customs requirements;
- a satisfactory system of managing commercial records;
- proven financial solvency (where appropriate); and
- appropriate security and safety standards (where applicable).

The incentive for the operator to reach this status is the benefit of experiencing fewer custom controls. This concept has been operational since the beginning of 2008 and has reportedly generated a substantial interest.[8] As the C-TPAT, the Community Customs Code and the AEO status are voluntary concepts, simultaneously, they demand a significant amount of investment and, for this reason, many, mostly small, operators continue to provide their services without complying with the AEO prerequisite measures.

In 2004 the European Council asked the European Commission to prepare an overall strategy to protect critical infrastructure. In response, the Commission put forward the notion of a European Programme for Critical Infrastructure Protection (EPCIP) and a Critical Infrastructure Warning Information Network (CIWIN).[9] Two years later, the Commission proposed a Directive that provides the main foundations for an EPCIP (CEU, 2006a) and a communication that contains non-binding measures designed to facilitate its implementation (CEU, 2006b). The scope is to protect those European infrastructures (i.e., physical resources, services, information technology facilities, networks and infrastructure assets or parts thereof) which if disrupted, or destroyed, would have a serious impact on socially critical functions (including the supply chain, health, safety, security, economic or social well-being) of two or more member states, or a single member state if the critical infrastructure is located in another member state (DG-TREN, 2006). Such critical infrastructures are identified in 11 different sectors with one of them

7. Regulation 648/2005, of 13 April 2005, amending Council Regulation 2913/92 establishing the Community Customs Code. OJ L 117, 13–19, 4 November 2005.

8. *Lloyd's List*, "EU inundated by early rush for the AEO status", by J. Stares, 19 February 2008.

9. For a definition of the Critical Infrastructure see DG-TREN (2006).

being the transport sector.[10] Those involved in the operation of these infrastructures are expected to develop a security plan, describing the security measures that have been taken and a relevant action plan.

This was a turning point regarding port infrastructures and the broader regime of EU (general or sectoral) security-related measures, as port infrastructures were outright excluded from the programme. The rationale of this exclusion is that in the case of European ports, relevant issues are covered by the Directive 65/2005 that focuses explicitly on port security. The heterogeneity of the structural and operational conditions in different member states was a key issue for this decision. The reason is that a common framework can only be effective if there is a uniform approach of determining critical infrastructure. In the absence of identical traditions, the EPCIP would have a distorting effect on the market whenever member states would define different protection regimes for identical infrastructure. This decision was also taken in the light of the strong reaction by European port authorities (see: ESPO, 2006a) and other stakeholders, who emphasised the potential of unnecessary financial burden and the formation of an overregulated market.

It has to be noted, however, that the adoption of this, still pending, proposal would result in the establishment of a national critical infrastructure protection authority, which would monitor the implementation of an action plan in each EU member-state, the mobilisation of expert groups at EU level, an information-sharing process, and finally a broader discussion towards the identification and analysis of interdependencies of the various European transport (and other) infrastructures. Taking into account that past decisions to exclude ports from transport-related measures were reversed due to the complementarities of transport modes (see the case of the trans-European networks in: Chlomoudis & Pallis, 2002), this situation might not be seen as irreversible.

Along with the initiatives that explicitly address maritime transportation, the EU moved towards measures to secure the landside part of transport chains. The Commission has proposed a regulation on enhancing supply chain security via the introduction of the secure operator status (CEU, 2006c). The suggested pattern is not a new one: operators fulfilling specific security requirements would be awarded a quality status and thus experience less security controls within the EU member states. This was the first EU attempt to secure the landside part of transport chains through a regulation solely dedicated to this part. As some port areas are embedded in supply chains and several operators interact within these areas, the endorsement of the regulation would undoubtedly affect ports as well; especially as it would imply that every individual business actor in the European transport market, including shippers, transportation companies, forwarders, and value-added operations (i.e., warehouse, storage facility, inland terminal etc.) would have

10. The other 10 identified sectors are: energy, nuclear industry, information and communication technologies, water, food, health, financial, chemical industry, space, and research facilities.

to fulfil certain security management requirements. These requirements would include physical security, access controls, procedural security, personnel security, documentation procedures, information security and education and training awareness.

The essence of the proposed regulation produced reactions by various stakeholders (cf. IRU, 2006). ESPO (2006b), the interest group representing all the European port authorities, welcomed the widening of the scope of EU security measures to all forms of transport but argued for the reduction of security checks along with clarity on how existing security legislation is applicable. ESPO stressed the importance of an appropriate minimum security standard applicable to all operators in the supply chain rather than a voluntary scheme which does not force weaker parts of the chain to participate. Besides, port authorities and other stakeholders advocated that with the relevant standards expanded, the application of the AEO security status for both international and intra-EU trade could, and should, offer sufficient possibilities for application to all the parts of the supply chains developed in the internal European market.

With the European transport sector stressing the substantial implementation costs and the potential of further negative effects upon their businesses, and advocating the need to avoid developing an overregulated transport market that would cripple small businesses while bringing only minor security benefits (Schilk et al., 2007), the EU decided to put the proposed regulation on hold. In particular, the Commission decided to re-evaluate the need for further action based on the experience of the AEO concept implementation and the assessment of whether this concept provides sufficient tools to increase the protection of the intra-EU transport supply chain against unlawful acts.

4. IS THERE A EUROPEAN APPROACH?

4.1 The initial "following the same path" approach

A comparison of the content and the main provisions of the reviewed US and EU security-related transport initiatives would suggest that in the early days decision-makers endorsed similar strategies. The fact that the EU measures were initiated and adopted at a more recent chronological point leads to the conclusion that in the policy field of security the EU followed the path designed by its geopolitical ally and trading partner.

The first target for both the US and the EU was to implement the international decisions in the strictest way possible. Having consent to, or even pioneering, the endorsement of the ISPS Code in the IMO, both the US and the EU adjusted the respective regional policy regimes in order to transform the Code to a mandatory national regulation framework. The fact that the US had adopted MTSA 16 months before the EU adopted a relevant regulation, might not be a clear sign of the US leadership and be attributed to the presence of a more complex European policy-making process. Yet, this sign is further enhanced by the fact that both of them expanded this international rule implementation in the same way, i.e., in coastal trade. Similar trans-Atlantic strategies are also identified when comparing the US C-TPAT and the EU Revised Customs Code which was launched two years later. As Table 13.1 illustrates, both policies aim at securing the landside of the transport chain, via a rewarding voluntary scheme that provide similar benefits to the qualified operators.

Table 13.1 Comparing the US C-TPAT and the EU revised customs code

	C-TPAT	*Revised Customs Code*
Launched	April 2003	April 2005
Aim	Securing the landside leg of the transport chain	Securing the landside leg of the transport chain
Applies to	US exporters, importers and their partners	Land transport operators
Scheme	Voluntary	Voluntary
Rewarding Operators	Green Lane Award	Authorised Economic Operator (AEO) Status
Requirements	Minimum security criteria based on the nature of the transport operation (air/sea/rail/highway/long haul carrier, foreign manufacturer, custom broker, Port Authorities)	(a) Appropriate record of compliance (b) System of managing commercial records (c) Financial solvency (d) Security and safety standards
Benefits	Fewer custom controls	Fewer custom controls

The early adopted policies dealing explicitly with port security provide further strategy similarities, as well as indications of a US leadership. The US, moved first via an initiative with a global effect, i.e., the CSI, and the EU followed in various ways. In particular, it signed a bilateral agreement with the US and two and a half years later it endorsed its first policy with the scope to enhance port security beyond the ISPS Code and Regulation 65/2005 provisions. On the one hand, this move was to a certain extent the European reaction to the respective US initiatives. On the other hand, the fact that this EU regulation does not have many common provisions with the US policies provided a first hint of an emerging EU differentiation.

In the same vein, the publication and endorsement of the NIPP was followed by the EPCIP proposal with the two rules sharing many common features. Both initiatives concentrate on the protection of infrastructures of vital importance in a wide variety of economic sectors putting the transport sector central stage. However, while the US initiative has been in place since June 2006, decisions regarding the EU initiative have been halted due to the presence of several stakeholders' reactions (see Pallis & Vaggelas, 2007). Irrespective of whether this halt is temporary or not, this is another indication of the fact that the relevant domestic scenes and policymakers' capacities to move towards the same direction are rather different on each side of the Atlantic.

4.2 Towards a distinctive approach

In recent times there have been clear signs that the EU approach has shifted towards a different path. Whereas in the US additional rule making in order to further enhance maritime transport and supply chain security is considered essential, policymakers and several stakeholders in Europe indicate their discontent with the introduction of further rules.

While the US has applied the TWIC programme, the European Commission decided to react by initiating a study on port-access regimes and a consultation process that examined the feasibility and the potential of introducing identification cards schemes in European ports. Stakeholders continue to object to the practical side of the rule. This is not least because neither the definitions of the "port" and the "port area" are easy, nor all ports are fence-proofed defined. Moreover, in the European case the general public attitude as regards the existing, or perceived, security policy gaps seems to be a minor issue, whereas cost implications of the rule are assessed to be substantial. Sceptical views regarding such a European scheme emerge from the fact that the EU port policy agenda considers the strengthening of the relationship between cities and their ports as a major issue. Promoting the image of European ports and by providing greater public access to them are subjects that have become a major concern of ports themselves, maritime European regions and member states. With the European Commission's recent European port policy review explicitly seeking ways to improve the image of ports and their integration with "their" cities (CEU, 2007), promoting access control issues, including requirements for pass surveillance systems, or the handling of information by the competent authority and/or the port/port facility, have frequently been considered as developments that further distance the port from its city. All these factors explain why the EU remains reluctant to adopt a regulation on access of personnel to sensitive security areas of ports and vessels.

Due to the reactions of many trans(port) stakeholders, the proposed EPCIP proposal which simply tries to establish a framework similar to that of the respective voluntary US C-TPAT, concluded in a stalemate. Controversies also resulted in the exclusion of ports from the draft rule. Stakeholders, including port authorities and freight forwards (see ESPO, 2006b; CLECAT, 2006), suggested that the proposed regulation corresponds neither to the peculiar characteristics of the European port market nor to the needs of the landside part of European supply-chains. Many transport companies in the EU are small and medium enterprises, thus the implementation costs of the

EPCIP would deteriorate their competitiveness and force many of them to exit the market.

The most recent indication of a distinctive EU approach is the explicit criticism of the SAFE Port Act as expressed by stakeholders, including port authorities (ESPO, 2007), forwarders (CLECAT, 2006), shipowners, member states (i.e., Belgium, France, Germany, Greece, Italy, Spain, the Netherlands and the UK) and the European Commission. SAFE requires every foreign port with US-bound containers to install the appropriate scanning equipment. A key criticism relates to the problems of the application, in particular the need for ports to separate US-bound containers in order to go through the scanning procedures. This impels extra surface areas in many port sections, such as terminals, storage areas etc., extra personnel, and investments in new scanning equipment. Other application-related criticism refers to the lack of scanning effectiveness or guarantees in order to handle the 100% container scanning. According to the European port authorities the major problem of SAFE is that this rule is not founded on a risk-based approach as any security-related policy should be.

The vital question seems to be the allocation of the implementation costs, i.e., whether this should be assumed by governments, port authorities, operators, or users. Estimations suggest that the cost of the scanning equipment will exceed $100 million for every European port.[11] There are already concerns that this will eventually impose an undesirable regulatory barrier to entry (De Langen and Pallis, 2007) in the market, and the biggest ports will be the only ones that could bear the relevant costs and thus the ones to dominate container trade with the US. Foremost, with this rule being a unilateral one, US producers and exporters whose cargoes are not subject to a scanning process, gain a significant cost advantage vis-à-vis their non-US located competitors. With estimates that the rule affects the $500 billion US commerce and about 600 foreign ports (WSC, 2007), a number of reactions and sceptical views regarding the SAFE Port Act are expressed by stakeholders and decision-makers in several countries worldwide (i.e., China, Singapore, and Canada)[12] and even within the US (see GAO, 2007b).

These cost-related concerns as well as questions regarding the necessity of a reciprocal application of the rule are shared by policymakers in Europe.[13] The expectation of a negative impact on the EU balance of payment, in particular the bilateral EU-US trade, and the stakeholders' opposition limited the potential of a similar EU rule. They also resulted in a campaign to get the US authorities to revise the specific regulation.[14] Furthermore, there are objections to the collection and foremost the sharing of the data produced via

11. *The Wall Street Journal*, "New shipping law makes big waves in foreign ports", 26 October 2007.
12. *Lloyd's List*, "China backs Europe on US box scanning", by J. Stares, 4 February 2008.
13. *Lloyd's List*, "Brussels reveals cost of US box scans", by J. Stares, 12 May 2008.
14. *Lloyd's List*, "Europe takes box scanning fight to US Congress", by J. Stares, 18 February 2008.

the scanning process, and this is not least because SAFE does not determine who collects, maintains, disseminates and analyses the apparently sensitive data. These objections are strongly related to the fact that this process safeguards a third region without the port state enjoying any immediate benefit. The common denominator, however, is the advocacy that the rule is imposing an unnecessary burden, whereas the European port industry does not experience any substantial security policy gaps.

Following the adoption of a core maritime transport security-related policy framework that enhances the uniform and most extended possible application of the relevant international rules, the pace towards additional and, inevitably, overlapping to a certain extent, has slowed down. Further signs of this EU approach on trans(port) security are provided by the absence of EU rules that would correspond to US initiatives like the 96-hour rule. Even the implementation of the respective EU "advanced cargo declaration scheme",[15] the EU's version of the 24-hour rule, is behind schedule and it is increasingly doubtful that the July 2009 deadline will be met. The opposition of stakeholders remains firm and explicit, with European shippers arguing that this is "another unnecessary bureaucratic burden" that demands the exchange of commercially very sensitive information with trading partners and thus seeking their exemption from the scheme.[16]

Overall, beyond the limited willingness to participate in information-sharing regimes, several stakeholders in Europe emphasise the substantial costs for implementing additional efforts to strengthen trans(port) security. A recent study by UNCTAD (2007) provides a global survey on the costs of meeting security in ports. Based on survey responses, UNCTAD estimated the port-related expenditures of the ISPS Code to range between about $1.1 billion and $2.3 billion initially and $400 million and $900 million annually. These expenditures would be equivalent to increases in international maritime freight payments of 1% and 0.5% respectively. A frequently highlighted difficulty is on the potential mobilisation of appropriate, public or private capital in order to guarantee implementation of any further security-related rules. It might be worth comparing this attitude with the most recent empirical evidence (Brooks, 2008) that in North America stakeholders advocate the need to raise awareness and force their partners in the supply chain to adopt security measures, and do so even though they acknowledge that security requirements have been costly and have put up more barriers to conducting normal business.

Cost implications are not, however, similar for all the stakeholders. Shipping companies face a small implementation cost compared to the overall investments required for operating a vessel (Rotterdam Maritime Group, 2005). The scene in the port industry is quite complex. Security costs differentiate

---

15. Regulation 1875/2006, of 18 December 2006, amending Regulation (EEC) No 2454/93 laying down provisions for the implementation of Council Regulation (EEC) No 2913/92 establishing the Community Customs Code.

16. *Lloyd's List*, "EU shippers seek '10+2' scheme waiver", by J. Stares, 10 January 2008.

according to the size of the port (i.e., small or large ports) as well as the type of cargo they facilitate (i.e., container, dry cargo, etc.). The example of the ISPS Code application is illustrative. As recently estimated (Dekker & Stevens, 2007), the average investment needed for financing the requirements of the ISPS Code are €464,000 per port, and the annual running costs are €234,000. The largest share of the initial investments is dedicated to landside accesses-entrances and electronic systems and the largest share of the annual maintaining costs is absorbed by the personnel (almost 60% of the total), with the total compliance investments needed differing remarkably between European port facilities according to the scale of the port or the type of market(s) served. The financial regimes to address these costs range from a full funding by the port authority to market driven mechanisms. In general, the mechanisms might include an increase in port tariffs, and/or a security charge levied on every port user, and/or government assistance. Out of a sample of 27 EU port facilities, 23% received subsidies in order to finance the security measures. Another 19% used an increase in port tariffs and 55% introduced a security tariff. This variety in financing schemes makes the creation of a balanced level playing field among the EU ports difficult.

In the US, the overall annual cost of the TWIC rule (i.e., enrolment, issuance, threat assessments, IDMS, card production and programme support) is estimated at $189 million. The SAFE Port Act requires $400 million every year. Public funds are available to be used by the port sector, even though the 2009 US budget provisions for port security financing were reduced compared to the respective provisions of the 2008 US budget.[17] In the EU, the security financing regime is different. While the first two of the mentioned financial mechanisms are in line with the EU internal market rules, government support is not an option. Such support would be considered an interference in pricing mechanisms and a distortion of competition in the case of a remarkable heterogeneous industry (see Pallis, 2007; also Farantouris, 2008). Even though some might consider security as a public good, the potential of the EU allowing public financing of the security measures seems remote.

Some of the US security policies aiming to secure the entire transportation systems and supply-chains have a significant impact beyond the US borders. Several stakeholders in Europe have expressed their discontent with the impact they have on the EU (maritime) transport systems and trade. Moreover, following a long-standing practice of maritime policy developments (cf. Aspinwall, 1995; Pallis, 2006), the preference of maritime interest groups representing stakeholders at a European level stands for the relevant policies to be made at international (i.e., the IMO) rather than regional level. The framework of standards for supply chain security which was recently adopted (2007) by the World Customs Organisation (WCO) is indicative. The so-called SAFE framework (WCO, 2007) is based on the European Customs

---

17. *Lloyd's List*, "Port short-changes in US security budget", by R. Josh, 7 February 2008.

Code and establishes standards that enhance the supply chain security through the voluntary co-operation of the stakeholders. The framework applies a risk-management approach to the case of the cargoes and containers handled in the WCO member states seeking, among others, for an international application of the AEO status. As already detailed, the latter is in line with the provisions of the EU Revised Customs Code. This internationally agreed rule provides an illustrative example of the different policy making approaches observed in the US and the EU: while the EU promotes security initiatives to the international organisations, it is reluctant to respond to calls for further regional policy initiatives.

4.3 Comparing policy-making and implementation regimes

Figure 13.1 presents both the main US security policies and the authorities which are responsible for each of them. Following the events of 11 September and the subsequent reorganisation of security agencies, the USCG acts as the separate entity within the DHS that deals with maritime security issues. DHS supervises the major security-related public authorities and also manages the majority of the US security policies and programmes. This figure illustrates however, the complex US security scheme in place, providing the base for comparisons to the respective non-US security schemes. Figure 13.2 presents the EU policy-making regime and the responsible authorities for the enforcement and monitoring of the regulations and programmes that constitute the backbone of the EU security policy framework.

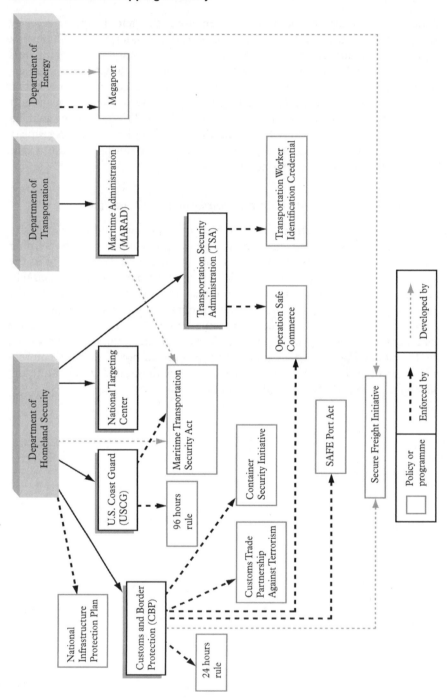

Figure 13.1 The US maritime transport related security regime

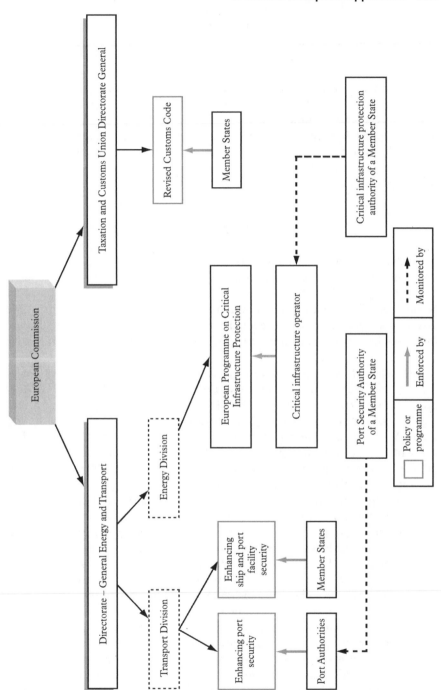

Figure 13.2 The EU security policy framework

Compared to the US regime, the EU security policy framework is a more centralised one. Two Directorate Generals (DGs) of the European Commission are responsible for proposing all the security-related transport policies, to be then decided according to the standard EU legislative process (i.e., involving consultation with the stakeholders, the participation of the European Parliament, and the final decision of the Council of (Transport) ministers). The enforcement of some of the EU policies is a responsibility of the EU member states. As regards the rest of the security policies, the implementation responsibility lies with the operators of the transport infrastructures, i.e., port authorities, terminal operators, etc., with national administrations monitoring their application.

5. CONCLUSIONS

This chapter examined the EU regime dealing with the enhancement of maritime transport security, and compared to this regime the respective policy developments in the US. In recent times, especially since the events of 11 September, EU policies aiming to minimise risk and increase the security and operational reliability of the sector have been central stage. Some of these initiatives have been transformed to EU laws, regulations and administrative provisions while others are still under discussion.

The relevant EU policies were initially developed as a result of major security incidents which occurred worldwide and the subsequent security initiatives undertaken at international (IMO, ILO, etc.), and peripheral levels. The findings of the chapter suggest that the US led this trend, with the EU following a similar strategy and, to a certain extent, copying the actions of its geopolitical ally and trading-partner. Both the US and the EU adopted the broader possible application of the ISPS Code, and then brought in security initiatives aiming to safeguard the entire transport process.

The comparative analysis also indicated that progressively policymakers and stakeholders in Europe became uneasy with this strategy. First, the potential of further rules, in particular those recently discussed in the European context, has been challenged by stakeholders, thus policy proposals failed to be transformed to EU legislation. The dominant assessment is that any additional rules to the established EU regime would prove to be an unnecessary bureaucratic burden potentially overlapping the security policies that are in place. The list of reasons contributing to the discontent with the US approach also includes the significant implementation costs involved; the difficulties to finance the implementation of security-related policies, especially due to the presence of a remarkably heterogeneous European port industry; and, not least, the different levels of willingness to share sensitive commercial information for security reasons. This discontent is extensive enough to generate demands to the US to overturn its own recent policy initiatives (i.e., the scanning of containers in foreign ports).

The presence of different schemes of policy-making regimes and implementation processes on each side of the Atlantic further emphasises the emerging *sui generis* European approach. Yet the themes of these two distinctive approaches remain interlinked, as neither of them can ignore the global structures of the maritime (trans)port industry, and thus the common security demands of these structures.

CHAPTER 14

PORT SECURITY IN ASIA

Koi Yu Adolf Ng and Girish C. Gujar

1. INTRODUCTION

The 11 September terrorist attack had cruelly exposed the potential brittleness of the transportation system. A terrorist event involving the system could lead to unprecedented disruption of the global trade system (Flynn, 2006) which would not only involve human casualties, but also economic, political and social impacts, notably the breakdown of the global supply chains and potentially global economic recessions (Greenberg et al., 2006). Indeed, the attack had served an important indicator in raising the awareness of security along the transportation system (Kingdon, 1995).

Being the nodal points, the security of ports was arguably regarded as pivotal in ensuring the smoothness and efficiency of intermodal logistical supply chains with increasing complexities (Robinson, 2002; Ng, 2007). In this sense, port security could be understood as all security (including the protection of cargoes, passengers and crew, as well as fighting crime like smuggling and drug trafficking) and counter-terrorism activities which fell within the port domain, including the protection of port facilities and the protection and coordination of security activities when ship and port interact, although counter-terrorism had been the core focus after 11 September. Although a number of studies on maritime security, both academic and industrial, had been carried out, e.g., OECD (2003), King (2005), Greenberg et al. (2006), Zhu (2006), etc., works dedicated to port security had, so far, remained scarce. The contribution of previous port security-related studies with, for example, Bichou (2004), Kumar and Vellenga (2004) and Bichou et al. (2007) providing significant insight on the subject concerned is not trying to be downplayed. Nevertheless, the mentioned works had mainly being technical in nature, e.g., operational efficiency, IT security systems, calculating the cost of compliance with international guidelines, etc. where comprehensive analysis on how such international guidelines can be applied in a regional or local perspective, including its problems, obstacles and solutions, remained scarce. Even within these few works, attention was often focused on western societies, e.g., Ng (2007), Pallis and Vaggelas (2007), etc., while comprehensive analysis on Asian port security remains largely untouched, or simply descriptive rather than analytical, e.g., Huxley (2005), Tan (2005). Given the importance of Asia and its major ports in contemporary global trade, it was perhaps quite surprising that, more than half a decade since 11 September, such a large research gap has yet to be addressed.

Recognising such deficiency, this chapter provides an analysis on how Asian countries and regions have attempted to comply with the mandatory international requirements on port security, mainly the ISPS Code. Here it is important to note that this chapter's analysis on port security mainly focuses on counter-terrorism, with core attention being paid to the situation of selected Asian countries and regions in complying with the mandatory requirements found in the ISPS Code, while other non-compulsory/US-oriented initiatives, like Container Security Initiative (CSI), Custom-Trade Partnership Against Terrorism (C-TPAT) and other national and regional initiatives, are only used in further enhancing understanding on the issue, if deemed necessary.

After this introductory section, section 2 briefly introduces the ISPS Code, with special focus on the mandatory requirements related to port security. Section 3 discusses the current situation of port security in Asia, with empirical evidence from the APEC member economies, followed by a critical review on the major obstacles and challenges of Asian countries, regions and ports in complying with the international guidelines in section 4. Finally, section 5 summarises the major findings and analysis, as well as providing some constructive recommendations on how the current situation in Asia can be significantly enhanced in the foreseeable future.

Last but not least, this chapter contributes significantly to enhancing understanding on how geographical unevenness and political variations can pose difficulties to decision-makers during the implementation of international guidelines and standards. This chapter not only offers valuable insight to an increasingly important issue on the maritime sector, but also provides an excellent case in enhancing knowledge on the dynamics of political geography and global development.

2. THE ISPS CODE AND PORT SECURITY

The ISPS Code, adopted by the IMO in December 2002 and fully effectuated in July 2004 (IMO, 2002b), is the major and most important international response to the proliferation of the importance of maritime security since the 11 September terrorist attack and provides better protection against terrorism for ships and port facilities. Based on the amendments made in December 2002 to IMO's International Convention for the Safety of Life at Sea (SOLAS) 1974 as amended, as well as the addition of Special Measures in Enhancing Maritime Security (Chapter XI-2) to SOLAS (IMO, 2002a), quoting IMO's official website (2008), the ISPS Code can be understood as "a comprehensive set of measures to enhance the security of ships and port facilities, developed in response to the perceived threats to ships and port facilities in the wake of the 9/11 attacks in the US . . . In essence, the [ISPS]

Code takes the approach that ensuring the security of ships and port facilities is a risk management activity and that, to determine what security measures are appropriate, an assessment of the risks must be made in each particular case. The purpose of the [ISPS] Code is to provide a standardised, consistent framework for evaluating risk, enabling Governments to offset changes in threat with changes in vulnerability for ships and port facilities through determination of appropriate security levels and corresponding security measures".

The aim of the ISPS Code is to address the vulnerability of maritime (and supply chain) security due to poor preventive measures, as well as the ineffective response after the attack, i.e., ineffective crisis management system. Given such concerns, deliberate address and guidance on maritime security, including ports, had been included in the ISPS Code. The code was initiated by the US Coast Guard as part of the US government's response to 11 September with the target of creating a consistent security programme for ships and ports (and their operators and governments) to identify and deter threats from terrorists more effectively. Under the ISPS Code, all ships over 500 gross tonnages as well as port facilities are required to conduct vulnerability assessments and develop security plans to deter potential terrorist attacks, e.g., passenger, vehicle and baggage screening procedures, security patrol, the establishment of restricted areas and its execution, procedures for personnel identification, access control, installation of surveillance equipment, etc. The main objectives of the ISPS Code include: (i) detecting and identifying potential security risks; (ii) implementing security measures, e.g., protection systems, procedures, communications, etc.; (iii) collating and promulgating information related to maritime security; (iv) providing a reliable methodology in assessing maritime security risks; (v) developing detailed security plans and procedures in reacting to changing security levels; and (vi) establishing security-related roles and responsibilities for contracting governments (and their administrations), ship companies and port operators at national and international levels, including the provision of professional training.

The ISPS Code consists of two major parts. Part A provides minimum mandatory requirements that ships (and their respective companies) and ports (and the contracting governments) must follow and is binding to contracting governments, while Part B provides more detailed, but not compulsory, guidelines and recommendations in the implementation of security assessments and plans. The section outlines of the two parts are largely equivalent, of which Part A mainly illustrates the principles that maritime stakeholders need to follow, while Part B mainly discusses how such principles should and can be put into practice. Here three aspects are especially related to port security: (i) at all times, a three-tier security level system (from MARSEC1 to MARSEC3) must be introduced at all ports within the territory of the contracting government based on an assessment on the degree of credibility, collaboration, specific and imminent nature of the threat information, as well as the potential consequence of such an incident; (ii) contractual governments of IMO should appoint a designated authority dedicated for security affairs within ports and establishing a supporting administrative structure. The designated authority should then set security levels in accordance with Part A of the ISPS Code and provide guidance from security incidents taken place in ports, especially necessary and appropriate instructions to affected ships and port facilities in the case of higher security levels; and (iii) contractual governments should also establish the requirements when a Declaration of Security (DoS) is necessary when ship and port facilities interact.[1]

Complied ports are required to act in accordance with security levels set by their respective contracting governments, of which the degree of protective measures should be increased with changing security levels in all security-related issues. Apart from daily routine operation, contracting governments (or its designated authorities) must periodically assess port facilities, namely the Port Facility Security Assessment (PFSA), and report the outcomes (or approve the report if done by a separate designated authority), of which a Port Facility Security Plan (PFSP) should be developed for each port facility, with provisions in addressing the three security levels in the issues including: measures to prevent weapons and dangerous devices from being introduced in the port, authorised access to restricted areas, effective security of cargo and cargo-handling equipment and security of security information; procedures in responding to security threats, new/amended security instructions, evacuation, interfacing with ship security activities, periodic review and updating of PFSP, reporting security incidents, audition of the plan and facilitation of shore leave for ship's personnel or personnel change; as well as identification of port security officer and the duties of security-related personnel. Finally, a Port Facility Security Officer (PFSO) should be appointed for each designated port facility and is responsible to ensure that the PFSAs and PFSPs are well-prepared and being carried out effectively. The PFSO also acts as the liaison between the contracting government and the shipping companies, often through the Ship Security Officers (SSOs) and Company Security Officers (CSOs).

---

1. The purpose of DoS is to ensure that agreement can be reached between interfacing port facility and ships as to the respective security measures each side will undertake in accordance with the provisions of their respective approved security plans. The most important part of the DoS consists of a table clearly indicating the division of security responsibilities between the two sides, including: (i) ensuring the performance of all security duties; (ii) monitoring restricted areas to ensure that only authorised personnel have access; (iii) controlling access to the port facility; (iv) controlling access to the ship; (v) monitoring of the port facility, including berthing areas and areas surrounding the ship; (vi) monitoring of the ship, including berthing areas and areas surrounding the ship; (vii) handling of cargo; (viii) delivery of ship's stores; (ix) handling unaccompanied baggage; (x) controlling the embarkation of persons and their effects; and (xi) ensuring that security communication is readily available between the ship and port facility. The decision on whether a DoS is necessary is usually decided by the contracting government, although a ship can also request the completion of a DoS under outstanding circumstances, e.g., the ship is operating at a higher security level than the port it is interfacing, a security threat/incident is involved in the ship/port, etc. (IMO, 2002b).

Finally, it is important to highlight that, however, there is no international certification scheme for the ISPS Code for ports, but rather a statement of compliance by the contracting government subsequently endorsed by IMO. Thus, unlike ships, it is the contracting government, rather than IMO, which bears the ultimate decision on whether their port(s) have complied with the required standards and regulations. Such a system would have significant implications, as it implies that a high level of co-operation and commitment to security from the contracting government is required to ensure that ports are actually complying with the ISPS Code, especially within countries and regions where security is not necessarily prioritised in the political agenda, including Asia.

3. THE SITUATION: EVIDENCES FROM APEC MEMBER ECONOMIES

Before discussing the major characteristics of port security in Asia, this section is going to provide readers an overview of the situation in Asia by providing some empirical evidences from the APEC member economies (Figure 14.1)[2] in pushing their ports to comply with the ISPS Code. Until now, no port security-dedicated regional co-operation has existed within the Asia-Pacific region, and the only regional effort in addressing maritime security (including some aspects on port security) was the Security Trade in the APEC Region Programme (STAR Programme) initiated by the US (as an APEC member economy) during the 10th APEC Economic Leaders' Meeting (held at Los Cabos, Mexico in 2002). In the 2002 Leaders' Declaration, all APEC member economies agreed to endorse the importance of fighting terrorism as the latter had posed a profound threat on APEC's vision of free trade and investments (APEC, 2002), of which terrorist threat was regarded as one of the major obstacles standing in-between. Since then, the STAR conference had been organised annually, and until 2007, five STAR conferences had been held in different cities within different APEC member economies, namely Bangkok,

2. Asia-Pacific Economic Cooperation (APEC) is an inter-governmental forum for 21 Pacific Rim countries/regions to discuss the regional economy, co-operation, trade and investments, with its membership (usually called "member economies", given the fact that not all its members are sovereign countries or globally accepted as independent countries, like Hong Kong and Taiwan respectively) accounts for approximately 41%, 56% and 49% of the world's population, GDP and trade respectively. All activities, including year-round meetings of the member economies' ministers, are coordinated by the APEC Secretariat. The organisation conducts the APEC Economic Leaders' Meeting (AELM), an annual summit attended by the heads of government of all APEC members except Chinese Taipei (Taiwan) (which is represented by a ministerial-level official). The location of the summit rotates annually among the member economies, and a famous tradition involves the attending leaders dressing in a national costume of the host member. For further details, refer to APEC official website: www.apec.org

Thailand (2003); Vina del Mar, Chile (2004); Incheon, Korea Republic (2005); Hanoi, Vietnam (2006) and Sydney, Australia (2007).

Figure 14.1 The Indian subcontinent and APEC member economies in Asia

Similar to the EU's Regulation 725/2004,[3] the STAR Programme emphasised heavily on the inscription of the ISPS Code into regional standardisation of security measures. Under the STAR Programme, all APEC member economies were required to submit a Counter Terrorism Action Plan (CTAP) which provided a concise checklist of counter-terrorism measures undertaken by these member economies to achieve the key elements of the conference, with aspects including maritime security. A template of the CTAP can be found in Appendix 1, of which two sub-areas are directly related to port security, namely: (i) cargo protection and (ii) protection of ships engaged in international voyages.[4] Note that, however, no sub-areas had directly addressed port security. Also, in the CTAP, apart from setting the objectives and expected outputs, the APEC member economies were requested: (i) to provide a timeframe on when the planned measures could be accomplished; (ii) to list out the difficulties that the member economy concerned would likely tackle in the accomplishment of such tasks, if any; and (iii) to identify any required assistances from other APEC member economies, if any.

3. The core objective of EU's Regulation 725/2004 was to inscribe the ISPS Code into EU laws and regulations. Although largely adopted in accordance with the ISPS Code, the regulation also extended the ISPS Code to European ports dedicated for intra-European short sea shipping.

4. A full CTAP covers five core areas: (A) enhancing secure trade in the APEC region; (B) halting terrorist financing; (C) promoting cyber security; (D) energy security; and (E) protecting the health of communities. Among these areas, cargo protection and ship protection in international voyages belong to the first two sub-areas of Area A.

Although not dedicated towards port security, given the nature of this exercise, through investigating the CTAPs of different APEC member economies, it would be possible to assess the status of their ports in complying with the ISPS Code, as well as identifying the problems and challenges in the process of compliance. Given the theme of this chapter, here attention was only paid to the APEC member economies lying within East and Southeast Asia. Also, the focus was on freight transportation (containerised cargoes), while other types of terminals (like cruise terminals) were not investigated. Some major ports within these APEC member economies, of which many of them are the most important global ports (in terms of tonnage), can be found in Table 14.1.

Table 14.1 The major ports lying within the APEC member economies in Asia

Member economy	*Major ports*
Brunei Darussalam	Muara
China PR	Dalian, Fuzhou, Guangzhou, Qingdao, Shanghai, Shenzhen, Tianjin, Xiamen
Chinese Taipei	Keelung, Kaohsiung
Hong Kong, China	Hong Kong
Indonesia	Jakarta, Surabaya
Japan	Kobe, Nagasaki, Nagoya, Osaka, Yokohama, Yura
Korea Republic	Busan, Gwangyang, Hyundai, Ulsan
Malaysia	Penang, Port Klang
The Philippines	Manila
Singapore	Singapore
Thailand	Bangkok, Laem Chebang
Vietnam	Ho Chi Minh City (Saigon Port)

This section investigated whether the governments of their respective member economies (of which all of them were IMO members, either full or associate) were able to comply with the mandatory requirements of the ISPS Code since its enactment in July 2004. The status of APEC member economies in the approval and implementation of PFSPs in compliance with the ISPS Code between 2004 and towards the end of 2006 can be found in Table 14.2.

Table 14.2 Status of APEC member economies in Asia in the approval and implementation of PFSPs in compliance with the ISPS Code

Member economy	2004	2006
Brunei Darussalam	F	(N.A.)
China PR	F	F
Chinese Taipei	F	F
Hong Kong, China	F	F
Indonesia	P$^{£}$	P$^{£}$
Japan	F	F
Korea Republic	F	F
Malaysia	N	N
The Philippines	N	N
Singapore	F	F
Thailand	P*	P*
Vietnam	N	(N.A.)

Remarks: F—full compliance with the ISPS Code; P—partial compliance; N—not yet/ in the process of complying; ;£ Only Tanjung Priok Harbour had obtained the ISPS Code Compliant Certification; * Had only approved PFSPs for MARSEC1.
Source: APEC (2008).[5]

As shown in Table 14.2, Brunei Darussalam, China PR (hereafter called "China"), Chinese Taipei, Hong Kong, Japan, Korea Republic and Singapore had successfully approved and implemented their respective PFSPs when the ISPS Code was fully effectuated in July 2004. Partial compliance had been accomplished in Indonesia and Thailand (mainly concentrated within the major ports), while Malaysia, the Philippines and Vietnam had yet to or were in the process of preparing their respective PFSPs. Given their differences in economic development stages, it was perhaps not too surprising to find that Southeast Asian countries found it more difficult to finish this task on time. The interesting phenomenon, however, was that such situation had virtually remained stagnant and those who failed in meeting the deadline in 2004 still found it difficult to finish the mandatory task by the end of 2006. Here it would be interesting to investigate the major difficulties that these member economies had been facing in complying with the ISPS requirements. Table 14.3 illustrates different types of assistances required from different countries/ regions in accomplishing the planned measures as indicated in their respective CTAPs.

5. Note that the assessment of compliance as reported in Tables 14.2 and 14.3 is done by APEC, while from the IMO's perspective, all such ports are in full compliance with the ISPS Code. Indeed, this reflects a typical example of inconsistency in compliance and reporting.

Table 14.3 Different types of assistance required from APEC member economies in accomplishing the planned measures as indicated in their respective last updated CTAPs

Member economy	Last updated	Capacity	Finance	Training	Information sharing
Brunei Darussalam	Feb 05	(N.A.)	(N.A.)	(N.A.)	(N.A.)
China PR	Jan 07	–	✓	✓	✓
Chinese Taipei	Apr 07	–	–	–	–
Hong Kong, China	Apr 07	–	–	–	–
Indonesia	Mar 07	✓	–	✓	✓
Japan	Jan 07	–	–	–	–
Korea Republic	Jun 07	–	–	–	–
Malaysia	Feb 06	✓	–	✓	✓
The Philippines	May 06	✓	–	✓	✓
Singapore	Jun 07	–	–	–	–
Thailand	Jan 07	–	–	✓	✓
Vietnam	Apr 07	✓	–	✓	✓

Remarks: A tick indicates that the member economy concerned has noted that it requires significant assistance in accomplishing the planned measures as indicated in its respective updated CTAP.
Source: CTAP of respective APEC member economies.

Except China, member economies which had already fully complied with the requirements since 2004 did not indicate any significant problems in their respective CTAPs, nor had any of them required any assistance from other APEC member economies. On the other hand, for the member economies which had failed to comply so far, their major difficulties seemed to lie in the fact that they had inadequate knowledgeable personnel as all of them had indicated the need to seek opportunities in training qualified officers, as well as the importance of information sharing (like attending international security-related workshops and seminars). On the other hand, while all these member economies had indicated that they were still lacking the capacity in complying with the requirements, interestingly, except China, none of them had actually laid down in their respective CTAPs requesting financial assistance from the national governments or other APEC member economies, probably due to the fact that most such member economies had been receiving security financial aids since 2003, mainly from the US,[6] notably Thailand, the Philippines and Indonesia (Huxley, 2005).[7]

6. Such phenomenon could be partly explained by the diversity between different APEC member economies in terms of the extent and strictness that their respective ports needed to comply with international standards and regulations. See next section.

7. Despite US's concern over Indonesia's human right records (Huxley, 2005), US had remained an active supporter in helping Indonesia to improve its security standards since 2002.

From this section's analysis, two major observations can be identified. First, it was clear that various Asian countries found difficulty in complying with the requirements. Secondly, among them, most had cited training, information sharing and capacity-building as the factors requiring the most external assistance and it seemed that the problem was more related to the "soft" rather than "hard" aspects.[8] To enhance understanding on this issue, in the next section a detailed analysis on the challenges and obstacles of various Asian authorities in complying with the ISPS Code and other security guidelines is undertaken.

4. OBSTACLES AND CHALLENGES

Despite being the world's biggest continent with huge landmass, unlike North America, Asia is a massive region with more than 30 countries and regions with different political interests (sometimes at loggerheads), and with no empowered governmental organisation above national authorities (to a certain degree, at least) in addressing and implementing international standards and issues in a regional perspective. Another difference is that, unlike the US and the EU, Asia mainly consists of developing/industrialising, rather than highly developed, economies. With such fundamental geographical and demographic differences, it is not surprising that Asian ports are likely to experience additional difficulties when complying with the ISPS Code and other counter-terrorism port security measures. Indeed, empirical evidence from APEC member economies has clearly indicated that various Asian countries, especially developing countries, have found it difficult in ensuring that their ports fully comply with the ISPS Code and the pace of compliance had often been slow, if not completely stagnant. It seems that there are various issues which have acted as obstacles in preventing Asian ports complying with the ISPS Code. With such understanding, this section undertakes a detailed analysis on the major obstacles of the implementation of port security in Asia. Apart from the APEC member economies, analysis in this section is also supported by examples and cases from the Indian subcontinent (Figure 14.1). Apart from literature and documental reviews, analysis in this chapter is also based on information obtained from semi-structured in-depth interviews conducted between the second half of 2007 and the beginning of 2008, with various industrial players directly involved in Asian port security affairs, including government officials, managing directors of port operators, academic scholars, etc., hereafter called "anecdotal information". To assist readers' understanding, the regions and ports which have been used as examples in this section are illustrated in Figure 14.2.

---

8. Note that an additional source of non-compliance can also be due to the problem stemming from ports reporting or the lack of security incidents/accidents.

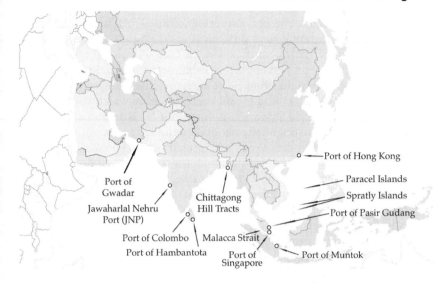

Figure 14.2 The locations of the regions and ports being used as examples in section 3

The first major problem for many Asian ports in complying with the international mandatory requirements was the scarcity of regional co-operation, including information sharing. Despite the efforts by APEC, given the often lack of coherence between different member economies, there was a genuine lack of supra-national co-ordination of port security issues in Asia which had affected information flow and sharing. According to anecdotal information, the sharing of security information between different countries and ports was, to say the least, scarce and was often restricted to a number of maritime security conferences and/or workshops organised by non-governmental organisations, of which two examples can be found in Appendix 2. Despite the existence of some limited bilateral co-operation, like Indonesia-Malaysia-Singapore joint efforts in fighting piracy and terrorism along the Malacca Straits, security co-operation within Asia remained largely potential rather than actual (Chin and Singh, 2005). Indeed, even the only pan-Asian-governmental programme, the STAR Programme, was very much a US-initiated programme with other Asian counterparts simply following suit, and the emphasis of the programme was mainly compromising regional standards rather than, like EU's Regulation 725/2004, establishing more binding maritime (including port) security requirements, not to mention any further measures in enhancing port state control, critical infrastructure protection and the role of ports in supply chain security (Pallis and Vaggelas, 2007). Such failure was mainly due to the fact that Asia is made up of many countries and regions with highly conflicting national interests, resulting in the fragmented and piecemeal nature of the implementation of port security in Asia, of which the tensions between China and various Southeast Asian countries (Vietnam, the Philippines, Indonesia et al.) in controlling the South China Sea and the archipelagos lying within, notably Paracel and Spratly Islands, served as excellent examples illustrating such difficulty.

Conflicts between different countries and the lack of regional co-operation would naturally impinge on perceptions of what security should be and that international guidelines would often be re-interpreted by different countries due to diversified political, economic and social interests which subsequently affected what should be prioritised. As pointed out by Kingdon (1995), the prioritisation of different issues on the national political agenda was very much decided by how a given condition was interpreted, and responses were often subject to social, political and institutional constraints (Jacobs and Hall, 2007), and it was clear that the concept of security was interpreted very differently in Asia and was typified in the Indian subcontinent. Due to its unique historical, demographic and religious background, coastal gateways, i.e., ports were not perceived by the Indian national government as providing the main sources of terrorist threats.[9] When human casualties from terrorist attacks were classified geographically, it became easy to understand the Indian government's prioritisation of land over maritime security, of which fatalities were highly concentrated within the inland provinces bordering Pakistan and Bangladesh (Table 14.4), not helped by the fact that none of the 66 post-11 September terrorist attacks (until January 2008) within India were maritime-related (SATP, 2008).

Table 14.4 Human casualties caused by terrorist attacks in India, 1994–2007*

Province	Civilians	SFP^	Terrorists	Total
Jammu and Kashmir	10,996	5,025	18,549	34,570
Northeast Provinces#	7,958	2,135	5,736	15,829
Punjab	89	2	91	182
All other regions	715	12	34	761
Total	19,758	7,174	24,410	51,342

Remarks: * Figures here do not include casualties caused by left-wing extremists, e.g., CPI-Maoist, CPI (Marxist Leninist) Janashakti, etc.[10]; ^ SFP means security force personnel; # The Northeast Provinces include Assam, Manipur, Meghalaya, Nagaland and Tripura.
Source: SATP (2008).

9. In India, there were over 150 million Muslims who by and large have been ignored by the successive governments and who did not really find a place within the mainstream society and did not enjoy the benefits of growth of the country. There were several reasons for this phenomenon, but what was the most important was the fact that this scenario had made Indian Muslims resentful, compounded by the almost daily occurrence of the clashes between the majority Hindus and the minority Muslim communities. Such sense of injustice had sometimes been inflicted by some of its neighbours through providing some members of the Muslim extremist societies (like HuJI and JuM) with arms and explosives (albeit mostly indirectly). For further details, visit South Asia Terrorism Portal's (SATP) website: www.satp.org

10. According to the Ministry of Home Affairs of the Government of India, between 2002 and 2006, most of the terrorist attacks and thus human casualties initiated by left-wing extremists (87%–89%) took place in states with hardly any significant maritime interests, notably Andhra Pradesh, Bihar, Chhattisgarh and Jharkhand. For more information, see SATP (2008).

As a consequence, despite the intensified need for hi-tech scanners for container inspections at Indian ports ever since 11 September, given the reluctance of the Indian authorities in setting aside necessary funds to acquire such equipment, until recently, except Jawaharlal Nehru Port (JNP),[11] no other Indian ports had been equipped with such systems, and even the discovery of live rocket shells hidden in several containers coming from Iran in JNP in 2006 was unable to alter such reluctance.

Even within the maritime sector, the definition of maritime (including port) security could be highly diversified and ambiguous. During the conference entitled Maritime Security in the Asia-Pacific (held in Singapore in 2004, hereafter called the "MSAP Conference"), speakers pointed out that, within the Asian-Pacific region, the meaning of maritime security could range from traditional power rivalries between nation states, control of trunk shipping routes, to contemporary economic and social issues, e.g., environmental degradation, weapon proliferation, drugs and human smuggling, etc. (IDSS, 2004). In the Indian subcontinent, for example, the denial of security clearance of Hutchison Port Holdings (HPH) in bidding for a port construction project in Mumbai in 2006 by the Indian national government served as a textbook example illustrating that port security could be extended to a much wider political spectrum than just deterring smuggling, trafficking and counter-terrorism (Herald Tribune, 2006),[12] especially given the perceived Chinese strategy of "enveloping" India by collaborating with Pakistan and Sri Lanka (through HPH) in the development of their respective ports of Gwadar and Hambantota, not helped by the Sri Lankan government's decision to shortlist HPH in the final round of the bidding war for the construction of a three-berth container terminal in the port of Colombo in October 2007. Indeed, within the MSAP Conference, rather than conventional, US-defined terrorist activities (like deterring Al Qaeda's activities), speakers generally agreed that the most urgent matter related to maritime security within Southeast Asia was piracy (IDSS, 2004), which was supported by Huxley (2005), and thus more resources should be allocated in fighting pirates, rather than deterring terrorism within the region. A further example could be found in Bangladesh, of which given its own political situation, the maintenance of security was more being understood as fighting internal rebellions (like the Chakma tribal rebels along the Chittagong Hill Tracts since the late 1970s) and the preservation of social order rather than deterring international terrorists using its ports as tools in smuggling arms in and out of the country (SATP, 2008). Given such diversified interpretation of security, the conventional international understanding of port security in deterring terrorist attacks and

11. In India, JNP is also widely known as *Nhava Sheva*.
12. It was widely believed that the main reason for barring HPH from the project was due to the existence of a major Indian naval base proximate to the planned construction site, thus causing serious concerns within the Indian authorities, given the perceived close relation between the Chinese national government and Mr. Li Ka Shing, the Hong Kong tycoon who owned HPH through his business empire, the Cheung Kong Group.

activities was often lowly prioritised in Asian authorities' political agendas because the identified conditions, in some cases, were not even regarded as problems at all.

Such ignorance was understandable given the fact that no maritime-related terrorist attacks of any real significance had taken place in Asia so far[13] and thus little human consequence (Greenberg et al., 2006) of any significance had ever existed in this region which could trigger public attention, while the potential economic implications (like property damage and decline of world trade) were still largely hypothetical to the general public.[14] As a consequence, the level of emergency of introducing efficient security measures in ports was often low, especially when the psychological impression of 11 September started to fade away as time went by, while other more pressing issues started to emerge. Such perception was reflected by the fact that the PFSO (or security manager) often occupied a rather junior position within many port facility operators. In Hong Kong, for example, according to anecdotal information, none of the PFSOs/security managers in any of the port facilities had reached the senior/general manager grades, and that the responsibilities of security officers were often execution rather than decision making in nature. Due to such perception, governments and port facility operators were often quite reluctant to devote substantial financial commitments in enhancing port security, especially given the potential substantial financial requirements in complying with the ISPS Code,[15] especially the secondary ports.[16] This was not surprising, given that Asian government's budget allocations in the development of efficient maritime infrastructure were often lacking (Zhu, 2006) and, inevitably, wrangling existed over who would finally bear the costs of maintaining enhanced port security requirements (Asia Pacific Foundation of Canada, 2004).[17] Using the example of Hong Kong again, the HKSAR

13. The only post-11 September maritime-related terrorist attack in Asia took place in the Middle East in the port of Aden, Yemen, where the French tanker *Limburg* was attacked. In the following years, Aden port had suffered significant decline in terms of cargo throughputs.

14. A number of scenarios after terrorist attacks had taken place had been simulated in the last few years, like the *Port Security War Game* carried out by Booz Allen Hamilton (2003) which indicated that every day of diminished trade activity would need multiple days for restoration, where during the period of disruption following a terrorist attack, ships would be forced to wait for anchorage, trade would slow down and losses would build with, for example, the explosion of a dirty bomb would cost the US economy US$58 million (Seidelmann, 2007). However, until now, all these scenarios are still completely restricted to simulated, rather than realistic, scenes.

15. For example, based on Krishna's calculations (2006), the installation of a combined, effective container scanning system in a port (including systems with different strengths, e.g., GaRDS, 9MeV, TNA, PFNA, etc.) would cost as much as US$12 million.

16. According to a survey conducted by UNCTAD investigating how global ports complied with the ISPS Code, the initial average unit costs of small, medium and large ports would be US$386,000, 287,000 and 181,000 per ISPS port facility respectively, while they would need to spend annually US$128,000, 105,000 and 81,000 respectively to operate each ISPS port facility (Benamara and Asariotis, 2007).

17. Note that there had been no efforts at all in addressing the financial aspect of port security in Asia. For example, in 2004, the Asian Development Bank (ADB) had established a trust fund to support technical assistance in enhancing transport security, including ports, and combating money laundering and terrorist financing in developing countries (ADB, 2004).

government[18] was not prepared to provide a port security budget and all port facility operators were expected to cover all the financial costs in the execution of their respective PFSAs, the preparation of PFSPs and actions. Indeed, during the second Port Area Security Advisory Committee (PASAC)[19] committee meeting, the chairman had made clear to all committee members that the HKSAR government would not subsidise, or providing any loans, to any port security projects, and port facility operators had to be financially responsible for all upcoming items (PASAC, 2003). Such phenomenon was not dissimilar to the observations by Kingdon (1995) who indicated that serious attention paid to solving a transport problem by public authority took place only in response to an occurrence of nearby, recognisable crisis, and Asia had none, leading to an indifferent, or even hostile, attitude when addressing port security, especially given that the production of such expensive port security systems (and thus profits) was dominated by North American and European companies (Figure 14.3) and the frequent use of security by the US as a reason to continue military deployment in various Asian regions, notably Southeast Asia (Huxley, 2005). Quoting an interviewee from a major Asian port: "International terrorist attacks were mainly targeting the US and the West . . . those maritime security international guidelines were actually established with the core objective of protecting them . . . and what was the point for us to commit such substantial financial obligations? It was simply the tactics of the West in shifting part of their burden [to Asian countries and regions] so as to protect their own interests". This comment had very much represented the suspicion and prejudice by considerable Asian ports on the rationale of complying with the ISPS Code and other port-related counter-terrorism initiatives.

18. Since the return of Hong Kong to China in 1997, the Hong Kong Special Administrative Region (HKSAR) was established under the principle of 'one country, two systems'. From then on, the government of Hong Kong was often referred as the 'HKSAR government'.

19. PASAC was an ad hoc committee, established under (and chaired by) the Marine Department of the HKSAR government, in providing security-related advice to the port of Hong Kong. Its members composed of both public and private sector representatives within Hong Kong's port industry, including the port facility operators.

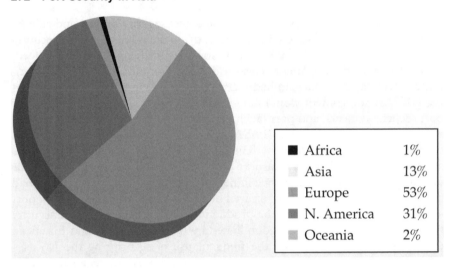

■ Africa	1%
Asia	13%
■ Europe	53%
■ N. America	31%
Oceania	2%

Source: WorldSecurity-index.com (2008).

Figure 14.3 A division of port security systems manufacturers by continents

Such indifferent and/or hostile attitude was not helped by the existence of regional/local interests, which often found the need for improving port security confronting. While the willingness to pay for personal security was seldom in question, the situation became more complicated about national or institutional security as such willingness would often be interfered by established privileges and egos. Since 11 September, striking the optimal point between fighting terrorism but without compromising smooth and cost-effective supply chain had always been one of the major dilemmas for policymakers and industrial stakeholders in setting port security policies. For example, in Japan, despite substantial pressure from the US, the authorities concerned were still reluctant to install radiation detection systems in their ports due to opposition from local facility operators about the possible slowdown of turnaround time which, in turn, could affect the competitiveness of respective terminals (Pilling and Mitchell, 2006). Together with the lack of an inter-governmental framework and the existence of a significant gap between different Asian economies, the degree of strictness between different countries/regions (or even different ports within one country/region) could vary significantly, not helped by the fact that many Asian ports often found it difficult to comply with even the basic mandatory requirements of the ISPS Code (not to mention the optional requirements), leading to mediocre performance in maintaining even the required minimum standards. Such situation confirmed Kingdon (1995) where the inability to solve a problem could cause a problem to fade from the political agenda which largely explained the stagnancy of some APEC member economies in complying with the ISPS Code. For example, in the Indian subcontinent, although most major port facilities had submitted and approved

PFSPs, in practice, many such plans had never been fully implemented, even among the major ports, and the port security system was often being exploited by the authorities as a convenient channel to generate additional private revenues, of which the criteria on how long and how detailed inspections would take was largely based on rent-seeking behaviours. For example, since most shippers would be more than willing to bribe so as to ensure that their cargoes would not be delayed, only less than 10% of the containers passing through JNP were actually inspected (both directly and indirectly) (Krishna, 2006), with the custom officers largely turning a blind eye to it.[20] The problem of such mediocre performance was exposed in 2007, when four containers owned by Oriental Overseas Container Lines (OOCL) were stolen from JNP's premises through the use of fake cargo documents, driver licences and vehicle registration plates (OOCL, 2007).[21] Another case illustrating such poor quality could be found in Southeast Asia. Despite Indonesia's vow to tighten maritime security within the region and intensified co-operation with Malaysia and Singapore against piracy and counter-terrorism (Huxley, 2005; Tan, 2005), in 2005, a cargo ship carrying tin ingots departing from the Indonesian port of Muntok, originally destined for Singapore, was hijacked by pirates while sailing along the Malacca Strait, where the pirates managed to get access to Muntok port's premises, and then got onboard (and hid in) the ship before its departure without being noticed by the Indonesian authorities at all, even though the ship had already docked there for two days. In this incident, apart from Indonesia, the effectiveness of Malaysia's port security system was also called into serious question on how the pirates managed to obtain the necessary documents to unload and store the robbed cargoes in a warehouse within the port of Pasir Gudang's premises.

The above problem was partly due to the lack of well-trained, qualified people, not only critical to the technical aspects like the approval of threat assessments and plans and the verification of PFSA procedures, but also who understood the importance of effective implementation of the security system in ports. In India, for example, even with the installation of the scanning system in JNP, they were mostly operated by junior level officers who had little or even no effective training on the system, especially since the government had yet to agree with the industry on whether the government or the port facility operators should be financially responsible for these training programmes, with both sides reluctant to pay. The result was poor security management, as exemplified by the earlier illustrated example concerning the disappearance of four OOCL containers from JNP's premises. Here IMO was

20. According to anecdotal information, in reality, the figure was much worse, with less than 1% of the containers passing through JNP being actually inspected.

21. JNP is not only the most important container port in India, handling 48% of the country's container traffic (in terms of TEUs) in 2005–06 (Indian Ports Association, 2008), but also one of the earliest ISPS-complied ports (since June 2004), as well as by far the only Indian port with hi-tech security inspection systems being installed. Thus, it would not be difficult to imagine the seriousness of the incident, as well as the situations in the secondary and minor ports.

partly to blame. In 2002, IMO had launched a number of technical programmes dedicated to Asia through its Integrated Technical Co-operation Programme (ITCP) in promoting the awareness of maritime security threats, while various seminars and workshops had also been organised for various APEC member economies, e.g., Indonesia, the Philippines, Thailand, Vietnam, etc. However, based on student feedbacks, such programme seemed unable to transfer all necessary practical knowledge to learners in dealing with the ISPS Code. For example, in evaluating the feedbacks from students about the programme, an important insight was that while the programme had covered the topic of maritime security well, it had largely overlooked the practical aspects, notably on how to implement the ISPS Code when it came into force in 2004, e.g., the preparation of PFSPs and PFSAs, how to enhance the awareness in identifying suspicious cargoes, etc. (Zhu, 2006). As indicated in the last section, the lack of training was actually regarded as one of the biggest problems for the APEC member economies which persistently failed to comply with the international security regulations. The lack of qualified personnel had made compliant work alone difficult to execute, not to mention any further steps in enhancing inspection efficiency, e.g., balancing sampling and risk-taking, risk management systems, etc.

Given the growing export trade and the negative economic impacts of non-compliance of ISPS Code (as well as the potential booming of international trade), many Asian authorities regarded complying with the ISPS Code as a burden/responsibility, having no real alternatives but ostensibly complying, even when many were not really enthusiastic. For many, the main goal of complying with the ISPS Code and other counter-terrorism measures was to avoid the political and economic consequences due to non-compliance like losing the US market, with the issue starting to fade away from the agenda as a problem being solved once the basic requirements had been fulfilled. Thus, the issue of port security often only occupied a backseat role within the national political agenda and regional efforts, including information sharing, had often been paralysed by confronting political interests as well as the reluctance of genuine efforts in promoting it. As a consequence, in implementing the ISPS Code, Asian ports were largely followers and innovative actions and outputs, like the Port Facility Security Toolkit (PFST) initiated by the port of Rotterdam (PoR),[22] remained extremely scarce, if anything at all, which was perhaps not surprising given that, so far, little empirical evidence, if any, had indicated convincingly that better port security would result in more business. The lack of genuine regional co-operation, diversification in the prioritisation of security issues, the scarcity of financial and technical

22. PFST was a web-enabled software tool initiated by PoR (in co-operation with Aon Netherlands) with the objectives of providing users: (i) a uniform interpretation of the ISPS code, which simplifies supervision of compliance; (ii) prepare PFSP within a limited period of time; (iii) modify PFSAs and PFSPs immediately if any additional measures were taken; and (iv) overview the status of the PFSPs within ports. Further details can be found in PFST's website: www.portsecuritytoolkit.com

resources and the embryonic stage of the risk management culture had ensured the stagnancy of compliance. Given such deficiency, authorities in Asia were generally, to say the least, indifferent in complying with the ISPS Code and other counter-terrorism initiatives, of which the focus of port security was closely embedded within regional/local political, economic and social realities.

5. CONCLUSIONS

This chapter has provided a detailed analysis on the development of Asian countries and regions in pushing their ports in complying with the ISPS Code, which was adopted and effectuated in 2002 and 2004 respectively. Using examples from the APEC member economies in Asia and the Indian subcontinent, this chapter argued that while some countries and regions could address the issue effectively, at the same time, a number of them, especially the developing countries and regions, found it difficult to fully comply with the mandatory requirements, mainly due to the lack of information sharing, technical know-how, regional co-operation and the low priority of port security issue on the political agenda, not helped by the influence of various local and regional interests which could significantly jeopardise the effectiveness of implementation. In Asia, it seemed that most governments still regarded port security as a problem to solve rather than establishing the philosophy that good security could be good business (PoR, 2007). As a consequence, the process of compliance had remained stagnant in many Asian countries, while for others the issue seemed to have quickly faded once the basic mandatory requirements had been fulfilled, as one interviewee put it, "problem-solved". While beware not to over-generalise, but based on this chapter's analysis, it would be fair to argue that the concept and focus of port security in Asia was significantly different from that of the western, developed countries and regions. Since 11 September, while the latter had put its security focus on fighting terrorism, it was certainly not the case in Asia, and the commitment to comply with the ISPS Code was often half-hearted, and the notion that higher security would enable ports an opportunity in creating additional values to shippers (Robinson, 2002; Jacobs and Hall, 2007; Srikanth and Venkataraman, 2007) was simply overlooked. Indeed, Mr Wong Kan Seng, Singapore's then-Minister of Home Affairs, was right when he argued that the greatest challenge of counter-terrorism in Asia was "in the realm of the mind and the heart" (Tan, 2005). For many Asian authorities, the core attention was still embedded by local social and political realities, thus constraining them into addressing alternative security-related issues rather than counter-terrorism, e.g., geopolitics, smuggling, drug trafficking, etc., and a proper port security culture in deterring terrorism has yet to blossom, not to mention the wider spectrum about the role of ports in contributing to supply chain security (Bichou, 2004). Similar to other aspects of port development like institutional reforms (Ng and Pallis, 2007) and port-city spatial relationships (Lee et al., 2008), an "Asian" perspective existed in the development of port security systems.

Port security in Asia served as an excellent case illustrating that excessive international standards might not be an effective way to ensure more security if regional and local circumstances and the "soft" aspects had been continuously overlooked. Looking to the future, it seems that Flynn (2006) was right describing port security in Asia as still being "a house of cards" with enormous room for improvements. Given the understanding that the problem of Asian ports in complying with the security requirements is more related to attitude, during the implementation of the ISPS Code and other security initiatives, it is important for policymakers to be aware about the existence of regional and local cultural and political circumstances which can significantly affect the effectiveness of changing ports' status quo (Ng and Pallis, 2007). Apart from the financial costs and technical aspects of compliance, mutual trusts between different authorities and the perception of security are playing an equally, if not more, important role in deciding how effective Asian ports can fully comply with IMO's initiatives on port security. Attention should not be focused on just the hardware of technological improvements and legal documents, but encouraging the development of the soft issues, notably international co-operation, cross-national information sharing, education and know-how transfer and, perhaps most importantly, altering the indifferent and/or even hostile feeling towards port security. Finally, IMO should also co-operate with contracting governments to reform the current compliance system which largely relies on the commitment and co-operation of contracting governments, where the introduction of annual random inspection visits to selected ports within IMO members can be a good starting point in gradually improving the system to become a global certification scheme with general standards agreed globally.

Last but not least, this chapter has shed some light on the issue when international requirements were put into practice in a regional and local perspective, notably the potential obstacles and challenges that policymakers would possibly face. It is sincerely hoped that this chapter provides readers with a valuable view on the subject concerned, as well as offering policymakers an opportunity to review their existing approaches in addressing the problem of port security. As the critical intermodal nodal points along global logistical supply chains and thus the blood veins of the global economy, it is extremely important for policymakers to ensure that the issue of sustaining secure ports will not be overlooked and that the right approach can be employed in tackling existing obstacles and challenges in Asia.

APPENDIX 1: A TEMPLATE OF THE CTAP (SECTIONS A1 AND A2 ONLY)

ECONOMY: _____

A.1 Protect Cargo:

Contact Point: Name: _____ Title: _____

Telephone No.: _____ Fax Number: _____ Email Address: _____

OBJECTIVE	EXPECTED OUTCOME	MEASURES UNDERTAKEN OR TO BE COMPLETED IN (*YEAR*)	FURTHER MEASURES PLANNED (indicate timeframe)	CAPACITY BUILDING NEEDS TO MEET AGREED TARGETS

A.2 Protect Ships Engaged in International Voyages:

Contact Point: Name: _____ Title: _____

Telephone No.: _____ Fax Number: _____ Email Address: _____

OBJECTIVE	EXPECTED OUTCOME	MEASURES UNDERTAKEN OR TO BE COMPLETED IN (*YEAR*)	FURTHER MEASURES PLANNED (indicate timeframe)	CAPACITY BUILDING NEEDS TO MEET AGREED TARGETS

APPENDIX 2: SELECTED INTERNATIONAL MARITIME SECURITY CONFERENCES HELD IN ASIA

Conference	**GOVSEC Asia, Asia Law Enforement and Asia Ready! Summit**
Organisers	National Trade Productions, Inc, and Infoex-World Services Ltd.
Dates	28–29 March 2006
Host city	Hong Kong
Keynote speakers contributed from	– Hong Kong Police Force – Good Harbour Consulting – US Drug Enforcement Administration (Hong Kong Country Office) – Security Division, FBI – Singapore Civil Defence Force – Strategy and Innovation, Faculty of I.T., Queensland University of Technology – Motorola Asia Pacific Ltd. – Terrorism Studies, Strategic and Defence Studies Centre, The Australian National University – US Department of Homeland Security

Conference	**Maritime Security Asia 2006**
Organiser	Marcus Evans
Dates	18–19 April 2006
Host city	Singapore
Keynote speakers contributed from	– International Centre for Political Violence and Terrorism Research – Port of Rotterdam Authority – Hutchison Port Holdings, Hong Kong – US Coast Guard – Maersk Sealand, Indonesia – "K" Line – Institute of Defence and Strategic Studies – Maritime Institute of Malaysia – Det Norske Veritas – Singapore Maritime Academy – East Asia Response Ltd.

CHAPTER 15

LANDSIDE CARGO THEFT

Eric Custar

1. INTRODUCTION

This chapter provides an analysis of maritime cargo theft at the landside. That is, cargo that has been stolen at some point either between its origin and stowage on a vessel at a port or between its discharge from a vessel at a port and its ultimate destination. Historically, cargo theft such as stealing a tractor-trailer to acquire its goods has been reported as auto theft. Ultimately, the criminal is prosecuted according to the guidelines of auto theft irrespective of the intention to steal valuable cargo. The spirit of the law is similar around the world but each country or region has unique definitions of cargo theft.

In two US states where cargo theft is most endemic, California and Florida, each one has taken the matter seriously and created clear definitions of "cargo theft". The California Penal Code 487h(b) defines "cargo" as "any goods, wares, products, or manufactured merchandise that has been loaded into a trailer, railcar, or cargo container, awaiting or in transit" and establishes a link between "cargo" and the act of taking it criminally.[1] Florida defines "cargo" as "partial or entire shipments, containers, or cartons of property which are in or on a trailer, motor truck, aircraft, vessel, warehouse, freight station freight consolidation facility, or air navigation facility".[2] In Europe, each member of the EU has its own definition of "cargo theft". For instance, it may simply state, "to permanently deprive the owner of that item", as it does in England, or more elaborately in Greece, "the removal (totally or partially) of a movable property from the possession of another person with a view of illegally appropriating it".[3] The intention of these definitions is that theft involves one person intentionally taking a thing which belongs to another person without that other person's knowledge or consent.

Coincidentally, a private insurance firm more clearly defines cargo theft as "a peril which is defined as either the forcible or clandestine taking of an entire shipping package, including a container, or shipment, not just the taking of the

---

1. http://info.sen.ca.gov/pub/03–04/statute/ch_0501-0550/ch_515_st_2004_ab_1814
2. "The Florida Anti-Fencing Act", Florida Statute, Title XLVI Crimes, Chapter 812, Theft, Robbery, and Related Crimes, 812.012, Definitions www.flsenate.gov/statutes/index.cfm?App_mode=Display_Statute&Search_String=&URL=Ch0812/SEC012.HTM&Title=>2007->Ch0812->Section%200120812.012
3. "Theft of Goods and Goods Vehicles", European Council of Ministers of Transport, 26 April 2001, p. 16

contents of a shipping package or container". Included in this rather broad category is hi-jacking, defined as "the forcible, normally by armed assailants, taking of a truck, trailer or container".[4]

A potential conflict arises, however, when considering the impact of cargo theft on the Just-in-Time cycle. In a Just-in-Time business environment, the goal is to reduce or eliminate the inventory cycle and avoid warehousing altogether by delivering a container full of a particular item that will be put into process immediately upon arrival at the manufacturer's plant. The danger to a business in this environment of losing a container, for example, to theft means that it has no immediate backfill from its own inventory or from that of the manufacturer. The time to replace the shipment may be weeks or months but the economic impact to the plant is felt instantaneously and may cause severe harm to the firm through lost contracts, tarnished reputation, and financial loss.

There are a few words, while loosely familiar in discussion, that have unusual but logical origins that are important to understanding their true meaning and providing insight on their use today. The etymology of "fence" traces its beginning to turn-of-the-eighteenth-century thieves' slang referring to the clandestine nature of their stolen goods dealing "under defense of secrecy".[5] "Heist" is an Americanism of "hoist" dating to the 1920s and defined as a robbery or "lift[ing] another on one's shoulders to help him break in".[6]

This chapter first examines the evolution of cargo theft from the break-bulk era to the age of containerisation and then quantifies the extent of its economic and social impact. Next is an investigation of the process of cargo theft, the illegal actors, and the victimised legitimate parties. The *modus operandi* of the thief and the fence will be developed as well as how they victimise the shipper, carrier, and warehouse. The role of insurance also will be discussed to understand its participation in the process. Finally, the focus will turn to deterring cargo theft with an overview of the differing technologies, education, and information dispersal as positive deterrents to cargo theft. Also, the steps being taken by governments to legislate against cargo theft and mandate actions to deter it will be discussed.

2. THE EVOLUTION OF CARGO THEFT

Fighting cargo theft is as old as the process of cargo transportation itself. In the days prior to container shipping, general cargo was transported in palle-

---

4. "Ocean Cargo Insurance Glossary of Terms", Chubb Group www.chubb.com/businesses/cci/chubb5810.pdf
5. "Etymology and variations of 'fence'", Online Etymology Dictionary, www.etymonline.com/index.php?search=fence&searchmode=none
6. "Etymology and variations of 'heist'", Online Etymology Dictionary, www.etymonline.com/index.php?search=heist&searchmode=none

tised break-bulk units requiring large gangs and many days to work a vessel while in port. This process, in turn, required trans-loading the cargo into a railcar or truck before arriving at its final destination. This time-consuming, labour-intensive lading and unlading process of hoisting one pallet at a time left the unsecured cargoes as tempting and easy targets for pilferage and theft. The desire to obtain something that one does not own and to take it intentionally, depriving the rightful owner of it, at a time when the opportunity is present is the crux of the problem: unsecured goods exposed to the hands of an opportunistic criminal.

In order to understand contemporary inland cargo theft and its prevention, it is helpful to understand the basic purpose of theft in pre-industrial and modern manufacturing societies. Prior to today's more efficient production and manufacturing techniques in which goods are mass-produced and transported quickly, theft was generally for personal consumption. This is attributed in part to a smaller transportation infrastructure, an inability to mass-produce identical products, and poor communication systems. Hence, there were relatively few buyers, a limited supply of transport resources, and an ease with which stolen property could be identified.[7] In addition, during the break-bulk era, palletised cargoes were unsecured and more easily accessible to thieves. This is not the case today where more sophisticated tools rather than a cutting knife are required to access the goods in a container. Yet, there are several tactics that continue to be used that have remained unchanged since the break-bulk era of cargo theft. These tactics will be examined later.

Until the advent of the Malcolm McLean's shipping container, break-bulk shipment of cargo was the *de facto* method of shipping general goods. Break-bulk requires the pallet-by-pallet, or piece-by-piece, movement of cargo to and from a vessel by crane and is labour and time intensive. The open pallets of unprotected individual units provide opportunities for pilferage during the loading, unloading, and warehouse distribution processes. Each step requires gangs of longshoremen to assist in assembling goods (such as boxes of cigarettes) on pallets in the warehouse, moving them to the quay, and then working below decks to stow the pallets.[8]

In 1953, the Port of New York-New Jersey established the Waterfront Commission of New York Harbor in response to pilferage, corruption, and ties of unionised stevedore operations to organised crime. Gang foremen were often career criminals who formed gangs with men who would provide a kickback for the privilege to work; loan sharking was readily available to help

---

7. Blakey, G. Robert, Michael Goldsmith, "Criminal Redistribution of Stolen Property: The Need for Law Reform" , *Michigan Law Review*, Vol. 74, No. 2, August 1976, pp. 1511–1512.
8. Shinnick, Joseph, "Thinking Inside the Box, Fifty Years of Containerization", *PortViews*, March/April 2006, p. 3. www.panynj.gov/DoingBusinessWith/seaport/pdfs/portviews_0306.pdf

the men with their financial shortfalls. Guards working the docks were ineffective in controlling cargo theft and "public loaders" at the warehouse coerced truck drivers to hire them to load and unload their trucks.[9]

In the 1960s, cargo theft was a major source of revenue for organised crime, focusing on cargoes moving through the airports, seaports, and warehouses. Adding to the growing cargo theft problem were small insider operations around the country. By the early 1970s, cargo theft was so endemic that the US federal government directed the US Department of Transportation to work with the private transportation industry to combat the problem. In 1981, the government had become satisfied that its efforts had sufficiently curbed cargo theft. The following year, the National Cargo Security Council was formed to create a voluntary organisation to develop education programmes and to coordinate private industry theft deterrence efforts with government initiated programmes.[10]

Today, consumers shop for stereo equipment, computer hardware, clothing, and food items but do so often without considering the factors influencing prices or the item's likely international voyage inside a shipping container. The direct and indirect costs of cargo theft are built into the market price of these goods without the consumers' awareness that theft drives up product costs. Generally, cargo theft is regarded as a victimless crime because its economic impact is spread across many consumers, a sort of criminal economy of scale, rather than as a single loss to a shipper, where insurance covers the replacement cost.

With little doubt, Malcolm McLean's container is the catalyst behind globalisation and global trade.[11] The introduction of the standardised container has resulted in innovations by port, rail, and trucking industries that streamline the delivery cycle. Even though a container is moved easily among various modes of transportation (ship, truck, and rail), criminals can readily exploit the container transportation system by virtue of its vastness and complexity.

To fully understand the efficiency-driven nature of containerisation, it is useful to consider it in numerical terms. Worldwide in 2006, ports made more than 440 million TEU[12] moves, more than 128 million TEUs were in circulation,[13] and slot capacity for ships on liner trades exceeded 11.7 million

9. "Why the Commission was Created in 1953", Waterfront Commission of New York Harbor History, www.wcnyh.org/history.htm

10. Badolato, Edward, *Cargo Security: Avoiding Theft and Loss in the New Millenium [sic]*, 21 September 1999, pp. 2–3.

11. A good source to learn more about McLean's concept is: Levinson, Marc, *The Box: How the Shipping Container Made the World Smaller and the World Economy Bigger*, Princeton University Press, Princeton, NJ, 2006.

12. TEU = Twenty-foot Equivalent Unit. This refers to a standard container measuring 20 ft (length) × 8 ft (width) × 8.5 ft (height). FEU = Forty-foot Equivalent Unit. The standard FEU measures 40 ft (length) × 8 ft (width) × 8.5 ft (height).

13. "Annual Container Market Review and Forecast 2007/08", Drewry Shipping Consultants, Ltd., September 2007, www.drewry.co.uk/news.php?id=9

TEUs.[14] The complement to the container vessel's scale efficiency is the port's ability to handle increasingly larger-sized vessels and maintain quick turn times not only for the vessel itself but for trucks and trains. In the case of Hong Kong, "a vessel arrives or departs every 1.2 minutes [and] one TEU is handled every two seconds".[15]

Beginning its journey in the Asian hinterlands (Figure 15.1), a container may be filled with hundreds of small items to be sold in stores in other parts of the world. From the factory, a full container rolls away, securely fastened to a trailer or chassis, on its way to a rail yard where a train hauls the container to another rail yard hundreds of miles away, to be trans-loaded to a truck before finally arriving at the port for its ocean voyage. Or, the small items may leave the factory bound for a distribution centre to be consolidated in a container with other commodities and then sent to the port via truck. At the port, the container may sit for a day or two waiting to be stowed on the vessel. The container in its journey to its final destination is exposed to numerous individuals with numerous opportunities for its theft or pilferage.

Herein lies the inherent risk of freight transportation in general: trust must be given to every individual in the supply chain that he/she will act honestly and accurately report the contents of the container (in the case of the shipper) and transport it without incident (in the case of the truck driver, for example) or resist the pressure to become involved as an insider supporting the theft (in the case of a port worker or warehouseman, for example). The movement of a container on the tractor trailer is the mode most vulnerable to cargo theft. In Asia, for example, before a container is loaded on a ship bound for the US, it will typically pass through more than 12 waypoints.[16] In the US, for example, there have been no significant background checks on the nearly 11,000 owner/operator truck drivers who enter container terminals every day and will remain so until the Transportation Worker Identification Credential (TWIC) becomes fully implemented on 15 April 2009.[17]

14. "ASX-Alphaliner Top 100 Operated Fleet as of 19 January 2008", www.axsmarine.com/public/top100/index.php

15. Coulter, Daniel Y., "Globalization of Maritime Commerce: The Rise of Hub Ports", www.ndu.edu/inss/books/Books_2002/Globalization_and_Maritime_Power_Dec_02/08_ch07.htm

16. Flynn, Stephen, "The Continued Vulnerability of the Global Maritime Transportation System", 9 March 2006. www.cfr.org/publication/10074/continued_vulnerability_of_the_global_maritime_transportation_system.html

17. *Ibid.*

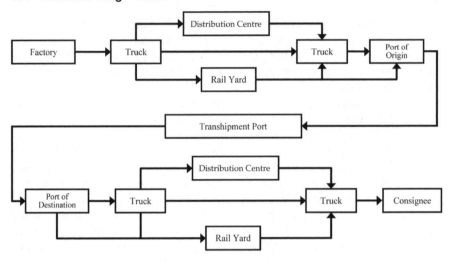

Figure 15.1 The travel path of a container from origin to destination

Estimates indicate that world-wide "approximately 5% of all container move-ments result in theft, damage, or excessive delays"[18] and the annual financial loss due to cargo theft and pilferage in the US alone is approximately $15 billion and the international loss at least $50 billion.[19] However, if all direct and peripheral costs related to cargo theft in the US alone are factored into the cost calculation, it could feasibly account for as much as 1% of the US GDP.[20,21]

18. "Clarkson Professor Helps Speed Global Cargo Security System to Market", Clarkson University, web2.clarkson.edu/news//view.php?id=1420

19. Hoffman, William, "Cargo Theft Rising", *Journal of Commerce*, 17 December 2007, Vol. 8, No. 50, p. 38.

20. Wolfe, Michael, "In this case, bad news is good news", *Journal of Commerce*, 26 July–1 August 2004, p. 38.

21. This estimate is determined upon the following and establishes a baseline GDP of about $11 trillion: The US Department of Transportation presented a report which included the cost of claims administration and investigations to the value of the stolen cargoes. Their estimate is $20–$60 billion. Wolfe rightfully assumes that official cargo theft statistics are low and do not reflect the unreported figures. While the official law enforcement assumption is that as much as 60% of all thefts go unreported, creating a direct loss of $45 billion, Wolfe hedges that figure in favour of a more conservative 40% representing a direct loss of $30 billion. He then includes the indirect costs: "sales lost to stolen goods, damaged brand value", the impact on insurance coverage, etc., a cost estimated to be "three to five times greater than the direct costs of the loss". This now provides a range of $90 to $150 billion for the indirect costs, or: one percent of US GDP. The total value of all goods transported via all forms of trucking (for-hire and not-for-hire) in 2002 equalled 6.2 trillion dollars (2002 Economic Census, Transportation, Commodity Flow Survey, p. 16) and a 2002 estimate by the Transportation Research Board estimated that the US transportation industry itself represents more than 11% of US GDP ("Critical Issues in Trans-portation, 2002", Transportation Research Board, p. 2).

3. THE PROCESS OF CARGO THEFT

Cargo thieves typically seek high-tech equipment, consumer electronics, computer components, clothing and shoes, alcohol and cigarettes, cosmetics, and pharmaceutical goods. The objective is to find low volume and high-value cargoes (such as home stereo equipment) that have a ready black market distribution network, and are not easily identifiable as stolen (such as a bar of soap).[22,23]

As in the legitimate market, the illegitimate market is dependent upon a supply chain driven by consumer demand and met by producer supply. In this case, the demand is created by an organised crime ring which identifies goods to be stolen and criminals who steal them. Concerned with an efficient turn around and a tax-free, all-cash income flow, the criminal underworld has developed an appropriate means to this end. The concept and the process of cargo theft is a complex set of risk analysis, both business and personal.

3.1 The fence

There are three components of the cargo theft market: the customer (who knowingly or unknowingly purchases stolen goods), the criminal, and the fence. "The magnitude of [cargo] theft is so great . . . the only reasonable outlet must be to legitimate consumers".[24] The thief probably does not have a personal need for a container full of tyres or shoes and is likely to sell the goods to a criminal distributor, the fence. The fence usually has a market willing to purchase stolen goods at a low price providing the fence with a low-risk profit.

There is a synergistic relationship between the thief and the fence; one is dependent upon the other to sustain his business. The thief, who is eager to be rid of the stolen goods, needs a market to take possession of it. The fence is either an outright seller of stolen goods to individuals or fills the shelves of a legitimate business with the items. The motive of a fence to use stolen merchandise in his business operations is twofold: first, to increase profit margins by acquiring goods at a cost less than the legitimate wholesale cost, and second, to undercut competitors with lower prices. Likewise, the thief may have a ready supply of fences available as receivers of stolen goods. Efficiency in the stolen goods market place is crucial to the viability and sustainability of the cargo theft industry. "Goods hijacked at 4:30 p.m. may be on retail shelves by 5:15 pm that same day".[25]

---

22. "Mitigating Transit Theft", Chubb Group, p. 1, www.chubb.com/businesses/cci/chubb1100.pdf

23. Hoffman, William, "Cargo theft rising", *Shipping Digest*, 24 December 2007.

24. Blakey, G. Robert, Michael Goldsmith, "Criminal Redistribution of Stolen Property: The Need for Law Reform", *Michigan Law Review*, Vol. 74, No. 2, August 1976, p. 1518.

25. *Ibid.*, p. 1541.

Historically, the amount of compensation that a thief can demand is roughly one-third of the value of stolen goods; he knows that he cannot get a half, which is the standard wholesale ratio value.[26] In some instances, thieves determine the legitimate wholesale value of stolen goods in order to avoid receiving lower prices for the goods from fences than otherwise.[27]

Ideally, the fence would like to have low-volume, high-value stolen goods. However, they are more likely to deal in high-volume, low-value goods such as clothing, food, and cigarettes. The fence determines prices just as a legitimate business would. They must take into consideration the price paid for the stolen goods, their current legitimate market price, and storage and transportation fees. However, assuming that a person who knowingly consumes stolen goods will be charged a lower price than someone who purchases a legitimately sold item, the fence must also incorporate the cost of legitimising the goods for sale, such as the removal of product labels or falsifying purchase orders.[28] The fence will continue a particular operation until a point at which his prices reach equilibrium with legitimate market prices for the same goods.

The fencing operation has many similarities to the legitimate supply chain. Blakey and Goldsmith have identified distinct types of fencing operations.[29] The first, and perhaps most distant from the theme of maritime cargo theft, is the Neighbourhood Connection fence. This fence typically deals within its own neighbourhood and only with small amounts of goods provided directly by the thief.[30] Occasionally, neighbourhood fences may increase the scope of their operation and organise a customer-specified heist or develop relationships with other fences. The Outlet Fence is a business that may or may not know that it is the conduit for selling stolen goods. The legitimate businesses do not deal directly with thieves but instead receive repackaged goods from other fencing operations via apparently legitimate wholesalers.

The Professional Fence typically poses as a legal retail establishment, and may actually perform some or even a substantial amount of legal transactions. But in reality it acts as the primary distribution channel for stolen goods. This fence may also organise heists to meet a particular customer's needs and is heavily dependent upon insider information that provides detailed information, for example, on container numbers, the distribution centre where a particular container is destined, or the state of security surrounding a particular container.

26. Blakey, G. Robert, Michael Goldsmith, "Criminal Redistribution of Stolen Property: The Need for Law Reform", *Michigan Law Review*, Vol. 74, No. 2, August 1976, p. 1515. See footnote 18.

27. *Ibid.*, p. 1515.

28. *Ibid.*, p. 1526.

29. *Ibid.*, pp. 1529–1542.

30. In this instance, the thief is typically a shoplifter or an employee at a warehouse, for example.

The Master Fence has multiple roles: a middle-man between two other fencing operations or the organiser of theft operations. As the organiser, the fence is diligent to keep his distance from the stolen goods themselves but makes arrangements for the stolen goods' storage, legitimisation, and delivery. The Master Fence "relies upon his paid connections, such as a dock employee of a manufacturing company or a dispatcher of a trucking outfit, to provide detailed information on shipments of valuable merchandise".[31] Since these heists are planned according to a customer's specific order, they will move quickly through the underground supply chain. Furthermore, because a Master Fence typically has ties to or is directly involved in organised crime, their success is an indicator of the extent to which organised crime is involved in their operations.

The Syndicated Crime fence is the ultimate cargo theft operation that utilizes a network of criminals and informants that focuses mainly on large-scale heists. Organised crime is able to capitalise on its vast financial and logistical resources as well as connections to smaller fencing operations to maintain its prominence in the stolen cargo market. They use truck drivers to employ the "give-up" tactic (discussed in the next section) or coerce drivers to assist by calling in their gambling or loan debts. The bosses of these organisations often keep themselves distant from the actual perpetration of crime and the stolen goods.

3.2 The thief

The complementary partner to the fence is the person who has decided to be the thief of stolen goods. Thieves are individuals who see the potential reward of stealing to outweigh the potential risk, whether the reward is financial compensation or personal satisfaction.

Whether an individual will be a thief of stolen goods will depend upon the:[32]

- expected payoff;
- direct costs incurred to obtain stolen goods, e.g., paying-off an insider;
- opportunity cost of being legitimately employed (which is likely to be significantly lower than the income generated by stealing);
- likelihood of being caught;
- potential time and monetary punishment if caught and prosecuted; and

---

31. Blakey, G. Robert, Michael Goldsmith, "Criminal Redistribution of Stolen Property: The Need for Law Reform", *Michigan Law Review*, Vol. 74, No. 2, August 1976, p. 1536.

32. Ehrlich, Isaac, "Crime, Punishment, and the Market for Offenses", *The Journal of Economic Perspectives*, Vol. 10, No. 1. (Winter, 1996), p. 46.

- one's preference for crime—determined by one's moral values, proclivity for violence, and preference for risk.

Therefore, a person will be willing to commit a crime if overall benefit of the crime exceeds its risk.

There are two motivators, positive and negative, to compel a person not to commit a crime. A positive motivator is the enticement for a person to seek a lawful alternative to committing a crime, e.g., seeking legitimate employment and income. A negative motivator is the deterrent of a harsh and long prison sentence in committing a crime.[33]

3.3 The modus operandi

To steal cargo, criminals employ a variety of tactics ranging from crude and destructive to fraudulent manipulation. In the US, common strategies that have been used by cargo thieves are:[34,35]

- driver "give-away": a truck driver receives a minimally acceptable cash payment (or satisfies a debt) from a criminal group to become an accomplice and simply gives them the truck and cargo; the accomplice driver reports the incident as a hijacking, thereby being absolved of any wrongdoing;
- insider collusion: an employee of a firm that deals directly with cargo and transportation documentation, passes such information to a criminal group;
- blackmailing, bribing, or coercing employees: the accomplice is forced into participation rather than being enticed by compensation;
- fraudulent shipping documentation: this tactic is used by a truck driver who, with insider help, presents counterfeit documents to facility personnel for a pre-targeted, high-valued cargo;
- "grab and run": high-valued cargo transiting streets is identified by a gang and pursued; when the truck stops, several members quickly jump out of their vehicle, open the container, for example, and pilfer as much cargo as they can before the truck begins to roll again;[36]

---

33. Ehrlich, Isaac, "Crime, Punishment, and the Market for Offenses", *The Journal of Economic Perspectives*, Vol. 10, No. 1. (Winter, 1996), p. 44.

34. Cullen, David, "Shining a light on Cargo Theft", *FleetOwner*, 1 August 2006, p. 26.

35. Badolato, Edward V., "Cargo Security: Avoiding Theft and Loss in the New Millennium", presented at the Supply Chain Solutions 1999 conference, p. 3, www.iiainc.net/articles/Supply%20Chain%20Presentation.doc

36. Anecdotal note: on the Northeast corner of 39th Street and Wentworth (next to the Dan Ryan Expressway/I-90/94) on the Southside of Chicago, one can generally observe a Chicago Police cruiser parked on the sidewalk continuously patrolling that intersection. This intersection is notoriously known for "grab and run" activity. This intersection is an entrance to a major railhead and warehouse district.

- warehouse burglary and theft of goods;
- warehouse for stolen cargo: a gang's central storage location for stolen cargo, trucks, containers, and trailers; may be an abandoned warehouse, a public storage facility, or a residence.

3.3.1 Document fraud

Document fraud has various methods of implementation. For example, an inside informant who has access to a container terminal's electronic records looks for high-valued cargoes in these records. The informant notifies a trucking accomplice of the high-valued cargo and its container serial number. A false document is then created including every detail necessary to locate and retrieve the targeted container.

The International Union of Marine Insurance (IUMI) found that there is a tendency in the cargo insurance industry to set a dollar value threshold below which claims tend not to be thoroughly investigated.[37] The rationale is that a claim below the threshold does not warrant an adjuster's in-depth claim investigation. Instead, the adjuster merely reviews the claim followed by payment to the claimant. This process may be known and thus exploited by criminals.

A scenario in which a criminal group exploits this weakness may involve several accomplices in the supply chain.[38] For example, an accomplice may intentionally short-load a container, i.e., loaded with less than the declared quantity of goods. At the container's destination port, surveyors and Customs agents open the container, observe the shortage, and verify the shortage against the container's manifest. A claim is then filed for a value below the insurance company's minimum investigation threshold. The accomplice shipper subsequently receives a claims payment against the now documented and, in reality, falsified shortage.

This criminal strategy may be continued for many months before the scam is detected. Underwriters will eventually notice a pattern and link the activity to the shipper and subsequently refuse to further insure the company's shipments. However, given the confidential nature of the insurance business and its drive to capture market share, another firm is usually willing to take on a new client. If so, it will become the next victim of the scam. A cargo theft ring may successfully execute a given scam for many years by exploiting one insurer after another before word is spread throughout the insurance industry about

37. Mukundan, Pottengal, "Marine Cargo Fraud", International Union of Marine Insurance, Cargo/Cargo Loss Prevention Workshop, 14 September 1999, p. 5, www.aimu.org/IUMI%20 PAPERS/CARGO%20&%20CARGO%20LOSS%20PREVENTION/ Marine%20Cargo%20Fraud.pdf
38. *Ibid.*

this group's tactics. The critical issue in this circumstance is that insurance firms tend not to share information with each other about known crime rings and their *modus operandi*.

Another type of document fraud has been identified in the UK, where organised crime groups are involved in a tactic called "VAT (Value Added Tax) Carousel Fraud". This is a relatively simplistic scheme in which the same load of electronic goods is repeatedly "imported" with a VAT refund claimed for each imported load.[39]

3.3.2 Warehouse theft

Cargo theft organisations have also ventured into distribution and ware-housing, where they have direct or indirect access to high-valued and high-demand cargoes. Surprisingly, in spite of the proliferation of advanced on-site security technology, the gangs that target warehouses and distribution centres still rely on old-fashioned breaking and entry techniques unmodified since the break-bulk era.

A cargo theft ring without insider help may spend weeks observing key aspects of a warehouse's characteristics. For instance, knowing the centre's hours of operation, visible security measures, access routes to and from major roadways, and frequency of police patrolling helps establish a pattern around which the ring can plan its attack.

In order to gain insider access to the facility, cargo theft rings have been known to infiltrate a warehouse by using a member to apply for a job (e.g., as a forklift operator) at the warehouse or act as a vendor or contractor. Once infiltrated, the individual may directly observe and analyse the security sys-tems in place and become familiar with the floor plan and the warehouse's access points. Generally, the operation involves a highly specialised team consisting of a truck driver, forklift operators, surveillance personnel, and alarm system technicians to conduct a theft.[40]

It is not unusual for the warehouse's managers to be profoundly surprised that their deterrence efforts against cargo thefts have been thwarted. The security system industry itself has often failed to understand the operating methods employed by cargo theft gangs. Thus, the industry's clients believe falsely that they have purchased and implemented sufficient security meas-ures. Furthermore, the security system industry typically includes caveats in its contracts, absolving them of responsibility and limiting their liability should their systems or its employees fail to protect the cargo of its clients.

39. "Fighting Lorry Load Theft—A Partnership Approach", Essex Police, IUMI Paper, September 2000, p. 2.

40. Brandman, Barry, "Cargo Theft: A Costly Epidemic", *Loss Prevention Magazine*, February-March 2007, www.lpportal.com/archives_view.html?id=1736

4. THE ROLE OF INSURANCE

Cargo insurance, like any other insurance product, is detailed and laden with caveats. The purpose of this section is not meant to provide a comprehensive exploration of cargo insurance nuances, but rather to discuss the practice of insuring cargo during its landside movement and the efforts of insurers to educate members of the cargo supply chain on means to reduce or deter opportunities for cargo theft.

The nature in which international maritime containers are transported provides cargo thieves with many opportunities to deprive cargo owners of their goods. A container may experience an interruption in its journey for a number of reasons and thus become sitting prey. As the adage goes, "A sitting cargo is cargo at risk". Because cargo owners have little control over their goods during transit, it is in their best interest to shift the risk of a loss to an insurer. Cargo insurers have worked with the shipping industry and law enforcement to create new cargo protection methods and technological innovations to prevent cargo theft.

Insurance firms often disseminate information about theft occurrences to their clients and provide tips on how to better secure their goods or to create a transparent paper trail in their supply chain. For securing goods in containers, insurers often recommend to their clients that they make the contents of containers as plain and anonymous as possible. To avoid handlers becoming familiar with shippers' bills of lading, shippers are advised to frequently change coding schemes and avoid routine schedules. Also, shippers are advised to insist that their containers be removed from a storage or marshalling yard and be transported to the consignee as soon as possible. Further, if a theft is detected, the insurer and law enforcement should be contacted immediately to minimise the time between theft and response.

One method to reduce exposing a container's contents is to ship the container door-to-door, thereby avoiding the possibility of trans-loading, where the contents of one container are removed and consolidated with other cargoes in another container. By shipping port-to-port and door-to-port, containers are more likely to spend time in storage at a port.

Insurance is a contractual agreement between the insurer and the assured in which the insurer agrees to reimburse or indemnify the assured for a loss occurring under the conditions of the contract. Cargo insurance is a complex process that provides financial remuneration for the actual loss or declared value of the goods to a party who pays for coverage. However, it is ultimately the responsibility of the buyer and the seller to determine who is responsible for coverage at every point in the journey of the goods.

The shipper is under certain obligations to truthfully assess the insurance needs for a particular shipment. For example, the shipper may see a need to negotiate with the insurer to acquire an endorsement that covers cargo theft by its employees, known as "employee infidelity", and verify that every carrier in every mode used in transporting its cargo is indeed covered by an insurance policy.

The shipper should not assume that carriers and warehouses are adequately insured to pay for losses due to theft. The insurance liability of carriers to recompense cargo owners for their losses is usually a maximum financial limit set forth in the cargo's bill of lading (determined by the carrier's or warehouse's tariff). In the US, a trucking firm's liability is limited to about $.50 per pound of cargo shipped, whereas the liability for the warehouse and railroad is determined by each particular firm.[41]

Typically, shippers purchase an "All-Risks" policy covering the shipment from the seller's facility to its arrival at either the port of destination or the buyer's warehouse. The owner of the goods in transit usually supplements the cargo with "shipper's interest coverage" as All-Risks may not provide adequate coverage. The shipper may also choose to purchase "warehouse storage coverage" for the goods that are either pre- or post-transit or are experiencing an extended interruption and must remain in storage.[42]

A warehouse-to-warehouse insurance clause states specifically when the insurance coverage begins and when it finishes. It remains in effect while the goods transit from the warehouse of origin to the warehouse of destination and continues during a transit delay only if the assured notifies the insurer in a timely manner and then pays any additional premiums.[43]

Carrier insurance policies may not in certain situations provide sufficient insurance for cargo that they transport. That is to say, the policies may exclude carrier insurance on shipper cargo under certain situations, for example in the case of "theft from an unattended vehicle, unless parked overnight in a public garage or locked private garage, and at all times, unless the loss is the direct result of visible, forcible entry". Another possible exclusion is for a carrier incident that occurs when the vehicle used in the transportation of cargo is not the vehicle recorded in the carrier's insurance policy. Also, it is not uncommon for an insurer to absolve itself of any obligation to provide coverage for a cargo that has been conveyed to someone posing as the true recipient of the cargo even if the carrier believed that it was dealing with the true recipient.[44]

Although a carrier is obligated to provide insurance coverage for its customers' cargoes, the shipper is also expected to use due diligence by having its cargo sufficiently insured from origin to destination. The amount of coverage

41. "Cargo Insurance Manual", Roanoke Trade Services, Inc., 2006, p. 1–1, www.roanoke-trade.com/pdf/marinetemplates/Cargo%20Insurance%20Manual%202006.pdf

42. The extended storage may be due to a logistics problem or it may include a firm that stores inventory off-site as part of a Just-In-Time process. "Cargo Insurance Manual", Roanoke Trade Services, Inc., 2006, p. 7–7, www.roanoketrade.com/pdf/marinetemplates/Cargo%20Insurance%20Manual%202006.pdf

43. "Cargo Insurance Manual", Roanoke Trade Services, Inc. 2006, p. 26, www.roanoke trade.com/pdf/marinetemplates/Cargo%20Insurance%20Manual%202006.pdf

44. Augello, William J., Esq., "So You Think Your Freight is Insured?" *Logistics Management*, 1 May 2003, www.news.thomasnet.com/IMT/archives/2003/06/the_ins_outs_of.html?t=archive

and the policy exclusions are expected to be understood by the shipper and carriers prior to the cargo beginning its journey.

An Open Cargo Policy can assure cargo in foreign trade from the seller's warehouse to the buyer's warehouse. The policy typically has three clauses: a Perils Clause; at least one Average Clause; and an additional basic coverage clause such as the Warehousing and Forwarding Packages Lost in Loading Clause.[45]

The insurance industry estimates that "for every $1 of direct cost recovered from insurance, another $4 is lost to non-reimbursable indirect costs related to lost sales, replacement shipments, customer dissatisfaction, and implementation of deterrents".[46] Many larger insurers have risk management departments that work with clients in analysing the integrity of their cargo security initiatives and methods for theft prevention and deterrence. By working with clients, losses can be monitored and reduced.

To reduce the likelihood of cargo theft, shippers may demand from carriers: (1) direct routeing of their cargo from origin to destination; (2) elimination of as many stops and transhipment points as possible in the transportation of their cargo; (3) real-time tracking capabilities; and (4) the use of tamper-evident seals on containers. Shippers should consider hiring carriers that conduct background checks of their employees but also should be wary of carriers that subcontract the transportation of cargo without the shipper's consent.

Shippers should also scrutinise cargo-theft vulnerabilities within their operations. For example, they should not label a box of goods with a company logo or any other conspicuous indicator of the content in the box and use a tamper-evident tape when sealing boxes. Further, shippers should limit the description of the cargo (to the extent possible) on the cargo's manifest or bill of lading. In regions of intense theft, say in underdeveloped countries, shippers may request that carriers use an escort service.[47] The insurance industry believes that it is the shipper's responsibility to utilize reliable transportation carriers. In turn, the shipper purchases insurance from an insurer in order to shift the risk and burden of cargo theft to the insurer.

Warehouse insurance is less complicated than cargo insurance. In general, warehouse insurance policies fall into one of two categories, Warehouseman's Legal Liability and Bailees' Customers, where the latter supplements the former.

The Warehouseman's Legal Liability policy is issued by the American Association of Insurance Services and limits the extent to which the warehouse is financially liable for customers' goods in storage. The policy states that goods must be stored in the warehouse or within 100 feet of it. The

45. "Guide to US Cargo Insurance", American Institute of Marine Underwriters, 2005, p. 7.

46. "Mitigating Transit Theft, Chubb Group, p. 1, www.chubb.com/businesses/cci/chubb1100.pdf

47. *Ibid.*

"Fraud and Deceit" extension to this policy protects the assured in the event that it is led to believe that it is releasing cargo to the true owner; the extension provides a limited liability of $1,000. However, in the event that an employee of a warehouse participates in cargo theft, the policy will not cover the loss.[48]

The Bailee's Customers policy starts where the Warehouseman's Legal Liability ends. It would be purchased to protect and maintain the warehouse's goodwill and reputation with a client whose cargo has been stolen from a warehouse. Bailees are persons who have custody of another's property. If a bailee does not "exercise the ordinary, prudent care which a reasonable man would presumably give to his own property", he has acted negligently and will be liable for his negligence.[49] For example, if a client's cargo is stolen from a warehouse and the warehouse was not adequately protected from theft, such as in the case of an alarm system not being activated at the end of the day, the legal liability of the warehouse would be limited to no more than $1,000. However, wishing to maintain its goodwill, the warehouse would previously have purchased supplemental coverage, i.e., the Bailee's Customers policy, to provide financial coverage above the $1,000 offered in the legal liability policy, i.e., the Warehouseman's Legal Liability policy.

5. LAW ENFORCEMENT

The move to integrate international crime data and to streamline reporting procedures has been underway in the EU since the 1990s. In the US, however, it was not until 2007 that the federal government introduced and implemented legislation setting the foundation for uniformity in reporting cargo crimes.

The European Conference of Ministries of Transport (ECMT) is a European organisation of 41 transportation ministries, established in Brussels in 1953 to facilitate discussion about transportation problems and to reach joint solutions that ensure "rational development of European transport systems of international importance". ECMT's purpose is to create a "political bridge between the European Union and the rest of the continent at a political level" while creating an integrated, economical, and technically efficient transportation infrastructure. As of 2002, the ECMT sought "the development and implementation of a pan-European transport policy; the integration of Central and Eastern European countries into the European transport market; specific issues relating to transport by rail, road, and waterway" among other topics.[50]

48. "AAIS Warehouse Legal Liability Coverage Form", American Association of Insurance Services, www.roughnotes.com/pfm/300/..%5C100%5C142_1500.htm

49. Block, Huntington T., "Insurance in the Conservation Laboratory", *Bulletin of the American Group. International Institute for Conservation of Historic and Artistic Works*, Vol. 1, No. 2, April 1961, p. 5.

50. "Crime in Road Freight Transport", European Conference of Ministers of Transport, 2002, p. 3.

In 1997 and again in 1999, ECMT agreed to further investigate and make recommendations to counter the growing trend of transportation crime in Europe. The ECMT created the Steering Group on Combating Crime in Transport whose membership includes representatives of Transportation and Economics Ministries, national and international police organisations, customs agencies, and the insurance and transportation industries. The Group's first, and perhaps most significant, undertaking was to standardise a database of transport crime. Second, the Group investigated technological solutions to crime deterrence and prevention. Furthermore, it acknowledged that the terrorist attacks of 11 September 2001 uniquely tied supply chain and cargo security to global counter-terrorism objectives.

The Group compiled the report, "Crime in Road Freight Transport", which includes country-specific information and statistical analysis of criminal events. However, there were fundamental and inherent problems in creating a uniform code for reporting cargo crimes. Each EU member has a unique method of reporting and investigating crimes.

The report indicates that, throughout Europe, up to 1% of the vehicles engaged in cargo transportation are stolen annually. In Sweden, the trucking industry is experiencing a dramatic increase in cargo thefts and it is extending into the hinterland areas. In response, the Swedish trucking industry and its customers are looking for solutions to the problem. Customers are either hiring trucking firms that specialise in high security transportation, offer high-tech protection, or employ escort service providers. A problem in addressing the cargo thefts in Sweden is that foreign truck carriers who experience a theft incident in Sweden may prefer to report the theft to authorities in their home country rather than to the Swedish government.

The ECMT has also found that larger carriers typically report cargo thefts while smaller carriers are reluctant to do so, perhaps because of the likelihood of experiencing higher insurance rates in the future. Further, cargo theft is subject to under-reporting. However, "reporting errors are likely to be proportional to the true crime rate".[51] A victim of a crime is more likely to report the crime if it is known that the criminal will be severely punished or if the victim receives compensation for information leading to an arrest.[52]

In the US, as in other countries, government and law enforcement agencies do not have databases that include records of cargo thefts. If these databases are available, they often have incomplete information on the extent of the cargo thefts. Uniform and accurate reporting of cargo thefts by carriers and shippers to local, national, and international governments is expected to dramatically enhance the capabilities of law enforcement to combat cargo thefts. The reporting would provide governments and law enforcement agencies with information for detecting trends in the thefts: (1) of certain types of

---

51. Ehrlich, Isaac, "Crime, Punishment, and the Market for Offenses", *The Journal of Economic Perspectives*, Vol. 10, No. 1 (Winter, 1996), pp. 58–59.

52. *Ibid.*, p. 59.

commodities; (2) at specific ports or distribution centres; and (3) true dollar value.[53]

6. PRIVATE SECTOR DETERRENCE MEASURES

Rather than government, the private sector may be more effective at preventing cargo theft. A notable private sector initiative to combat cargo theft is the Transported Asset Protection Association (TAPA) that began in 1997 as an initiative by the security managers of the US companies Intel, Compaq, and other high-tech manufacturers.[54] Today, TAPA is a global association of 400 private firms that seeks to be a unifying, common front among shippers, freight forwarders, security managers, and manufacturers that share the common goal of reducing losses from cargo theft. The members openly share information to facilitate preventative security theft measures through industry best practices.

A TAPA goal is to establish a minimum level of cargo security standards for logistics service providers, carriers, and handlers throughout the supply chain, while developing and maintaining strong relationships with domestic and international law enforcement agencies. Furthermore, TAPA is actively involved in helping to shape the regulatory requirements set forth by national governments and customs agencies.

TAPA-EMEA (TAPA-Europe, Middle East, Asia) has undertaken numerous efforts to eradicate cargo theft. It seeks to foster a secure supply chain from beginning to end via its two transportation operating standards, the Freight Security Requirement (FSR) and the Truck Security Requirement (TSR).

FSR is a qualitative cargo security standard and certification developed in 2000 to ensure a minimum acceptable level of cargo security for storage and warehousing facilities. Further, methods to maintain this qualification are specified. TAPA uses its network of auditing agencies (e.g., Bureau Veritas, Germanischer Lloyd, Lloyd's Register Quality Assurance, and SGS) to determine whether a facility adheres to FSR requirements.

Unlike FSR, TSR only requires a self-assessment of TAPA-EMEA compliance, e.g., truck carriers would determine whether they provide TAPA-EMEA's minimum level of cargo security. TAPA-EMEA members would then choose truck carriers based upon whether, in their opinion, the carriers have met the minimum level of cargo security.

The TAPA-EMEA is also actively involved in securing rest areas for truckers. The secure parking initiative, Secured European Truck Parking Operational Services (SETPOS), combines the knowledge and security efforts of key European players in cargo movement. In 2007, a secured truck parking

---

53. Edmonson, R.G., "Keeping track of cargo theft", *Shipping Digest*, 24 April 2006.
54. All information found at their homepage: www.tapaemea.com

facility was developed in France, the first of about 50 to be built around Europe. SETPOS is seeking to have all truck rest areas in a Trans-European network to be modelled after the park in France, each meeting a minimum standard of quality and safety established by the TAPA Secure Parking Working Group (WESP).

TAPA-EMEA also provides a central incident data collection point as a service to its members. The Incident Information Service (IIS) collects crime incident data that is analysed to alert members of new trends or problem locations. IIS also serves as a crime database that reports uniform information quarterly in a newsletter.[55] The 2007 second quarter newsletter reported 79 incidents of cargo theft and one incident of fraud. The thefts of laptops and PDAs occurred most often. Cargo thefts occurred most often in the North Rhine-Westphalia region and the least in the Baden-Württemberg region in Germany. France topped the list of countries where the most thefts occurred, 25 incidents, while Belgium experienced the fewest, four.[56]

In South Africa, TAPA is helping manufacturing and transportation industries to more effectively combat a widespread cargo theft epidemic. Between April 2006 and March 2007, there were 893 cargo hijackings reported. However, two problems block South African firms from joining TAPA: cost of membership and, perhaps more insidious, fear, apprehension, and uncertainty about sharing confidential information.[57] The South African TAPA initiative is focused on air cargo crime, especially at the Johannesburg airport (JNB). Between 2005 and 2006, there were 200 reports of cargo thefts at JNB. The next closest airport, statistically, was Schiphol, Belgium with 18 incidents.[58]

7. TOOLS FOR CONTAINER PHYSICAL SECURITY

Because containers allow a shipment of cargo to be transported in a single conveyance without the need for transhipment, containers reduce cargo susceptibility for theft. While containers add a significant layer of protection against cargo being stolen or pilfered, its protection is only as good as the means of keeping it secured within the box and the reliability of the people in the supply chain.

Since the terrorist attack in 2001, the Advanced Container Security Device (ACSD) has been a primary focus of the Department of Homeland Security's Science and Technology department.[59] One of the ACSD developments, the

---

55. The information is gathered in three sections: (1) incident category definitions lists and defines the type of crime committed, e.g., hi-jacking or fraud, (2) *modus operandi* lists and defines how the crime was committed, e.g., forced stop or internal, and (3) location types lists and defines where the crime was committed, e.g., en route or non-secured parking.

56. *Quarterly News Update*, TAPA-EMEA, Issue 2, 2007, p. 13.

57. *Ibid.*, p. 9.

58. *Quarterly News Report*, TAPA-EAMA, Issue 1, 2007, p. 3.

59. Edmonson, R.G. "Creating the smart container", *The Journal of Commerce*, 13 December 2004, p. 12.

Smart Container, was a collaborative effort between two German organisations to provide secure cargo transportation in Europe. The value-added technology allows shippers to track their cargo location as well as monitor the state of the contents using Radio Frequency Identification (RFID) and Global Positioning (GPS) technologies. RFID tags are strategically placed inside a container to spread a signal over the entire box and continuously monitor the condition of the box and its contents and then transmit this data to a small onboard computer. This information is then linked to the geographic location data provided by an onboard GPS unit and is streamed wirelessly to the shipper via the Internet for real-time monitoring.[60]

The cost of implementing this tool may be tied to the value of the cargo or to the urgency of needing a device for a particular container. However, the shipper should consider the opportunity cost of the device. Would the funds needed to purchase and use the device be better spent for additional cargo insurance?

A survey conducted in 2004 by Eyefortransport (an organisation that routinely conducts transportation industry surveys and conferences) asked whether the government, shippers, consignees or transportation providers should be responsible for the cost of anti-terrorism efforts in securing the supply chain security and cargo theft. In response to anti-terrorism, the respondents suggested that the onus belongs to the shipper and the government.[61] However, when combating cargo crime, the respondents indicated that the responsibility lies evenly across all entities, but placed a heavy responsibility on transportation providers. The indications are that more than half of the respondents are bearing the cost of security while nearly 40% are financing this cost through increased prices to their customers. Despite the strong opinion that cargo and supply chain security is vitally important to the industry and its customers, more than half of the study's respondents budget less than 1% of company revenue for cargo crime prevention and anti-terrorism measures.

When assessing the economic impact of implementing cargo security, the industry and regulators must ask whether it is enough to simply require minimal levels of security. It is myopic to only view the cost of security without also considering the cost of that security requirement to the overall cost of business. The security measure must also provide economic benefit. Likewise, government bodies need to take the economic impact on business into consideration when drafting security legislation that influences business operations and commerce. The negative result could lead to strong industry resistance if the cost is excessive.

Nevertheless, it is possible that security measures can return significant benefits to industry players. For example, the 24-hour pre-departure submission to Customs and Border Patrol requirement of a vessel's manifest,

60. "NEWS: Thinking outside the box", *The Engineer*, 11 July 2005, p. 14.
61. "Eyefortransport, North American Supply Chain Security, An Analysis of eyefortransport's Recent Survey", July 2004, pp. 16–22.

demanded by C-TPAT,[62] allows vessel planners to complete their tasks a day earlier and terminal operators to streamline their yard operations.

8. CONCLUSION

Cargo crime is a pervasive event that will likely be a persistent component of society, irrespective of deterrence measures. Given both the complexities and the efficiencies created by intermodalism, the ease of container cargo theft poses an economic threat. Criminal rings rely on the fact that, unless law enforcement agencies increase their force sizes or better deter or pursue and punish the criminals, there will be a growing inverse relationship between the number of containers in transit and the number of legal and law enforcement counter measures. While police and government organisations are constantly struggling with an under-developed and under-funded intelligence response, the push towards a standardised cargo-theft reporting system must continue. Standardisation in crime reporting likely provides more reliable information for combating cargo theft.

A container is vulnerable throughout its journey. Hence, a deterrent to stealing its cargo is needed. However, a deterrent is only as good as the efforts to implement it and properly utilize it. The private sector is able to quickly find solutions to combat cargo-theft problems while bureaucratic organisations tend to take considerably longer to achieve effective legislation and programmes. Private industry response, such as TAPA and SETPOS, indicate both a discontentment of the slow bureaucratic process to accomplish meaningful cargo-theft results and a desire to control losses and costs immediately. It is not surprising to see more effective cargo-theft programmes coming from the private industry. Ultimately, the cargo-theft industry is a threat to legitimate businesses and governments given costs that cargo theft places on the economy.

62. (C-TPAT) is a voluntary compliance programme that extends US security to the point of origin by establishing a minimum standard of security criteria for shippers, NVOCCs, freight forwarders, etc. When in compliance, the C-TPAT member is considered low risk and is afforded benefits such as expedited processing and less likely to be examined by Customs and Border Patrol (CBP). To remain in compliance, they must work continuously with CBP to maintain the integrity of the secured supply chain and present security action plans that align their supply chain with the objectives of C-TPAT.

LIST OF REFERENCES

Chapter 2

Abe, M. (2000). "Classification societies: Their roles, duties and responsibilities", *BIMCO Review 2000*, p. 116.

Ashburner, W. (1909). *The Rhodian Sea Law*, Oxford, Clarendon Press.

Bergantino, A. & Marlow, P. (1996). "An analysis of the decision to flag out", Seafarers' International Research Centre, University of Wales, Cardiff.

Boczek, B. (1962). *Flags of Convenience—an International Legal Study*, Harvard University Press, Cambridge, MA.

British Parliamentary Papers, 1970. *Committee of Inquiry into Shipping (Rochdale Report)* CMND 4337 (London: HMSO).

Bureau of Infrastructure, Transport and Regional Economics (BITRE) (2007). *Australian Trade Statistics 2007*, BITRE, Canberra, ACT.

Campbell, R. D. (1980). "The Ship's Register, a History of British Ships Status and Registration Procedures including their Adoption in New Zealand", Ministry of Transport, Marine Division, Auckland.

Goss, R. (1993). "Safety in sea transport", *Journal of Transport Economics and Policy*, January 1994.

Gunton, P. (2008). "IMO casualty code could mean 'major change' for shipping", in *Fairplay*, Vol. 362, Issue 6471, 6 March 2008, pp. 10–11.

International Chamber of Shipping (ICS) website www.marisec.org/shipping facts/worldtrade.php (accessed 13 February 2008).

Llacer, M. (2003). "Open Registers, past, present and future", *Marine Policy*, Vol. 27, Issue 6, pp.513–523 (Elsevier).

Nielsen, D. (2004). "Should Flag States Assume responsibility, or The case for Flag State Implementation", paper presented at Safer Ships Conference, National Maritime Museum, Greenwich, 22–24 March 2004, Greenwich, UK.

Resolution A. 739 (18) "Guidelines for the authorisation of organisations acting on behalf of the administration", as amended, www.imo.org/includes/blastDataOnly.asp/data_id%3D15582/208%2881%29.pdf (accessed 27 March 2008).

Resolution A. 789 (19) "Specifications on the survey and certification functions of recognised organisations", www.imo.org/Safety/mainframe.asp?topic_id=361, (accessed 27 March 2008).

UNCTAD (2007). *Review of Maritime Transport*, Geneva.

http://ec.europa.eu/justice_home/doc_centre/criminal/environmental/doc/com_2008_134–en.pdf (accessed 26 March 2008).

http://goliath.ecnext.com/coms2/gi_0199–6118941/GL-panel-rejects-BV-takeover.html (accessed 27 March 2008).

www.austlii.org/au/journals/ANZMLJ/2004/7.pdf (accessed 28 March 2008).

www.britanniapandi.com/circulars/14188_Britannia_Marpol.pdf (accessed 26 March 2008).

www.cdlive.lr.org/psc/psc.asp (accessed 29 Feb 2008).

www.iacs.org.uk (accessed 6 March 2008).

www.igpandi.org/downloadables/submissions/iopc_fund/Sept_92a10–32_e.pdf (accessed 27 March 2008).

www.imo.org/about/mainframe.asp?topic_id=106&doc_id=1755 (accessed 27 March 2008).

www.law.cornell.edu/uscode/18/1001.html (accessed 25 March 2008).

www.lr.org/corporate_information/brief_history.htm (accessed 8 March 2008).

www.marisec.org/flag-performance (accessed 19 March 2008).

www.parl.gc.ca/common/Bills_ls.asp?Parl=38&Ses=1&ls=C15 (accessed 26 March 2008).

www.tokyo-mou.org/ANN06.pdf (accessed 29 February 2008).

www.usdoj.gov/ag/readingroom/sarox1.htm (accessed 26 March 2008).

www.usdoj.gov/usao/eousa/foia_reading_room/usam/title9/crm00923.htm (accessed 25 March 2008).

www.usdoj.gov/usao/eousa/foia_reading_room/usam/title9crm1729.htm (accessed 26 March 2008).

Chapter 3

ABS (2002). "Prestige Casualty—Information Update No. 5", ABS Press Release, American Bureau of Shipping, 3 December.

Card, J. Haugland, B.K. and Pomeroy, V. (2004). "Developing the Next Generation of Classification Rules for Oil Tankers, *Proceedings of the International Conference on Design and Operation of Double Hull Tankers*", The Royal Institution of Naval Architects, London.

Cowley, J. (1995). "The Concept of the ISM Code", *Proceeding of Management and Operation of Ships: Practical Techniques for Today and Tomorrow*, The Institute of Marine Engineers, 24–25 May, London.

Eleye-Datubo, A.G. (2006). "Integrating Risk-based Assessment Modelling of Safety-critical Marine and Offshore Applications", PhD Thesis, Liverpool John Moores University, UK.

Eleye-Datubo, A.G., Wall, A., Saajedi, A. and Wang, J. (2006). "Enabling a Powerful Marine and Offshore Decision-Support Solution through Bayesian Network Technique", *Risk Analysis*, Vol. 26, No. 3, pp. 695–721.

House of Lords, (1992). "Safety Aspects of Ship Design and Technology

(Carver Report)", Select Committee on Science and Technology, 2nd Report, HL Paper 30-I, February.

HSE, (1995), "Generic Terms and Concepts in the Assessment and Regulation of Industrial Risks (Discussion Document DDE2)", *Health and Safety Executive*, HSE Books, Suffolk, UK.

IMO, (1997a), "Formal Safety Assessment: Trial Application to High Speed Passenger Catamaran Vessels", Final Report, DE 41/INF.7, submitted by IMO UK, IMO Sub-Committee on Ship Design and Equipment, 41st Session, Agenda Item 5, London, UK.

IMO, (1997b), "Interim Guidelines for the Application of Formal Safety Assessment to the IMO Rule-Making Process", IMO/MSC Circular 829, London, 17 November.

IMO, (1998a), "Bulk Carrier Safety, Proposal for a Formal Safety Assessment of Bulk Carriers", MSC70/4/Add1, submitted to the IMO by the UK MCA.

IMO, (1998b), "Trial Application of Formal Safety Assessment to Dangerous Goods on Passenger/Ro-Ro Vessels", MSC69/INF.24, submitted by IMO Finland.

IMO, (2002a), "International Collaborative FSA study on Bulk Carriers —Step 2 of FSA (Risk Analysis) WP 11—Develop Risk Contribution Tree Components", MSC 75/INF.22, submitted by France to IMO London, UK.

IMO, (2002b), "International Collaborative FSA Study—FSA step 3 (Risk Control Options)", MSC 76/INF.8, submitted to the IMO by IMO UK.

Kuo, C., (1998), *Managing Ship Safety*, LLP, London.

Liu, J., Yang, J.B., Wang, J., Sii, H.S. and Wang, Y.M., (2004), "Fuzzy Rule-based Evidential Reasoning Approach for Safety Analysis", *International Journal of General Systems*, Vol. 23, No. 2–3, pp. 183–204.

Lois, P., (2004), "Cyprus and Mediterranean Cruise Market: A Financial and Economic Appraisal", PhD Thesis, Liverpool John Moores University, UK.

Lois, P., Wang, J., Wall, A. and Ruxton, T., (2004), "Formal Safety Assessment of Cruise Ships", *Tourism Management*, Vol. 25, pp. 93–109.

Loughran, C., Pillay, A., Wang, J., Wall, A. and Ruxton, T., (2003), "A Preliminary Study of Fishing Vessel Safety", *Journal of Risk Research*, Vol. 5, No. 1, pp. 3–21.

MCA, (1993), "Formal Safety Assessment", submitted by the UK to IMO Maritime Safety Committee, Marine Safety Agency, MSC66/14.

MSC, (1998a), "Notes on the Experience Gained on Formal Safety Assessment", informal paper submitted by UK to IMO/MSC, 69th Session, 12 February, (IMO/MSC 69/INF14), UK.

MSC, (1998b), "Formal Safety Assessment for Bulk Carriers (Including Annexes A-I)", informal paper submitted by UK to IMO/MSC, 70th Session, 27 November (IMO/MSC 70/INF PAPER), UK.

Pillay, A. (2001). "Formal Safety Assessment of Fishing Vessels", PhD Thesis, School of Engineering, Liverpool John Moores University, UK.

Pillay, A. and Wang, J. (2003). "A Risk Ranking Approach Incorporating Fuzzy Set Theory and Grey Theory", *Engineering Reliability & System Safety*, Vol. 79, No. 1, pp. 61–67.

PVA (1997). *A Guide to Improving the Safety of Passenger Vessel Operations by Addressing Risk*, Arlington, pp. 1–28.

Rosqvist, T. and Tuominen, R. (2004). "Qualification of Formal Safety Assessment: An Exploratory Study", *Safety Science*, Vol. 42, pp. 99–120.

Sekimizu, K. (1997). "Current work at IMO on Formal Safety Assessment", *Proceeding of Marine Risk Assessment: A Better Way to Manage Your Business*, The Institute of Marine Engineers, 8–9 April, London.

Sii, H.S. (2001). "Marine and Offshore Safety Assessment", PhD Thesis, Staffordshire University/Liverpool John Moores University, UK.

Sii, H.S., Ruxton, T. and Wang, J. (2001). "A Fuzzy-logic-based Approach to Qualitative Safety Modelling for Maritime Systems", *Reliability Engineering & System Safety*, Vol. 73, No. 1, pp. 19–34.

Spouse, J.R. (1997). "Risk Criteria for Use in Ship Safety Assessment", *Proceeding of Marine Risk Assessment: A Better Way to Manage Your Business*, The Institute of Marine Engineers, London, 8–9 April.

Trbojevic, V.M. (2002). "Risk-based Methodology for Safety Improvement", *Journal of Hazards Materials*, Vol. 71, pp. 467–480.

UK DpT (1987). "MV Herald of Free Enterprise—Fatal Accident Investigation", Sheen Report, Report of Court No. 8074, UK Department of Transport, HMSO.

Vie, R.H. and Stemp, J.B. (1997). "The Practical Application of Risk Assurance Technology Techniques to Cruise Vessel Design and Operation", *Proceeding of Marine Risk Assessment: A Better Way to Manage Your Business*, The Institute of Marine Engineers, London.

Wang, J. (1997). "A Subjective Methodology for Safety Analysis of Safety Requirements Specifications", *IEEE Transactions on Fuzzy Systems*, Vol. 5, No. 3, pp. 418–430.

Wang, J. (1999). "A Review of Design for Safety Methodology for Large Marine and Offshore Engineering Products", *Proceedings of the Institution of Mechanical Engineers Part E, IMechE Journal of Process Mechanical Engineering*, Vol. 212, pp. 251–261.

Wang, J. (2001). "Current Status of Future Aspects of Formal Safety Assessment of Ships", *Safety Science*, Vol. 38, pp. 19–30.

Wang, J. (2002). "Offshore Safety Case Approach and Formal Safety Assessment of Ships", *Journal of Safety Research*, Vol. 33, No. 1, pp. 81–115.

Wang, J. (2006). "Maritime Risk Assessment and its Current Status", *Quality and Reliability Engineering International*, Vol. 22, No. 1, pp. 3–19.

Wang, J. and Foinikis, P. (2001). "Formal Safety Assessment of Containerships", *Marine Policy*, Vol. 25, No. 2, pp. 143–157.

Wang, J., Sii, H.S., Yang, J.B., Pillay, A., Yu, D., Liu, J., Maistralis, E. and Saajedi, A. (2004). "Use of Advances in Technology for Maritime Risk Assessment", *Risk Analysis*, Vol. 24, No. 4, pp. 1041–1063.

Wang, J. and Trbojevic, V.M. (2007). *Design for Safety of Large Marine and Offshore Engineering Products*, Institute of Marine Engineering, Science and Technology (IMarEST), London, UK.

Wang, J., Yang, J.B. and Sen, P. (1995). "Safety Analysis and Synthesis Using Fuzzy Set Modelling and Evidential Reasoning", *Reliability Engineering & System Safety*, Vol. 47, No. 3, pp. 103–118.

Wang, J., Yang, J.B. and Sen, P. (1996). "Multi-person and Multi-attribute Design Evaluations Using Evidential Reasoning Based on Subjective Safety and Cost Analyses", *Reliability Engineering & System Safety*, Vol. 52, No. 2, pp. 113–128.

Yang, J.B., Liu, J., Wang, J., Sii, H.S. and Wang, Y.M. (2005a). "Belief Rule-base Inference Methodology Using the Evidential Reasoning Approach —RIMER", *IEEE Transactions on Systems, Man and Cybernetics—Part A: Systems and Humans*, Vol. 36, No. 2, pp. 266–285.

Yang, Z.L. (2006). "Risk Assessment and Decision Making of Container Supply Chains", PhD Thesis, Liverpool John Moores University, UK.

Yang, Z.L., Bonsall, S., Wall, A. and Wang, J. (2005b). "Reliable Container Line Supply Chains—A New Risk Assessment Framework for Improving Safety Performance", *Journal of World Maritime University*, Vol. 4, No. 1, pp. 105–120.

Yang, Z.L., Bonsall, S., Wang, J. and Phipps, J. (2007a). "Fuzzy Rule-based Bayesian Network Approach for Failure Mode, Effects and Criticality Analysis", Proceeding of the 7th International Conference on Reliability, Maintenance and Safety, 22–26 August, Beijing, China.

Yang, Z.L., Bonsall, S. and Wang, J. (2007b). "Use of Hybrid Multiple Uncertain Attribute Decision Making Techniques in Safety Management", *Expert System with Applications*, doi: 10.1016/j.eswa.2007.11.054.

Chapter 4

Anderson, E.E. and W.K. Talley (1995). "The oil spill size of tanker and barge accidents: determinants and policy implications", *Land Economics*, 71:216–228.

Cohen, M.J. (1995). "Technological disasters and natural resource damage assessment: an evaluation of the *Exxon Valdez* oil spill", *Land Economics*, 71:5–82.

Cohen, M.A. (1987). "Optimal enforcement strategy to prevent oil spills: an application of a principal-agent model with moral hazard", *Journal of Law and Economics*, 30:23–51.

Epple, D. and M. Visscher (1984). "Environmental pollution: modeling occurrence, detection, and deterrence", *Journal of Law and Economics*, 27:29–60.

Grau, M.V. and T. Groves (1997). "The oil spill process: the effect of coast guard monitoring on oil spills", *Environmental and Resource Economics*, 10:315–339.

Greene, W.H. (1997). *Econometric Analysis*, 3rd Edition, Prentice Hall, Upper Saddle River, NJ.

Grigalunas, T.A., J.J. Opaluch, J. Diamantides and M. Mazzotta (1998). "Liability for oil spill damages: issues, methods, and examples", *Coastal Management*, 26:61–77.

Jin, D., H.L. Kite-Powell and J.M. Broadus (1994). "Dynamic economic analysis of marine pollution prevention technologies: an application to double hulls and electronic charts", *Environmental and Resource Economics*, 4(6):555–580.

Jin, D. and H.L. Kite-Powell (1995). "Environmental liability, marine insurance and an optimal risk sharing strategy for marine oil transport", *Marine Resource Economics*, 10(1):1–19.

Jin, D. and H.L. Kite-Powell (1999). "On the optimal environmental liability limit for marine oil transport", *Transportation Research Part E: Logistics and Transportation Review*, 35(2):77–100.

Jin, D., H.L. Kite-Powell and W.K. Talley (2001). "The safety of commercial fishing: determinants of vessel total losses and injuries", *Journal of Safety Research*, 32(2):209–228.

Jin, D., H.L. Kite-Powell, E. Thunberg, A. Solow and W.K. Talley (2002). "A model of fishing vessel accident probability", *Journal of Safety Research*, 33(4):497–510.

Jin, D. and E. Thunberg (2005). "An analysis of fishing vessel accidents in fishing areas off the northeastern United States", *Safety Science*, 43(8):523–540.

Kim, I. (2002). "Ten years after the enactment of the Oil Pollution Act of 1990: a success or a failure", *Marine Policy*, 26:197–207.

Kite-Powell, H.L., D. Jin and S. Farrow (1997). "Expected safety benefits of electronic charts and integrated navigation systems", *Journal of Transport Economics and Policy*, 31(2):147–162.

Kite-Powell, H.L., D. Jin, J. Jebsen, V. Papakonstantinou and N. Patrikalakis (1999). "Investigation of potential risk factors for groundings of commercial vessels in US ports", *International Journal of Offshore and Polar Engineering*, 9(1):16–21.

Millar, I.C. (1980). "The need for a structured policy towards reducing human-factor errors in marine accidents", *Maritime Policy and Management*, 6:9–15.

Talley, W.K. (1996). "Determinants of cargo damage risk and severity: the case of containership accidents", *Logistics and Transportation Review*, 32(4):377–388.

Talley, W.K. (1999). "Determinants of the property damage costs of tanker accidents", *Transportation Research Part D (Transport and Environment)*, 4:413–426.

Talley, W.K. (2000). "Oil spillage and damage costs: US inland waterway tank barge accidents", *International Journal of Maritime Economics*, 2:217–234.

Talley, W.K. (2001). "Determinants of the property damage cost of bulk barge accidents", *Maritime Policy and Management*, 28(2):175–186.

Talley, W.K. (2002). "Vessel damage cost differentials: bulk, container and tanker accidents", *International Journal of Maritime Economics*, 4(4):307–322.

Talley, W.K., D. Jin and H.L. Kite-Powell (2001). "Vessel accident oil spillage: post US OPA-90", *Transportation Research Part D: Transport and Environment*, 6(6):405–415.

Talley, W.K., D. Jin and H. Kite-Powell (2004). "Post OPA-90 vessel spill differentials: transfers versus vessel accidents", *Maritime Policy and Management*, 31(3):225–240.

Talley, W.K., D. Jin and H. Kite-Powell (2005a). "Determinants of crew injuries in vessel accidents", *Maritime Policy and Management*, 32(3):263–278.

Talley, W.K., D. Jin and H. Kite-Powell (2005b). "Post OPA-90 vessel oil transfer spill prevention: the effectiveness of coast guard enforcement", *Environmental and Resource Economics*, 30(1):93–114.

Talley, W.K., D. Jin and H. Kite-Powell (2005c). "The US Coast Guard vessel inspection programme: a probability analysis", *Maritime Economics and Logistics*, 7(2):156–172.

Talley, W.K., D. Jin and H. Kite-Powell (2006). "Determinants of the severity of passenger vessel accidents", *Maritime Policy and Management*, 33(2):173–186.

Talley, W.K., D. Jin and H. Kite-Powell (2008a). "Determinants of the severity of cruise vessel accidents", *Transportation Research Part D: Transport and Environment*, 13(2):86–94.

Talley, W.K, D. Jin and H. Kite-Powell (2008b). "Determinants of the damage cost and injury severity of ferry vessel accidents", *WMU Journal of Maritime Affairs*, 7(1):175–188.

Wikipedia 2008. *Exxon Valdez* oil spill, http://en.wikipedia.org/wiki/Exxon_Valdez_oil_spill (accessed 19 February 2008).

Chapter 5

Babione, R., Kim, C.K., Rhone, E., and Sanjaya, E. (2003). "Post 9/11 Security Cost Impact on Port of Seattle Import/Export Container Traffic", University of Washington: GTTL 502 Spring session, 4 June 2003.

Bichou, K. (2004). "The ISPS code and the cost of port compliance: an initial logistics and supply chain framework for port security assessment and management", *Maritime Economics and Logistics*, 6(4), 322–348.

Bichou, K. (2005). *Maritime Security: Framework, Methods and Applications*, Report to UNCTAD, Geneva: UNCTAD, June 2005.

Bichou, K., Bell, M.G.H. and Evans, A. (2007). *Risk Management in Port Operations, Logistics and Supply Chain Security*, Informa, London, 2007.

Bichou, K. and Evans, A. (2007) Maritime Security and Regulatory Risk-Based Models: Review and Critical Analysis, in Bichou, K., Bell, M.G.H. and Evans, A. (2007), *Risk Management in Port Operations, Logistics and Supply Chain Security*, Informa: London, 2007.

Bichou, K., Lai, K.H., Lun, Y.H. Venus and Cheng, T.C. Edwin (2007). "A quality management framework for liner shipping companies to implement the 24-hour advance vessel manifest rule", *Transportation Journal*, 46(1), 5–21.

Bier, V.M. (1993). "Statistical methods for the use of accident precursor data in estimating the frequency of rare events", *Reliability Engineering and System Safety*, 42, 267–280.

Brooks, M.R. and Button, K.J. (2005). "Market Structures and Shipping Security", *Proceedings of the 2005 Conference of International Association of Maritime Economists*, Limasol: Cyprus, June 2005.

Damas, P., "Supply chains at war", *American Shipper*, November 2001, pp. 17–18.

Diop, A., Hartman, D. and Rexrode, D.(2007), *C-TPAT Partners Cost/Benefit Survey*, CBP: Washington, DC.

Evers, P.T. and Johnson, C.J. (2000). "Performance perceptions, satisfaction, and intention: the intermodal shipper's perspective", *Transportation Journal*, 40(2): Winter 2000.

Flynn, S. (2004). *America the Vulnerable: How our Government is Failing to Protect us from Terrorism*, NY: HarperCollins Publishing.

Fung, M.K., Cheng, L.K. & Qiu, L.D. (2003). "The impact of terminal handling charges on overall shipping charges: an empirical study", *Transportation Research Part A*, 37(8): 703–716.

Gooley, T.B. (2004). "C-TPAT: Separating hype from reality", *Logistics Management*, 1 August 2004.

Hummels, J. (2001). *Time as a trade barrier*, Mimeo: Purdue University, 1–40.

International Monetary Fund (IMF). (2001). *World Economic Outlook: The Global Economy after September 11*, (www.imf.org/external/pubs/ft/weo/2001/03 (accessed December 2005)).

Kruk, B. and Donner, M.L. (2008). *Review of Cost of Compliance with the New International Freight Transport Security Requirements*, World Bank Transport Papers, TP 16: 1–58, February 2008.

Lee, H.L. and Whang, S. (2005). "Higher supply chain security with lower cost: lessons from total quality management", *International Journal of Production Economics*, 96(3), 289–300.

Organisation for Economic Co-operation and Development (OECD). (2002). "The Impact of the Terrorist Attacks of 11 September 2001 on International Trading and Transport Activities", Working Party of the Trade Committee, OECD: Paris (TD/TC/WP(2002)9/FINAL).

Organisation for Economic Co-operation and Development (OECD). (2003). *Security in Maritime Transport: Risk Factors and Economic Impact*, Maritime Transport Committee, Paris: OECD.

Phimister, J.A., Bier, V.M., Kunreuther, H.C. (2004). *Accident Precursor Analysis and Management: Reducing Technological Risk through Diligence*, Edited book, National Academy of Engineering, Washington D.C.: The National Academies Press.

Rabadi, G., Pinto, C.A., Talley, W. and Arnaout, J.P. (2007). "Port recovery from security incidents: a simulation approach", in Bichou, K., Bell, M.G.H. and Evans, A. (2007). *Risk Management in Port Operations, Logistics and Supply Chain Security*, Informa: London, 83–94.

Richardson, M. (2004). Growing vulnerability of Seaports from Terror Attacks, to protect ports while allowing global flow of trade is a new challenge, *Viewpoint*, Institute of South east Asian Studies, www document www.iseas.edu.sg/viewpoint

Russell, D.M. and Saldana J.P. (2003). "Five tenets of security-aware logistics and supply chain operation", *Transportation Journal*, 42, 4, 44–54.

UNCTAD (2007). "Maritime Security: ISPS Implementation, Costs and Related Financing", Report by the UNCTAD Secretariat, Geneva: UNCTAD.

Walkenhorst, P. and Dihel, N. (2002). "Trade Impacts of the Terrorist Attacks of 11 September 2001: A Quantitative Assessment", Workshop on the Economic Consequences of Global Terrorism, DIW/German Institute for Economic Research: Berlin.

Wilson, J., Mann, C., and Otsuki, T. (2003). "Trade Facilitation and Economic Development: Measuring the Impact", *The World Bank Economic Review*, 17, 367–89.

Chapter 6

Burnett, John S. (2002). *Dangerous Waters, Modern Piracy on the High Seas*, New York: Dutton.

Greene, W.H. (1997). *Econometric Analysis*, 3rd Edition, Upper Saddle River, NJ: Prentice Hall.

Grinter, Mike (2005). "Fury as Japanese Insurers Slap on Malacca Strait Premium", www.lloydslist.com (26 August).

Hand, Marcus (2005a). "Terrorists Could See Ports as Soft Targets: Successes of Pirates in Supposedly Secure Areas Cause Alarm", www.lloydslist.com (21 October).

Hand, Marcus (2005b). "Nations Unite on Malacca Security Pact", www.lloydslist.com (9 September).

Hand, Marcus (2005c). "Malacca Strait Stakeholders Join Forces on IMO Safety", www.lloydslist.com (8 September).

Hand, Marcus (2005d). "Add Piracy to ISPS Code, Says Japan", www.lloydslist.com (12 September).

Harismo, A. (1999). "Dark Alliance Rules the High Seas", *Bangkok's, The Nation*, 13 April.

Harris, A. and Fiddler, S. (2005). "Pirates hold Malacca Strait Shipping Hostage to Fortune". *The Financial Times*, 24 June, pp. 2 and 16.

International Chamber of Commerce (2005). Annual Death Toll From Piracy Rises, www.iccwbo.org/home/news_archives/2005/piracy-92.asp (July).

International Maritime Organization (various years). *Reports on Acts of Piracy and Armed Robbery*, London: IMO.

Marlow, Peter B. and Gardner, Bernard M. (2006). "The Marine Electronic Highway in the Straits of Malacca and Singapore—An Assessment of Costs and Key Benefits", *Maritime Policy and Management*, Vol. 33, No. 2 (May 2006), pp. 187–202.

Chapter 7

Abhyankar, J. (2002). "Piracy and maritime violence: a global update", pp. 9–25 in Proshanto K. Mukherjee, Maximo Q. Mejia, Jr., Gotthard M. Gauci (Eds.), *Maritime violence and other security issues at sea*, Malmö, Sweden: WMU Publications.

Abhyankar, J. (2005). "Maritime crime", pp. 201–243, in Maximo Q Mejia, Jr. (Ed.), *Contemporary issues in maritime security*, Malmö, Sweden: WMU Publications.

Beckman, R.C. (2002). "Combating piracy and armed robbery against ships in Southeast Asia—the way forward", *Ocean Development and International Law*, 33(3/4): 317–341.

Birnie, P.W. (1987). "Piracy—past, present and future", *Marine Policy*, 11(3): 163–183.

Brittin, B.H. (1986). *International Law for Seagoing Officers* (5th Edition), Annapolis, Md.: Naval Institute Press, p. 116.

Brown, E.D. (1994). *The International Law of the Sea*, Dartmouth, UK: Aldershot, Hants, p. 299.

Derek Johnson, Erika Pladdet, Mark J. Valencia (2005). Research on Southeast Asian Piracy, in *Piracy in Southeast Asia: Status, Issues, and Responses*, IIAS/ISEAS Series.

Dillon, D. (2005). "Maritime piracy: defining the problem", *SAIS Review*, XXV(1): 155–165.

Dubner, B.H. (1980). *The Law of International Sea Piracy*, The Hague: Martinus Nijhoff Publishers.

Farley, M.C. (1993). "International and regional trends in maritime piracy 1989–1993", unpublished master's dissertation, Monterey, CA: Naval Postgraduate School.

Geneva Convention on the High Seas (1958), Art. 15; United Nations Convention on the Law of the Sea (1982), Article 101.

Halberstam, M. (1988). "Terrorism on the high seas: the *Achille Lauro*, piracy and the IMO convention on maritime safety", *American Journal of International Law*, 82: 269–286.

ICC International Maritime Bureau (2006), "Piracy and armed robbery against ships: annual report 1 January–31 December 2005", Essex: ICC International Maritime Bureau.

International Maritime Bureau (2006), Annual report 2005, p. 29.

International Maritime Organization (1999). *MSC/Circ. 622/Rev.1*, "Recommendations to Governments for preventing and suppressing piracy and armed robbery against ships", London: IMO, p. 1 in Annex.

International Maritime Organization (1999). *MSC/Circ. 623/Rev.3*, "Guidance to shipowners and ship operators, shipmasters and crews on preventing and suppressing acts of piracy and armed robbery against ships", London: IMO, p. 3 in Annex.

International Maritime Organization (2002), *Resolution A.922(22)* "Code of practice for the investigation of the crimes of piracy and armed robbery against ships", London: IMO, p. 4.

Mak, J.N. (2002). "Incidents at sea: shipjacking, maritime muggings and thefts in Southeast Asia", Paper presented at the Intercargo Roundtable Discussion on Piracy, Singapore, 4 February 2002.

Mejia, M.Q., Jr. (2003). "Maritime gerrymandering: dilemmas in defining piracy, terrorism and other acts of maritime violence", *Journal of International Commercial Law*, 2(2): 153–175.

Menefee, S.P. (1999). "Anti-piracy Law in the Year of the Ocean: problems and opportunity". *ILSA Journal of International and Comparative Law*, 5(2): 308–318.

Menefee, S.P. (2005). "Under-reporting of the problems of maritime piracy and terrorism: are we viewing the tip of the iceberg?", pp. 245–263, in Mejia, M.Q., Jr. (Ed.), *Contemporary Issues in Maritime Security*, Malmö, Sweden: WMU Publications.

Mukundan, P. (2005). "The scourge of piracy in Southeast Asia: can any improvements be expected in the near future?", *Piracy in Southeast Asia. Status, Issues, and Responses*, IIAS/ISEAS Series.

Ormerod, H.A. (1997). *Piracy in the Ancient World*, Baltimore: The John Hopkins University Press.

Oxford University (1987). *The Compact Oxford English Dictionary* (2nd Edition), Oxford: Oxford University Press, p. 1349.

Rubin, A.P. (1998), *The Law of Piracy* (2nd Ed.), New York: Transnational Publishers.

Sestier. J.-M. (1880). *La Piraterie Dans L'antiquité*, Paris.

Sundberg, J. W. F. (1999). "Piracy," pp. 803–817, in Bassiounni M.C. (Ed.), *International Criminal Law* (2nd Ed.), Ardsley, New York: Transnational Publishers.

Yun M.S. (2004). "Decomposition moment in the first moment", *Economics Letters* 82, pp. 275–280.

Chapter 8

Abrams, Herbert. (2001). "A Short History of Occupational Health". *Journal of Public Health Policy*, Vol. 22, No. 1, 34–80.

AFL-CIO. (2003). *Death on the Job: The Toll of Neglect*, 12th Edition.

Alderton, Patrick. (2005). *Port Management and Operation*, 2nd Edition, Informa.

Allen, Dan. "Automated Mooring Systems, Is It the Future?" Presentation at 2007 Facilities Engineering Seminar and Expo, American Association of Port Authorities, http://aapa.files.cms-plus.com/SeminarPresentations/07%5FFACENG%5FAllen%5FDan.pdf (8 November 2007, 29 January 2008).

American Society of Safety Engineers. White Paper, "The Return on Investment for Health and Environmental Management Programs" (8 June 2002).

APM Calls for a "Global Safety Day." APM Terminals Press Release (24 October 2007).

Baker, Susan P., et al. (1992). *The Injury Factbook*, 2nd Edition, New York: Oxford University Press.

Basel Convention. (2005). "Basel Convention on the Control of Transboundary Movements of Hazardous Wastes and Their Disposal", www.basel.int/text/con-e-rev.pdf (22 February 2008).

Cargo Handling. (2007). Encyclopedia of American Industries Online, Advameg Inc, www.referenceforbusiness.com, Path: Marine Cargo Handling (11 January 2008).

Conway, H. and Svenson, J. "Occupational injury and illness rates, 1992–96: why they fell", *Monthly Labor Review*, November 1998.

Davis, Colin J. (2003). *Waterfront Revolts—New York and London Dockworkers, 1946–61*, University of Illinois Press.

Dibenedetto, Bill. "Cleaning the air in the PNW", *Journal of Commerce* (New York) 8 February 2008, pp. 32–33.

EcoPorts Foundation. "Port Environmental Review System", www.ecoports.com/page.ocl?mode=&version=&pageid=90 (2 February 2008).

Finlay, William. (1988). *Work on the Waterfront*, Temple University Press.

Gallagher, John. "The Cost of Going Green", *Traffic Weekly*, 2 July 2007: 1, ABI/INFORM Global, ProQuest, Perry Library Old Dominion University, Norfolk, VA (20 February 2008), www.proquest.com

Goldblatt, Louis. (1963). *Men and Machines: A Story about Longshoring on the West Coast Waterfront*, San Francisco: International Longhoremen's and Warehousemen's Union and Pacific Maritime Association.

Harrison, Daniel. Personal Interview, 28 January 2008.

Hensel, Jr., Bill. (2001). "Getting them Home Alive", *Journal of Commerce Review and Outlook*.

Higgins, Thomas, Randolph Hall, Maged Dessouky. "Comparison of Attributes and Characteristics of Strategic Ports to Agile Port Models", Department of Industrial and Systems Engineering, University of Southern California, Los Angeles, California (22 February 1999).

Hong Kong International Terminals. "Our Operations, Our Safety, 2007", www.hit.com.hk/4fac/safety.asp (20 February 2008).

Hong Kong News. "Training set for container-yard operators", www3.news .gov.hk/isd/ebulletin/en/category/atschool/050601/html/050601en02002 .htm (1 June 2005, 22 January 2008).

Hospitals in the Port. PORTCities London, www.portcities.org.uk/london/ server.php?show=ConGallery.33 (13 February 2008).

International Dockworkers Council. Position Paper on a European Port Policy, www.empa-pilots.org/pdf/IDCPortPolicyFinal.pdf (12 July 2007, 28 December 2007).

International Labour Organization. 1996–2008, 8 January 2008 www.ilo.org/ global/About_the_ILO/lang-en/index.htm.

International Longshoreman Association, AFL-CIO, 2006, www.ila2000.org/ index.htm (6 February 2008).

International Longshore and Warehouse Union, 2005, www.ilwu.org/history/ ilwu-story/ilwu-story.cfm (6 February 2008).

International Longshore and Warehouse Union Local 19, Seattle, Washington, www.ilwu19.com/history/contents.htm (9 February 2008).

Kearney, Barry J., Memo issued by the NLRB Division of Advice, 25 January 2005.

Koutitas, Christoforos, Eva Vafaki, and George Palantzas, 17 June 2005. First International Conference on Harbours and Air Quality, Genova, Italy, www.fisica.unige.it/atmosfera/HAQ/download/Koutitas-Vafaki-Palantzas. pdf (8 January 2008).

LA/Long Beach Port Programme will Reduce Pollution by 80%, Government Technology, www.govtech.com/gt/articles/104992 (16 April 2007, 13 February 2008).

Landon, Felicity, "Dust-busters", *Port Strategy*, 1 April 2007.

Leigh, James, et al., "Global Burden of Disease and Injury Due to Occupational Factors", *Epidemiology*, September 1999, Vol. 10, No. 5.

Lettman, Amy, *Monthly Labor Review*, October 1989, Vol. 112, Issue 10, pp. 37–38.

Liberty Mutual Group. "Despite 6.2% fall in the number of serious workplace injuries, their financial impact on employers remains huge", 20 September 2005.

Litwin, Adam Seth, "Trade Unions and Industrial Injury in Great Britain, August 2004", Centre for Economic Performance, London School of Economics and Political Science, London.

Lou, Kok-Yong and Cher-Hiang Goh, "Design and Real-time Implementation of a Control System for Port AGV Application", DSO National Laboratories, Computational Intelligence in Robotics and Automation, 16–20 July 2003, Kobe, Japan.

MacLaury, Judson. (1984). "The Occupational Safety and Health Administration, A History of its First Thirteen Years, 1971–1984", US Department of Labor, 9 February 2008, www.dol.gov/oasam/programmes/history/mono-osha13introtoc.htm.

Maglen, Krista, "The First Line of Defence, British Quarantine and the Port Sanitary Authorities in the Nineteenth Century", *Social History of Medicine*, 2002, Vol. 15, No. 3, pp. 413–428.

Martens, Horst, "Dock Safety at Saudi Arabian Seaports", *Professional Safety*, November 1989, Vol. 34, Issue 11, ABI/INFORM Global, p. 33.

McNamara, Thomas, M.J. and Sean Tarver (1999). "The strengths and weakness of dock labour reform, ten years on", *Economic Affairs*, 19(2), 12–17, doi: 10.1111/1468–0270.00151.

Mongelluzzo, Bill, Shippers Attack LA/LB Plan, *Traffic World*, 22 October 2007: 1, ABI/INFORM Global, ProQuest, Perry Library, Old Dominion University, Norfolk, VA, www.proquest.com (20 February 2008).

National Center for Injury Prevention and Control (2006). *CDC Injury Fact Book*, Atlanta (GA): Centers for Disease Control and Prevention.

National Council on Compensation Insurance Inc. Annual Statistical Bulletin for Workers Compensation Insurance, 2007, Boca Raton, Fl, USA.

National Institute for Occupational Safety and Health. NIOSH Health Hazard Evaluation Report: HETA #2003–0246-3013 Joint Pacific Marine Safety Code Committee, Centers for Disease Control and Prevention; August 2006.

"Navigating the Longshore and Harbor Workers' Compensation Act into the 21st Century". Coalition for the Longshore Act Reform, February 2007.

NMSA/OSHA Safety Alliance. National Maritime Safety Administration. July 2006. 31 January 2008, www.nmsa.us/nmsa_home.html.

O'Neill, Rory. "When it comes to health and safety, your life should be in union hands", Labor Education. (ILO Bureau of Workers' Activities-ACTRAV), No 126, 2002.

"On the Edge". *Maritime Workers Journal*, Maritime Union of Australia.

January 2004. 9 February 2008, www.mua.org.au/journal/janfeb_2004/twistlocks.html.

Porter, Janet. "Ships steer clear of Southampton", *Lloyd's List*, 19 February 2008.

"Put safety first and give productivity a head start". *Lloyd's List*. Insights and Opinions, 10 March 2006, 2 February 2008, Perry Library Old Dominion University Library, http://global.factiva.com

Raine, George. "Shipping's Dirty Cargo—Port pollution poses huge health threat, says union", *San Francisco Chronicle*, 4 March 2006, Page C-1.

Safe and Sound Port. Malaysia: *New Strait Times*, 28 June 2005. Factiva, Perry Library Old Dominion University, Norfolk, VA, 15 January 2008, http://global.factiva.com.

Sansbury, Tim. "Greater Protection". *The Journal of Commerce* (New York), 24 July 1997. ABI/INFORM Global, ProQuest, Perry Library Old Dominion University, Norfolk, VA, 31 January 2008, www.proquest.com

Secretariat of the Pacific Community. Regional Maritime Programme, Pacific Maritime Legislation & Regulations, Chapter 3, Port Safety Act, Port Administration and Port Safety, Vol. 4, 3 January 2002.

Sengupta, Ishita et al. "Workers' Compensation: Benefits, Coverage, and Costs, 2003", July 2005, National Academy of Social Insurance, Washington, D.C.

Spielman, Kord. "Better safe than sorry". *The Journal of Commerce* [New York] 13 Aug 2007, 1. ABI/INFORM Global. ProQuest. Perry Library Old Dominion University, Norfolk, VA, 4 December 2008, www.proquest.com

Swedberg, Claire. "APM Terminals Readies Its RFID System", *RFID Journal*. 9 May 2006, 15 January 2008, www.rfidjournal.com/article/articleview/2323.

"The APM Terminals Virtual Safety Organization", *Quay Words*, APM Terminals, Fall 2007, p. 21.

"The most disabling workplace injuries cost industry an estimated $48.3 billion", from *Research to Reality*, Liberty Mutual Research Institue for Safety, Vol. 11, No. 1 (Winter 2008).

Twistlocks. Besco. 2002. 9 February 2008, www.besco.de/lao_sha_info1.htm.

"Union Take Safety to Global Forum". (2007). *Maritime Workers Journal*. Maritime Union of Australia, 16 November 2007, www.mua.org.au/journal/sum_2007/safety.html.

United States Department of Labor. Bureau of Labor Statistics. "Injuries and Accident Causes in the Longshore Industry", 1942, Washington, GPO, 1944.

United States Department of Labor. Bureau of Labor Statistics. "National Census of Fatal Occupational Injuries in 2005", 9 August 2007, Washington, 28 February 2008. www.bls.gov/news.release/pdf/cfoi.pdf

United States Department of Labor. Occupational Health and Safety Admini-stration, "Safety and Health Regulations for Longshoring", Chapter 29, Standard 1918.85, www.osha.gov.Path: Containerized cargo operations

Vis, Iris F.A., Ismael Harika. "Comparison of vehicle types at an automated container terminal", *OR Spectrum*, Heidelberg: February 2004, Vol. 26, Issue 1, pp. 117, 27 pages, 9 January 2008.

Walker, Roma E. "Nursing on the Waterfront", *The American Journal of Nursing*. August 1959, Vol. 59, No. 8, pp. 1139–1141.

Warde, John. "Home Improvement", *New York Times*, 15 June 1989.

Webb S. and Webb, B. (1902). *Industrial Democracy*, 2nd edition, Longmans, Green and Co, London.

Winslow, Calvin. (1998). *Waterfront Workers, New Perspectives on Race and Class*. University of Illinois Press.

Witt, Steve. National Maritime Safety Association Meeting, 23 June 2005, Carlsbad, CA, www.osha.gov/pls/oshaweb/owadisp.show_document?p_table=SPEECHES (retrieved 31 January 2008).

World Health Organization. "Hazard Prevention and Control in the Work Environment: Dust". August 1999, 12 February 2008, www.who.int/occupational_health/publications/en/oehairbornedust.pdf

World Health Organization. Occupational Health. 2008, 26 July 2008. www.who.int/occupational_health

Chapter 9

Alderton, T., Winchester, N. (2002). "Flag states and safety: 1997–1999", *Maritime Policy and Management*, 29(2), pp. 151–162.

Cariou, P., Mejia, M.Q., Jr., Wolff, F.C. (2007). "An econometric analysis of deficiencies noted in Port State Control inspections", *Maritime Policy and Management*, 34(3), 243–258.

Cariou, P., Mejia, M.Q., Jr., Wolff, F.C. (2008). "Evidence on target factors used for Port State Control inspections" (forthcoming).

Cariou, P., Mejia, M.Q., Jr., Wolff, F.C. (2008). "On the effectiveness of port state control inspections", *Transportation Research Part E*, 44, pp. 491–503.

Degré, T. (2008), "From Black-Grey-White detention-based lists of flags to Black-Grey-White casualty-based lists of categories of vessels, using a multi-variate approach", *The Journal of Navigation*, 61(3), September (forthcoming).

Fields, G. (2003). "Accounting for income inequality and its change: a new method with application to the distribution of earnings in the United States", *Research in Labor Economics*, 22, 1–38.

Kasoulides, G.C. (1993). *Port state control and jurisdiction: evolution of the port state regime*, Kluwer Academic Publishers, Dordrecht, p. 42.

Knapp, S. (2007). *The econometrics of maritime safety—recommendation to enhance safety at sea*, Doctoral Thesis, Erasmus University, Rotterdam.

Knapp, S., Franses, P.H. (2007). "A global view of port state control: econometric analysis of the differences across port state control regimes", *Maritime Policy and Management*, 34(5), 453–484.

Li, K.X. (1999). "The safety and quality of Open registers and a new approach for classifying risky ships", *Transportation Research Part E* 35, pp. 135–143.

Li, K.X., Wonham, J. (1999). "Who is safe and who is at risk: a study of 20-year record on accident total loss in different flags", *Maritime Policy and Management* 26(2), pp. 137–149.

Chapter 10

Alderton, P. M. (2004). *Sea Transports: Operations and Economics*, London: Adlard Coles Nautical.

Akten, N. (2004). "Analysis of shipping Casualties in the Bosphorus", *Journal of Navigation*, 57(3), 345–356.

Christou, M. D. (1999). "Analysis and control of major accidents from the intermediate temporary storage of dangerous substances in marshalling yards and port areas", *Journal of Loss Prevention in the Process Industries*, 12(1), 109–119.

Dabra, R.M. and Casal, J. (2004). "Historical analysis of accidents in seaports", *Safety Science*, 42(2), 85–98.

De, P., and Ghosh, B. (2003). "Causality between performance and traffic: an investigation with Indian ports", *Maritime Policy and Management*, 30(1), 5–27.

Dft (2006). *Port Marine Safety Code*, March 2006, Department of Transport, UK.

Fujii, Y. (1982). "Recent trends in traffic accidents in Japanese waters", *Journal of Navigation*, 35(1), 90–99.

Greene, W. H. (2008). *Econometric Analysis*, 6th Edn, Upper Saddle River, NJ: Prentice Hall.

Harrald, J. R., Mazzuchi T. A., Spahn J., Van Dorp R., Merrick J., Shrestha S. and Grabowskib M. (1998). "Using system simulation to model the impact of human error in a maritime system", *Safety Science*, 30(1–2), 235–247.

IMO (2002). *Guidelines for the application of formal safety assessment (FSA) for use in the IMO rule-making process*, Marine Safety Committee MSC/Circ. 1023, MEPC/Circ. 392, London: International Maritime Organisation (IMO).

ISL (2006). "Shipping Statistics and Market Review". Bremen, Germany: Institute of Shipping Economics and Logistics.

IWR (1999). *Analysis of US Coast Guard Accident Data*, Aug 1999, Institute for Water Resources, US Army Corps of Engineers.

Kite-Powell, H.L., Jin, D., Jebsen, J., Papakonstantinou, V. and Patrikalakis, N. (1999). "Investigation of potential risk factors for groundings of commercial vessels in US ports", *International Journal of Offshore and Polar Engineering*, 9(1), 16–21.

Kristiansen, S. (2005). *Maritime Transportation: Safety Management and Risk Analysis*, Elsevier.

Lam, S. Y. W. and Yip, T. L. (2008). "The role of geomatics engineering in establishing the marine information system for maritime management", *Maritime Policy and Management*, 35(1), 53–60.

Lewison, G.R.G. (1978). "The risk of encounter leading to a collision", *Journal of Navigation*, 31(3), 384–407.

Liu, C. P., Liang, G. S., Su, Y. and Chu, C.W. (2006). "Navigation safety analysis in Taiwanese ports", *Journal of Navigation*, 59(2), 201–211.

LRS (1962–93) (1994–98) *Serious Ship Casualties, World Fleet 1962–93 & 1994–98*, London: Lloyd's Register of Shipping.

MaritimeNZ (2006). *Accident Book—Maritime Accidents 2003–2004*, Maritime New Zealand.

Marlow, P. B. and Gardner, B.M. (2006). "The marine electronic highway in the Straits of Malacca and Singapore—An assessment of costs and key benefits", *Maritime Policy and Management*, 33(2), 187–202.

Pillich, B., Pearlman, S. and Chase, C. (2003). "Real time data and ECDIS in a web-based port management package", *Proceedings of Oceans 2003*, 4, 2, 227–233.

Ronza, A., Felez, S., Darbra, R.M., Carol, S., Vilchez, J.A., and Casal, J. (2003). "Predicting the frequency of accidents in port areas by developing event trees from historical analysis", *Journal of Loss Prevention in the Process Industries*, 16(6), 551–560.

Talley, W. K. (2002). "Maritime safety and accident analysis", in Grammenos, C. T. (Eds.) *The Handbook of Maritime Economics and Business*, LLP, Chapter 9, pp. 426–442.

Talley, W. K., Jin, D. and Kite-Powell, H. (2005). "Determinants of crew injuries in vessel accidents", *Maritime Policy and Management*, 32(3), 263–278.

USCG (1999). *Regulatory Assessment Use of Tugs to Protect Against Oil Spills in the Puget Sound Area*, Nov 1999 (summarised in Annex 5), United States Coast Guard.

Wang, J. (2002). "Offshore safety case approach and formal safety assessment of ships", *Journal of Safety Research*, 33(1), 81–115.

Wang, J. (2006). "Maritime risk assessment and its current status", *Quality and Reliability Engineering International*, 22(1), 3–19.

Yip, T.L. (2008). "Port traffic risks—A study of accidents in Hong Kong waters", *Transportation Research Part E*, 44(5) 921–931.

Yip, T.L., Zhang, D.H. and Chwang, A.T. (2002). "Environmental and safety considerations for design of a perforated seawall", *Proceedings of the 12th*

International Offshore and Polar Engineering Conference (Kitakyushu, Japan, 25–31 May 2001), 3, 758–763.

Chapter 11

Adler, R.M. and J. Fuller (2007). "An Integrated Framework for Assessing and Mitigating Risks to Maritime Critical Infrastructure, Technologies for Homeland Security", 2007 IEEE Conference, 252–257.

American Association of Port Authorities (2008). *Emergency Preparedness and Continuity of Operations Planning: Manual for Best Practices*, www.aapa-ports. org/home.cfm (last accessed 16 June 2008).

Anonymous (2007). "The JoC Top 50 World Container Ports", *Journal of Commerce*, 30 June, 46–54.

AON (2007). *Global Risk Management Survey 2007*, Chicago: AON Corporation 2007.

Barnes, P. (2004). "Crisis Management Capabilities in Maritime Trading Systems", in *Proceedings The Australian New Zealand International Business Academy Conference: Dynamism and Challenges in Internationalisation*, Canberra, Australia.

Bennett, A.C. and Y.Z. Chin (2008). *100% Container Scanning: Security Policy Implications for Global Supply Chains*, Masters of Engineering in Logistics, Cambridge MA: MIT.

Bichou, K. (2004). "The ISPS Code and the Cost of Port Compliance: An Initial Logistics and Supply Chain Framework for Port Security Assessment and Management", *Maritime Economics and Logistics*, 6(4), 322–348.

Brooks, M.R. and K.J. Button (2006). "Market Structures and Shipping Security", *Maritime Economics and Logistics*, 8, 100–120.

Brooks, M.R. and K.J. Button (2007). "Maritime Container Security: A Cargo Interest Perspective", in *Port, Maritime and Supply Chain Security: Frameworks, Models and Applications*, Bichou, K., M. Bell and A. Evans, (eds.), London: Informa, 221-236.

Brooks, M.R., J.R.F. Hodgson and J.D. Frost (2006). *Short Sea Shipping on the East Coast of North America: an Analysis of Opportunities and Issues*, Halifax: Dalhousie University, http://management.dal.ca/Research/ShortSea.php

Cambridge Systematics Inc. (2007), *Cross Border Short Sea Shipping Study: Final Report Phase II*, Prepared for the Whatcom Council of Governments, January, www.wcog.com/library/imtc/sss2report.pdf

Cummings, E. (2008), "Cummings Tells Lockheed Martin, Coast Guard to Fix Delays in TWIC Enrollment" (Press Release) 23 January 2008, www.house.gov/list/press/md07_cummings/20080123twic2.shtml

Customs and Border Protection (2004), *Securing the Global Supply Chain: Customs-Trade Partnership against Terrorism* (C-TPAT Strategic Plan), November.

Customs and Border Protection (2008), Container Security Initiative Ports, www.dhs.gov/xprevprot/programs/gc_1165872287564.shtm (last accessed 30 April 2008).

Drewry Shipping Consultants (2004), *Annual Review of Global Container Terminal Operators—2004*. London: Drewry Shipping Consultants.

Fanguy, M. (2008), "Transportation Worker Identification Credential (TWIC): Testimony before the United States House of Representatives Committee on Transportation and Infrastructure, Subcommittee on Coast Guard and Maritime Transportation", 23 January 2008, downloaded 28 January 2008, http://transportation.house.gov/Media/File/Coast%20Guard/20080123/Fanguy%20testimony.pdf

Flynn, S. E. (2006). "Port Security is Still a House of Cards", *Far Eastern Economic Review*, 169(1), 5–11.

Flynn, S. E. (2007). "Nature of the Border". Presentation to the *Homeland Security and Canada-US Border Trade* conference, Windsor, ON, 25 October.

Government Accountability Office (2005). *Cargo Security: Partnership Program Grants Importers Reduced Scrutiny with Limited Assurance of Improved Security*, D-05–404, Washington, DC: Government Accountability Office.

Government Accountability Office (2006). *Risk management: Further refinements needed to assess risks and prioritize protective measures at ports and other critical infrastructure* (GAO-06–91), Washington, DC: Government Accountability Office.

Government Accountability Office (2007a). *Maritime Security: Observations on selected aspects of the SAFE Port Act* (GAO-07–754T). Washington, DC: Government Accountability Office.

Government Accountability Office (2007b). *Port Risk Management: Additional Federal Guidance Would Aid Ports in Disaster Planning and Recovery* (GAO-07–412). Washington, DC: Government Accountability Office.

Government Accountability Office (2008a). *The SAFE Port Act: Status and implementation one year later* (GAO-08–171T). Washington, DC: Government Accountability Office.

Government Accountability Office (2008b). *Supply Chain Security: Challenges to Scanning 100 Percent of US-Bound Cargo Containers* (GAO-08–533T). Washington, DC: Government Accountability Office.

Haveman, J., H. J. Shatz, and E. Vilchis (2004). *An Overview of US Port Security Programs*, Public Policy Institute of California Working Paper No. 2004.15 (http://papers.ssrn.com/sol3/papers.cfm?abstract_id=638361).

International Maritime Organisation (2002) *The Safety of Life at Sea, 1974, As Amended Mandatory Requirements Regarding the Provisions of Chapter XI-2 of the International Convention For the Safety of Life At Sea, 1974, as amended*, London: IMO.

Kshetri, Nir (2005). "Pattern of Global Cyber War and Crime: A Conceptual Framework", *Journal of International Management*, 11, 541–562.

Lirn, T.C., H.A. Thanopoulou, M.J. Beynon and A.K.C. Beresford (2004). "An Application of AHP on Transhipment Port Selection: A Global Perspective", *Maritime Economics and Logistics*, 6, 1, 70–91.

Malak, Patricia (2007). "Capabilities-based Planning for the National Preparedness System", *TR News*, May-June, 250, 4–8.

Maritime Transportation Security Act of 2002, Public Law 107–295 (2002), 25 November.

Newman, D. and J.H. Walder (2003), "Federal Ports Policy", *Maritime Policy and Management*, 30, 2, 151–163.

Ng, Koi Yu Adolf and Girish C. Gujar (2009). "Port Security in Asia", in *Maritime Safety, Security and Piracy*, Wayne K. Talley (ed.): London: Informa.

Nott, J. (2006). *Extreme Events: A Physical Reconstruction and Risk Assessment*, Cambridge UK: Cambridge University Press.

Ojah, M. (2005). "Securing and Facilitating US Land Border Trade: A Critical Analysis of the C-TPAT and FAST Programs", *Transportation Research Record*, 1938, 30–37.

Organisation for Economic Cooperation and Development (2004). *Security in Transport: Report on Transport Security Across the Modes* (CEMT/CM(2004)22), Paris: OECD.

Pallis, Athanasios A. and George Vaggelas (2009). "EU Maritime and Port Security Strategy: Developing a Distinctive European Approach", *Maritime Safety, Security and Piracy*, Wayne K. Talley (ed.): London: Informa.

Pantouvakis, A. (2006). "Port-Service Quality Dimensions and Passenger Profiles: An Exploratory Examination and Analysis", *Maritime Economics and Logistics*, 8(4), 402–418.

Peck, Helen (2005). "Drivers of Supply Chain Vulnerability: An Integrated Framework", *International Journal of Physical Distribution and Logistics Management*, 35(4), 210–232.

Peck, Helen (2006). "Reconciling Supply Chain Vulnerability, Risk and Supply Chain Management", *International Journal of Logistics Research and Applications*, 9(2), 127–142.

Pinto, Ariel, Ghaith Rabadi and Wayne K. Talley (2009). "Port Security in the US", in *Maritime Safety, Security and Piracy*, Wayne K. Talley (ed.): London: Informa.

Sarathy, Ravi (2006). "Security and the Global Supply Chain", *Transportation Journal*, 45(4), pp. 28–51.

Security and Accountability for Every Port Act of 2006 (SAFE Port Act), Congress of the United States; H.R. 4954

Thibault, Marc, Mary R. Brooks and Kenneth J. Button (2006). "The Response of the US Maritime Industry to the New Container Security Initiatives", *Transportation Journal*, 45(1), 5–15.

US Department of Homeland Security (2006), "DHS and DOE Launch Secure Freight Initiative", Press Release 7 December, www.dhs.gov/xnews/releases/pr_1165520867989.shtm (last accessed 23 June 2008).

US Department of Homeland Security (2007), "Strategy to Enhance International Supply Chain Security", July 2007, downloaded from www.dhs. gov/xlibrary/assets/plcy-internationalsupplychainsecuritystrategy.pdf (last accessed 23 June 2008).

US Department of Homeland Security Office of the Inspector General (2006), "Audit of Targeting Ocean Going Containers (OIG-07-09)", Washington DC: Department of Homeland Security, November.

US House of Representatives Committee on Homeland Security (2008), "Homeland Security Committee Gets Its Answer on the Transportation Worker Program", 2 May, http://homeland.house.gov/about/sub committees.asp?ID=365&SubSection=0&Issue=0&DocumentType=0& PublishDate=0&subcommittee=8 (accessed 14 May 2008).

US House of Representatives Committee on Transportation and Infrastructure, Subcommittee on Coast Guard and Maritime Transportation (2008). *Summary of Subject Matter*, 22 January, downloaded 28 January 2008, http://transportation.house.gov/Media/File/Coast%20Guard/20080123/SSM_CG.pdf

UNCTAD (2006), *Maritime Security: Elements of an Analytical Framework for Compliance Measurement and Risk Assessment*, Geneva: United Nations Conference on Trade and Development.

Chapter 12

Cooperman, S. (2004). "Tracking Cargo", *Security*, 41, 20–22.

Government Accountability Office (2003). *Homeland Security: Preliminary Observations on Efforts to Target Security Inspections of Cargo Containers.* Washington, D.C.: US Government Printing Office.

Government Accountability Office (2007). *Homeland Security Grants: Observations on Process Department of Homeland Security Used to Allocate Funds to Selected Urban Areas.* Washington, D.C.: US Government Printing Office.

Government Accountability Office (2008). *Homeland Security: DHS Improved its Risk-Based Grant Programs' Allocation and Management Methods, But Measuring Programs' Impact on National Capabilities Remains a Challenge.* Washington, D.C.: US Government Printing Office.

Keane, A. G. (2005). "Applauding C-TPAT's Reach", *Traffic World*, 25 April, pp. 9–10.

Makrinos, S. T. (2004). "United States Port Security in the War Against Terrorism", *Sea Technology*, 45, 33–34.

National Archives and Records Administration (2006). *Code of Federal Regulations 33, Sub-chapter H, Part 101, Navigation and Navigable Waters*, revised, 1 July 2006.

Natter, A. (2007). "Reading the Cards". *Traffic World*, 23 July, 15.

Pinto, C.A. and W.K. Talley (2006). "The Security Incident Cycle of Ports", *Maritime Economics and Logistics*, 8, 267–286.

Rabadi, G., C.A. Pinto, W. K. Talley, J.-P. Arnaout (2007). "Port Recovery From Security Incidents: A Simulation Approach", *Risk Management in Port Operations, Logistics and Supply Chain Security*, eds., Bichou, K, M.G.H. Bell, and A. Evans, London: Informa, 83–94.

Staff (2004). "Ports: Does Compliant Mean Secure?" *Marine Log*, 109, 12–14.

Talley, W. K. (2006). "An Economic Theory of the Port", in Cullinane, K. and W. K. Talley, eds., *Port Economics: Research in Transportation Economics*, 16, Amsterdam: Elsevier, Ltd., 43–65.

Thibault, M., M. Brooks and K. Button (2006). "The Response of the US Maritime Industry to the New Container Initiatives", *Transportation Journal*, 45, 5–15.

US Army Corps of Engineers Waterborne Commerce Statistics Center (2005). *Waterborne Commerce of the United States for Waterways and Harbors (5 Parts)*. Washington, D.C.: US Government Printing Office.

US Department of Homeland Security (2007a). *The Post-Katrina Emergency Management Reform Act of 2006 (Title VI)*, Washington, D.C.: US Government Printing Office.

US Department of Homeland Security (2007b). *Port Security Grant Program—Award Comparison by Port Area*, www.dhs.gov/xgovt/grants/gc_1178831744366.shtm (retrieved 10 March 2008).

US Department of Homeland Security (2008). *Press Release: National Response Framework Released*, US Department of Homeland Security Press Office, 22 January 2008.

US House of Representatives Homeland Security Committee (2008). *Compilation of Homeland Security Presidential Directives (HSPD) through 31 December 2007*, Washington, D.C.: US Government Printing Office.

US Maritime Administration (2002). *Report of the United States Mobile Training Team: Regional Course on Port Security for Caribbean Countries*, Washington, D.C.: US Government Printing Office.

Chapter 13

Aspinwall, M. (1995). *Moveable feast: Pressure group conflict and the European Community shipping policy*, Aldershot: Ashgate.

Brooks, M.R. (2008). "North American Freight Transportation: The Road to Security and Prosperity", Cheltenham: Edward Elgar.

Brooks, M.R. and Button, K.J. (2007). "Maritime container security: A cargo interest perspective", in: Bell, M., Bichou, K. and Evans, A., (Eds). *Risk management in Port Operations, Logistics and Supply Chain Security*. London: Informa, 219–234.

CBP (Customs and Border Protection US) (2007). Fact Sheet, October 2007, Washington, D.C. Available at www.cbp.gov (accessed March 2008).

CEU (2001). White Paper—European transport policy for 2010: time to decide, Com (2001)370 final. Brussels, 12 September 2001.

CEU (2004). Customs: EU and US adopt measures to strengthen maritime container security. IP/04/1360. Brussels, 15 November 2004.

CEU, (2006a). Proposal for a directive of the Council on the identification and designation of European Critical Infrastructure and the assessment of the need to improve their protection. COM (2006) 787 final, 12 December 2006. Brussels.

CEU (2006b). Communication on a European Programme for Critical Infrastructure Protection. Com (2006)786 final. Brussels, 12 December 2006.

CEU (2006c). Proposal for a regulation of the European Parliament and of the Council on enhancing supply chain security. Com (2006)79 final, Brussels, 27 February 2006.

CEU (2007). Communication on a European Ports Policy. Com (2007)616 final, Brussels, 18 October 2007.

CLECAT (European Association for Forwarding, Transport, Logistics and Customs Services) (2006). Discussion paper 6 August 2006, Brussels: CLECAT.

Chlomoudis, C.I. and Pallis A.A. (2002). *European Port Policy: Towards a Long Term Strategy*, Cheltenham: Edward Elgar.

De Langen, P.W. and Pallis, A.A. (2007). "Entry Barriers in Seaports", *Maritime Policy and Management*, 34(5), 427–440.

Dekker, S. and Stevens, H., (2007). "Maritime security in the European Union—Empirical findings on financial implications for port facilities", *Maritime Policy and Management* 34(5), 485–499.

DG-TREN (2006). Minutes of the Expert Group meeting on Critical Maritime Infrastructure, 28 March, Brussels: CEU.

Dupont, C. (2007). "EU Maritime Security: From adoption to consolidation", WSO Conference, Prague, February 2007.

ESPO (2006a). Green Paper on Critical Infrastructure: ESPO's initial views, available at www.espo.be, accessed December 2007.

ESPO (2006b). ESPO reaction on the Commission proposal for a Regulation on enhancing supply chain security, August 2006, www.espo.be, accessed February 2008.

ESPO, (2007). Implementing recommendations of the 9/11 Commission Act of 2007. Letter to Commissioner for Taxation and Customs Union, 26 September, Brussels: ESPO.

Farantouris, N. E. (2008). "Public Financing in the port sector and State aid rules", paper presented at the 5th European Colloquium on Maritime Law Research, Athens, Greece, May 2008.

Fritelli, J.F. (2005). "Port and maritime security: Background and issues for Congress". The Library of Congress, 27 May.

GAO (US Government Accountability Office), (2007a). "Maritime security. The SAFE Port Act and efforts to secure our nation's seaports", 4 October, Washington, D.C.

GAO (US Government Accountability Office), (2007b). Maritime security.

One year later: A progress report on the SAFE Port Act. Statement of Stephen L. Caldwell, Director Homeland Security and Justice Issues, GAO-08-171T, 16 October, Washington, D.C.

Greenberg, M., Chalk, P., Willis, H.H., Khilko, I., Ortiz, D.S. (2006). "Maritime terrorism. Risk and liability", RAND Center for Terrorism Risk Management Policy. Santa Monica, CA, USA.

Johnston, V.R. (2004). "Transportation security and terrorism: Resetting the model and equations—epilogue", *Review of Policy Research*, 21, 379–402.

ILO (2003). Seafarer's Identity Documents Convention (Revised), No. 185. Geneva: ILO.

IMO-ILO (2003). "Code of practice on security in ports", Tripartite meeting of experts on security, safety and health in ports, Geneva.

IRU (International Road Transport Union) (2006). "IRU position on supply chain security", 13 November, Geneva.

ISO (2004). "Ships and marine technology—maritime port facility security assessments and security plan development", ISO/PAS 20858, First edition, 2004-07-01, Geneva.

ISO (2005). ISO/PAS 28000. "Specification for security management systems for the supply chain", First edition 15–11-2005, Geneva, Switzerland.

Lee, H.L., Whang, S. (2005). "Higher supply chain security with lower cost: Lessons from total quality management", *International Journal of Production Economics*, 96(3), 289–300.

Notteboom, T.E., Rodrigue, J.P. (2005). "Port regionalization: Towards a new phase in port development", *Maritime Policy and Management*, 32, 3, 297–313.

OECD (2004). Report on container transport security across modes. Available at: www.oecd.org/dataoecd/29/8/31839546.pdf

Pallis, A.A. (2002). *The Common EU Maritime Transport Policy: Policy Europeanisation in the 1990s*, Aldershot: Ashgate.

Pallis, A.A. (2006). "Institutional dynamism in the EU policy-making: The evolution of the EU maritime safety policy", *Journal of European Integration* 28(2), 137–157.

Pallis, A.A. (2007). "EU Port Policy Developments: Implications for Port Governance", in: Brooks, M.R. and Cullinane, K. (eds.), *Devolution, Port Governance and Performance, Research in Transport Economics Series No. 17*, London: Elsevier, 161–176.

Pallis, A.A., and Vaggelas, G.K. (2007). "Enhancing Port security via the enactment of EU policies", in: Bell, M., Bichou, K. and Evans, A., (Eds). *Risk Management in Port Operations, Logistics and Supply Chain Security*, London: Informa, 303–334.

Power, V. (1992). *The EC Shipping Law*, London: Lloyd's of London Press.

Robinson, R. (2002). "Ports as elements in value-driven chain systems: the new paradigm", *Maritime Policy and Management*, 29(3), 241–255.

Rotterdam Maritime Group (2005). Study on maritime security financing. Final report TREN/05/ST/S07.48700. In co-operation with the Swedish Maritime Administration and CETEMAR.

Schilk, G., Blumel, E., Recagno, V., Boeve, W. (2007). "Ship, port and supply chain security concepts interlinking maritime with hinterland transport chains", International Symposium on Maritime Safety, Security and Environmental Protection, 20–21 September, Athens, Greece.

Thai, V.V., Grewal, D. (2007). "The maritime security management system: Perceptions of the international shipping community", *Maritime Economics and Logistics* 9(2), 119–137.

UNCTAD (2007). Maritime Security: ISPS Code Implementation, Costs and Related Financing, UNCTAD/SDTE/TLB/2007/1, of 14 March 2007, Paris: UNCTAD Secretariat.

World Customs Co-Operation Council (WCO) (2004). "Resolution of the customs co-operation council on global security and facilitation measures concerning the international trade supply chain", June, Geneva: WCO.

WCO (2007). SAFE: Framework of Standards. June, Geneva: WCO.

WSC (World Shipping Council) (2007). Statement regarding legislation to require 100% container scanning, 30 July.

Chapter 14

ADB (2004). "ADB Establishes Regional Fund to Strengthen Port Security and to Combat Money Laundering and Financing of Terrorism in Developing Asia", Manila: ADB, www.adb.org/Documents/News/2004/nr2004073.asp.

APEC (2002). APEC 2002 Leader's Declaration, The Tenth APEC Economic Leaders' Meeting, 27 October, www.apec.org/apec/leaders_declarations/2002.html.

APEC's website: www.apec.org (last accessed February 2008).

Asia Pacific Foundation of Canada (2004). New security measures challenge competitiveness of Asian ports, *Asia Pacific Bulletin*, 30 April, www.asiapacificbusiness.ca.

Benamara, H., and Asariotis, R. (2007). "ISPS Code implementation in ports: costs and related financing", in: K. Bichou, M.G.H. Bell and A. Evans (eds.): *Risk Management in Port Operations, Logistics and Supply Chain Security*. London: Informa, pp. 281–301.

Bichou, K. (2004). "The ISPS Code and the cost of port compliance: an initial logistics and supply chain framework for port security assessment and management", *Maritime Economics and Logistics*, 6: 322–348.

Bichou, K., Bell, M.G.H., and Evans, A. (2007). *Risk Management in Port Operations, Logistics and Supply Chain Security*, London: Informa.

Booz Allen Hamilton (2003). *Port Security War Game: Implications for US Supply Chains*. New York: Booz Allen Hamilton.

Chin, K.W. and Singh, D. (2005). Introduction, in: K.W. Chin and D. Singh (eds.): *Southeast Asian Affairs 2005*, Singapore: Institute of Southeast Asian Studies, pp. ix–xiv.

Flynn, S.E. (2006). "Port security is still a house of cards", *Far East Economic Review*, Jan/Feb 2006 (www.feer.com/articles1/2006/0601/free/p005.html).

Greenberg, M.D., Chalk, P., Willis, H.H., Khiko, I., and Ortiz, D.S. (2006). *Maritime Terrorism: Risk and Liability*, Santa Monica: RAND.

Herald Tribune (2006). "India bars Hutchison from port project in Mumbai", *Herald Tribune*, August, www.iht.com/articles/2006/08/30/business/ports.php

Huxley, T. (2005). "Southeast Asia 2004 stable, but facing major security challenges", in: K.W. Chin and D. Singh (eds.): *Southeast Asian Affairs 2005*, Singapore: Institute of Southeast Asian Studies, pp. 3–23.

IDSS (2004). *Maritime Security in the Asia-Pacific: Report of a Conference Organized by the Institute of Defence and Strategic Studies (IDSS)*, Singapore, 20–21 May.

IMO's website: www.imo.org (last accessed February 2008).

IMO (2002a). *Amendments to the Annex to the International Convention for the Safety of Life at Sea, 1974 as Amended*, London: IMO, SOLAS/CONF.5/32, adopted in December 2002.

IMO (2002b). *International Code for the Security of Ships and Port Facilities*, London: IMO, SOLAS/CONF.5/34, adopted in December 2002.

Indian Ports Association's website: www.ipa.nic.in/oper.htm (last accessed February 2008).

Jacobs, W. and Hall, P.V. (2007). "What conditions supply chain strategies of ports? The case of Dubai", *GeoJournal*, 68: 327–342.

Krishna, G. (2006). Gamma sleuths, *Business World*, 26 June, (www.rapiscan.com).

King, J. (2005). "The security of merchant shipping", *Marine Policy* 29: 235–245.

Kingdon, J.W. (1995). *Agendas, Alternatives and Public Policies* (Second Edition), New York: Longman.

Kumar, S.H. and Vellenga, D. (2004). "Port security costs in the US: a public policy dilemma", Proceedings of the Annual Conference of the International Association of Maritime Economists (IAME), Izmir, Turkey, July.

Lee, S.W., Song, D.W. and Ducruet, C. (2008). "A tale of Asia's world ports: the spatial evolution in global hub port cities", *Geoforum*, 39: 372–385.

Ng, K.Y.A. (2007). "Port security and the competitiveness of short sea shipping in Europe: implications and challenges", in: K. Bichou, M.G.H. Bell and A. Evans (eds.): *Risk Management in Port Operations, Logistics and Supply Chain Security*, London: Informa, pp. 347–366.

Ng, K.Y.A. and Pallis, A.A. (2007) "Differentiation of port strategies in addressing proximity: the impact of political culture", *Proceedings for the International Congress on Ports in Proximity: Competition, Cooperation and*

Integration, Antwerp, Belgium and Rotterdam, The Netherlands, 5–7 December.

OECD (2003). *Security in Maritime Transport: Risk Factors and Economic Impact*, Paris: OECD Maritime Transport Committee.

OOCL (2007). "Four containers stolen from JNPT", *OOCL's Local News* (www.oocl.com).

Pallis, A.A. and Vaggelas, G.K. (2007). "Enhancing port security via the enactment of EU policies", in: K. Bichou, M.G.H. Bell and A. Evans (eds.): *Risk Management in Port Operations, Logistics and Supply Chain Security*, London: Informa, pp. 303–334.

PASAC (2003). Minutes of the Second Meeting of the Port Area Security Advisory Committee, Hong Kong: Marine Department, HKSAR Government, September.

PFST's website: www.portsecuritytoolkit.com (last accessed February 2008).

Pilling, D. and Mitchell, T. (2006). "US official urges Asia to improve port security", *Financial Times*, 28 March.

Robinson, R. (2002). "Ports as elements in value-driven chain systems: the new paradigm", *Maritime Policy and Management*, 29(3): 241–255.

PoR (2007). "Security programme: Port of Rotterdam", Presentation given at Erasmus University Rotterdam, Rotterdam, The Netherlands, March.

SATP's website: www.satp.org (last accessed May 2008).

Seidelmann, C. (2007). "Developing and implementing global interoperable standards for container security", in: K. Bichou, M.G.H. Bell and A. Evans (eds.): *Risk Management in Port Operations, Logistics and Supply Chain Security*. London: Informa, pp. 55–60.

Srikanth, S.N. and Venkataraman, R. (2007). "Strategic risk management in ports", in: K. Bichou, M.G.H. Bell and A. Evans (eds.): *Risk Management in Port Operations, Logistics and Supply Chain Security*. London: Informa, pp. 335–345.

Tan, A.T.H. (2005). "Singapore's approach to homeland security", in: K.W. Chin and D. Singh (eds.): *Southeast Asian Affairs 2005*. Singapore: ISAS, pp. 329–362.

WorldSecurity-index.com's website: http//worldsecurity-index.com (last accessed February 2008).

Zhu, J. (2006). "Asia and IMO technical co-operation", *Ocean and Coastal Management*, 49: 627–636.

INDEX